PROBLEMS IN EDUCATION—XI
EDUCATION AND MENTAL HEALTH

Titles in the series *Problems in Education*

EDUCATION
AND MENTAL HEALTH

by W. D. WALL

UNESCO

GEORGE G. HARRAP & CO. LTD.
182 High Holborn, London, W.C.1

All our lives long, every day and every hour, we are engaged in the process of accommodating our changed and unchanged selves to changed and un-changed surroundings; living, in fact, is nothing else than this process of accom-modation; when we fail in it a little we are stupid, when we fail flagrantly we are mad, when we suspend it temporarily we sleep, when we give up the attempt altogether we die. In quiet, uneventful lives the changes internal and external are so small that there is little or no strain in the process of fusion and accom-modation; in other lives there is great strain, but there is also great fusing and accommodating power; in others great strain with little accommodating power. A life will be successful or not according as the power of accommodation is equal to or unequal to the strain of fusing and adjusting internal and external changes.

The trouble is that in the end we shall be driven to admit the unity of the universe so completely as to be compelled to deny that there is either an external or an internal, but must see everything both as external and internal at one and the same time, subject and object—external and internal—being unified as much as everything else. This will knock our whole system over, but then every system has got to be knocked over by something.

Much the best way out of this difficulty is to go in for separation between internal and external—subject and object—when we find this convenient, and unity between the same when we find unity convenient. This is illogical, but extremes are alone logical, and they are always absurd; the mean is alone practicable and it is always illogical. It is faith and not logic which is the supreme arbiter. They say all roads lead to Rome, and all philosophies that I have ever seen lead ultimately either to some gross absurdity, or else to the conclusion already more than once insisted on in these pages, that the just shall live by faith, that is to say that sensible people will get through life by rule of thumb as they may interpret it most conveniently without asking too many questions for conscience' sake. Take any fact, and reason upon it to the bitter end, and it will ere long lead to this as the only refuge from some palpable folly.

The Way of All Flesh, by SAMUEL BUTLER

Published in 1955 by the United Nations
Educational, Scientific and Cultural Organization
Place de Fontenoy, Paris-7e
Reprinted in 1956, 1959, 1960 and 1964
by IFMRP, Paris

PREFACE

The fine publication to which I have been asked to write an introduction results from the work of the Regional Conference on Education and the Mental Health of Children in Europe, which was organized by Unesco in Paris in 1952, in pursuance of a resolution adopted by the General Conference of the Organization in 1951.

The central idea of those who drafted that resolution and those who organized the regional conference to which it led was that the balanced development of the individual, intellectually, emotionally and socially, is now constantly threatened by the disturbance of the community's values owing to the two wars of which Europe has been the theatre, and that means of solving this problem must be sought by reconsidering our methods of education in the light of the present data of child psychology.

Expressed in more practical terms, the starting point of the work described in this publication was the idea that mental development is an uninterrupted process and that it is never too early to take steps to avoid possible causes of a disturbed balance, if we are finally to achieve that flowering of the personality and that readiness to co-operate which are the two main aims of education. For this reason, since they were ultimately concerned with social adaptation and international understanding, the author of this volume and the experts invited to the regional conference did not hesitate to turn their attention to early childhood. They were rightly convinced that the internal conflicts which may be caused in the kindergarten or in the home by mistaken methods or failure on the part of adults to understand the child, may have a greater effect than is generally imagined on his later development. For this reason, too, they made a detailed study of the basic problem of co-ordination between school and home, and devoted special attention to the general evil of overstrain at school, the serious nature of which is not fully realized by those responsible for public education. Such overstrain gives rise to maladjustment which must militate against the ideals pursued, or which should be pursued, by the school. For this reason, lastly, they laid stress on all the opportunities for co-operation and team work to be found in the new type of education and on all the opportunities for practical activity which have been opened up by the reform of teaching methods. The distinguishing feature of all this work is the close connexion made by each of the experts between educational considerations and the results of the most recent research in child psychology, especially in the sphere of the emotional life. The present book might be said to be, from one point of view, a study in psychology applied to education and, from another, a survey of the new ideas on education and the reforms being carried out, judged in the light of child psychology. This leads to the laying of considerable stress not only on the social responsibilities of the school and the teacher, but also on the importance of psychology in the training of teachers and in the development of sound methods of education. It is this dual concern with education and psychology that gives the volume its unity.

This unity of inspiration is all the more remarkable because so many people have collaborated in producing the work. It is a successful example of the operation of that spirit of international co-operation which adults would like to inculcate into children even while they do not always manage to practise it among themselves. The working papers (summaries of investigations) on which it is based were prepared by 15 experts from 8 different countries, by 4 National Commissions for Unesco, and by 2 Specialized Agencies of the United Nations. In addition, 14 international, and 4 national, non-governmental organizations sent in reports and suggestions. Thirty-eight experts and delegates, belonging to 13 European countries and 3 non-European countries, were thus able to take part in the regional conference. The manuscript to which all these contributed in the first stages was later commented upon and expanded by further information supplied by more than 60 experts from 20 different countries. All these combined efforts went to the making of this study.

But the fact that this volume is not simply a hotch-potch, despite the similarity of ideas inspiring all those who contributed to it, the fact that it succeeds in condensing so much work into so few pages, and above all, the fact that it is readily intelligible to any educated reader, even if not a specialist—laying stress on practical achievements and, wherever possible, avoiding theoretical treatment and the expression of any views not founded on practical considerations or experiment— is of course due to the excellent work of co-ordination and clarification that went on behind all the authors and experts consulted. In this connexion, I cannot conclude this brief preface without warmly congratulating Unesco on the great success it achieved in organizing this regional conference, and on the no less great success of this volume. My congratulations must go, in particular, to the two psychologists on the staff of the Department of Education, Dr. W. D. Wall and his colleague Miss U. M. Gallusser, to whom most of the credit for this double success is due.   JEAN PIAGET

LIST OF ABBREVIATIONS

Am. Journ. Orthopsychiatry.	*American Journal of Orthopsychiatry*
Arch. Dis. Child.	*Archives of the Diseases of Childhood*
Brit. Journ. Ed. Psych.	*British Journal of Educational Psychology*
Brit. Journ. Soc.	*British Journal of Sociology*
Brit. Journ. Psych. Stat.	*British Journal of Psychology—Statistical Section*
Bull. Int. Sci. Soc.	*Bulletin international des sciences sociales*
El. Sch. J.	*Elementary School Journal*
Eug. Rev.	*Eugenics Review*
Int. Soc. Sci. Bull.	*International Social Science Bulletin*
J. Abnorm. Soc. Psych.	*Journal of Abnormal and Social Psychology*
J. App. Psych.	*Journal of Applied Psychology*
J. Ed. Psych.	*Journal of Educational Psychology*
J. Soc. Iss.	*The Journal of Social Issues*
Psych. Bull.	*Psychological Bulletin*
Psych. Rev.	*Psychological Review*
R. belge de Ps. Péd.	*Revue belge de psychologie et de pédagogie*
Rev. suisse Psych.	*Revue suisse de psychologie*
Teach. Coll. Contr. Educ.	*Teachers' College Contributions to Education*
Times Ed. Suppt.	*The Times Educational Supplement*
Train. Sch. Bull.	*Training School Bulletin*
Wiener Arb. z. päd. Psychol.	*Wiener Arbeiten zur pädagogischen Psychologie*
Zeitschr. f. ang. Psychol.	*Zeitschrift für angewandte Psychologie und Charakterkunde*
Zeitschr. f. päd. Psychol.	*Zeitschrift für pädagogische Psychologie und Jugendkunde*

CONTENTS

INTRODUCTORY NOTE

This book summarizes the results of a conference convened by Unesco in Paris in November-December 1952.[1] During three weeks, some thirty educational administrators, educators, psychologists, social workers and psychiatrists from 13 European countries worked together in four multi-disciplined groups discussing a lengthy agenda and studying an extensive series of documents specially prepared for them on various aspects of the mental health of children by scholars and organizations throughout the Continent. They were joined by experts from Latin America, India and the United States. The representatives of 14 international non-governmental organizations, and seven individual consultants, were also invited to spend a short time discussing special aspects of the agenda, with the working groups into which the conference divided. In all, if we include the authors of working papers, and participants in preparatory groups called together by Unesco National Commissions and by the Non-Governmental Organizations, rather more than a hundred of the leading European authorities in the fields of education and psychology contributed in some way to the work of the conference.

Not unexpectedly, a subject so wide provoked an analysis of the whole of the education of children, and gave rise to a great many specialized reports. Naturally, the treatment of some important topics was superficial, of others deeper than the general reader, parent, teacher or administrator, could be expected to go. The written reports and documents from the conference are being circulated in Europe and elsewhere; criticisms, additions and the reports of further discussions are being received by Unesco, and everywhere there are signs that the important subject of the contribution which can be made by the school to the mental health of the European community is under study.

The present work is an attempt to give stimulus and direction to this activity. It is a first synthesis of the work of the conference itself, of the material prepared for it and of the reports of other discussions which have gone on since the Conference closed. The subject is too large and the areas of our exact knowledge too small for an exhaustive or

---

1. For fuller detail, see Appendix IV A.

complete treatment to be possible. Theoretical discussion has been kept to a minimum as have illustrative examples; only the basic psychological theses on which most workers would be agreed have been presented as a foundation for the practical discussions and suggestions. This at times may give a false air of dogmatism which, it is hoped, will be corrected by the bibliographies given at the end of each chapter.

There is ample room for difference of opinion over the best means of securing the healthy mental and emotional development of children; and, while the broad lines of our knowledge of child development are firm enough, on many of the most practically important pedagogic, familial, and social aspects of mental health, there is insufficient research knowledge to guide our judgments. It is a field where confident assertions are apt to abound in proportion to the absence of evidence; but in any concrete case there may be a number of solutions each with peculiar disadvantages, and each adapted more or less to the culture in which it arises. Healthy mental development is possible within widely differing systems of values and beliefs; and while the psychologist may point out the costs or advantages of any system of cultural regulation, judgments on the ultimate value of the beliefs on which the system depends fall into the province of religion, morals and ethics. Here an attempt has been made to present the major controversial issues fairly, reconciling if possible conflicting viewpoints and, if not, stating differences frankly and indicating their implications for mental hygiene.

An attempt too has been made to secure as much freedom from unconscious bias as possible. As a whole or in parts, this publication—itself based upon the collective thinking of the conference participants, witnesses and the contributors of working material—has been circulated in draft for discussion and comment to those who took part in the conference and to those mentioned in the Acknowledgements—rather more than sixty people in all. Many of the views expressed were conflicting, some would have carried the discussion too far into realms of theory or philosophy for so small a book; from them all, however, much was gained, which enriched and gave balance to the discussion of controversial issues and recommendations. Some readers will complain that the book goes too far; others that the views expressed lack boldness and originality. An average is always open to criticisms from the extremes, and while this is not the book which any one European authority would write, it does represent a statement of current European thinking in a difficult and controversial field.

The book is intended to provoke discussion and practical action. It has accordingly been written as far as possible in non-technical terms and without accepting, explicitly or implicitly, any of the current theoretical frames of reference. More technical discussion and references to the research evidence will be found in the footnotes or in the appendixes. At the end of each chapter will be found a short bibliography containing the principal European works not already cited in the text and which may make the starting point for further study. These bibliographies have been established in collaboration with those who took part in the conference and with other European authorities. They contain, as far as we have been able to ascertain, only those books which make an original contribution to some aspect or other of the problem under discussion; and in general, works of popularization have been omitted, as have research papers appearing in scientific journals. Only the sparsest reference has been made to the American literature, since in almost all the fields treated considerable bibliographies and abstracts exist already.

It is hoped that the non-technical nature of the text and the bibliographies will together make the book of value to teachers, parents, administrators, and youth leaders, who have in fact far more to contribute to the healthy mental development of children than the professional mental health workers, and that the book will serve as a kind of stocktaking of our ideas on which the next move forward may be planned.

ACKNOWLEDGEMENTS

The Secretariat of Unesco wishes to express its gratitude to all the participants in the conference (listed in Appendix III) who read and commented upon at least those sections of the book which concerned the work of their group, and in particular to the chairman, Professor F. J. Th. Rutten (Holland), the vice-chairmen, Dr. H. M. Cohen (United Kingdom), Professor R. Gal (France), Professor W. Olson (U.S.A.), Professor A. Rey (Switzerland), and the rapporteurs, Dr. M. Duncan (United Kingdom), Mr. R. Mallet (France), Dr. M. Revault d'Allonnes (France) and Dr. P. Volkov (United Kingdom), who read the entire work.

The Secretariat of Unesco also wishes to thank the many educational, medical and psychological specialists who generously gave of their time, experience and knowledge but whose contributions cannot be acknowledged in detail in the text, though everywhere this book has benefited from their comments. A particular debt is owed to the following—those marked with an asterisk (*) have read substantially the whole manuscript: Dr. H. J. Abraham, Unesco Relations Staff, State Department, Washington, U.S.A.; Dr. Hans Aebli,* Oberseminar des Kantons, Zürich, Switzerland; Professor Sylvia Bayr-Klimpfinger, University of Vienna, Austria; Dr. and Mrs. F. Boutourline-Young, Harvard-Florence Research Project, Florence, Italy; Sir C. Burt,* Emeritus Professor of Psychology, University of London, United Kingdom; Mrs. W. E. Cavenagh, Department of Social Science, University of Birmingham, United Kingdom; Prof. A. H. El Koussy,* Institute of Education, Cairo, Egypt; Dr. Adolf Ferrière,* founder and vice-president of the International New Education Fellowship, Switzerland; Pastor H. Flensmark, president, Danish Branch, World Organization for Early Childhood Education, Denmark; Dr. M. C. L. Gildea,* chairman, APA Committee on Child Psychiatry, U.S.A.; Mr. N. Gillett, Dudley Training College, Dudley, United Kingdom; Mrs. S. Herbinière-Lebert, world president, World Organization for Early Childhood Education; Prof. F. Hotyat,* Centre de Travaux de l'Institut Supérieur de Pédagogie de Morlanwelz, Morlanwelz, Belgium; Prof. O. Klineberg, Columbia University, New York, U.S.A.; Mr. R. R. Leeper, associate secretary, The Association for Supervision and Curriculum Development, U.S.A.; Miss I. Lézine, Laboratoire de Psycho-biologie de l'Enfant, France; Miss M. M. Lindsay, H.M.I., Ministry of Education, United Kingdom; Prof. W. Line, Department of Psychology, University of Toronto, Canada; Prof. G. Mialaret, Ecole Normale de St. Cloud, Paris, France; Mr. B. S. Morris, director, National Foundation for Educational Research, United Kingdom; Rabbi Munk, Agudas Israel World Organization, France; Mr. M. Norman, and the Medico-Psychological Commission of the Bureau Catholique de l'Enfance, Paris, France; Mr. R. O'Brien, secretary, and members of the Catholic Education Council, United Kingdom; Miss D. Pye, headmistress, United Nations Nursery School, Paris, France; Dr. Ilse Rother, Pädagogische Hochschule, Celle, German Federal Republic; Prof. C. W. Valentine,* Emeritus Professor of Education, University of Birmingham, United Kingdom; Mr. A. van Waeyenberghe, Chargé de Cours à l'Université Libre de Bruxelles, Belgium; Prof. P. E. Vernon,* Professor of Educational Psychology, Institute of Education, United Kingdom; Prof. R. Zazzo,* directeur du Laboratoire de Psycho-biologie de l'Enfant, Paris, France. Naturally, opinions expressed in this book are those of the authors and do not necessarily reflect the views of Unesco.

CHAPTER I

MENTAL HEALTH AND
INTERNATIONAL TENSION

INTRODUCTORY

International tensions, like tensions between individuals, do not arise solely from rational causes. They are coloured by, and indeed may sometimes spring from deep, unconscious feelings of insecurity, and from maladjustments and hostilities in the lives of the men and women who constitute nations and the leaders of nations.

The family, the school, the community, the nation, are aggregates of individuals, whose behaviour and attitudes are influenced by unconscious elements and by the interplay of personalities in ways as yet obscurely known.

If these groups are made up of men and women who are markedly anxious and insecure, it is relatively easy for one among them—the leader—to focus that anxiety and insecurity on some kind of external bogey-man, and eventually to induce the group to become overtly aggressive. If, however, every person is essentially free of anxiety except that which is normal in the face of a real danger, then imaginary fears are less likely to be heeded. In the course of their development, most human beings acquire some anxieties which are not rationally caused—which are in fact 'neurotic'; in modern societies, unhappily, many acquire such anxieties and insecurities, and on a scale sufficiently intense to be described as maladjustment. Their unconsciously determined feelings of guilt and aggression, of anxiety and insecurity, are such that even in normal daily life, situations arise from which they must retreat or from which they feel they must escape by aggression. Quarrels between individuals, trouble at the office or factory, marital breakdown, industrial and political strife, and other similar situations as well as their immediate cause, have roots in the developmental history of those who participate in them. This is not to minimize the economic and social reasons for strife; but questions of living space, of food and of personal or economic survival have no relevance except in so far as they are reflected in human psychology, shape human development and provoke human reactions. The removal of objective causes of anxiety will not remove anxiety if it is neurotically caused. The pathologically anxious *seek* objects for their fears—and such objects can always be found.

One at least of the marks of mental health is freedom from fears and anxieties which are not justifiably caused. Coupled with this is the security which comes from a knowledge of what to do to free one's self from a real threat. The child crossing the busy street should feel some fear, as a stimulus to alertness; but if he has also been taught the precautions to take, his fear will quickly pass and he will cross it safely. Many of the situations which provoke fear, anxiety and insecurity in modern societies are not such as can be solved by individual effort alone. Few men can protect themselves single-handed from hunger or unemployment; and few indeed can grasp and interpret the interplay of all the factors which make up the large group in which they live. Hence all look to some kind of leadership, political or religious, by an individual or an elected group, which will indicate the collective precautions and techniques to deal with threatening situations or to achieve the desired ends.

GROUP LOYALTY

One of the functions of a group is to contain and render innocuous the hostility of its members towards each other. Loyalty to a common symbol—a totem or a national flag—in fact provides a sentiment which overrides inter-personal hostilities, especially when the group is under an external threat. The danger of such a partial loyalty arises when it is used to rally aggression against another group. Where the members of a group are free of neurotic insecurity, their loyalty will be relatively objective and it will be difficult for its leader to rouse an aggressive feeling towards another group in the absence of a real threat; where, however, the group is composed partly of men and women who are in a state of easily aroused fear, then it is not difficult to persuade them to project their anxieties upon another group and for their loyalty to intensify their aggression.

LEADERSHIP

In modern complex societies the groups are many, their loyalties partial, with normally an overriding national loyalty; and their leaders are many and of differing relative importance. Usually leadership comes to those who possess, in the eyes of the group, in a concentrated and well defined form, certain apparent qualities which themselves correspond to the group's values, aspirations and fears, both consciously held and unconsciously determined. Just as it has been said that a country gets the government it deserves, so we may say that a group tends to reflect an intensification of itself in its leadership. Yet it does happen not infrequently that a group throws up leaders who are more liberal and gifted and who may therefore not only give the group a security that in itself it lacks but in many ways 'educate' it out of adverse attitudes and towards valuable positive action.[1]

Accumulating experience however shows us that no human group can for long exist by gifted leadership alone. In a period of stress, an unhealthy society is likely to reject leaders who counsel moderation and restraint since the fears aroused from unconscious levels overwhelm any objectivity of thinking. To survive without hostility to others, the whole mass of a society must be fundamentally healthy, composed of stable men and woman free of neurotic fears, anxieties and tensions, aware of their own prejudices and with positive attitudes of friendliness to others. Such a healthy society is likely to reject, as eccentric and unbalanced, individuals, however gifted, who are themselves maladjusted and who claim leadership. The danger to peace is at its most acute, as we have seen, when a nation of predominantly unbalanced people seeks and finds maladjusted leaders who, by playing on deep fears and anxieties, rouse and maintain hostility to other groups. Anything therefore which contributes to the healthy emotional development of human personality, which frees men's minds from prejudice and from fear is a direct contribution to the maintenance of peace.

INTERNATIONAL UNDERSTANDING AS A DYNAMIC ATTITUDE

This is the foundation without which no adequate superstructure can be erected. Peace and international understanding are not founded, however, upon a vague good will without dynamic. Respect for human rights and dignity, a sense of the solidarity of mankind, international co-operation and the like are empty and dangerous terms if they remain

---

1. It has been pointed out (K. Mannheim, *Diagnosis of our Time*. London, Paul, Trench, Trubner, & Co. Ltd., 1943) that nowadays political power and leadership can more readily be both concentrated in the hands of a few and perpetuate itself against the wishes of the ruled, because of the much closer interdependence of modern society and because modern technology, scientific, industrial and social, fosters centralization. Hence, by a skilful use of social and psychological techniques, a leader or a leadergroup may be built up to appear to embody the fears, aspirations and values of a nation. Once accepted, such an individual or group can then rule unchecked by public opinion; creeds, beliefs and behaviour can indeed be superimposed which do not correspond with the real nature of the citizen. One of the major modern problems is that of passing from a laisser-faire society composed of small, relatively unorganized groups whose interplay assures the survival of liberty to a centralized or at least planned society (which seems the inevitable result of technological advance) without falling into dictatorship. Mannheim argues powerfully that this is largely a function of the values consciously accepted by society, that these result in part from individual strivings and in part from social pressures. Without discussing the source of the values—spiritual, philosophic or social—it can however be seen that the acceptance by the individual and ultimately by his society of any set of values and the action to which they lead individually or collectively are intimately related to processes of psychological development and adjustment.

intellectual concepts subscribed to but not passionately believed. If they are to affect action and to inhibit war, they must be rooted as fundamental attitudes in the very core of personality and permeate the whole texture. As such they are not something which can be grafted on by a process of teaching facts; they must inform the entire atmosphere in which the child grows and develops. Many such attitudes—for example an attitude of respect for the intrinsic value of human personality, a recognition of the worth of a human being because he is human—will develop within the family and the school, provided that the child is himself handled well by those around him. These attitudes, however, will not operate beyond a personal circle unless they are broadened by knowledge and by a widening experience of increasingly complex human societies. Mental health in the modern world cannot be secured simply by cultivating one's garden. Many of the great anxieties of the present are international and none of us can live in indifference to what goes on beyond our national frontiers. The home and the school are directly involved in the task of providing adequate information, of aiding the child consciously to generalize his experience, and, most important of all, of helping him steadily to expand his social horizons from family to school, from school to nation, and from nation to the world community.

EDUCATION IN FAMILY, SCHOOL AND COMMUNITY

Conceived as the whole shaping process of development, education in the family, the school and the community has, therefore, a heavy responsibility. Satisfactory human development depends upon the success with which the fundamental emotional needs of each individual are met within the framework of the demands of the society in which he grows up. To this problem each culture has its solutions, traditionally determined and embodied in systems of child upbringing, of education, and of general social expectations. The solutions chosen by any society involve some cost to the individual, some frustration, and perhaps some distortion of the free development of the human personality. Some systems of education have been consciously aimed at so indoctrinating the minds of children and adolescents that continuing hostility towards other peoples has been the result; others without deliberate intention inculcate ideas of superiority of race, religion, culture and the like; and few as yet attempt deliberately to break down hostility to the stranger or to those who are different in their customs and habits. Some impose upon children demands which they cannot meet without undergoing severe stress and acquiring negative and adverse attitudes to themselves and others, which lie at the root of personal and social tensions.

20

THE CHANGING SCHOOL

Underlying many post-war educational reforms lies recognition that the task of the school has considerably changed in the past 50 years, and that the old formulae and attitudes are insufficient for current needs. The modern school is not an instrument simply for the training of the mind; it is not purely a machine of instruction; it is more and more consciously seen to be an institution which reflects and thus perpetuates and shapes the entire social group in which it exists. The nineteenth and early twentieth century reformers hoped that, through the school alone, they could remould the world to their heart's desire. We are more cautious. We know that a good part of a child's education takes place in the early years long before he passes the doorway of the school and that all experience which he undergoes outside as well as inside the classroom, for good or for ill, shapes his attitudes and his personality. We know too that because of this, and because of the invincible individuality enshrined in every child, the claims which may be made for the school as a social instrument are more modest.

Nevertheless the school is society's formal instrument for moulding the young, for transmitting the cultural heritage, for inculcating these values, ideals and modes of behaviour on which both the continuity and the evolution of humanity depend. This mission was easier to fulfil when the schools existed only for a limited group selected in some special way—by social caste, by intellectual level, by religious, or by political belief. Then school, home and community presented to the child a united and coherent scheme of values, and the task of each was clearly defined. In the mixed and developed cultures of Europe, the concept of education for all has thrown on the schools an immensely more complex task not always clearly realized by teachers and parents, by administrators or philosophers.

There is first the fact that because no family unit or small community now can give all that a child needs for his personal development, we can no longer equate school education with instruction. The inculcation of the basic techniques of reading and calculation or a purely intellectual training is not a sufficient supplement to the work of the immediate family. Moreover, however much in our theory and philosophy we may attempt to isolate the task of the school as one of a purely intellectual discipline and formation, we cannot escape the fundamentally emotional aspect of all learning. From the choice which the teacher makes as to what to teach and what to omit, from the values implicit in the curriculum, from the pedagogical method, from the rewards and sanctions used to evoke effort, the child, not perhaps always consciously but surely none-the-less, draws his own conclusions. He reacts to the values implicit in his school and to some extent incorporates them into his growing personality.

THE AIMS OF EDUCATION

We are not however agreed upon the content or the aims of education. Many schools exist in more or less of a void, reflecting roughly the values of the world outside their walls, emphasizing roughly what accumulated experience and tradition assert to be valuable, and avoiding too definite an expression of what contribution they should bring to the growth of their pupils. As an avoidance of indoctrination this has merits; yet the absence of clear guidance for growing children and adolescents may present them with grave problems of anxiety if the society in which they live also presents them with problems to which there are no solutions, with situations for which there are no accepted techniques of behaviour, and with moral crises before which the adult world itself is perplexed, anxious and undecided. If the child's own home provides him with a stable confident environment, all may be well; and the school may continue without a declared or implied philosophic or moral aim. Many educators would affirm that much more depends upon the spirit and atmosphere of the school, upon the personal relationships among the staff and between them and the pupils than upon any declared philosophy or system of belief. It is indeed arguable that many degrees and kinds of belief and unbelief should be presented to the child during his education so that, by the free play of differences, he may be led to reflect and choose for himself without the risk of indoctrination. This however is a situation markedly different from one of indecision; and if the school merely reflects the indecision of the home and of the surrounding world we have an atmosphere of grave anxiety for the child, the seed-bed of emotional difficulty and a most serious menace to mental health.

NATURE AND NURTURE

Human development is a complex process in which genetic endowment, elements arising from the inner life, forms of acquired response, and stimuli from the outside world are combining and recombining. Every child is born with certain innate potentialities some of which are malleable while others strongly determine, at least, the limits of his growth. He is equipped with tendencies to laugh, to play, to imitate, to respond to more or less general stimuli like the desire for food, for sleep, for defecation, for self-assertion and submission. As he develops, such general innate trends grow into dispositions to react in certain ways, and he may acquire others which have all or more than the force of the fundamental biological drives.[1] Many of these dispositions,

---

1. G. W. Allport, *Personality. A Psychological Interpretation.* London, Constable & Co. 1937, ch. VII.

whether based on innate or acquired tendencies are, certainly in the early years, highly plastic and little specific, subject to considerable environmental modifications, to deflection but rarely to complete suppression. They constitute the sources of energy, the motive force of the personality.

Even in the most primitive circumstances, a child is born into a society, and hence as well as a purely personal maturation there is always an element of socialization in his growth. As he gets older, the social pressures upon him increase and the process of development is that of reconciling his crude biological drives with the needs both of individual and of social living; human societies may be viewed as means to the satisfaction of instinctive propensities within a framework which reconciles the ego-centricity of the individual with the needs of his group.

The interplay between the child and his human and material environment continually involves some frustration. In his earliest months the amount of such frustration may be relatively small; he is fed, sheltered and allowed to sleep; he can exercise his limbs, as a rule, free from marked restraint; and he is cherished physically and emotionally by his mother. The tempo of his development is set by maturational factors, but even thus early, elements enter which are in part cultural and common to all or most children in the same tribe or group and in part arise from the personalities and attitudes of his parents and constitute the beginnings of his unique experience.

SECURITY AS THE BASIS FOR ADVENTURE

This bio-social situation has two distinguishable major aspects which reverberate in the child's emotional life and colour his development. Whenever his activity attains a satisfying end, whenever his impulses towards the outside world meet with success, his tendency to repeat the activity and to value it positively is increased. Whenever he is frustrated by his environment in the satisfaction of his primordial needs, then he will react with aggression or retreat or both and will have the tendency to regard the frustrating circumstance as 'bad'. Successful contacts with his world tend to reinforce his feelings of being safe; unsuccessful and frustrating ones tend to be perceived as threats to his security.

It is probably a general innate characteristic of human beings that, unless frustration is too severe and too painful or unless it continues over a long period, they tend to seek other acceptable outlets for primordial drives. Indeed, McDougall[1] defined 'persistency with varied

---

1. *An Introduction to Social Psychology.* London, Methuen, 1908. *The Energies of Men.* London, Methuen, 1932.

effort' as the mark of an innate propensity of an instinctive kind. The very young child is able to do scarcely anything for himself; but even so he is far from passive. However imperfectly, he is an agent and as he develops physically he shows a growing independence. Bühler,[1] in her observation of children's smiles, notes that from about nine months onward babies begin to be independent and selective in their response to a smiling face. Valentine[2] puts it even earlier than the ninth month. This independence is greatly increased by the child's ability to crawl and later to walk, but even before he can do either some observers notice an introvert-extravert rhythm[3] in his reaction to his environment.

This thrust towards independence inevitably brings him up against physical impossibilities and an increasing number of prohibitions imposed by his family. Children vary, probably innately, in emotional stability and in their ability to tolerate these and other frustrations. Some few seem, even in favourable circumstances, destined to become maladjusted; others seem able to survive even when their environment is markedly adverse. In general, whatever the level of frustration tolerance of the individual, healthy development will only be assured if acceptable outlets for his basic drives are offered by his environment and if the affection of his mother and family are there to sustain him. For child and adult alike the most emotional, and therefore formative, situations are those which lead to a successful discharge of energy or those which threaten his physical or psychological security. In a very fundamental sense the whole education of children, and indeed the whole of mental hygiene, turns upon the solutions sought and found to the twin problems of maintaining personal security and of moving forward to resolve the continual challenges presented by the environment. That the willingness to take a risk depends upon feeling safe enough to do so is only apparently a paradox—at least in the psychology of growing children. Freedom from fears and anxieties which are not directly related to the objective situation is itself a mark of mental health; and it is to the achievement of a state of dynamic equilibrium in a social environment that the upbringing and education of children should be directed.[4]

FRUSTRATION AND OUTLET AS INSTRUMENTS OF CULTURAL SHAPING

This however is not to say, as some have done, that children should

1. *Kindheit und Jugend.* 3rd ed., Leipzig, Hirzel, 1931.
2. *The Psychology of Early Childhood.* London, Methuen & Co., 1943.
3. A. L. Gesell and F. L. Ilg, *Infant and Child in the Culture of Today.* New York and London, Harper, 1943.
4. On this whole field see A. H. El Koussy, *Usus al-sihhah al-nafsiyah* (Fundamentals of Mental Hygiene). 4th ed. Cairo, Librairie de la Renaissance, 1952.

not under any circumstances suffer frustration. Life in society implies frustration; and one of the marks of satisfactory development is a growing ability to tolerate, without retreat or aggression, an immediate check to a desire while an acceptable outlet is found. This implies that upbringing should progressively provide the child with acceptable habits and techniques of expression for the forces of his personality. It is also the mark of a healthy society that it is rich in adequate outlets for the energy of the innate drives of its participants and at the same time, recognizing the range and variety of human endowment, that its practices of child upbringing permit for all children and adults a smooth adjustment to the environment, human and circumstantial.

It is in fact by the manner in which frustrations are imposed, by the outlets provided and by the selection of responses which gain approval, that a culture sets its mark upon the individual, giving him the distinctive 'national' cast of personality. Culturally speaking, this is what the social psychologist means by education. It is a process which begins at birth and continues throughout life. Artificially we may divide it between various agencies—the family, the school, the milieu; to the human being it is a process taking place in different physical environments perhaps and in terms of relationships with different groups of people, but none the less continuous and rendered coherent by the continuity of the experiencing self.

In this cultural or social sense there are likely to be as many definitions of mental health as there are different ways of life. If we attempt to move beyond such an operational definition, we leave psychology for ethics, philosophy or revealed truth. An adequate definition of mental health in general terms would involve also a statement of the values prized by society.

It would however have to be something more than this. While innately remarkably variable and, at least affectively, markedly modifiable, human beings have certain needs and drives which in themselves are neither good nor bad but the complete denial of which renders any satisfactory adjustment to life impossible. The process of education is the means by which society specifies acceptable outlets for these innate needs and capacities of the individual and at the same time ensures that they will enrich his personal life as well as serve his society.

MENTAL HYGIENE IN TERMS OF HUMAN NEEDS

Functionally therefore it is possible to base certain principles of mental hygiene upon our developing knowledge of human psychological needs, and on an evaluation of the means of satisfying them. Any given culture, any cultural custom—for example, the weaning of the infant—can be evaluated in terms of the outlets which it offers for the instinctive

25

tendencies or fundamental drives called into play and in terms of the relationship it sets up between the challenges to the individual and the means it provides of restoring the psychological equilibrium.

Development is not however a matter merely of imposed choices. The child is himself an agent from the moment of birth. As well as being challenged he challenges. Early in his life much of his activity seems to be random and only some of it brings him into positive relationship with his physical environment. As he grows his activity becomes more and more purposive, more and more defined and more and more integrated. Every successful or unsuccessful piece of activity teaches him something which he incorporates into a growing notion of himself as distinct from others, into a notion of values and into a series of patterns which he tends to repeat. Thus almost from the outset of his life, he develops a past which colours the immediate present, tending to give a prepotence in any given situation to one of a number of possible modes of response.

What distinguishes a response which is healthy in terms of future stability from one which militates against mental health, is whether it in general brings the child into an acceptable and satisfactory relationship with his environment or tends to withdraw him from it. This is a statement which needs some qualification, particularly in terms of the stage of development of the child and the precise circumstances. It is however important that the majority of situations in which a child finds himself should be those in which a forward-looking behaviour is possible and in which socially acceptable forms of success can be achieved by an effort within his compass. For young children, in particular, this demands some degree of modification both of the adult environment and of the expectations and attitudes of those responsible for him.

As the child matures he develops attitudes and patterns of behaviour which become steadily harder and harder to change. In part these patterns are the result of his unique experience and in part they reflect norms imposed by the culture in which he lives. In every response to each new challenge however there is an element of novelty, a new integration. It is essentially in the formation of such new integrations, their shaping and direction, that the two aspects of development—maturation and education conceived in its fullest sense—play their most important part.

EDUCATION AS A REFLECTION OF THE CULTURE

Education is the means of shaping maturation in accordance with the changing series of cultural choices which every society, partly as a result of ecological factors, partly from unconscious causes, partly

26

through its history and traditions, progressively makes. A society agrees to sanction certain kinds of behaviour—for example the acquisition of wealth through work—and to outlaw others—for example the acquisition of wealth and power through brigandage. Some of these choices appear logical and consistent; some arbitrary or irrational: they range from the acceptance of moral and philosophical values to the smallest details of convention and etiquette; they affect every aspect of the individual's growth and life; their sum total is what is usually understood by 'a way of life'; and their impact on the personality, 'national character'.

Thus in any society, every growing child has to learn to conform more or less to a series of cultural norms; and his ideas of 'good' and 'bad' are based, in his early years, on what he finds to be acceptable or unacceptable to the adults round him. Since his sense of personal security is very nearly bound up with an easy, warm and well defined relationship to those with whom he lives, it will be seen that he has the strongest of all motives for conformity. In this way his growth is shaped in one direction rather than in another which may be, psychologically speaking at least, equally satisfactory.

It is in this context of dynamic growth and of interaction between the unique individual and his social environment that we must consider the principles of mental hygiene and the means to promote a healthy society. Since, even in an area as relatively homogeneous as Europe, or indeed even within any one nation, there are wide differences in cultural choices and cultural sanctions between groups and between generations, we cannot hope to establish universally applicable rules or definitions. The most that can be done is, by a study of growing children and of the impact upon them of their total environment, home, school and community, to point out some of the principles that should be applied and some of the practical measures which might be taken by those who see that the sum of human happiness and adjustment is no small item in the arithmetic of peace.

BIBLIOGRAPHY

ADORNO, T. W., FRENKEL-BRUNSWICK, E. et al. *The authoritarian personality.* New York, Harper, 1950. 990 p.

ALLPORT, G. W. *The resolution of intergroup tensions.* New York, The National Conference of Christians and Jews, 1952. 48 p.

BRACHFELD, O. *Les sentiments d'infériorité.* Genève et Annemasse, Ed. du Mont Blanc, 1945. 310 p.

CANTRIL, H. *Tensions that cause wars.* Urbana, University of Illinois Press, 1950. 303 p.

CLAPAREDE, E. *Psychologie de la compréhension internationale.* Paris, XIth International Congress of Psychology, 1937. 8 p.

Democracy in a world of tensions. Paris, Unesco, 1951. 540 p.

KISKER, G. W. *World tension. The psychopathology of international relations.* New York, Prentice Hall, 1951. 324 p.

KLINEBERG, O. *Tensions affecting international understanding.* New York, Social Science Research Council, 1950. 227 p.

Mental health and world citizenship: a statement prepared for the third international congress on mental health. London, 1948. World Federation for Mental Health, 1948. n.p.

MYRDAL, G. "Psychological impediments to effective international co-operation", *The journal of social issues,* supplement series no. 6, 1952. 32 p.

"National stereotypes and international understanding." *International social science bulletin,* vol. III, no. 3. Paris, Unesco, 1951.

"Nouvelles méthodes pour l'étude des stéréotypes." *Bulletin international des sciences sociales,* vol. III, no. 3. Paris, Unesco, 1951.

CHAPTER II

HOME, SCHOOL AND COMMUNITY

I. THE ROLE OF THE FAMILY IN MENTAL HEALTH

LEARNING AS A PROCESS WITH EMOTIONAL, MATURATIONAL AND INTELLECTUAL ASPECTS

Psychologists have come to regard as a commonplace that human learning has important maturational and emotional components as well as intellectual ones. How these three aspects are related to one another depends of course upon the age of the human being and upon the circumstances in which learning takes place. For example a child learns to walk only when readiness has been achieved though physiological maturation. The success or failure which attend his early efforts, the attitudes of over-protective fear, or of encouragement and praise shown by the parents, however, affect him emotionally in a way which not only tinges the immediate experience but may colour his attitude to subsequent situations of effort and achievement. It is probable that, at least up to late adolescence, there is a maturational element, both intellectual and emotional, in much of the formal and informal learning, social or academic, that takes place. It seems certain too that to a greater or lesser degree, however intellectual the process may seem, all learning has emotional correlates and leads to a modification of attitudes, sometimes, especially in childhood, affecting them very profoundly and in ways most unexpected to the naïve observer. How profound this modification is, depends upon a multiplicity of inter-related factors past and present, interior to the person and exterior to him, which constitute what might be likened to a field of force.

In the case of children under the age of 3 the intellectual aspects of learning may be relatively very small compared for example with adult learning. It is indeed only at a comparatively late stage that intelligence becomes a fully effective instrument in the analysis of experience and the choice of response. Even in the adult, while the intellect may appear to function in an atmosphere of pure reason, it in fact rarely does so. The selection of what to observe, the weight given to the various factors in a situation, and the choice of action will all be heavily influenced by prior affective experience, by feelings and emotions and by sets or attitudes deep-rooted in the personality and unamenable to rational analysis.

In a primary biological sense, learning is a process of adaptation set in train either by a drive such as hunger originating from a change within the organism or by an alteration in the environment which the experiencing person sees as a challenge or a threat; and it is characteristic of human beings that they are more variable in their responses, more capable of learning and more dependent upon it, than animals or insects. By the time a human being in a modern society reaches maturity, however, primary biological learning has been highly sophisticated by the growth in intelligence, by the effects of individual experience and cultural conditioning. Steadily from the moment of birth, the human child acquires a past and integrates his experience in a complex system of attitudes, sets, and habitual responses. An adult has learned the adaptive habits and attitudes that enable him to adjust quickly and efficiently to most of the circumstances in which he normally finds himself. He can also adapt himself within certain limits to the new and unfamiliar. Only in special circumstances, as when he is conscripted into the army during wartime or when a social upheaval affects the entire framework of his daily life, does his environment radically change and force him profoundly to modify all his habitual attitudes and responses. When such situations do arise and affect a large proportion of a group the whole structure of society tends to change irreversibly, since the new circumstances have in fact irreversibly changed the individuals who compose it.

One has only to study the effects of rapid industrialization on agrarian communities, the impact of a new country upon immigrants, or the changes brought about by a war to see that, in such circumstances, the emotional tension of the individual rises and for a time at least many of the old habits break down; adults become insecure and on the *qui vive* like animals that scent danger. If the modifications demanded are too great or the emotional tension too high, many may break down neurotically; alternatively, for a time there may be a retreat into earlier forms of behaviour, many of them anti-social, or partaking of the magical thinking of childhood—such as the revival of superstition during war. As genuine adaptation takes place, so the individuals develop new habits, and the group of which they form part achieves a new stability.

Situations of rapid change are relatively rare in the lives of adults. Children however find themselves daily—in the first year, one might almost say hourly—in novel situations for which they have few developed habits. The very process of growth steadily provides further challenges to their powers of adaptation. They learn to sit up, to speak, to walk, to feed themselves, to make social contacts in an ever-widening sphere, to go to school, to travel unaccompanied ever further and further afield. Their developing physical strength and co-ordination, and their growing intellectual power put more and more things within their grasp; and at the same time, the environment represented at first by parents and their immediate family and then by the world beyond the home, increasingly shows that there are expectations which they have to fulfil. Many of these are things acquired slowly and with difficulty; some of them are outside the child's immediate capacity and therefore bring him the negative feeling of failure; some are achieved only after strenuous effort and bring him the warm positive experience of success; from all of them he learns something more about the people, events, and things in his surroundings and more about himself, his capacities, and his limitations.

THE VULNERABILITY OF CHILDREN TO EXPERIENCE

Young children too, because of their imperfect grasp of the distinction between reality external to themselves and their own wishes and fantasies, tend to confound their inner imaginary and the outer 'real' or 'phenomenal' worlds. They may believe, for example, that wishes will come true in a way which, to an adult, is magical. An imperfect grasp of the laws of cause and effect in the physical world, a lack of knowledge of the difference between themselves and other living things and between both and inanimate objects, lead them to project on to their surroundings the feelings and even the impressions made by events of their own mental life. Because the demands to adapt which are hourly being made upon them keep children in a state of emotional alertness, and because so much of what they experience is new, they are all the time, with the imperfect experience at their command, attempting to interpret and thus to learn.

The child's world is a continuous one of which he is the centre. Less even than the adult can he analyse it into separate independent compartments. His learning is global and all his keenly felt experience is educative, reverberating through all he is and does. Much of his learning goes on in situations which parents and teachers do not usually regard as educative ones. The little girl playing apparently quietly on the floor, while her mother in a hushed voice discusses with a neighbour the death of the man down the road, will respond, though she may not immediately show it, to the anxiety in her mother's tones and manner. The little boy who has frequent experience of inter-personal hostility even though it is not directed against himself (for example quarrels between his parents) will endeavour with his immature knowledge to interpret what is happening and incorporate his ideas of it into his own developing attitudes.

Conversely, children do not always learn what the adult sets out to teach; what is selected from a situation, its meaning, is likely to be highly subjective and incomplete. To take a superficial example, a child whose mother prematurely tries to teach him not to make a mess as he eats, and who grows angry at his failures, may learn to fear any new thing he is asked to do, because he expects to fail. Examples of this type could be multiplied from the case histories of many childish maladjustments which have sprung from situations emotionally disturbing to the child, imperfectly understood by him, and in which he has been unable to meet satisfactorily what he dimly perceives as a threat to his own security.

THE IMPORTANCE OF THE FAMILY IN LEARNING

From birth the child has strong physical and psychological needs which he is powerless to supply without the aid of his mother, and his first learning takes place in connexion with her. The satisfaction of a need—for food, for example, or for warmth—enhances a feeling of security; the denial of a need—for example a loss of physical support—is likely to be felt as a threat to mere survival and a cause of anxiety. Quite early in his life the child begins to respond to other than merely biological stimuli; the very regularity of the major events of his day, the comings and goings of his mother, the way in which she handles him, speaks to him and cares for him, assume an importance psychologically as part of the framework within which he begins to feel safe or in which somehow he feels threatened. In a dim unspecific way he reacts to the satisfactions or dissatisfactions of his mother, to her confident consistency or anxious preoccupation.

MOTHER AND CHILD

The importance of the mother-child relationship as the source of security in the development of children is emphasized by a considerable body of recent work.[1] Food, warmth and protection from danger can readily be assured in their purely physical sense, and not necessarily through the agency of the family. But recent work has confirmed what psychologists long suspected, that impersonal satisfaction of a child's material needs is insufficient for his growth. What appears to be essential is a close, warm, affectionate and, at least for the first three or four years, permanent tie between the mother or mother substitute and the child. Many mothers for a variety of reasons provide this only imper-

---

1. See Appendix III B.

fectly if at all, at least for the first child. In other cases, babies are early abandoned or separated from their natural mothers entirely, or suffer prolonged separation during the day whilst mother is at work. Where the mother-child tie does not exist, or is ruptured, and where the child is not speedily allowed to form a new and permanent relationship to some one mother substitute, he may suffer an apparently irreversible warping of his emotional development and be unable throughout his subsequent life to form adequate relationships with other human beings.[1] In some extreme cases, though probably his innate intellectual capacity is unaffected, he may be markedly slowed in intellectual development and appear to become mentally defective, developing even tics and stereotyped mannerisms.

The symptoms of severe suffering are not solely psychological in their manifestation. The incidence of rhinolaryngitis and of infantile diarrhoea and the death rate from this and other diseases among very young children in orphanages and crèches where material conditions are good but where they cannot attach themselves to any one member of the staff, has been shown to be higher than among normal children or those in homes organized to provide separate family groupings in family buildings and an adequate permanent substitute for the mother.[2] Even a relatively short period in hospital may, for example in the case of a child of 2, cause so severe an emotional disturbance as to affect at least for a considerable time the child's whole attitude to others.[3]

We are thus led to a closer examination of the role of the mother in the child's earliest years. In the first few months mother and child form a close biological unit and baby's security depends upon the mother's attitude and upon her physical handling. If she is loving and consistent the baby will thrive whether breast-fed or bottle-fed, whether to a schedule or on demand and whether cleanliness training is begun a few weeks after birth or left until the middle of his second year. There is no reliable proof that any one method of infant care is more beneficial than another from the point of view of mental health,[4] though different methods may bring about differences in personality structure.

For the child's subsequent mental health, the essential is the development and reinforcing of his sense of security, his feeling of always being loved and acceptable to his mother. On the whole the studies indicate that gratification is preferable to deprivation, acceptance

1. The relevance of this to international understanding hardly needs to be underlined.
2. R. Lefort, 'Étude des troubles somatiques des enfants séparés, vivant en institutions'. Unpublished, duplicated material, Centre International de l'Enfance, Paris.
3. cf. film, A Two-year-old Goes to Hospital. J. Roberts, Tavistock Clinic, London, U.K.
4. H. Orlanski, 'Infant Care and Personality', Psych. Bull. vol. 46, p. 1-48, Evanston, Ill., American Psychological Association, 1949; W. H. Sewell and P. H. Mussen, 'The Effects of Feeding, Weaning, Scheduling Procedures on Childhood Adjustment and the Formation of Oral Symptoms', Child Development vol. 23, p. 185-91, 1952.

better than rejection, and permissiveness superior to coercion. But it is necessary to interpose the condition of 'other things being equal' since the development of personality seems to be an interactive process. Children differ substantially in the equipment or characteristics with which they are born but the implications of these differences for subsequent growth in personality vary according to how others react towards them. The emphasis in upbringing at home and at school should therefore be to adjust expectancies and pressures to individual differences. It should also be added that, while a child should only cautiously and sparingly be put into situations which arouse anxiety or make him fear loss of love, it is not primarily upon the methods used that his mental health depends but upon the meaning which the incidents of his daily life have for him; and more than anything else in his early years this will be conditioned by the mother's attitudes as he senses them.

FATHER

The importance of the mother's role in the first years of life has tended to obscure the important contribution of the father. Economically his part is clearly defined in most cultures. Not always so clearly perceived however is the importance of his relationship to his wife, on which so much of her emotional security and thus indirectly that of her child depend. If he can accept the woman's inevitable preoccupation with the new baby without being jealous, he can do a great deal to help his wife to accept and rejoice in her maternity. On the other hand he may react in terms of his own unresolved childish conflicts and—to the point of outright rejection—complicate the mother's response to her child.

After the first year of life, the infant becomes less and less exclusively dependent upon his mother and the part played by the father becomes more direct. In some groups he is a remote figure of authority, even a bogey man; in others he plays with his children but takes little part in their physical care or in the domestic work of the home.[1] In yet others he represents intellectual and social demands and is a source of more or less benevolent discipline. Current trends, especially in cultures of Anglo-Saxon origin, tend more and more to bring father to share in the whole life of the family. Children too begin quite early to interpret their own sex role in terms of the parent of like sex and at the same time to experience relationships between the sexes in terms of what they intuitively feel or comprehend of their parents' married life and their

---

1. J. Boutonier, 'Child Development Patterns—France', in *Child Rearing Practices and Social, Intellectual and Emotional Growth of Young Children*. Evidence submitted to the conference by the World Federation for Mental Health.

own reactions to the parent of opposite sex. Thus at the core of a child's attitudes to others lie his attitudes to his parents and his perceptions of their attitudes towards each other. In this, the masculine element as represented by father is as important psychologically as the feminine one, and becomes increasingly so as the child moves into adolescence.

Here we may draw attention to the fact that economic changes affect the psychological atmosphere of the family directly. For example the absence of domestic help in most homes, the need in many for the mother to work, and similar factors, have tended to involve the father more and more in the daily domestic tasks and hence have brought many closer to their children. The very isolation in which so many modern families live, their smallness, and the intensity of the relationships to which they give rise, magnify the impact of any changes in parental role and underline the importance, for the healthy development of children, of a consistent loving gentleness in the attitudes of mother and father towards them.

SECURITY IN PARENTHOOD

The confident acceptance of parenthood, upon which a sound family life is based, is a subtle thing dependent upon factors in the parents' own personalities, their relationships to each other and to their own past and present environments. Maternal and child health services in most of the European countries have done much to improve the health of children and to give mothers confidence in their physical handling of infants. The steady increase too of various social and welfare services —maternity grants, schemes of home help for nursing mothers, child allowances—has removed many of the immediate sources of anxiety. On the other hand, such services are themselves contributory to the almost universal phenomenon of the breakdown of the old patterns of child-rearing within which parents found the security of ways established and hallowed by tradition. In the past many parents had themselves frequently been members of large families, and the mother, as an adolescent, had had an apprenticeship to motherhood in caring for a younger brother or sister. Many modern mothers have their first contact with young children when they themselves have a baby. Such an undivided responsibility, for which they are totally unprepared by previous training or experience, may be provocative of anxiety and even be severely disturbing. Some parents too are made unsure of themselves by the conflicting advice—frequently sensational and ill considered—poured in upon them from many quarters, by books, magazine articles, newspapers and even by medical and welfare workers misdirected, improperly, or even untrained in mental hygiene principles, who pass on advice without co-ordination and without full realization of its effect in increasing the mother's anxious uncertainty.

The very search for advice and the willingness to accept it may reflect excessive anxiety or parental aspirations for their children, itself a feature of a society undergoing rapid change. Progress is of course not possible without some anxiety; the danger to the mental health of children arises when this anxiety is allied to a confused and often inconsistent intellectual knowledge divorced from the deep feeling and spontaneity which marks sound personal relationships.[1] Thus even though the advice given be sound, this alone is insufficient to prevent its being applied, particularly in middle-class and professional families, in a coldly scientific way.[2]

The important point to note is that more and more 'experts' of various types and from various disciplines are replacing the grandmother who passed on and sanctioned the folk ways, habits and customs of the culture. This is a process which has been going on for a long time but which has recently greatly accelerated. Our admittedly scanty knowledge of the impact of childish experiences connected particularly with feeding, defecation, sleep and contact with the mother would suggest that any practice advocated, for example on the grounds of physical health, should be carefully examined in the light of its implication for the development of the child's own personality, and through that, of the society in which as an adult he will participate. Similarly propaganda in the name of hygiene or psychology aimed at improving the handling of young children should be carefully controlled, since it is apt to arouse parents' anxiety and uncertainty rather than to reassure them in their own ability. This seems to be especially true when, instead of dealing with concrete examples of behaviour in terms of everyday human sympathy and values, articles are written in a pseudo-scientific style with an emphasis on the abnormal.

EXTERNAL ANXIETIES

Associated with the accumulating effects of urbanization and the social change und uncertainty which it induces, there are conditions directly detrimental to children and their parents. The small apartment which is far from sound-proof and in which children cannot adequately play,

1. J. Roudinesco, 'Comparative Study of French Case Material', in *Child-Rearing Practices and Social, Intellectual and Emotional Growth of Young Children*, loc. cit. supr.
2. J. Boutonier, 'Child Development Patterns—France', loc. cit. sup.

the long journeys of the adults by crowded trains and buses to and from work, the tiredness of the mother who has another job, poor sleeping conditions and curtailed rest, especially of the children, the frequent necessity of living with relatives or in lodgings with unsympathetic people, these and many similar conditions contribute to fatigue, irritability and tension in all members of the family, making each more vulnerable to emotional disturbances of all kinds. In the small flat, childish mess and untidiness are crimes. The child who wakes at night crying is apt to get a smack for disturbing his parents' and the neighbours' rest, rather than the reassurance he may need. Quite apart from the possibly detrimental experience of sleeping in the parents' bedroom, children in the small house or flat are continuously exposed to interparental frictions, to the anxieties and worries of mother and father. They are too closely and too continuously under adult supervision, and their needs too much and too continuously in conflict with those of their parents, for a relaxation of tension to be possible.[1]

In such a situation, more or less typical of any of the European urban centres, the great external anxieties of our time have their most devastating effect. Economic worries, the threat of unemployment, high living costs, the menace of war, conflicting politics which play upon fears as well as upon aspirations, advertisements for various specifics with their emphasis upon disease, all these and many others bear upon parents and through them affect the healthy mental growth of their children. It is not often realized how closely the total psychological atmosphere in which a child lives affects his whole attitude to himself and to others both at the moment and in his future; nor how even the concealed anxieties of parents are sensed by their children whose whole stability is dependent in the early stages upon the reassurance that nothing terrible can happen if mummy and daddy are there.

Modern conditions demand of parents more than has ever been demanded before or than most are able to give without considerable help and reassurance. The mentally healthy upbringing of children in a restricted living space by parents rendered uncertain themselves by the great and small anxieties and difficulties of our time is rarely achieved by the simple light of nature or, as has been suggested, by the coldly scientific application of rules deduced from psychoanalysis or even from child-development studies. It requires a deeply emotional insight into the nature and needs of children, a readiness to compromise on adult requirements and a spontaneous sympathy which cannot be built by lectures, occasional advice and a flood of more or less well informed pamphlets. The adverse circumstances of modern life affect children in their early formative years largely in proportion to the parents' own uncertainties and anxieties, expressed or unexpressed.

1. Evidence offered to the Conference by the World Union of Catholic Women's Organizations.

If mother and father, through a calm and accepting temperament, through a religious faith or a working philosophy can reassure their children and meet their emotional needs in all but the most impossible circumstances, then experience has shown that even, for example, extreme poverty or the terrors of aerial bombardment, can be passed through without permanent mental damage to children. Conversely, even where no objective cause for anxiety exists, parents often fail to appreciate how their words will arouse their children's fears. In many middle-class families, for example, parents mention in front of their children their day-to-day financial difficulties, but forget to mention what they know and their children do not—the financial assets which would in fact provide against the starvation the children may imagine to be near. The imperfect knowledge and experience of the young make them vulnerable to anxieties in a way few adults understand.

THE FAMILY GROUP

We have so far discussed the parts played by the parents in some isolation. It should be emphasized however that rarely is the child's relationship with any person an uncomplicated *egoïsme à deux* and then probably only in the first few weeks of his life. Normally the child enters what is in fact a social gestalt of interacting personalities. As he develops, the important role of mother, and the supplementary one of father, merge into that of the family group.

In the psychological nature of such groups there is a wide range of variation, even within any one of the developed cultures of Europe. The least 'complete' family is the isolated mother and her child—a phenomenon which shows some tendency to increase. More typical is that by-product of industrial development and a rising standard of living—the small family consisting only of two generations, the parents and one, two or three children living in greater or lesser psychological isolation from other similar families. This pattern has been emphasized by the type of housing to which it, and economic factors, have given rise—the small flat or apartment or the self-contained house in the city suburbs. Recently through social planning and through economic measures such as child allowances, there have been attempts to increase the numbers of children born into such families and to decrease the social isolation in which many of them live.

At the other extreme are what might be called patriarchal families, which consist of at least three generations—grandparents, parents and children—and which, from the child's point of view, provide affective relationships not merely with his immediate parents and siblings but with related groups of cousins, of aunts and uncles. He grows within a system of complex equalities and hierarchies. Essentially the patriarchal or matriarchal family is based upon property or upon territory, e.g. an ancestral home or a village, and some of the reasons for its tendency to disappear are to be found in the greater mobility of the working population and the changing nature of work. There are, however, certain factors—for example the great ease of modern travel—which may permit a family of a more or less patriarchal type to exist simply on the basis of a common kinship though without property or a shared daily life.

A EUROPEAN COMMUNITY AND ITS PROBLEMS

In Europe will be found all gradations between the more or less 'incomplete' family and the family community; but in spite of social legislation and propaganda the demographic tendency seems still to be towards a relatively low birthrate, a small family with two or three children only, and an ageing population. In a study specially written for Unesco[1] Lang describes the situation in Austria where these tendencies have perhaps gone further than elsewhere. He states that in Austria with a birthrate of 15 per thousand of the population, the family with three or four children has practically ceased to exist. Moreover the factor of tradition is lacking owing to the disappearance from children's lives of grandparents, whose generation has been subject to severe trials. Consequently the children are much too attached to their parents. The problem of a reduction of the size of the family is complicated also by the number of orphans. Of the 856,554 children of compulsory school age attending Austrian schools, 153,000 (18 per cent) were orphans. He calls attention also to the fact that 80 per cent of newly wed women in one of the larger towns of Austria declared their intention of continuing work after marriage.[2]

Similar tendencies are found in rural populations, where the average number of children in peasant families has fallen from 6.4 in the previous generation to 3.6 in the present. This shrinkage is accompanied by a migration to the towns; before 1938, 50 per cent of the Austrian population were landworkers; the present figure is less than 25 per cent Thus, accompanying changes in the size and structure of the family, are found changes in its milieu. Communities which, especially in the west of Austria, formerly consisted solely of peasants have been transformed into worker-cum-peasant communities, and country children are growing up in an environment which has been completely transformed.

One of the results of this change has been a considerable development in the social tasks undertaken by the school and in the educational as

1. L. Lang, 'The Pedagogical Position in Austria'. Vienna, Ministry of Education.
2. In England (1953) one wife in four goes to work. *Ministry of Labour Gazette*. London, HMSO, 1953. Many of the industrialized countries of Europe probably show a very similar tendency.

distinct from the instructional effort of the teacher.[1] The whole educational system has been administratively reformed and attempts are being made to bring curricula into closer relation to the constant evolution of modern life; a school psychological service is in process of development; school record cards *(psychologische Schülerbeschreibungsbogen)* have been introduced to encourage teachers to make thorough psychological observations of children, and the average number of children in each class has been reduced since 1947 from 44 to 34. Perhaps the most striking and socially significant change is the increase in the number of nursery and infant schools (kindergarten and *Kinderhorte*). In the last six years the number of such schools has increased by 95 per cent (from 573 schools in 1945-46 to 1,117 in 1951-52) and the number of pupils in them by 130 per cent (from 27,281 in 1945-46 to 62,734 in 1951-52).

This picture of change in Austria and of a vigorous attempt to use the educational, social and medical services to supplement the work of the home is in many ways typical of modern Europe, and of social processes which have been gathering way since the turn of the century. Psychologically speaking the family is a buffer, a filter and a bridge for the child. It should protect him from too harsh a contact with realities throughout his growing period; it should interpret to him the culture in which he lives; and it should act as a base from which he can launch out into the more impersonal world outside the protection of his home. As societies grow more complex and their heritage of skills, techniques and knowledge is enriched, it becomes increasingly difficult for the family—even the patriarchal family group—to discharge completely these responsibilities in the upbringing of its children. Just as economic development alters the nature of the family's food-getting activities and even displaces much of its responsibility, so more and more aspects of the process of shaping children's personalities, their ethical and intellectual standards, are passed into the hands of adults outside the family.

FAMILY AND COMMUNITY

It is doubtful whether, even in the most primitive tribal organization, the social adaptation of the child and his preparation for the life of an adult rested entirely with the family, even with the patriarchal family

---

1. 'The schools to which a majority of the older children go are now often called "Erziehungsschule" (school intended to educate and not merely to teach facts) and "Leistungsschule" (achievement school). The name "Erziehungsschule" is used in order to emphasize the special duties which, owing to the decline in the educational functions of the family, are now incumbent on the school and require it to adopt new educational methods appropriate to school life in the true sense of the term. With the "Leistungsschule" the emphasis is on the concrete and visible results that school work must produce.'—Lang, op. cit.

group. In the ordinary sense the education of the primitive child is short, informal, and acquired in the course of the normal amusements of childhood. At the threshold of puberty however he is often admitted at the hands of his elders to adult status by some kind of initiation ceremony which contains an element of formal instruction. Developed societies commence the initiation of the young early and tend to prolong it well beyond puberty; in most, compulsory education begins when the child is between 5 and 7 years old and continues until somewhere between 12 and 16, and the age of full legal responsibility and independence is not attained until 21.

The extent and direction of this conscious cultural shaping of children, certainly after the age of 2, varies markedly from one human group to another; and even, within a nation broadly homogeneous in its pattern, from one social milieu to another. So too, does the balance between the role of the child's immediate family and that of the community in general. However, in the earliest years, it is in general through the interpretations of the mother and the immediate family that the surrounding culture, whether it be tribal or urban-industrial, moulds the child. As the child achieves a measure of physical independence, he begins the process of psychological weaning which brings him into more direct contact with a widening section of the community life. It is as this process grows and develops that the great intercultural differences begin to make themselves most felt, through implicit and rarely more than vaguely expressed expectations, through custom and tradition, and through conscious community organization backed by legislative sanctions.

CONFLICTING TENDENCIES IN SOCIAL ACTION

We may distinguish in modern Europe three important and possibly conflicting tendencies. There is first the prolongation of the child's economic and psychological dependence which has the effect of intensifying the influence of the family; secondly, and partly as a consequence of the first, there is the attempt to provide services to help the family in its more complex task; and thirdly we find that some communities, recognizing the inability of the family to discharge its educative task unaided, tend to remove children more and more from the home and thus in fact to undermine the influence of the parents. The last of these warrants careful examination since there are serious dangers, both to the mental health of children as individuals and to the moral and political health of communities, in any measure which breaks the affective link between a child and his natural parents, particularly in the case of the very young, or which removes from the family the final responsibility for its children.

A child's family is important to him throughout the whole of his development—under modern conditions, throughout the period from birth until at least the early twenties. Because of the evident importance of the first five or so years of life there has been a tendency to concentrate attention and support upon the educative activity of the parents of the very young child. This has led to a neglect of middle and later childhood and adolescence or at least to the assumption that agencies outside the home—school and leisure groups—can look after this, provided the foundations are laid aright in the early years. Certainly the broad bases of personality are laid in childhood when, through inexperience and intellectual immaturity, the child is liable to intensely emotional experiences with which he is unable to grapple alone. But life steadily thrusts the growing child forward into novel situations and, in the teens particularly, when physiological factors combine with environmental stimuli to provoke another profoundly emotional and therefore formative period, he needs the continuing support and understanding of his family. For the development of a mentally healthy personality and for all that is normally meant by character, the second decade of life is at least as important as the first and offers what may be the last opportunity of setting right any misdevelopments which have taken place earlier.

This suggests that efforts to improve the mental health of communities should be confined neither to the first few years of a child's life nor to the remedying of maladjustments when they have arisen. An essentially preventive mental health service will begin with the family before the child is born into it and will aid—principally through the family— the child and adolescent throughout his formative years. It is in the light of this that we are led to suggest that legislative, administrative, economic and social action should be initiated and evaluated in terms of whether it tends to strengthen and support the family in its task of ensuring the healthy personal, emotional, and physical growth of its children and whether it brings outside agencies, such as the school, the medical and social services, into active co-operation with parents throughout the whole of the child's period of psychological growth.

II. HOME AND SCHOOL

THE COMPLEMENTARY NATURE OF THE SCHOOL AND THE HOME

After the first years of childhood, the school is the most important single organization which could work with the child and his family. Its influence can be exerted not only on the fathers and mothers, but directly and indirectly in the preparation of the next generation of parents. It occupies a vantage point from which the many other services, medical, social and psychological, could be brought into relationship with the family and its pupil.

So far, however, co-operation between homes and schools and between schools and the community generally has not (for a variety of reasons) developed as fully as it might in Europe; yet all three are necessarily complementary agencies in the education of children, and parents and teachers have different but supplementary tasks. Mothers and fathers, for example, have a far closer and deeper tie with their children than the teacher has; they know them more intimately and possess a fuller knowledge of the whole pattern of previous growth. The teacher on the other hand should have been trained to know the psychology of children in general; he should be able to draw comparisons from one child to another, to estimate what is normal and what deviates from the average; his attitude to any particular child should be more detached and objective than that of a parent, and he should be able to allay unnecessary anxiety and put the individual child in the perspective of his wide experience.

The child-in-school is in many ways a different person from the child-at-home; his attitude and behaviour towards his parents are markedly different from those towards his teacher. The two environments however interact and what happens in the one will influence behaviour in the other. Many parents, for example, are ignorant of the way in which too heavy a demand on the help of a girl or boy with family chores may prevent satisfactory progress in school; many teachers are unaware that the tasks they set for homework may rouse antagonism in the parents or provoke mother or father to undertake the job of a supervisor of studies. Sometimes, newer teaching methods or educational aims are not understood by parents; a subtle or overt opposition to the school begins at home and quickly puts the pupil in a conflict of loyalties. The teacher may treat as lazy a child who goes so late to bed that he has no energy left for work, or fail to understand the irritability, aggressiveness or stubborn non-co-operation of another whose energies are absorbed in anxious fantasies provoked by a mother's illness or the unexplained birth of a baby.

THE GENERAL TASK

There is thus a general task to be discharged—that of building up mutual knowledge and understanding between school and home, the initiative in undertaking which, by virtue of his training and his position of responsibility towards a number of children, will normally fall to the teacher. Invitations to parents to visit the school and see what goes on, talks and discussions on educational method, upon changes in conception and technique which have taken place since the parents went to school, and upon innovations which are about to be made, demonstrations and suggestions as to how, without playing the amateur teacher, parents can help their own children to learn and how they can complement the lessons which are given, these and activities like them will bring parents into an understanding participation in the teacher's work.

It is more difficult for the teacher, especially in the urban school, to get to know the homes of his pupils and something at least of the personalities and attitudes of parents. Where custom is not antagonistic to it, and where time permits, a visit to the homes of his pupils will tell the alert and observant teacher a great deal that he could not otherwise know. In the case of children who experience difficulties in their educational or personal development, such a direct contact with the home is indispensable and will often go far to explain the cause of the difficulties. Much of the necessary understanding however can be obtained by other means; by personal conversations with the parents; through the reports of school welfare officers, attendance officers, social workers and the like; and through the teacher himself making a careful study of the community in which he lives and works, so that he may come to understand the preoccupations of the families of the children he teaches, and the kinds of experience which his pupils are having outside the classroom.

In the course of a child's school career there are, too, a number of occasions when consultation between parents and teacher should be close and where, in the majority of instances, the initiative to bring it about will have to be taken by the teacher. We may list as examples, the child's first entry to school or change from one school to another; the times at which he has to be guided in his choice between alternative courses of study; and, as schooling draws towards a close, when the adolescent's future career is discussed. In such circumstances and others like them, it is the task of the teacher to act as adviser to the parent, to present as objectively as possible the facts which bear upon, for example, the choice of a vocation, and to help the parent to come to a decision.

PARENT-TEACHER ASSOCIATIONS [1]

It is at least partly from an awareness of these facts that the last 50

---

1. Much of what follows is based on information contained in a report by the World Confederation of Organizations of the Teaching Profession on 'Parent-Teacher Co-operation', Washington, 1953, and in a study specially prepared for the Conference by the International Union of Family Organizations on 'Co-operation between Parents and Teaching Staff'.

years have seen a considerable growth both in general public interest in the social tasks of the school and in the development of parent-teacher activity as means of promoting the general growth of children.

In some countries[1] associations of parents or parent-teacher societies are established by law; in others,[2] legislation or official policy encourages co-operation and even goes so far as to suggest appropriate forms for it; in yet others, responsibility for action is left entirely to the initiative of teachers or parents themselves. Hardly anywhere in Europe do the schools now function in complete isolation from the families of their pupils, though contacts may range from the most rare and casual consultation to highly organized and effective collaboration.[3]

Attitudes in the teaching profession as a whole are not unanimously favourable. Not a few teachers—and especially, but not solely, those from countries where religious conflict maintains a dual system of education with the fears, rivalries and jealousies that this sometimes means—fear that organizations of parents, especially if they are federated on a national level, will act as political pressure groups. Others see a tendency for parent associations to infringe on the professional liberty of the teacher, and are anxious lest there be a direct interference in school organization, curricula, and methods by those who are not fully aware of the complex problems involved. Yet others, perhaps from bitter experience, complain that parents' meetings induce ill-informed and hostile expressions of opinion about the school and about individual teachers. Some few think that close contact between parents and teachers may make children insecure and self-conscious.[4]

There is no doubt that such fears and doubts have some justification. Moreover in the ranks of the teaching profession itself there are members whose dictatorial manner or clumsiness in personal relationships are likely to provoke rather than allay stresses and tensions between the school and the home. There are individual parents who are too fearful, too indifferent and, sometimes, too hostile to co-operate in the education of their children. There may well be local or even national situations in which co-operation on an organized basis, is undesirable; though it is difficult to imagine circumstances in which informal and personal contacts between members of a school staff and the parents of particular pupils do not have value.

In spite of the difficulties encountered and the fears expressed, most teachers and teachers' organizations recognize that for the good of individual children and for the progress of education as a whole, the home and the school should be brought close together and that they

---

1. For example: France, Holland and Norway.
2. For example: Belgium, Sweden, U.K., Zürich (Switzerland).
3. See 'Councils and their Schools: II', *Planning* vol. XV, no. 288, 27 Sept. 1948.
4. For an examination of the opinions of a group of teachers on parent-teacher co-operation see: W. D. Wall, 'The Opinions of Teachers on Parent-Teacher Co-operation', *Brit. Journ. Ed. Psych.* vol. XVII, pt. II, June 1947.

should jointly exercise their complementary functions. As to how it should be done opinions and practice vary. Probably in the majority of European schools, it is at least partially achieved by casual meetings between a parent and the headmaster or headmistress, or the teacher of the child's class. In many schools, the head is available to parents by appointment at certain times or invites them for interview whenever particular problems arise. In addition, parents may be invited to school occasions—prize days, exhibitions of work, sports days, concerts and the like—during which personal contact with the school staff is possible.

Many heads and teachers feel that such individual and informal contacts are all that is justified or necessary. For rural schools where the teacher is known to and knows the local community, they are probably sufficient. In towns or where the school draws its pupils from a wide area, such more or less casual contacts are rarely enough to give the teacher real insight into the home circumstances of the pupils, to help the parent to understand the aims and methods of the school or for teachers and parents together to exercise a decisive influence upon the improvement of the total education of children. Hence, usually on the initiative of the head, or of individual teachers, meetings of all parents or of the parents of pupils in a particular class[1] are called on specific occasions, such as first entry to school and when a choice of future studies is to be made, or regularly at intervals of a month or more. The principal object of such group meetings is informational: and, while there is interchange between teachers and parents, they most usually take the form of lectures by the head, his staff or outside experts.

From such regular meetings to the development of a formal parent-teacher association is a relatively small step; and in a great many European countries associations exist on a regional basis or in connexion with particular schools. The advantage of a formal association is that it makes initiatives by the parents themselves easier and, suitably constituted with a carefully defined field of activities, provides an organization which can give direct and material support to the school. Parent-teacher associations undertake money-raising activities to provide for such things as school expeditions and equipment[2] which would not normally be supplied by the education authorities; they organize social activities, study groups, parent-teacher meetings of informal kinds and arrange for visiting lectures on special topics. More important however is the framework they give for parent education, for the creating of an informed public opinion on educational matters,

---

1. As in the *classes nouvelles* in France.
2. In at least one case (the Russelokka Elementary School, Oslo) parents, teachers and pupils combined to rebuild and re-equip a school destroyed during the war (see WCOTP pamphlet cited on 44).

and for bringing parents and teachers, through working together and educating each other, to realize the significance of the social task of the school in its community.

LINKS WITH OTHER SERVICES

There is a limit to what parents and teachers can achieve alone and a link should be established between the parent-teacher association, or the school, and the more specialized services and resources of the community. This should be a functional co-operation which ensures that research in child development, knowledge of social and medical welfare work, developments in educational technique and the like are harnessed to the practical and constructive task of improving the all-round education and upbringing of children. The emphasis should be on normality, upon the everyday problems and upon ways of improving patterns of family and school education rather than upon maladjustments, subnormalities and psycho-therapeutic treatment. Hence the psychologists, social workers, specialized educators, school medical officers and others who may be called in to help, must train themselves in the difficult art of speaking directly to parents and teachers in terms of daily life and experience rather than of the clinic or laboratory. Much can be done by the publication of pamphlets, by lectures and demonstrations, by newspaper articles, and by radio programmes if these are very carefully controlled and framed. Many parent-teacher associations seek and obtain help from university departments of education and psychology, from school psychological and medical services, and from the vocational guidance bureaux, in arranging courses of talks which can then be followed up by discussions.

An interesting initiative, in France,[1] Switzerland[2] and Luxembourg, is the École des parents et des educateurs. In its developed form, this type of organization provides a full programme of lectures by educators, medical specialists and psychologists, on various aspects of the physical, mental, and, especially, the psychological development of children.[3] The lectures, supplemented by pamphlets[4] and illustrated folders[5] each bearing upon a concrete problem of development are published and made available to parents and teachers. As an essential corollary to this general dissemination of information, these organizations have

---

1. Lyons, Paris, Strasbourg.
2. Geneva, Neuchâtel.
3. For example the Conférences de l'École des Parents in Paris included, in 1952-53, lectures under the four main headings 'L'adolescence', 'Psychologie du mariage', 'Quelques influences premières sur la formation du caractère' and 'L'enfant à l'école'.
4. For example: *L'esprit d'indépendance, L'enfant aîné, Les parents nerveux, La colère, Si vous vous séparez de votre enfant.*
5. For example: *Tournants dangereux, Paquet-de-nerfs, Un petit frère, Toto mouillait son lit.*

47

developed the small discussion group of parents under the guidance of a specialist and an individual service of consultations open to parents and teachers.

SOME TECHNIQUES[1]

Properly developed and under the guidance of teachers who have been more adequately trained than is usual at present for this particular task, the parent-teacher association aided by other services, can perform a most valuable part in the mutual education of parents and of teachers; indeed the teaching staff are likely to draw as much profit from it as the parents themselves. Yet it will largely fail to fulfil the tasks earlier described if it concentrates its activities upon the provision of information acquired at a purely intellectual level. The transition from knowledge to spontaneous practice, from intellectual concepts to intuitive wisdom in handling the growth problems of children and still more in shaping their whole education towards the needs and conditions of the future, is difficult to make. Parent and teachers alike behave towards children more in terms of their own past experience, in terms of barely conscious fears, anxieties and wishes, than in terms of objective psychological insight. General information on child rearing and child development disseminated by lectures and pamphlets may, however carefully framed, do more harm than good if it merely raises doubts and uncertainties, if it undermines an already precarious security in family upbringing, without providing both parents and teachers with the capacity to respond spontaneously as well as correctly to the children in their charge.

The education and orientation of parents and teachers begins long before adulthood and depends more upon directed and analysed experience than upon factual information intellectually acquired. The little girl caring for a younger child is learning some of the responsibilities and joys of parenthood; and girls' secondary schools, as well as teaching the elements of cookery, housecraft and domestic economy, could arrange for their adolescent pupils to have some care of young children, even of babies, in the nearby nursery school or crèche. The expectant or young mother, in the maternity hospital or through the

---

1. The following contain representative suggestions of a practical kind useful for parent-teacher activities and discussion; R. Drouineau, *Vade mecum à l'usage des organisations de cercles de famille*. Paris, Union Nationale des APEL, 1944; K. E. D'Evelyn, *Individual Parent-Teacher Conferences*. New York, Bureau of Publications, Teachers' College, Columbia University, 1945; E. McHose, *Family Life Education in School and Community*. New York, Teachers' College, Columbia University, 1952; National Congress of Parents and Teachers, *Study-Discussion Group Techniques for Parent Education Leaders*. Chicago, Illinois, 1951; G. H. Pumphrey, *Juniors: a book for Junior School Parent-Teacher Groups*. Edinburgh, Livingstone, 1950.

ante- and post-natal clinic [1] can be trained (and not merely instructed) in meeting the psychological needs of her child. In this, demonstration, free and frank discussion, carefully arranged experiences under skilled psychological guidance are worth more than lectures or than the rapid didactic consultation with a busy paediatrician not always well informed on psychological matters. The nursery school, with its relaxed atmosphere and its staff trained to put children's needs first can, by welcoming the participation of mothers and fathers, rouse questions in their minds and affect the handling not merely of one child at the school, but others in the family.

The parent-teacher association provides the logical framework for a continuation of this process. We are still relatively ignorant of the techniques necessary to ensure that men and women from different social and educational levels will assimilate psychological knowledge and will modify their own attitudes, prejudices and behaviour to children. But it is becoming clear that one means to this end is the discussion group, which systematically explores, from both the home and school standpoints, concrete examples of child behaviour. Such groups should be small—8 to 12 persons as a maximum—informal, and, as soon as possible, conducted in an atmosphere of complete frankness. This atmosphere will develop only gradually as the participants work together and gain knowledge and security in their relations with each other. Much depends upon the skill with which such a group is initiated and conducted. The ideal is to have someone fully trained in psychology who can at the beginning suggest topics, act as a reference point, and as leader and who can delicately bring the group to understand something of the dynamics of their inter-personal reactions. [2] The fact that such skilled personnel are not available need not however prevent the development of such groups within parent-teacher associations. One member—usually, but not invariably, the teacher—might accept the task of choosing one or two topics for discussion, and of gathering the necessary information both on child development and—of almost equal importance—upon the psychology of small groups. Effective points of departure may be found too through carefully chosen films and filmstrips, especially those of the open-ended variety which lead dramatically up to a practical situation in parent-child, parent-teacher or teacher-child relationships, but break off before a solution is offered. These have the advantage that they can be presented to a large audience which can then subdivide into small

1. Partial and promising initiatives of this kind have been undertaken by the Mutterschule, Winterthur, Switzerland, the Hôpital St-Antoine, Paris, and Queen Elizabeth Hospital, Birmingham, U.K.
2. See J. Bierer (ed.), *Therapeutic Social Clubs*. London, Lewis, 1948. Also the second part of W. D. Wall, 'École et famille en Angleterre', *École des parents*. Paris, no. 10, Oct. 1953.

groups to continue an intimate discussion; and it is not beyond the resources of a school staff or parent-teacher association to produce such filmstrips themselves or to dramatize incidents of their everyday experience in the form of a radio play recorded on the tape- or wire-recording apparatus possessed by many schools.

In all this work, whether the leader is a trained psychologist, a teacher or a parent, it is important that, even in the initial stages, the leadership should not be too directive. The earliest opportunity should be seized of letting the group collectively develop and guide its own discussions.

Some parent-teacher associations have gone beyond this into what is rather pretentiously called psycho-drama or socio-drama. The essence of this technique is that incidents of adult-relationships or adult-child relationships are more or less spontaneously dramatized by parents and teachers themselves without an audience, and as a means of having, at first hand as it were, the emotional experience involved. Carefully handled and with a group which has passed beyond its initial self-consciousness, this can be a most formative and valuable technique. It can even be applied to the many problems of relations between adolescents and their families and teachers, with the direct participation of the adolescents themselves. A further development is for one group, having evolved and discussed a spontaneous drama of its own creation, to construct alternative endings to it and then to present the whole to an audience of parents for discussion.

The success of such techniques depends upon the readiness of participants to accept them, and this is in part a function of individual resistances and self-protective attitudes and in part of the cultural patterns of the particular national or social group. The more an activity penetrates in its effects to the emotional life, the more 'dangerous' is it likely to appear to the adult and the greater the resistance to be expected. In such matters the rule is to hasten slowly; tactfully to encourage the development of frank discussion, of socio-drama and the like rather than to impose them.

Meanwhile there are many other ways in which parents can be drawn into a participation which is something more than passively listening to a lecture. Every form of activity which tends to diminish the isolation of the individual family or parent or which brings teacher and parent together on a creative task contributes directly to mentally healthy living for the adult and thus, indirectly, to that of the child. The principal need of many adults is for the outlet of doing something constructive, of joining in musical, craft or artistic activities with others, of learning how to learn, and discovering that excitement and satisfaction in a finished and complete product of which their daily lives rob them. The social and cultural activities of a good parent-teacher association therefore are as valuable as the directly educational ones, and may, indeed, by the relief and relaxation they bring, be the essential preliminary to more overtly educational work.

III. COMPREHENSIVE SERVICES

CO-ORDINATION

The value of parent-teacher activity has been dwelt on because potentially it can span the largest part of the developmental period of children and because it can typify the principle of co-operative effort to help the family to help itself, without robbing it of responsibilities and initiative. The same principle should inform the educational activities of other agencies which aim to bring specialist help to parents or to the school. Services of medical and social welfare, of educational, vocational and psychological guidance and of the supervision of young workers in industry are all increasingly seen to be necessary. Unfortunately they are at present only too frequently unco-ordinated, partial in their action, and they tend to be absorbed primarily in the individual case where something has gone wrong. Moreover the nature of the conceptions by which they have grown frequently leads such services too readily to take over responsibilities which rightly belong to parents or to teachers, thus undermining with technical expertise a confidence which, by a more disseminated, co-operative and constructive educational function, they should be building up. If this is allowed to continue, and particularly if the services work in mutually exclusive compartments as they tend to do at present, the end result may well be worse than that of a policy of laisser-faire. Essentially, unless actual specialist treatment is involved, as in the case of a greatly disturbed or sick child, the specialist, individual or service, must remain the consultant or adviser to the parents and to the teacher. The aim must be to make it possible for the mother or father, for the schoolmaster or schoolmistress, to use effectively in their work the knowledge gained by the specialist; and the primary aim of any kind of service should be constructive and preventive, and only secondarily remedial.

Here we need to stress that the authorities should study ways of co-ordinating the various services: and, through the joint training of staff, especially in educational work with parents and in inter-disciplinary understanding and co-operation, efforts should be directed to ensuring that there is a comprehensive system working for the benefit of all children. In the educational field much could be done officially to stimulate and guide the establishment of parent-teacher associations or committees, to ensure that the training of teachers includes practical study both of the home and family life of children and of the methods of working with parents. Parent and teacher representatives might be invited to take part in the determination of educational policies, and continuous research of a practical kind into the most important educational needs of the community and the results of current educational methods should be promoted and financed.

High among the priorities should come the whole problem of how, in co-operation, school and home may lay the foundations for successful marriage and parenthood. Parents may make many mistakes in their handling without lasting damage to their children, if they remain affectionate, supporting and consistent. This however is just what many parents, without being 'problems', are not fully able to do; and the qualities necessary are those least easy to acquire late and in an intellectual manner. They are the mark of a fundamentally mature personality which has met and adjusted to the strains of its own development. Effective parent education is a lengthy and continuous process beginning long before adulthood, aimed at preparation for marriage and parenthood, helping the new father and mother to understand and to apply throughout the youth of their families and with a genuine spontaneity the intellectual knowledge which the science of child development is putting at our disposal.

The problems facing psychologists and educators are the closely related ones of the comprehension and interpretation of a swiftly changing culture and the development of techniques which help men and women emotionally to assimilate the knowledge so obtained. Such work implies co-ordinated services by many agencies which, respecting the individuality and responsibility of parents themselves and calling them into an active and creative partnership, co-operate to build up their confidence in parenthood. It means too that all who have to do with children and their families—nurses, doctors, teachers, social workers, police—are involved and should have both sound practical and at least some theoretical training in child psychology.

THE SOCIAL AND ECONOMIC BACKGROUND

Action of the type sketched above can only be truly effective if it is carried out within a social and economic framework which protects and fosters the real family. Hence while social and industrial organization should preserve the possibility for women to choose freely between making home life a career, having a career outside the home, or combining both, it should be possible for a mother to remain with her children, at least for the first two years of their lives, without being forced away from them by economic necessity. In particular the use of day nurseries for infants under one year should be discouraged except when it is totally impossible for the mother to give her child personal care. If, for any reason, a child has to be separated from his family this should be regarded as a very grave step, to be taken only after the most careful exploration of other possibilities. Moreover separation should be as short as possible and every effort should be bent to the restoration of the child to its parents, and where parents are inefficient, to assisting them to develop their skills. If a child cannot be restored to his natural family, he should be placed quickly and permanently in a substitute family or, failing that, in an institution run on family lines where he can find a genuine mother substitute. Since the inefficient or broken family is so fertile a seed bed of emotional disturbances, neurosis and delinquency, which repeat themselves in the next generation, legislative and administrative action should concentrate upon prevention and, where that fails, upon early discovery and speedy remedy.

The health of the family is however directly affected by many administrative measures over which individuals may have little control. Wherever, for example, authorities are concerned with the provision of adequate housing, they should bear in mind that the large family should not be penalized for being large, i.e. that provision should be made for them as well as for childless and small families; that in new housing estates it should be possible to develop a real sense of community; that families should not be isolated (though having privacy); and that children should not be removed from their natural surroundings. A satisfactory housing scheme would be based upon small communities with adequate shopping, social and recreational amenities, and with safe and accessible playgrounds for its children. It would in fact reproduce the best conditions of village life with the hygienic, labour-saving, and cultural advantages of a town. It would be utopian to hope that more than a small proportion of the families in Europe will be rehoused in such conditions in the near future, though many countries have begun to rebuild. It is however suggested that, even in adverse conditions such as exist in most of the great cities of Europe, much more might be undertaken at very little cost to foster a sense of community in small groups of families and to provide adequate playing space for the children who so sorely need it.[1]

The last decades have seen an increasing amount of money, public and private, spent in Europe upon attempts to cure mental ill-health with greater and lesser success. There are child guidance clinics, psychiatric clinics, family service units, social welfare services and a host of similar organizations engaged in attempts to remedy ills which arise mainly from faulty relationships and tensions within the family.

---

1. A good example has been given by the Community Centre movement in the Scandinavian countries and in the U.K., and by the provision of 'adventure playgrounds' for children in congested areas. See: Lady Allen, *Adventure Playgrounds*. King George's Jubilee Trust, 1953.

Normally little is done until a breakdown occurs. Then the cost to the community of one severely maladjusted person may well be astronomic, not merely in terms of money and skilled time, but in terms of an expanding circle of self-perpetuating maladjustment and unhappiness. In all forms of social work and particularly where the healthy emotional development of children is concerned a ton of prevention costs less in the long run than an ounce of cure; and its dividends spread over the whole community. Preventive and constructive mental health work requires co-ordinated thinking by all those concerned with the family whether as administrators, architects, teachers, psychologists, medical practitioners, social planners or legislators. The healthy growth of a community cannot be secured by a few specific measures, nor by appointing of a handful of experts. It requires, as well as the experts and facilities for the treatment of neurotic or maladjusted individuals, the realization in practice that every social measure has an implication for the life of the family, and through the family, for the development of the next generation of parents.

BIBLIOGRAPHY

ANDERSEN, O. et al. *Hjem og børn.* København, J. H. Schulz Forlag, 1947. 216 p.

ANSHEN, R. N. *The family, its function and destiny.* New York, Harper, 1948. 44 p.

ARLITT, A. H. *Family relationships.* New York & London, McGraw Hill, 1942. 277 p.

BAYLEY, N. *Mental growth during the first three years; a developmental study of sixty-one children by repeated tests; from the Institute of Child Welfare, University of California.* Provincetown, Mass., Journal Press, 1933. 92 p.

BENEDICT, R. *Patterns of culture.* Boston & New York, Houghton Mifflin, 1934. 290 p.

BENJAMIN, Z. *The young child and his parents.* London, University of London Press, 1947. 156 p.

BERGE, A. *Education familiale.* Paris, Aubier, Ed. Montaigne, 1936. 254 p.

———, *Les défauts de l'enfant.* Paris, Aubier, Ed. Montaigne, 1953. 220 p.

BLACKBURN, J. *Psychology and the social pattern.* London, K. Paul, Trench, Trubner, 1945. 157 p.

BOER, H. de. *Gezin en school; referaat gehouden op de Grondslagenconferentie van het Christelijk onderwijs te Birkhoven op 31 Oct. 1947.* 's-Gravenhage, Boekencentrum, 1948. 31 p.

BONNARDOT, J. *La collaboration des parents avec l'école.* Lyon, Ed. de la Maison Heureuse, 1933. 64 p.

BOURGUIN, F. *La protection sociale de l'enfant en France.* Paris, Masson, 1938. 184 p.

BOVET, L., GUEX, G., RAMBERT, M., RICHARD, G. *Parents et enfants.* Lausanne, Ed. du Groupe Esprit, 1943. 140 p.

BOVET, P. *Famille . . . Quelle famille?* Lausanne, La Concorde, 1942. 14 p.

BOWLEY, A. H. *The problem of family life.* 2nd ed. Edinburgh, E. & S. Livingstone, 1948. 99 p.

BRULÉ, H. *Le rôle de la femme dans l'éducation familiale et sociale.* Paris, Foucher, 1950. 132 p.

BURLINGHAM D. and FREUD, A. *Infants without families.* New York, International University Press, 1944. 128 p.

CHAMBRE, P. *Une école de parents.* Paris, Les Presses d'Ile de France, 64 p.

CHORUS, A. "Zuigeling en kleuter", in Rutten, F. J. Th. *Jaren der Jeugd* vol. I. Heemstede, De Toorts, 1942.

COHEN, E. W. *English social service.* London, G. Allen & Unwin, 1949. 170 p.

CONFERENCE OF EDUCATIONAL ASSOCIATIONS. *Annual report 1949, home and school.* London, Conference Office, 169 Strand, W.C.2, 1949.

Economie, psychologie dans la vie familiale. Journées familiales internationales, Rome, Sept. 1949. Paris, Union Internationale des Organismes Familiaux. 134 p.

EDGE, P. *Some parents' questions answered.* London, Faber & Faber, 1946. 76 p.

Enfance et famille. IVe Congrès du Bureau international catholique de l'enfance à Constance. Paris, Ed. Fleurus, 1953. 127 p.

EVELYN, K. E. D. *Individual parent-teacher conferences.* New York, Bureau of Publications, Teachers College, Columbia University, 1945.

FERRIÈRE, A. *L'éducation dans la famille.* 4e éd. Lausanne, Ed. du Secrétariat romand d'hygiène sociale et morale, 1935. 98 p.

——. *Vers une classification naturelle des types psychologiques.* Nice, Ed. des Cahiers

——. *Vers une classification naturelle des types psychologiques.* Nice, Ed. des Cahiers Astrologiques, 1943. 75 p.

FLUGEL, J. C. *The psycho-analytic study of the family.* 4th ed. London, Hogarth Press, 1939. 259 p.

GERRITSMA, W. E. *De school, ouders, besturen, onderwijzers.* Zeist, Gereformeerd Schoolverband.

GONTCHAROV, N. K. *Zaklady pedagogiky.* Moskva, Statne Nakladatel'stve, 1950. 409 p.

HART, I. K. *Education in the humane community.* New York, Harper, 1951. 172 p.

ILLINGWORTH, R. S. *The normal child: some problems of the first three years of life and their treatment.* London, J. and A. Churchill, 1952.

ISAACS, S. *Concerning children* [pamphlets] nos. 3-7. London, Univ. of London Institute of Education, and the Home and School Council of Great Britain, 1937.

KATHOLIEKE CENTRALE VERENIGING VOOR GEESTELIJKE VOLKSGEZONDHEID. *De geestelijke gezondheid van het gezin. Verslag van de jaarvergadering op 30 Mei 1949.* Utrecht, De Vereniging, 1949. 88 p.

KOHNSTAMM, P. *Schepper en schepping.* Vol. II. *Persoonlijkheid in wording.* Haarlem, F. Bohn, 1929.

KREVELEN, D. A. VAN. *Het enige kind; bijdrage tot de psychologie en psychopathologie van het kind.* Utrecht, J. Bijleveld, 1946. 374 p.

LACROIX, J. *Force et faiblesse de la famille.* Paris, Editions du Seuil, 1949. 159 p.

LEBEL, R. *L'enfant dans la famille.* Paris, J. Oliven, 1952. 191 p.

LIDBETTER, E. J. *Heredity and the social problem group.* London, E. Arnold, 1933. 160 p.

LINDNER, R. M. & SELIGER, R. V. *Handbook of correctional psychology.* New York, Philosophical Library, 1947. 691 p.

MEILI, R. "Beobachtungen über charakterologisch relevante Verhaltensweisen im dritten und vierten Lebensmonat", *Rev. suisse Psych.* 1953, vol. 12, no. 4, p. 257-75.

MENUT, G. C. *La dissociation familiale et les troubles du caractère chez l'enfant.* Paris, Ed. Familiales de France, 1943. 108 p.

NATIONAL SOCIETY FOR THE STUDY OF EDUCATION. "Nature and nurture", *27th Yearbook.* Bloomington, Ill., Public Publishing Co., 1928. 2 vols.

NØRVIG, A. M. *Det sunde barn og dets foraeldre.* 2. udg. København, E. Munksgaard, 1941. 208 p.

PARENTS' GUILD. *Parents working together.* London, Central Council of Parents' Guild, 1946.

PEYSSARD, L. *La famille regarde l'école.* Paris, Ed. Familiales de France, 1946. 109 p.

PRO JUVENTUTE. *Bericht über den Kongress Jugend und Familie.* Zürich, Zentralsekretariat Pro Juventute, 1942. 112 p.

RADKE, M. J. *The relation of parental authority to children's behavior and attitudes* (The Institute of Child Welfare, *Monograph series,* no. 22). Minneapolis, University of Minnesota Press, 1946. 123 p.

RIBBLE, M. A. *The rights of infants.* New York, Columbia University Press, 1943. 118 p.

SAYLES, M. B. *Substitute parents; a study of foster parents.* New York & London, The Commonwealth Fund; Oxford University Press, 1936. 309 p.

SCHIFF, H. *Elternfehler-Kinderschicksal; Formen der Fehlerziehung.* Wien, Braumüller, 1948. 104 p.

SCHMID, H. *Die Pädagogische Situation in der Kinderreichen Familie.* Dissertation. Freiburg, Schwarzenbach, 1948. 198 p.

TICHELEN, H. VAN. *Huis en school.* Gent, Boekh. Rombaut-Fecheyr, 1946. 195 p.

VIEHWEG, W. *Die Schule als Funktion der Gesellschaft.* Darmstadt, Schröter, 1949. 35 p.

WALLASEY EDUCATION COMMITTEE. "Children growing up", *Your child at school* (*Guidance for Parents,* pamphlet no. 14). Wallasey, WEC, 1953. 12 p.

WALLER, W. *The family; a dynamic interpretation.* New York, The Cordon, 1938. 621 p.

WATERINK, J. *De school aan de ouders.* Delft, W. D. Meinema.

ZIMMERMAN, C. C. *The family of tomorrow. The cultural crisis and the way out.* New York, Harper, 1949. 256 p.

PRE-SCHOOL EDUCATION[1]

SOCIAL NEEDS

The modern incomplete family with its restricted living space and its urban environment is often unable to give its children all that they need physically and psychologically for their fullest personal development. In a country village where there is ample play space, a supply of natural play materials, sand, water, mud, wood, in an environment free of serious hazards and where the child finds himself in a group of children of pre-school age, many of his needs are provided naturally. The town child is in a very different situation. Indoors his play space may well be confined; and in many homes it does not exist. His desire to experiment with his environment is restricted by a need for cleanliness and order which is incomprehensible to him. Outside his front door, the environment is dangerous—too much so for him to go far afield; and he may in fact have no contact at all with children or with adults other than his parents. In a real sense therefore the nursery school, which provides artificially the space, materials and the group of equals the child needs, is a necessary antidote to the restrictions imposed by urbanization. This is not to say that it is essential for all children or that the aim should be to remove any child from his family for the whole or even for the larger part of his waking hours.

PRE-SCHOOL EDUCATION IN EUROPE

The picture of organized pre-school education in Europe is a confused one, and the implicit or explicit aims of many institutions providing day-care for young children are conflicting. In many countries, the nursery school or kindergarten has grown out of the garderie or crèche and still retains or is even dominated by its function of social first-aid for

---

1. This chapter whilst it is based in general upon the deliberations of Group I, draws heavily in the first part (frequently verbatim) upon the working papers produced for the conference by H. Aebli and by the International Catholic Child Bureau.

children whose mothers cannot look after them in the pre-school years. In other countries, usually those economically more fortunate, the nursery school or kindergarten caters solely for the education of children between the ages of three or four and the beginning of compulsory schooling. In practice many pre-school institutions combine an educative function with that of physical and social protection, some as in France, having two separate staffs, one to conduct the relatively short daily period of pre-school education and the other to ensure the care of children from early in the morning until the end of the mothers' working day. Though the distinction is perhaps artificial in practice, it is necessary to point out the essential difference in conception between the nursery, garderie or crèche and the nursery school, kindergarten or infant school proper. The first concentrates primarily upon the physical care of young children, often of babies under the age of 2; its intention is only incidentally, if at all, educative and its staff rarely trained for an educational task. The second, the nursery school or kindergarten, has a primarily educational aim and its intention is to provide an environment and a specially trained staff devoted to the psychological and educational needs of children, enriching and adding to, but not acting as a substitute for, the education and, the physical care properly given by the mother at home. As such it should occupy only a few hours of the daily working time of the child. The extent to which the pre-school is forced to take over tasks not properly in its field will be a function of social and economic necessities which should be handled at their source by other means. Even the need for and extent of its more purely educative activities is conditioned by the capacity—not solely economic—of the parents, especially of the mother, fully and understandingly to educate children in the years before they enter the primary school.

It is here worth underlining that any measure which tends to separate the mother from a child under the age of 3 is usually undesirable from the point of view of the child's mental and emotional development. It seems better by social and economic measures to make it possible for a mother to devote her whole attention to her child, at least for the first two or three years and, if necessary, to help her in the task, rather than by the provision of crèches and garderies to encourage her to resume work as soon as physically possible after her child is born. Similarly the encouragement of large families by systems of family allowances and other means if this is not accompanied by other social measures which provide the family with the necessary conditions for educating its children, may result in an increasing load of maladjustment in the community. The tired and irritable mother, the sordid overcrowded flat, the lack of play space out of doors and other similar evils are provocative of marital dissension, of repressive methods of upbringing, and ultimately of various forms of social unrest, mental ill-health and delinquency. Taking young children for long periods out of such conditions may certainly be necessary but it is a palliative only, not a remedy.

It is also a form of social action different from that intended by the nursery school. For many children in Europe, particularly those from crowded homes in large cities, but also for those from middle-class flats whose home circumstances may be physically excellent, the three or four hours' daily experience with a group of contemporaries in an atmosphere of calm and space is a necessary adjunct to ensure their healthy development. In few countries, however, is the provision adequate, partly because the need is not recognized and partly because this type of education is expensive in space, in staff and in equipment. It is difficult to obtain reliable estimates of the proportions of children between the ages of say 3 and 5 or 6 who attend such schools but in reading what follows it must be borne in mind that in few countries does the percentage exceed 60 and in most it is as low as 10 to 15.[1] Moreover global figures conceal the fact that, in England for example as in other countries, the available nursery school places in publicly-provided schools are usually allotted to those whose family circum-stances make some form of day care imperative, or the schools themselves are sited in the poorer districts. On the other hand in many countries, privately organized and financed nursery schools and kindergartens receive the children of parents in good economic circum-stances. For children whose circumstances are between these extremes and whose needs, though different, may be equally great, little or no provision exists.

In what follows, at the risk perhaps of some confusion, stress is laid upon the ways of meeting some of the more urgent emotional, in-tellectual and social needs of children in the period before the start of compulsory schooling. Few children nowadays enjoy the ideal circum-stances of growth in a large family, living in a spacious home with a garden and presided over by an intelligent mother who has time and energy to spare for the education of her children. Most are denied even the supplementary opportunities of the nursery class. Parents however can, even where difficulties of space and time are great, do much to ensure a balanced emotional and intellectual growth for their children if they are helped to develop an insight into their needs, and ingenuity in meeting them. Therefore in discussing the whole problem of pre-school education, the tasks of home and school, of mother and

---

1. These figures are derived from data in *The World Handbook of Educational Organization and Statistics*. Paris, Unesco, 1951, and from a *Report on Pre-School Education in the World* prepared for the conference by the World Organization for Early Childhood Education. The proportions seem to be, as one might expect, roughly proportionate to the population density. Belgium, with a population density of 284 per sq.km (1951), has about 65 per cent of the age group 3-6 in nursery schools. France, with a mean density of 77 per sq.km (1951), has about 20 per cent; Norway (density 10 per sq.km), less than 3 per cent.

nursery school teacher, have deliberately been juxtaposed, since frequently the mother may have to fulfil as best she can both functions. Moreover, even where the nursery school cares psychologically and educationally for children entrusted to it, its full task is not discharged unless it also accepts an active part in helping the parents to develop their educative capacity.

SOCIALIZATION

From birth to the beginning of compulsory schooling at the age of 5 or 6, the growing child has a great range of developmental tasks, emotional, intellectual and physical to accomplish if he is later fully to realize his own potentialities. Many, for example crawling and walking, he achieves mainly by processes of physiological maturation; others, for example learning to talk, take place under social stimulus as a result of maturation. Every aspect of his early growth, every developmental accomplishment is coloured by the attitudes of those around him. He may be assisted in his growth in a great variety of ways with correspondingly different effects upon his attitudes to himself and to others and upon the shaping of his subsequent life.

Thus there is an element of the social even in apparently maturational accomplishments. As human communities grow at once larger and less isolated, it becomes more essential that self-realization should take place within a framework which emphasizes the need to contribute to the life and development of society as a whole. Hence, the task which, from the viewpoint of society, is of the utmost importance is that of the beginnings of the socialization of the child's crude egotistic impulses. From at least the age of 2 onwards he is normally able to speak and is therefore open to a much more intensive educational influence by his mother; it is at her hands that he should get his fundamental education in moral behaviour, in co-operation with others, in how to share things and persons with younger and older brothers and sisters and with his parents. Social and moral attitudes do not grow spontaneously from social interaction but are the results of education, especially of social experience in groups of children playing in the presence of a mother or nursery teacher who acts, not merely to regulate conduct, but to interpret the moral norms of society. The child has to learn to respect the rights of others and to conform to exigencies which are often contrary to his egoistic desires; he should come steadily more and more and in increasingly complex ways to experience and discriminate between situations in which he must abandon or modify a desire of his own in order to conform to the life of a group and others where he must defend his own rights.

The family provides the child with his first social group within which such give and take can take place, and, if the family is a relatively complete one, a natural society providing many other experiences of hierarchic and of equalitarian relationships. As the child's experience expands, he comes into contact with other family groups, and with neighbouring children of nearly his own age; later still, wider and different communities are presented to him; the nursery or infant class, the primary school. These latter, and particularly the primary school, are communities different from that of the family, less personal and intense in their relationships and with a greater emphasis on the relations between equals. The young child, however, cannot conceptualize a large group, even one as apparently little complex as a village or a suburb; but he can experience and come to understand direct relationships between a small band of friends or a class of some 10 or 15 others[1] of his own age and thence be introduced steadily to larger and larger units. It is in the context of such progressive experience, based first on the socialization he has learnt from his parents and brothers and sisters, that he will learn to orient himself more and more fully to others, lay the basis of a widening concept of himself in relation to society and develop moral attitudes and techniques which bring him into satisfying harmony with children and adults outside the tightly drawn family circle. Even a good home, well equipped to satisfy many of the personal needs of a child, can only in exceptional circumstances and by much forethought and self-denial on the part of mother provide him with such a graded social experience; and the very intensity of the bonds which unite him to his family, even those which go beyond the immediate parents, has an element of exclusiveness which may contribute to raise inter-personal barriers rather than to lower them.

At the age of entry to nursery school (in most countries between 3 and 4 years) the child is still naturally egocentric and obeys almost completely his own impulses. In so far as his attitudes are social they are adult centred. Piaget's early work[2], though to some extent reflecting the Montessori type of activity pursued by his subjects, has been confirmed by subsequent research.[3] Up to the age of 3 or

1. The class of 40 or even 60 children in a nursery school makes nonsense of pre-school education as a means of social training for the 3 or 4-year-old. In European schools, the average teacher-child ratio seems to vary between one teacher to 59 children and one to 18. In many countries, though one fully trained nursery school teacher may have 30 or more children under her charge, she is assisted by nursery helps or by parents who voluntarily undertake some of the tasks of supervision.
2. J. Piaget, *Le langage et la pensée chez l'enfant*. Neuchâtel, Delachaux & Niestlé, 1924, and (idem) *Le jugement et le raisonnement chez l'enfant*. Neuchâtel, Delachaux & Niestlé, 1924. See also the criticisms of C. Bühler, *Kindheit und Jugend*. 3rd ed., Leipzig, Hirzel, 1931, p. 161, and of M. Muchow, 'Psychologische Probleme der frühen Erziehung', *Akademie gemeinnütziger Wissenschaften zu Erfurt, Abteilung für Erziehungswissenschaft und Jugendkunde No. 19*. Verlag Stenger, Erfurt 1929, p. 54 ff.; W. Hansen, *Die Entwicklung des kindlichen Weltbildes*. München, Kösel u. Puslet, 1938 and 1949, p. 114.
3. C. and W. Stern, *Die Kindersprache*. 4th ed., Leipzig, J. A. Barth, 1928; S. Isaacs, *Social Development in Young Children*. London, Routledge, 1933, and (idem) *Intellectual Growth in Young Children*. 1930.

thereabouts, the child—unless he himself is markedly mature and his early education has provided exceptional opportunities—is scarcely able to take part in co-operative play; solitary and parallel activities dominate all others. Around 3, however the social integration of the child normally begins to make marked progress, and during the following two or three years he comes to participate more and more frequently in associative and co-operative play, which has been found to reach a first peak between the age of 5 and 7 years.[1]

Social behaviour, and the moral basis on which it rests, is, as has been pointed out, largely learned. In ideal circumstances and particularly where the child is a member of a large family in a community which provides opportunities for contacts with children outside the immediate group of brothers and sisters, such learning comes about more or less spontaneously, under the guidance of the mother and father. Where these opportunities are lacking, the nursery school must play an important part in its development.[2] The mere contact of a child with age-mates affords numerous occasions for social learning. Hetzer, on the basis of qualitative studies of the social needs of different children, suggests that they be placed in different play groups according to which aspect of their social behaviour should be fostered. The nursery school teacher or parent may be even more positive. She can not only provide the opportunities but can actively assist the child in his development from ego-centricity towards associative and co-operative activities, governed by freely accepted and understood common rules. Her comments and reactions to the social behaviour shown by children, the ways in which she encourages co-operation and self-sacrifice or settles disputes, her praise and blame, even the questions she poses, will train and regulate the behaviour of her charges.

In addition to the concrete and guided social experience which children gain by contact with each other under her guidance, she can help them to become familiar with all kinds of men and things which are foreign and strange. It has long formed part of good nursery—and primary—school practice to take children outside the confines of home or the school from time to time, interesting them in the

1. H. Hetzer, 'Das volkstümliche Kinderspiel', *Wiener Arb. z. päd. Psychol.* 1927, no. 6; M. Parten, 'An Analysis of Social Participation, Leadership and other Factors in Pre-school Play Groups' (unpublished Ph. D. thesis, University of Minnesota, 1929). The findings are published by the author in the following three articles: 'Social Participation among Pre-school Children', *J. Abnorm. Soc. Psych.* 1933, 27, p. 430-40; 'Social Play among Pre-school Children', *J. Abnorm. Soc. Psych.* 1933, 28, p. 136-47. A digest of the thesis will be found in R. G. Barker et al., *Child Behaviour and Development*. New York, McGraw-Hill, 1943, p. 509-25; C. Bühler, *Kindheit und Jugend*. op. cit.; L. A. Hattwick and M. K. Sanders, 'Age Differences in Behaviour at the Nursery School Level', *Child Development* 1938. 9, p. 27-47; W. Hansen, loc. cit. p. 14-34: 'Das Spiel in der Frühphase der Kindheit.'
2. K. L. McLauchlin, 'Kindergarten Education', *Encyclopedia of Educational Research* (rev. ed.). Ed. by W. S. Monroe. New York, Macmillan, 1950, p. 647-54.

activities of others, and to invite adults from outside. If there are foreigners in the locality, the teacher can try to bring them into friendly relationship with her children. Quite young children too, by means of pictures and stories, may come to know how, for example, Esquimaux and Africans live and, by singing in their original languages, songs from other countries, come to see that different people use different words to say the same things. It is too much to say that international understanding in the full sense can be trained in the nursery school; but by making the strange familiar, the teacher can help to diminish the aggressive or fearful reactions which foreigners provoke and actively link the socialization of young children with the development of attitudes favourable to other peoples. One should however insist that the fundamental contribution of the home and of the nursery school to international understanding consists, at this early stage, of building up the attitude of good will towards others. This is done fundamentally, not so much by learning about other peoples, but by learning good relationships to playmates.[1]

SECURITY AND INDEPENDENCE

The child's social development however is not only the product of experience with others. The way must be paved for it by the progressive satisfaction of other needs. From the moment of birth, normal psychological progress implies an increasing differentiation of the self from its human and physical surroundings, a steadily fuller distinction between the world of external reality and the realm of fantasy, and a growing physical and emotional independence. None of these processes is completely accomplished before the end of adolescence, and they will be accomplished only partially, if at all, if the child's early growth does not favour them.

The gentle, loving, consistent and reasonable mother lays the foundations of her child's security—the very basis on which his independence is built. Throughout the first two or three years of his life, it is she who meets his needs and at the same time takes a large part in adapting him to reality, giving and withholding satisfactions. It is within the secure framework of her affection for him that he is able to assert his independence; it is she whom he imitates and of whom he feels an inseparable part; and it is against her that from time to time he shows opposition. If the child's relationship with his mother is free

1. Evidence given by Mrs. Herbinière-Lebert, President of the World Organization for Early Childhood Education. For an illuminating empirical study of the development of children's ideas of their own and other countries, see: J. Piaget and A. Weil, 'Le développement chez l'enfant de l'idée de patrie et des relations avec l'étranger', *Bull. Int. Sci. Soc.* vol. 3, no. 3, p. 605-21, Unesco, 1951.

63

of anxiety and if his acceptance of the values of his family is healthy, his independence and opposition will be important factors in the growth of his personality and of his ability later to learn and form values of his own. Valentine[1] has shown how essential to subsequent character formation is the period of negativism which occurs normally around the age of 2 or 3. This oppositional tendency is likely to become extreme if the parents are over-indulgent or inconsistent; if they are over-rigid and dominating they may provoke rebellion, or, by suppression, turn their children into cowards or nonentities. In a stable family most children find enough security and independence for their needs, enough to identify with, and to oppose, for their healthy emotional and intellectual growth. Many parents however need guidance in how to deal with such things as temper tantrums, disobedience, contradiction, refusal of food, and the like, which occur as normal manifestations of opposition and developmental stresses. They need to come to see, too, that much childish disobedience, for example, is simple forgetfulness or due to the child's inability to delay a response; that some selfishness or rudeness or bad manners is merely a phase of development, a sign of normal immaturity. This does not of course mean that they should merely accept or excuse such behaviour; but that they should learn to respond rather in terms of the child's developmental needs than of their own convenience or irritation.

WIDENING RELATIONSHIPS

The parent-child relationship is highly emotional; and everything in the child's life is coloured by it. It is important that as soon as possible his experience of realtionships should be widened and his exclusive dependence on mother should be lessened. The little group of friends in someone else's garden or the more regular experience of the nursery school group containing children who are not his brothers and sisters and depending on an adult who is not his mother is thus an important step nearer to a wider reality for the child who enters it. He is obliged to compare the new environment with what he meets at home. The only child or the spoilt child find themselves no longer the centre; they have to share the adult's attention with other children; they may receive what, for many only children at all events, is the first experieuce of 'disillusionment' in that, in the behaviour of other children, they find indifference or aggression and, in the fact that mother leaves them, what may be the first shock of psychological weaning from her

---

1. *Psychology of Early Childhood* London, Methuen, 1942; *The Difficult Child and the Problem of Discipline*. 5th ed. London, Methuen, 1950.

exclusive care. For the mother too this may be a difficult experience. Many of the problems of adaptation of young children are due to the mother's inability to release them.

The child's experience of groups outside the home should be more than a series of negatives, however necessary these may be in his adaptation to reality. The nursery class offers the child a field of relationships different from those experienced at home, other kinds of interpersonal tensions and another experience in resolving them so as to bring himself harmoniously into adjustment with others. Positively, the nursery class can continue and enlarge the mother's task of offering acceptable and happy compensations for the relinquishment of infantile expectations and desires. It fosters the natural drive to independence and gives the children in the person of the mistress who is not mother but whom the children recognize as 'safe', an adult whom they can 'love' and 'hate' less intensely than their parents. Thus it enriches and makes more real their system of personal relationships. By providing them with a greater variety of concrete experiences with material and with persons than is possible in the average home, the nursery school further leads children forward from the lawless world of their own fantasy into the realm where they realize that others, children and adults, have the same feelings and needs as they and that the objective world is governed by laws of cause and effect independent of their own wishes and fears.

INTELLECTUAL GROWTH

In young children, emotional and social development go hand in hand with intellectual growth. The child who is insecure will not progress normally in his social development and may thus be held back intellectually. Conversely, as is evidenced by studies of children from institutions and lower economic groups,[1] retardation in intellectual acquirements, if not actual dulling of innate capacity, can be a consequence of a lack of stimulating experience and, through an imposed poverty of concepts and of words, in its turn inhibit social contacts.

The contributions of the home and the nursery school to the child's intellectual development should arise naturally out of the quality of the environment they provide rather than from any direct teaching

---

1. H. E. Jones, 'Environmental Influences on Mental Development' in *Manual of Child Psychology*. Ed. by L. Carmichael. London, Chapman and Hall, 1946, p. 582-632; M. F. Little and H. M. Williams, *An Analytical Scale of Language Achievement (Univ. Iowa Stud. Child Welfare)*, 1937, 13, no. 2, p. 49-94; H. M. Skeels, R. Updegraff, B. L. Wellmann and H. M. Williams. *A Study of Environmental Stimulation: An Orphanage Pre-school Project (Univ. Iowa Stud. Child Welfare)*. 1942, 15, no. 4.

such as may be given in primary or secondary schools. Nevertheless the mother or teacher should be aware how experience contributes to the child's intellectual growth and how, by what she offers and her own interventions, she may stimulate and guide, as well as follow and assist, the natural course of growth.

Language development and concept formation are closely interrelated and lie at the basis of intellectual development. The child takes terms and expressions from adult language, as he develops at least rudimentary concepts; on the other hand, adult language exercises, through its implicit content of view points and categories, a strong influence on the child's concept formation.

Studies of genetic psychology stress that thought is interiorized and systematized action. The young child frequently must act out in play what the adult can think internally and the objective adult image of the world evolves out of the child's physical and sensory activity where attitude, movement, excitation and his seeking for experience and satisfactions are steadily brought into a closer and closer relationship to each other to form the basis of an expanding and steadily more and more verbalized series of concepts or ideas.[1] Activity and experience are therefore the very food of intellectual growth, and the task of the home and of the school is to provide both in variety.

Reflections of this kind led Maria Montessori[2] to design play material engaging the child in concrete activities to be executed in an isolated manner. However, this type of activity, commonly called functional play (Piaget: 'Jeu d'exercice',[3] Bühler: 'Funktionsübung'[4]) has been shown to make up only a part of the child's spontaneous play. Role play (called also 'symbolic' or 'imitative' play) is even more characteristic of pre-school children.[5] It consists in imitating typical real life situations, where father, mother, animals, and naturally the children themselves play the main parts. Doll play is a most popular form of role play in many countries. Scenes and events taking place away from the house may be imitated also: playing 'train' or 'zoo' are good examples; and stories told by parents or teachers furnish further subjects for children's spontaneous dramatizations.

1. C. Bühler, op. cit.; K. Bühler, *Die geistige Entwicklung des Kindes*. 5th ed., Jena, 1922; W. Hansen, op. cit. p. 72-99, 235-63; H. Hetzer and B. Reindorf, 'Sprachentwicklung und soziales Milieu', *Zeitschr. f. ang. Psychol.*, Leipzig, Barth, 1928; O. Kroh, 'Über die intellektuelle Entwicklung der reifenden Jugend', *Zeitschr. f. päd. Psychol.* 1928, 29, p. 10-34; J. Piaget, *La psychologie de l'intelligence*. Paris, A. Colin, 1947; H. Wallon, *Les origines de la pensée chez l'enfant*. Paris, Presses universitaires de France, 1945. 2 vols.
2. M. Montessori, *Autoeducazione nelle Scuole Elementari*. 3rd ed. Rome, E. Loescher, 1916; *The Absorbent Mind*. Wheaton, Illinois, Theosophical Press, 1949.
3. J. Piaget, *La formation du symbole chez l'enfant*. Neuchâtel, Delachaux & Niestlé, 1945.
4. C. Bühler, op. cit.
5. The playing of different roles or the imitation of different persons immediately in the environment has been reported by most observers of young children. Piaget has subjected it to a most thorough analysis (see reference in footnote 3 above).

Properly guided, such activities markedly promote the intellectual development of the child. In, for example, playing at 'washing-day' or 'postman', in joining in household tasks with mother, he acquires new concepts in the field of hygiene, money, transportation and the like. Such concept formation is matched by the learning of new words and expressions and an increase in vocabulary takes place. In order that the children may carry on such activities, home or school should be equipped not only with clay, painting materials and simple picture-books, but also with toys for house-keeping, dolls, locomotor toys, large floor blocks and other simple equipment for dramatic play.

When such activities take place in company, children are led to talk to each other. In a study carried out by Van Alstyne,[1] certain materials appeared to have considerably more 'conversation value' than others. Doll play, blocks, etc., ranked high for the percentage of time that their use was accompanied by conversation. McCarthy indeed[2] makes the suggestion that attempts should be made to stimulate the linguistic development of children who are not naturally very talkative by interesting them in play materials which appear to be conducive to conversation.

THE PART OF THE ADULT

What should be the function of the teacher or parent in these activities? Certainly to help organize and prepare the material needed for the play. But besides that, should it be her tendency to let children carry out their play independently, or should she actively participate in it, even introducing ideas of her own, not spontaneously found by the children? Although for quite irrational reasons, some current educational thought fosters minimum adult participation, much experimental evidence tends to show that contact with grown-ups powerfully promotes the linguistic and intellectual development of the child.

McCarthy[3] found that children who associate chiefly with adults show marked linguistic acceleration. So do only children. At the opposite extreme, several researches show severe retardation in vocabulary development among children in institutions.[4] Furthermore,

1. D. Van Alstyne, 'The Environment of Three-year-old Children. Factors related to Intelligence and Vocabulary Tests', *Teach. Coll. Contr. Educ.* 1929, no. 366.
2. D. McCarthy, 'Language Development in Children', *Manual of Child Psychology*. Ed. by L. Carmichael. London, Chapman and Hall, 1946, p. 563.
3. D. McCarthy, *The Language Development of the Pre-school Child*. Minneapolis, University of Minnesota Press, 1930.
4. M. F. Little and H. M. Williams, *An Analytical Scale of Language Achievement (Univ. Iowa Stud. Child Welfare)*. 1937, 13, no. 2, p. 49-94; H. M. Skeels, R. Updegraff, B. L. Wellmann and H. M. Williams, *A Study of Environmental Stimulation: An Orphanage Pre-School Project (Univ. Iowa Stud. Child Welfare)*. 1942, 15, no. 4.

linguistic retardation is frequently found in young twins, who play mostly together and who may, in fact, develop a kind of jargon private to themselves and unintelligible to others.[1] The fact that their lag is generally reduced as they enter school points to a lack of stimulation in their early language development.[2]

From these findings, it seems reasonable to conclude that the adult should introduce into the children's activities, ideas and forms of conduct that lead them beyond the patterns of behaviour that evolve out of their natural growth. As far as under-privileged children are concerned, the need of such active and conscious educational influence, usually by the teacher, is all too obvious. Among children of higher social groups, the number of cases where a similar need exists is rapidly increasing. It is of course by no means implied that forms of activity be suggested that are totally unadapted to the child's developmental level or that they be introduced under heavy adult pressure. The teacher should simply do what good parents have always done: look forward to the next desirable stage of growth and guide the child in his search for more developed forms of action and thought. At the same time extremes should be avoided. There are games and activities in which the child has need of adult participation, stimulus and even direction; there are others, equally necessary, where adult interference disturbs the assimilative or other processes going on. The only child frequently suffers from a precocious development in some directions—particularly in language and, apparently, in judgment—through being too closely with adults and may later, having lacked the possibility to grow at his own pace and to consolidate his acquirements, regress to infantilisms he has not been allowed to outgrow. Generally, also, over-great association with adults means that the child has been deprived of the social experiences which he gains with his peers.

WORK ATTITUDE

Within the development of creative activities, the Viennese school of child psychology has been able to show certain trends of apparently wide generality and value in our culture. They pertain to what might be called the 'development of purposiveness' or of the 'work attitude'. Purposive behaviour can be defined as being governed, from the outset by a determinate objective, which the individual strives to attain in spite of obstacles and distractions. Normal progress in the development of such purposiveness is of high importance to the young child in our

---

1. I. Lézine, *Enfance* vol. 1, Jan. Feb. 1951.
2. E. A. Davis, *Development of Linguistic Skill in Twins, Singletons with Siblings, and Only Children from Age Five to Ten Years (Inst. of Child Welfare. Monograph. ser. no. 14)*. Minneapolis, University of Minnesota Press, 1937.

culture, for it is a determining factor in readiness to enter primary school and to accept more directive forms of teaching.

In her studies of the development of creative activities such as building with blocks, drawing, modelling with clay and using the 'Matador' construction material,[1] Hetzer found apparently genetic sequences which seemed to correspond to a law of development. An initial stage was characterized by mere functional activity, the child being unconscious of the fact that his product might represent something. Later on, he would discover the resemblance of his product with some person or object after having completed it as a mere functional exercise ('it's a tower', 'it's a man'). During a third stage, he gave his product a meaning while he was working at it, still after some trait accidentally engendered. Only during a final stage was the child found to mention his intention of representing this or that before he set to work and to make definite efforts to attain his objective.[2]

This stage of purposiveness *(Werkherstellung)* was reached in all fields of creative activity studied by Hetzer by the age of 5 or 6 years, activity with constructional material being the last to become purposeful. From that time onward, children were observed to set themselves certain tasks and to struggle towards their solution. When they have reached this stage they are capable of the first simple forms of 'work' as opposed to play, and of the fulfilment of tasks set by the teacher. In respect, therefore, to the development of a work attitude, Bühler considers them ready to enter primary school.[3]

Two conclusions concerning pre-school education whether at home or in the nursery school might be derived from these facts of child psychology. Since the stage at which purposiveness is attained seems to be specific for each form of activity and to depend to some extent on the mastery of its particular problems, informal training in the use of crayons, pencils, colours and clay will probably foster the child's readiness for their more purposeful use in primary school. The good home or nursery school will also, as well as developing the child's vocabulary, provide him with pre-reading material and activities—pictures, books, words written on cards and associated with objects and the like—familiarity with which paves the way for more formal learning of reading skills later. In the third place, the adult should help to orient the child's development in the direction of purposeful

1. H. Hetzer, 'Die symbolische Darstellung in der frühen Kindheit', *Wiener Arb. z. päd. Psychol.* 1926, no. 3; *Kind und Schaffen, Experimente über konstruktive Betätigung,* Jena, Quellen und Studien zur Jugendkunde. 1931, (The 'Matador' material consists of perforated boards and discs that can be joined by means of small sticks that fit the holes.)
2. It is to be asked however whether such purposiveness or work attitude is a cultural artefact, an imposed ideal of our culture and not a genetically determined or purely maturational process. In certain African groups for example it does not appear to develop. If this is indeed the case, then the function of parent and teacher in fostering it may be all important.
3. loc. cit. supr.

work. Mother and teacher should gently encourage him from about the age of 4 to finish the piece of work that he has begun and help him to become conscious of his aim in the early stages. In the period immediately prior to entry to the primary school, children might frequently be asked to state their objective before they set to work on any task and they should from time to time be given certain jobs well within their reach, and become steadily more accustomed to working with a number of others on a given task, the completion of which is a collective responsibility. Care for pets and plants, involvement in domestic duties, and the undertaking of regular responsibilities within the school or family have proved well suited to help children to develop some sense for the fulfilment of a task and of the beginnings, at any rate, of an idea that there are duties to be discharged in a spirit of service to others, independently of whether one wishes or not to do them.

PLAY AS A DEVELOPMENTAL MEDIUM

So far stress has been laid upon certain aspects and uses of play which have a direct and, to most teachers and parents, obvious value for the physical, intellectual and social development of young children. The part played by the teacher and parent in such play is more or less directive, providing situations and guiding the child's growth. Play, however, to the child is something deeper than this. Studies by psychologists of many schools have repeatedly shown, what the records of work with difficult or disturbed children confirm, that play is at once the language of the child's emotional life and one of the means by which he brings his fantasies into steadily closer relationship with the real world.

A young child is easily made anxious; his latent fears of loss of love, loss of security, and his inner anxieties about his own strong and ambivalent feelings may quickly become overt and appear as either hostility or withdrawal or both. His wishes and desires come into conflict with environmental demands; his imaginative life holds fears and threats and anxieties which are the more terrifying for being secret and unexpressed. At such times play is for him a means of expressing concretely the chimeras of his mind. He is not primarily constructing or exercising; he is exteriorizing his emotions and literally using the only means at his disposal to think. Sometimes he plays out in detail situations which have moved him deeply or he seems to be trying to solve through dolls and teddy bears, problems in his relation-

---

1. This section draws heavily and often verbatim on a working paper prepared for the conference by the New Education Fellowship and in particular on Section 4: 'The Therapeutic Value of Play in the School Situation', by E. Balint. See *New Era*, vol. 33, pt. 10, 1952.

ships to others. In this sense his play may be cathartic; he is purging his own emotions and unconsciously using a concrete means to the solution of his difficulties and to an understanding of himself and of his relationships to others.

During the recurrent periods of emotional conflict and corresponding behaviour disturbance which are a normal accompaniment of development, he has a special need for acceptance through an understanding relationship with adults. In a good home and in a good nursery school he is fundamentally acceptable to his parents and to his teacher when he is good and when bad, when well and when sick. He can rely on not being rejected. This is the cornerstone of the ability later to accept himself and consequently others which is one of the main essentials of mental health.[1] His play is not merely tolerated but is encouraged and welcomed. The good mother and the good teacher use the child's play to understand and help him almost intuitively in much the same way as the psychologist does. When, however, the child does not feel that he is loved, when he feels himself rejected or when the adults round him cannot accept the intensity and the reality to the child himself of the experience projected in play and where they react with distaste or aggression to the fears, desires and preoccupations of childhood, he may steadily play less and less until he is unable to accept help in the solution of his difficulties or even to play at all.

Free play is the child's own expression of himself, whether it be the trivial filling of time or the language of his deepest wishes. Approval and understanding of his product, whether it be a picture, a construction from junk material, a climbing feat or a relationship with another child, means to him approval and acceptance of him as a person. According to the type of play, this acceptance may mean to him acceptance of him in all his 'goodness', in all his ambition to grow up and be able to do and to understand more and more things, or it may mean acceptance of him as a person vulnerable and chaotic in the present, or perhaps of him in all his 'badness' in the past. For example, a child beating up a teddy bear may dimly be indicating the evil thoughts towards his new baby brother which he either cannot or dare not directly express. The wise mother or teacher though they may not fully understand this, by their acceptance of the play incident, by the remarks which they make and by the reassurance they give even while they say 'Poor Teddy—I shouldn't do that . . . it's not very nice', help the child to come nearer to real understanding of what is 'good' and what is 'bad'. Play of this type is often a child's way of testing his wishes and desires against adult norms and reactions and a means of learning through imagination what in reality he cannot and

1. See J. A. Hadfield, *Psychology and Morals*. London, Methuen, 1923.

should not experience. The attitude and remarks of the adult therefore have great importance for him.

The play of children after the earliest years is less and less frequently purely solitary. More and more they tend to play side by side or together; and to them, playing together often means among other things the sharing of a fantasy life. Through play they tell one another these fantasy truths; through being shared these intimate truths become realities, and fall into their true perspective, and the children become real people to one another. They use one another in their seeking to understand the external things around them and in their efforts to understand their own experiences.

Probably this assimilative and cathartic function of play is, from the point of view of constructive and preventive work for the healthy, emotional development of children, the most important. It demands an environment rich in possibilities, in space, in objects and materials (not necessarily nor even desirably, elaborate toys) and, since imposed play is a task, at times at least an atmosphere of freedom in which the adult intervenes, if at all, only with interpretive or regulative comment. There are some adults, parents and teachers, who find it difficult to allow children to play freely: perhaps because they have not come to terms with the child in themselves and fear the fantasies which may be released; perhaps because they have an intense distaste for 'dirt'; or because they consider play a waste of time and are anxious for their children to work hard and get on. It is necessary therefore to urge that children—and not only children of nursery school age—need time and space to play freely. Even though space is at a premium in many homes and in not a few schools, at least a corner and ample time must be allowed.

FAIRY TALES

Allied to the child's need to play out his problems and fantasies, is his interest in fairy stories. Many elements of the folk and fairy tales including the cruel and sadistic elements, match the child's own inner world, and he can easily identify himself and his circumstances with the story as it is told—the good king and queen with the 'good' aspects of his father and mother; the cruel things done by the 'bad' people who are often giants or wild animals with the 'bad' side of his parents and with his own unregenerate wishes, and the way in which evil is overcome by the cleverness or cunning of the weak and harmless, with his own desire to be 'good' and powerful.

One can readily observe in the responses of children to fairy tales, in their play, and in their relations with their parents, a need to experiment with all kinds of different feelings not only of love and happiness but of fear, of terror, of anger and aggressiveness. It is only by experience that the little boy or girl can learn to control these emotions and recognize how far they are caused by things which will never really happen. In this way the fairy tale can be regarded at once as cathartic, and, skilfully used, as a means of aiding the child's adaptation to reality, helping him to distinguish fantasy from truth.

Nevertheless, fairy tales vividly told by adults at home or in the nursery school, sometimes arouse acute anxieties and phobias in certain children; and the danger is particularly acute if the adult telling the story uses it to express her own sadistic fantasies. Many of the folk tales contain elements which, however told, are gruesome, terrifying or sadistic. Some educators therefore would have them either heavily censored or completely banished from the home and nursery school. We do not know, however, how each individual child reacts to various symbols and stimuli and it would be difficult to select an agreed list, though it is clearly necessary to exclude the obviously horrifying. When stories are told, in an atmosphere of security, by a beloved mother or by a teacher who is not herself carried away by the vividness and strength of her own fantasies, and when children are allowed to act out their feelings during and after the telling, fairy tales can be a valuable bridge between the lawless morality of the child's inner world and the more regulated morality expected of him both by his parents and in his kindergarten. They may even be a useful counterpoise to the very rationalistic and 'hygienic' regime of some modern families and pre-schools. Good current practice, whilst it does not banish the fairy tale, includes in the stories read or told to children, tales about animals and about children which illustrate positive and optimistic attitudes towards others and towards life. Even in the pre-school stage, children can benefit from true or realistic stories of daily life which serve as a basis for discussion between teacher or parent and the child, and from which the lessons drawn can be directly applied to his life.

DEATH, BIRTH, SEX

In the pre-school period, for most children and for their parents and teachers, certain special difficulties may arise, on the handling of which much of the child's subsequent attitudes and healthy development depend. Sooner or later the child has experience of the death of someone in his environment; sooner or later, questions occur to his mind about the mysteries of birth. To both these phenomena, adult attitudes are in general poverty-stricken, full of fears, ignorance and magical feelings and often heavily charged with guilt and anxiety. At first, at all events, the young child is spontaneous in his approach and ree of such anxiety or guilt; he can often talk about birth and death much more freely than his parents and teachers, and indeed often shocks adults by his casualness.

Over the death, even of a much beloved person, a child's grief is likely to be different from ours and he can express it with more sincerity. When asked incautiously whether he was sad about his granny's death, a 4-year-old answered 'Yes—*very*—before dinner!'. So many things and people come over and pass beyond the child's limited horizon that he cannot suddenly be aware of the irrevocable nature of death. The adult should try not to be shocked by this and to accept and respect the child's own way of coping with and expressing his feelings.

So too with problems of birth and sex, it seems always better to answer the child's questions as they arise and to avoid imposing a mystery where the child sees none. Many experienced workers feel that adults should merely answer the child's questions without proffering more information than the child actually demands. Grown-ups often, however, by the very way in which they answer the child's first question, make it difficult for him to ask others; and it may seem therefore safer to give rather more information (for example about the father's role in procreation) than the child appears to be demanding because we can be sure that he will put aside, until he is ready to accept them, those parts of what we tell him which are not relevant to his needs.

A purely physiological explanation of sex divorced from the context of the parents' loving consideration, support, and concern for each other and for their children, is quite insufficient and may even cause more anxiety than it allays. When for example the first child, before or after the birth of a sibling, asks about where it comes from, it is important to tell him not only the biological facts so far as he can grasp them, but that he too was carried for nine months by his mother and born of the parents' love: he may otherwise feel excluded.

In the home or the nursery school where children are encouraged to keep pet animals and still more in the country where the phenomena of sex, birth and death among domestic and wild birds and beasts are a daily commonplace, many questions are answered for children before they frame them and in a context unaccompanied by the intense and overwhelming emotion provoked by experiences in their own families. But children learn also from each other and gain ideas in such matters which are often fantastic or even terrifying—and this is more likely to be so amongst those who are deprived of the natural opportunities for observation.

Sex education is not solely a matter of providing natural opportunities to learn and of giving the right information at the right time. It is a part of the whole development of a child as a human being and later as husband or wife and as a parent. The relationships between

74

father and mother, their attitudes towards others, their willingness to give their child the information he asks for, not only on sex, but on other things, all shape his attitudes towards others. Even information which comes late, after a child has achieved a garbled idea of sex and of the relationships between parents, has value as a corrective and as a means of attenuating shocks caused by premature or erroneous enlightenment. The child's first training in these matters and his first questions come at home; and it is from his mother and father that his early education—good or bad—in intimate relationships between the sexes will come, whether they accept the task or shrink from it. Ideally the school should intervene only in a secondary role, supporting and enlarging the action in this as in other things begun by the family. In the current situation of ignorance and unhealthy attitudes among parents and in the community at large however, the school may have to do more than this and attempt to help parents to answer their children's questions and even give collectively or, preferably, individually the information that mother or father do not feel able to give.

More disturbing to many adults than questions children ask about sex, are the self-examination and sex play of pre-school children. Parents and sometimes teachers are apt to react with shock or angry moralizing. To the child, his behaviour may be exploratory, an expression of curiosity, or a source of comfort in loneliness or anxiety. The adult attitude most conducive to the child's sound mental development is not that of anxious suppression which can build up pervasive complexes of guilt, but that which accepts such phenomena as natural and gently diverts the child's attention to other preoccupations. The nursery class with its free atmosphere and casual opportunities permits this to happen naturally on the same level as many other more acceptable forms of training.

In all the situations which arise in the development of children's ideas of sex, birth and death, the essential is to respect the child's personality, to create and maintain his confidence in his fundamental acceptability whatever he may do or ask, and to give answers to his questions which are truthful. Much harm may be done by the parent or teacher who gives an apparently immediately satisfying but ultimately untruthful reply to a child, or who adopts a hypocritical attitude to his behaviour. An even worse situation can arise where home and nursery school are not in accord in the replies which they give to children's questions or in their reactions to children's behaviour. The school cannot act alone or in contradiction to what is done at home without the risk of provoking in the child seriously conflicting attitudes; nor can it provide all the experiences which are necessary to sex education in its widest sense. On this as on other matters a full understanding and co-operation between the home and the school is essential.

EARLY RELIGIOUS EDUCATION

Much the same order of problems may arise in the early religious education of children and, as with other important aspects of the child's life, there should be no conflict of ultimate values and practices between home and school. There is nothing in current psychological findings about the requisites for healthy mental growth that is contrary to basic Christian teaching and indeed the three great virtues of faith, hope and love can be regarded as fundamental to healthy personality development. And since the moral values of western Europe are essentially Judaeo-Christian, the humanist education desired by parents, who are not religious believers, will have much in common, at this early stage, with the simple and non-abstract education in behaviour that would be favoured by believers.[1]

Great care must be taken however, even while inducing a sense of right and wrong, not to make children feel unduly guilty (for example about sexual curiosity). Again certain of the Christian mysteries and symbols (especially that of the death of Christ, and many of the lives of the saints) should be introduced to the child in such a way that confidence and love, rather than perplexity and fear, take possession of his mind. A wrong emphasis can be deeply disturbing.[2] The crucial thing is the attitude of the adult. If, however fervent his own faith, the adult really respects the personality of the child, his immaturity, his imaginative suggestibility, his easily aroused anxiety and his need to be loved and forgiven, young children can get interest, reassurance and moral enlightenment from the stories of the Old and New Testaments. But moral education is more likely to proceed from imitation and from the acceptance of the values of their home and school than from precepts, and the question of the relative validity of spiritual and scientific or experiential truth is not likely to arise or be comprehended in the minds of pre-school children.[3]

DISCIPLINE

Parents and teachers of pre-school children are daily faced with developmental changes and difficulties occurring in their young

---

1. That such a common humanism exists and is a sound basis for education is the position of the State school system in France and other countries. Religious groups of various persuasions would go much further. A. Miehle, 'Die kindliche Religiosität', *Akademie gemeinnütziger Wissenschaften zu Erfurt, Abteilung für Erziehungswissenschaft und Jugendkunde.* Erfurt, Stenger, 1928. M. Pfliegler, *Der rechte Augenblick.* Vienna, Herder & Co., 1942. *Der Religionsunterricht.* Vol. II. Innsbruck, Tyrolia Verlag, 1935.
2. Evidence given by The Catholic Child Bureau.
3. See Hansen, op. cit. sup., p. 155-60; 329-36.

charges. The child's need to grow up, perhaps the most fundamental impulse in the whole of his being, is the one need that the adult cannot directly satisfy by reasoning, by argument, by physical care or by all the techniques and means at his disposal. Parents, teachers and adults generally can best help by being unobtrusive and tactful in their educational efforts and by frequently standing aside to let the child experiment alone in the exciting and dangerous business of living, intervening to help him interpret his experience in terms of social norms and attitudes and to save him when physical danger is clearly imminent.

Children do however need the support of adult authority, of a discipline imposed first as the framework of an orderly home life which compels by its law-abiding and regular fulfilment of physical needs; they need some few categoric and reasonable imperatives to set the boundaries to their own dangerous thoughts, impulses and desires; and they react with anxiety if such authority and order is withdrawn or is fluctuating and inconsistent. But authority, however consistent and rational, which is neutral or hostile provokes aggression and anxiety; many adults have a highly developed intellectual understanding of children but, failing to feel respect and deep affection for them, they do more ultimate harm to their development than is done by a loving ignorance which is equally swift to punish and to give affection.

Nowhere is this more clearly shown than in the handling of many childish difficulties. The child's first 'lie', his occasional nightmares, his periods of regressive behaviour, the feeding difficulties that arise from time to time, outbursts of aggression and rebellion, his interest in the phenomena of his own body, his first 'theft', his jealousy of a sibling—all or any of these normal manifestations may become through unwise handling the centre of a disturbance which deflects temporarily or permanently his forward movement to maturity. Many parents and teachers, made unduly anxious by the popularizers of child psychology and particularly by the more extreme exponents of psychoanalysis, see in every temporary deviation from 'normality' the signs of neurosis; and they show horror, shock or anxiety which merely intensifies the child's own problems. We know altogether too little in a scientific way of the distribution of 'abnormalities' among children of any age and less still of the outcome in subsequent development of most of the commonly observed behaviour patterns of childhood, to be as certain as some are, that whenever a child shows deviations and difficulties in growth, psycho-therapy is necessary. What, however, we do know is that human material is extraordinarily resilient and adaptable and that, given a stable and consistent home discipline, a rich variety of opportunity to play and a warm accepting atmosphere, all but a few children overcome by themselves the developmental stresses inherent in their drive to grow up. A primary requisite in parents and in teachers is confidence in children's capacity to work through their own difficulties. Teachers particularly must be at once sufficiently detached in their attitude to tolerate a wide range of difference among children in their growth patterns and yet have the ability to love children of many different kinds as human beings.

GROWTH AND ADJUSTMENT

For school and parents alike, it is important to grasp, and allow for, the dynamism of normal psychological growth. A child faced with a new demand—the birth let us say of a baby brother—may go forward to a new adjustment; or he may regress to an earlier form of behaviour. More often both reactions take place alternately or simultaneously. The child may perhaps accept greater responsibility for certain aspects of his own life so that mother may tend the new baby but at the same time revert to bed-wetting or some other infantile reaction which betrays his anxiety, and bids for the attention and love of which he feels himself deprived. Whenever a human being is faced with a demand that is difficult to meet or a renunciation that is difficult to make, there is a choice either to move forward and adapt to it or to regress to a mode of behaviour that was successful in the past. If the demand is greater than he can meet, then regression is almost certain; and all children and all adults at times move back into their own past. A healthy environment stresses and provides for the maximum of forward movement, fostering the positive adaptation. The wise parent and teacher watch the child's adaptation to new demands, rarely asking of him more than he—in terms not of the hypothetical average child, but of his own peculiar history and endowment—can give. They are ready to support, praise and make easier his attempts to adapt; and they make him feel that they understand and tolerate his temporary regressions.

FIRST ENTRY TO SCHOOL

The child's first entry to a group outside his family and especially to school whether it be a nursery school or the first-year primary class, may well be a critical challenge to his need to grow up. His experiences and reactions at the time may set the pattern of response to any subsequent change of environment. To him it often means the first lengthy separation from his mother and a consequent threat to his love for and dependence upon her. She too may view it with anxiety and may regard the teacher as a potential rival for the affections of her child.

If, in such a situation the child is suddenly introduced into a nursery or infant school and left there or abandoned to the care of an unfamiliar neighbour, despite tears and cries, he may react with an apparent submission which cloaks a real rejection of his mother for deceiving him or he may succeed in literally making himself sick so that he has to be restored to his mother often to her only half-concealed triumph. If the matter is left there, the child's subsequent ability to adapt to new situations, to wean himself psychologically from dependence on his mother, may be seriously impaired.

Such an example has been sketched to illustrate that the child can never be considered alone. He is always a child with a past which has left its impress upon him and he is always a child who has grown in relation to others with whom we have to reckon at every stage of his development. Children's growth imposes tasks and adaptations on their elders as well as upon the children themselves and this is nowhere more clearly seen than during such a period as entry to school. His acceptance of the new situation of leaving mother for three or four hours or longer each day will be conditioned by his reactions to previous attitudes of his mother and her handling of psychologically similar situations earlier in his life—by what happened when he was weaned from breast or bottle, by the way in which previous brief periods of absence from mother have been managed, by his experiences with other adults, maids, the woman next door, visitors to his home, and his visits to other children's homes. Around the age of 3 the normally developing child should have sufficient confidence in his mother's ultimate return to tolerate being left with someone else for several hours, and this tolerance is one of the criteria of readiness for entry to nursery school. Even so, the new faces, the new environment and the new adults may be too much if they are presented all at once. The child who has remained at home up to the age of 5 or 6 may experience similar problems in an even more complicated form. Hence the teacher should make every effort to get in touch with the home before the child comes to school, either, where the cultural pattern allows it, by a personal visit or by inviting mother and child to come and see round the school, perhaps to listen to a story, to join in a play group or to see some other aspect of the children's occupations. A third way is for the headmistress to call a special meeting of the parents of new children and talk to them informally about the school day, about what the teachers aim to do for the children and about the child's psychological preparation to take this major step forward from the shelter of his home into a wider and more impersonal world.

PARENT-TEACHER CONTACTS

Not infrequently a child's entry to school brings about the first contact between his parents and teachers. For many mothers, especially those from the poorer districts of large towns, the nursery or infant school-teacher may well be the only worker with whom they have an informal contact and who has a sufficient knowledge of the needs and development of normal children to help them with the daily upbringing not only of the child at school but of younger siblings. The ability of the teacher to take advantage of the keen interest of the mother in her young child depends however on the teacher's competence in the psychological and physical care of children, in her knowledge of household management as it has practically to be applied in working-class homes, and upon her ability to build a friendly and co-operative relationship with the mothers. Her work with parents must be based on respect for them as parents and a clear perception of the fact that the school and the teacher have as much to learn from mother and father about the individual child as they have to teach about children in general. The approach should from the outset be that of working together from different points of view rather than a didactic offering of advice. Even mothers who have most need of help do not readily accept it from a teacher, often unmarried, who, they think, cannot have their intimate experience of what it is like to have a child and what it is possible to do with limited space, time and money. One of the most effective techniques, as has been pointed out in Chapter II, is the small group of parents meeting with the teacher, herself well-trained in child psychology, to discuss freely their joint problems. In such a group the teacher plays her part along with the others on an equal footing and makes the distinctive contribution of one who is sufficiently detached and knowledgeable to lower the tension of the anxious and to put at the disposal of the group the best current thinking on child psychology and care. Where parents co-operate with the teaching staff on other matters and truly participate in the material and moral support of the school, such activity often arises spontaneously and can be guided into channels valuable to the parents and to their children.[1]

Clearly the possibilities and value of such co-operation as well as the most appropriate methods are a function both of the capacities and training of the teachers and the folk ways of the communities concerned. What is immediately possible in say a Scandinavian country may not be equally practicable in French-speaking countries and vice versa. The essential objectives however remain the same. The unity of the child's world must at all costs be preserved. Not merely

---

1. Such a technique has been developed with success at the United Nations Nursery School, Paris.

should home and school not be in open conflict: they should present the child with coherent and complementary experiences; and each in its several way should contribute to his growth and socialization. This implies that many methods which are objectively desirable from the viewpoint of child development may in fact have to be, temporarily at all events, modified if they do not accord with the local attitudes and traditions. For example, children from homes where the discipline is very strict and rigid, may not be able to tolerate a very permissive school atmosphere; similarly, the school may have for the time to accept that parents are not willing to let their children get as dirty as the teacher would wish to allow them to be. This is not to say that in everything the school should follow the standards set by the homes; it implies that the staff should make a direct contribution to the mental health of their community by winning the co-operation of the parents, by patiently explaining what they are trying to do and why they are trying to do it and by inviting parents to contribute to and share in the living experience of adapting education to the real needs of children.

This conception of the social and mental health task of the nursery or infant school is one which many gladly, if unconsciously, accept. It throws on the teacher however, and especially on the headmistress, responsibilities for which she is rarely adequately trained. Some of its implications for the selection, prior experience, and the content of training of teachers have already been discussed and set forth elsewhere.[1] Here we need only reiterate that in industrial Europe, the school which begins the education of young children may make so fundamental a contribution to the mental health of the future citizens for whom it cares and be so effective an instrument in the smooth assimilation of technological and social change, both by children and by parents, that no pains should be spared to attract the right type of teacher and no watertight administrative or professional compartments should prevent its drawing on all the available psychological, medical and social services that exist to help in the task.

BIBLIOGRAPHY

AGAZZI, A. *Il metodo italiano per la scuola materna.* Brescia, La Scuola, 1942. XX, 156 p.

AGOSTI, M. & CHIZZOLINI, V. *La scuola materna italiana.* Brescia, La Scuola, 1939. 144 p.

ALLEN, W. Y. & CAMPBELL, D. *The creative nursery center.* New York, Family Service Association of America, 1948. 171 p.

---

1. *Mental Hygiene in the Nursery School (Problems in Education, IX).* Report of a joint WHO/Unesco expert meeting. Paris, Unesco, 1953.

EDUCATION AND MENTAL HEALTH

ALLERS, R. *Das Werden der sittlichen Person.* 4 Aufl. Freiburg, Herder, 1935. 316 p.

AUDEMARS, M. & LAFENDEL, L. *La maison des petits de l'Institut J. J. Rousseau.* 2e éd. Neuchâtel, Paris, Delachaux & Niestlé, 1950. 56 p.

BENJAMIN, Z. *Emotional problems of childhood.* London, university of London Press, 1948. 178 p.

BERGERON, M. *Psychologie du premier âge.* Paris, Presses Universitaires de France, 1951. 139 p.

Børnehaven i reformpædagogisk Belysning. Sœrtryk af *Pædagogisk-psykologisk Tidsskrift,* Bd VII, H. F. I. København, Munksgaard, 1947. 40 p.

BOWLEY, A. *A study of the factors influencing the general development of the child during the pre-school years by means of record forms.* Cambridge, University Press, 1942. 104 p.

BOYCE, E. R. *Infant school activities.* 4th ed. London, Nisbet, 1946. 254 p.

BRADBURY, E. & SKEELS, E. L. *A bibliography of nursery education.* Detroit, National Association for Nursery Education, 1939. 68 p.

BRUNET, O. & LÉZINE, I. *Le développement psychologique de la première enfance.* Paris, Presses universitaires de France, 1951. 129 p.

BÜHLER, K. *Abriss der geistigen Entwicklung des Kindes.* 7te Aufl. Heidelberg, Quelle & Meyer, 1949. 180 p.

BUREAU INTERNATIONAL D'ÉDUCATION. *L'organisation de l'éducation préscolaire.* Genève, 1939, 216 p.

CASOTTI, M. *Il metodo Montessori e il metodo Agazzi.* 2a ed. Brescia, La Scuola, 1950. 60 p.

CHESTERS, G. *The mothering of young children.* London, Faber & Faber, 1945. 84 p.

DESCOEUDRES, A. *Le développement de l'enfant de deux à sept ans. Recherche de psychologie expérimentale.* 2e éd. Neuchâtel, Delachaux & Niestlé, 1930. 322 p.

Erziehung im Sowjetischen Kindergarten. Berlin & Leipzig, Volk & Wissen Verlag, 1947. 118 p.

FAURE, M. *Le jardin d'enfants.* Paris, Presses Universitaires de France, 1943. 163 p.

GARDNER, D. E. M. *Long-term results of infant school methods.* London, Methuen, 1950. 108 p.

——. *Testing results in the infant school.* London, Methuen, 1942. 158 p.

GESELL, A. et al. *The first five years of life.* New York, London, Harper, 1940. 58 p.

GRIFFITHS, R. *Imagination in early childhood.* London, Paul, 1935. 367 p.

Growth in vocabulary and expression in the first twelve months at school (Information Bulletin no. 25) 14 p; *Growth in vocabulary and expression in the first two years at school (Information Bulletin no. 29).* Melbourne, Australian Council for Educational Research, 1952 & 1953. 14 p.

GUTTERIDGE, W. V. *The duration of attention in young children.* Melbourne, University Press & Oxford Universty Press, 1935. 52 p.

HARTLEY, R. E. et al. *Understanding children's play.* London, Routledge, K. Paul, 1952, 372 p.

HETZER, H. *Kürschners deutscher Gelehrten-Kalender.* F. Bertkau & G. Oestreich. 7te Aufl. Berlin, Walter de Gruyter, 1950, XI-2. 534 p.

HUME, E. G. *Learning and teaching in the infants' schools.* London, Longmans, Green, 1952. 271 p.

ISAACS, S. *The nursery years.* London, Routledge, 1932. 138 p.

JONCKHEERE, T. *La pédagogie expérimentale au jardin d'enfants.* 5e éd. Bruxelles, M. Lamertin, 1949. 202 p.

KIETZ, G. *Das Bauen des Kindes.* Ravensburg, O. Maier, 1950. 48 p.

KNOCH, I. *Die pädagogischen Aufgaben des Kindergartens am schulpflichtigen, aber schulunreifen Einkinde.* Weimar, Böhlans Nachf., 1940.

Les écoles maternelles. Classes enfantines, cours préparatoires. Règlements, organisation, fonctionnement. Paris, Bourrelier, 1953. 176 p.

Lexikon der Pädagogik, vol. III. Bern, A. Francke, 1952. xiv + 624 p. C. Bühler, p. 71; J. Froebel, p. 156; M. Montessori, p. 315; J. Piaget, p. 361.

LISSA, L. DE. *Life in the nursery school.* London, Longmans, Green, 1944.

MELLOR, E. *Education through experience in the infant school years.* Oxford, Blackwell, 1950. 250 p.

MILLER, E. W. *Room to grow.* London, Harrap, 1944. 78 p.

MINISTÈRE DE L'INSTRUCTION PUBLIQUE. DIRECTION GÉNÉRALE DE L'ENSEIGNEMENT PRIMAIRE ET NORMAL. *Plan des activités éducatives à l'école gardienne.* Bruxelles, Moniteur Belge, 1952.

MUSU, A. M. "Il metodo Agazzi", *Il posto nel mondo.* Firenze, Marzocco-Bemporad, 1952. 56 p.

NIEGL, A. *Gegenwartsfragen der Kindergartenerziehung.* Wien, Österreichischer Bundesverlag, 1950. 334 p.

NØRVIG, A. *Kinderspiele und Beschäftigung.* Zürich, A. Müller.

Nursery-infant education. Report of a consultative committee appointed by the executive of the National Union of Teachers. London, Evans Brothers, 1949. 116 p.

OLSON, W. C. *Child development.* Boston, D.C., Heath, 1949. 417 p.

Play and mental health. London, The Puskhin Press, 1945. 30 p.

RUSK, R. *A history of infant education.* London, University of London Press, 1933. 196 p.

Schools for young children in twenty-seven countries. Chicago, International Committee of the National Association for Nursery Education, 1949. 50 p.

SIGSGAARD, J. *Barnets Verden.* København, Det Danske Forlag, 1945. 118 p.

STERN, W. *Psychologie der frühen Kindheit bis zum sechsten Lebensjahr.* Leipzig, Quelle & Meyer, 1914. 372 p.

SZUMAN, S. *Psychologia wychowawcza wieku dzieciçego.* Warszawa, Wyd., Nasza, Ksiçgarnia, 1946. 189 p.

THOORIS, A. *Pédagogie du nourrisson et du premier âge.* Paris, Doin, 1947. 184 p.

UNESCO. *The influence of home and community on children under thirteen years of age towards world understanding*, no. 6. Paris, 1949. 53 p.|*L'influence du foyer et de la communauté sur les enfants de moins de 13 ans vers la compréhension internationale*, no. 6. Paris, Unesco, 1949. 58 p.

WALLON, H. *Evolution psychologique de l'enfant.* Paris, A. Colin, 1941 222 p.

WATTS, A. F. *The language and mental development of children.* London, Harrap, 1944. 354 p.

WHEELER, O. A. & EARL, I. G. *Nursery school education and the reorganization of the infant school.* London, University of London Press, 1939. 172 p.

WOLFF, W. *The personality of the pre-school child.* London, Heinemann, 1947. 341 p.

WORLD ORGANIZATION FOR EARLY CHILDHOOD EDUCATION/ORGANISATION MONDIALE POUR L'EDUCATION PRÉSCOLAIRE. *Report of the 2nd World Conference/Rapport de la 2 ème Conférence mondiale*, Paris, OMEP, 1949. 68 p.

———. *Report of the 3rd World Conference/Rapport de la 3ème Conférence mondiale*, Paris, OMEP, 1950. 83 p.

ZULLINGER, H. *Heilende Kräfte im kindlichen Spiel.* Stuttgart, E. Klett Verlag, 1952. 136 p.

CHAPTER IV

THE PRIMARY SCHOOL: AIMS, METHODS AND MENTAL HEALTH

THE SCHOOL AS SHAPER OF DEVELOPMENT

Some twenty years ago it could be written that the period from about 5 or 6 years to 11 or 12 was 'the dark ages of childhood'. And it is true that even now less has been written and fewer researches have been undertaken[1] on the developments and formation of personality in middle childhood than in infancy or adolescence. Many researches have however been made into the psychological demands made by school subjects, into the intellectual aspects of learning, into growth in intelligence and in the power of concept formation and into interests of value to education; and numerous studies exist of the maladjustments which declare themselves as behaviour disorders during the early years of school.

Some confusion still exists as to the proper function of the school in the education and development of children between the ages of 5 or 6 and 11 or 12 and this is at least partly because we are agreed neither on the method nor on the aims of primary education. By whatever principles it is guided however, the school and its demands form a part, even a principal part, of the influences which shape children between 5 or 6 and 14 or even older.[2] This means that educational aims have to be accepted as important conditioning factors and that personality development cannot be regarded as an autonomous psychic process. Thus while curriculum and method should be 'child centred' in that they should consider and respect the individual needs and capacities of each pupil, they have also to be

---

1. Particularly in Europe. For American work see L. Carmichael, *Manuel of Child Psychology.* New York, J. Wiley, 1946; W. S. Monroe, *Encyclopedia of Educational Research.* New York, Macmillan, 1950, and the numerous curriculum studies, e.g. J. M. Lee and M. C. Lee, *The Child and his Curriculum.* New York, Appleton Century, 1950, and the annual reviews of research issued by the American Educational Research Association. For British work see C. A. Mace and P. Vernon. *Current Trends in British Psychology* London, Methuen, 1952; C. W. Valentine, *Psychology and its Bearing upon Education,* London, Methuen, 1950.
2. M. J. Langeveld in *Ontsporing en Correctie* by L. van Gelder. Jakarta, J. B. Wolters, 1953, p. 268.

'community centred'[1] in that schooling is a means to help the child live satisfactorily first as a child and later as an adult fully participating in and contributing to the development of the life of his human group. The argument and practice of many progressive educators is based upon the idea that discipline arises from the free play of natural tendencies in the children and the adults who form the community and that this free interplay imposes a kind of self-regulation and observance of the rules essential to social living. It is however arguable that there are tendencies to disorder in human beings—explained in Christian theology for example by the doctrine of original sin—and that at least in the early stages of growth children need the help of adults in coming to terms with these and controlling them. Some would-be 'progressive' schools, by allowing an unrestricted satisfaction of their pupils' needs, neglect two fundamentals of healthy mental development: the security which comes from knowing there are limits imposed by a benevolent discipline; and the ability to accept, without undue frustration or subservience, the restrictions which are a necessary prerequisite of social living.

We may agree that education should permit, even ensure the fullest possible realization of individual capacities; but self-realization, unshaped by social demands, is merely crude ego-centricity. Fortunately every school provides a community of some sort and thus imposes regulation; most schools are staffed by teachers who, whatever their faults, are representative of the adult society into which the child will later pass; and who, often be it admitted blindly and unhelpfully, impose some of the rules by which they themselves live. It is however suggested that satisfactory mental and emotional development is not ensured by a freedom closely resembling licence nor by a rigid and unhelpful discipline coupled with impossible demands.

CURRICULUM

This implies that the curriculum should be planned in terms of clearly understood objectives and that these should envisage all aspects of development and not merely the intellectual ones. It implies too that while the school's demands should be graded in terms of the child's capacity to learn and methods should be modified to enable him to do so, the curriculum, method and atmosphere created are, unavoidably, the expression of a more or less self-conscious philosophy on the part

---

1. Whether regulating conduct purely by social standards makes society, in a good or a bad sense, the end and norm of our conduct depends upon the values, proximate or ultimate, implicit in the society itself.

of the adult community.[1] That this should be so is by no means in-compatible with a respect for individuality, nor with the idea that children need to learn what interests them at their own level and for ends clearly perceived by them to be valuable. Indeed the wide range of differences in capacity between individuals whether infants, children or adolescents forbids uniformity; and our growing knowledge of the dynamics of emotional growth, with which intellectual growth is seen more and more clearly to be closely related, suggests that if children are pressed forward too fast and do not therefore live through the various stages of childhood, their whole development may be stunted or turned awry. Children who are too early forced into adult roles—for example the 'little mother' or the boys of 10 and 11 who become leaders of bands of homeless children in war-devastated Europe—are striking and obvious cases. More subtle examples of the same thing are harder to detect but regrettably frequent in occurrence. Parents and teachers often expect (and obtain) a level of social or intellectual maturity which, because it syncopates the processes of growth, is obtained at excessive cost and is paid for by later disequilibrium. An instance in the 'newer' educational methods is where children are given too soon and too great a responsibility for other children which may later—because of the anxiety it has caused—lead to a repudiation of responsibility for others. In the formalistic school, the demand for accuracy and scope in the knowledge of facts or for a mature appreci-ation of literature not infrequently has led to a rejection of anything resembling things taught at school, with a consequent impoverishment of the intellectual life.

BASIC SKILLS

In practice in Europe there is general agreement on many of the demands which should be made by the primary curriculum. The distinction often drawn between instruction and education is frequent-ly false and misleading but at the primary school level at least we may

---

1. cf. G. H. Bantock, *Freedom and Authority in Education*. London, Faber & Faber, 1952, p. 212. The nature of the philosophy which determines the educational aims is not always clearly seen or explicitly stated. In any one society—especially those of mixed religious faith—there is probably room for many philosophies; the danger arises when societies fail to realize that in freeing the State educational system of a particular bias they may in fact be by implication acting according to a philosophy. It is doubtful whether ultimate 'neutralism' is possible in the education of children. However, educational neutrality as conceived by its more thoughtful exponents is by no means the avoidance of doctrinal or other differences in the education of children. It is a deliberate attempt to bring together children and adults of all kinds of con-viction, from all kinds of social backgrounds and political or philosophic orientations in an atmosphere which respects their right to differ and provides a means of allowing individuals to come to understand and sympathize with (though not necessarily adopt) other viewpoints than their own. It has thus a clear philosophy of tolerance.

distinguish certain aspects of the programme which have a large element of formal skill and are therefore properly matters for instruction. As an instrument of receiving information from others, as the foundation of his subsequent intellectual development and as a means of entry into the garnered culture of his people, a child needs to learn how to decipher written and printed words. To communicate in a semi-permanent form he needs to write and to be able to put words together in a coherent grammatical order. For a number of adult purposes (but not nearly so many as is presupposed by most arithmetic courses)[1] a minimum of arithmetic skills is required.

In the early days of compulsory education, reading, writing and arithmetic were considered to constitute all that was necessary, and even yet many primary schools concentrate almost exclusively upon the attainment of a mechanical perfection in these basic skills. To them has been added in greater or lesser degree a body of knowledge, a series, rather, of more or less coherently organized facts—historical, geographical, literary, scientific; and certain other subjects or techniques have been included to provide mental discipline likely to train supposed mental faculties of use in later life.

FORMS OF THINKING

It seems both educationally and psychologically sounder to view the intellectual aspects of the early years of primary education as aiming to equip a child with certain modes or techniques of thinking and expression. For later learning as well as for full adult living, he needs a mastery of verbal thinking and verbal communication; he needs, for utilitarian and for intellectual purposes, the beginnings at least of a command of numerical thinking, ordering, enumeration, comparison of spaces, volumes and sequences; life in the modern world too demands not merely a minimum of scientific knowledge, but an enlightened curiosity and insight into the objective evaluation of observed facts which is the basis of empirical science and scientific thinking. To these we may and should add techniques of visual and manual self-expression, musical and physical skills not only for their own sakes but because practical activities bring children and adults closer to the exigencies of reality from which a largely academic education may allow them to escape in verbalism.

It is in such a context that learning through activity and experience has most relevance since it becomes obvious that a child will best learn

---

1. G. M. Wilson, M. B. Stone and C. O. Dalrymple, *Teaching the New Arithmetic*. New York, McGraw Hill, 1939. Ninety-five per cent of adult figuring is covered by the four fundamental processes (addition, multiplication, subtraction and division), simple fractions, elementary percentages and simple interest.

to think numerically on the basis of considerable number activity and real experience of quantities and quantitative relationships. He cannot learn the arts of communication without having experience or thought to communicate, and as he develops the primordial skills of visual and oral communication so he can be brought to acquire and appreciate reading, writing and visual art as more permanent if less direct media. Similarly the child's curiosity about the external world, his search for causation and crude attempts to predict effect are the basis on which the school can build the willingness to suspend belief, to test hypotheses empirically and to formulate laws founded on observed relationships.

At this early stage other knowledge, in the sense of an ordered and coherent body of facts called botany, biology, history, geography, grammar or the like, has little relevance in and for itself. Certainly education, even when conceived primarily as an instruction in techniques, cannot be without content. But the importance of facts in the primary school years lies much more in the stimulus which they give to particular modes of thinking, the raw material their inter-relationships give for the child's developing ability to conceptualize, to think, and to express, than to their place in a systematic adult construct. Nor should it be forgotten that facts can be 'inert' and remain so unless they are actual in their significance for the child.[1] Hence one at least of the teacher's tasks is to provide experience and to help the child to order and discipline that experience through thinking and expression. The motive power of learning is the emotional life, and interest is one of the ways in which the emotions point outwards to an analysis of the objective world. Active learning takes place when the whole emotional energy is concentrated on an interest and when intelligence is exercised in its service.

THE TEACHER AS TUTOR

Active methods do not imply undisciplined running about or even, invariably, overt action, they do not mean 'learning any old thing by doing any old thing'; they imply that through a varied and consciously guided series of experiences in which the child participates he is led to mental activity of varied kinds. The teacher should provide perhaps even most of these, though he should also take advantage of the child's out-of-classroom life; and he should see to it that these experiences are such as to evoke ever more complex and varied types of thinking. But his task does not end here. He has to teach; he has to use, to stimulate, and to shape the *élan*, and to show his pupils how from the specific

---

1. A. N. Whitehead, *Aims of Education*. New York, Macmillan Co., 1929.

relationships, or elements, or techniques, they may increasingly generalize. It is only in this way that a transfer of training of value to the whole mental development of the individual will take place. The teacher too has to be the guardian of standards and, while not carping at the imperfections of immaturity and the errors that increasing mastery will eliminate, to set goals immediate and more remote toward which the pupils will strive.

Demands which are clearly understood, goals which are attainable with effort and values which the child can appreciate, are not merely the marks of a curriculum and method which is educationally sound; they are the very framework within which the child can build a feeling of security and confidence at school. Children will learn because they are emotionally stirred by the situation in which they find themselves; and gradually if they have been trained by undertaking at first small tasks with an easily seen and relatively immediate result, and later, progressively tasks with more and more distant objectives, accepted by them as worth while, they will undertake the immediately unrewarding toil, because they feel confident that the remoter end towards which they work is both attainable and worth attaining. The fault of many of the traditional methods lies in that fear of blame and punishment is the motive which leads to learning. Not infrequently, if the learning takes place, it is joyless and often impermanent; where, in spite of his fear and sometimes because of it, a child fails, his morale may be completely undermined and he may well lose the will to try again. On the other hand, many modern methods fail because, relying solely on arousing the child's immediate interest, they do not lead him progressively to perceive and wish to attain steadily more remote ends through an effort which may not in and for itself be immediately rewarding.

WORK ATTITUDES AND MENTAL HEALTH

A healthy personality in no small measure depends upon certain positive attitudes, as well as on the avoidance of negative ones. The development of a sound work attitude, which is compounded of confidence in one's own power to succeed, and the willingness to accept immediate drudgery for a worth-while end, is one of the major mental health as well as educational goals of the primary school. The techniques of reading, of written and oral expression, and of arithmetic are means to this end; and the content of the curriculum has a value both in bringing children into closer relationship with objective reality and in giving them increasing experience and practice in those modes of thinking which will form the basis of their cultural and personal lives.

It is typical of the immediately pre- and post-war educational reforms in Europe[1] that they were intended to move schools and their methods nearer to the position outlined above. The instructions and programmes published by the Ministère de l'Éducation Nationale in France in 1947, the work of the Italian Commission of Inquiry in 1947, the Swedish School Reform Act of 1950, the English Education Act of 1944, the Boresse Reform advocated in Belgium in 1936 all tend towards a similar goal. Unhappily, though administrative measures can facilitate development, they cannot ensure it; reform, as the Italian Commission of Inquiry stressed, depends upon the willing, enlightened and intelligent co-operation of all. Without entering here into a discussion of the relative parts of home and school in the education of children—conceptions of which vary greatly in Europe— it is clear that schools, whatever the part assigned to them, in fact educate as well as train; and academic instruction cannot be given without consequences for personal development and mental health.

INDIVIDUAL DIFFERENCES

The emancipation of the curriculum from excessive and premature demands and the emphasis on goals attainable by children at the stage of growth in which they find themselves, will be nugatory unless teachers are fully aware of the immense range of individual variation between children, even at the age of 6 or 7, and the increasing differences which make themselves felt with advancing age. For example, in sheer intellectual power there may well be a range of four years or more of mental growth between the dullest and brightest of a group of 6-year-olds, a divergence which at 10 will have widened to some six or seven years. Similar but less measurable differences are apparent in the strength and organization of the emotional drives in the ability innate or acquired, to tolerate frustration, and in levels of aspiration. Some children at 6 are little more mature socially and emotionally than 4-year-olds, and where children are drawn from very dissimilar social backgrounds, their levels of development towards maturity will not only be different in degree but in kind. Physically and physiologically too there will be differences—differences in size, in suscepti-

---

1. L. Bauwens, *Code de l'enseignement moyen*. Brussels, Ed. Universelle, 1949, 266 p.; Commissione Nazionale d'Inchiesta per la Reforma della Scuola, *La conclusioni dell'Inchiesta Nazionale per la Reforma della Scuola*. Rome, 1950, 339 p.; H. C. Dent, *The Education Act 1944. Provisions, Possibilities and Some Problems*. London, University of London Press, 1944, 101 p.; J. Debiesse, *Compulsory Education in France*. Paris, Unesco; I. Düring (ed.), *The Swedish School Reform 1950*. Uppsala, Appelbergs Bokfryckeriaktiebolag, 1951; W. de Lange, *Education and Instruction in the Netherlands* (tr. H. V. Leopold). The Hague, 1946, 34 p.; Ministry of Education, Science and Art, Czechoslovakia, *School Reform in Czechoslovakia*. Prague, Orbis, 1949, 52 p. (published also in German, Polish and Spanish); Ministry of Education, Denmark, *Survey of Danish Education*. Copenhagen, 1947, 35 p.

bility to fatigue, in neuro-muscular control, in the acuity of the senses and in the psycho-physical developments which underlie such skills as visual and auditory analysis, fine muscular co-ordination, and the like, on which learning to read, to spell and to write in part depend. In verbal development, in range of spoken vocabulary, in sentence structure and in comprehension, social differences and differences of individual experience will show themselves as marked almost as differences in the sheer power of intelligence.

Even if the teacher is encouraged to regard his task as that of giving a lesson, the learning of which is the responsibility of the children he can not afford to ignore this variety in the human material in front of him. If on the other hand he fully accepts its implications, he is faced with developing a highly flexible programme, much study of each child and a grading of his demands to meet the capacities of each. This does not mean that he must wholly give up class teaching or group activities in favour of individual attention. A sum in simple arithmetic will show that the primary school teacher with a class of 45 children could devote only five or six minutes of individual attention to each one daily, if he worked without interruption.

THE CLASS LESSON

It means that he must scrutinize carefully his curriculum and decide which parts of it are appropriate for direct teaching to the whole class, which are appropriate for group activities and where individual attention is necessary. This can be done by no rule of thumb formula. It can only be based upon an assessment of the human material he is teaching, an examination of the goals set by his curriculum—and if necessary a discarding of some of them as impracticable—and a process of trial and error enlightened by his teacher's knowledge of the ways in which children learn. The class lesson should have as its core those relationships, facts or techniques which are essential and which can be grasped by the slowest learner; and it should contain meat even for the brightest. The Shakespearian play which appealed for different reasons to groundlings, men of the world and the literary critic is essentially a perfect example of what a lesson should be: something within the grasp of everyone and much to challenge the capacity of the most able. The object of a lesson is to cover ground relatively quickly and to add to the common stock of the class. As a lesson of this type proceeds the teacher is aware of the shortness of the attention span even of the brightest child and by variety of technique maintains interest: didactic, expository, questioning, inspirational by turns, the good lesson moves at a tempo determined by the class and differing from class to class. It is essentially a creative and artistic

91

activity in which the media are the children and the subject matter varies in ways, subtle or marked, every minute.

Grouping or the establishment of 'sets' has many uses within the large class. In its simplest form it is a way of dividing the whole body of pupils into sections each more homogeneous than the whole. For example it is common to have groups for reading or for arithmetic who are moving slower or faster than the average and for whom the instruction and the exercises are appropriately graded. This is a device not to be despised in practice unless it becomes rigid and in fact stratifies the form into the able, average and the dull by the criteria of the basic skills or—as is often the case—by only one of them. Development, in the early stages of primary school at all events, is so uneven that grouping by attainment and ability carried out systematically for each skill to be acquired, means differently composed groups for each, and a continuous process of interchange between groups. The overcrowded classroom or school makes grouping (and of course any work which involves movement by the pupils) much more difficult; some would say impossible. Yet the large class in fact makes grouping the more necessary. Provided children can all be seated in a classroom (even where the desks are of the three or four to a bench type) it is possible for all members of any one arithmetic or reading set to be in geographical proximity. In most circumstances too it is possible to turn the desks in different directions according say to four sets or to four co-operating cross-sectional groups and thus break up the spurious homogeneity and teacher-directedness of the usual classroom layout. In order to adapt instruction to the varying possibilities of his pupils and to ensure that the various groups progress with sufficient to challenge their activity and interest, a careful system of recording is necessary. Here the record card maintained by each pupil is of inestimable service for keeping track both of the work and practice done by the groups and of individual progress.

Grouping of a different kind has other educational uses. For instruction in arithmetic or in reading skills, the group needs to be homogeneous; but for wider educational purposes, the class may be divided into what may be called cross-sectional groups. Each of these should reproduce, as far as possible equally, the spread of ability in the whole class, and they should work as a series of teams, the members of which assist each other on joint projects. In this way certain important attitudes may be fostered and developed. The abler children come to realize that their better endowment imposes duties towards their fellows; the less able learn that they have a contribution to make. Competition between individuals, which is a usual incentive in the classroom, is destructive for the majority of children who, however hard they work, can rarely beat the few outstandingly able—and who therefore frequently lose heart. Competition between equally matched groups, however, is a different matter, since success depends upon a joint effort and upon the smoothness of the integration of the team.

INDIVIDUAL WORK

In the early stages of number work and reading considerable purely individual learning is necessary and this cannot readily be achieved solely by group work. What happens still in many schools is that the whole class repeats a lesson out loud—chants arithmetical tables or number combinations, and reads collectively or round the class. The result is that many children perform mechanically and little or no learning takes place, certainly if the method is frequently practised. If however the rhythmic chanting is considerably reduced and replaced by a series of very short assignments—for example, cards containing many of the number combinations up to 100 arranged as subtractions and additions or a short passage to read followed by questions to test comprehension, or lists of 5 or 10 words to learn to spell—then, working individually or in pairs, children can check and record their own increasing speed and accuracy, logging their results on their own record cards. They can be taught to maintain a graph of their own progress and thus be stimulated to compete against themselves.

If periods of class instruction are kept short and employed only when it can reasonably be expected that all children will follow them; if a careful distinction is made between the teaching of techniques to homogeneous groups and class or group activities which have a value in stimulating social and co-operative learning; and if skilful use is made of individual assignments progressively graded and as far as possible self-checking; then the teacher can be free to devote attention for short periods individually to those children who have an immediate difficulty or to those who through absence have missed a critical step. Such help prevents children from falling further and further behind, growing more and more discouraged until—at 10 or 11 they have developed major emotional difficulties as well as marked educational retardation.

Methods of the type suggested above lend themselves to a wide variety of uses within the primary school. They demand of the teacher considerable sensitivity to the particular class of children with whom he is working, some ingenuity in the preparation and production of material, and rather more attention to systematic recording than older methods. In the early stages at any rate the uniform textbook possessed

93

by each child in the class is inappropriate. What is needed is a wide variety of exercises of all types printed or duplicated, single examples of a range of books, small sets only of some, and plentiful raw material in the form of paper, cardboard and the like.[1] In countries where the primary school syllabus and even the textbooks are prescribed by the central or local authorities the initiative of the progressive teacher may be somewhat hampered. Even so, individual and graded group work, self-checking and self-testing devices, the stimulation of self-competition, and intergroup competition and the elimination of direct competition between individuals are not impossible objectives.

FAILURE

The establishment through success of the child's confidence in his power to learn, the elimination of the total failures which are so painful and destructive of morale, and the adjustment of educational demands to the pupil's capacity to learn are important, indeed fundamental contributions to mental health. This does not mean that children should never be allowed to fail, nor that they should never be challenged by tasks which are somewhat outside their immediate possibilities. Failure is educative and even the most able among us has to learn not to be destroyed by it. The balance of a child's experience, especially in his early years, should be on the side of success: the watchful teacher will see to it that the failures incidental to learning are not total, that they act as a spur to further effort which is ultimately successful. This again demands careful grading in terms not merely of each pupil's intellectual capacity but of his ability emotionally to tolerate failure.

ADULT CONSISTENCY

Enough has been said to indicate that the social climate of the class-room and the emotional impact of the methods used by the teacher are likely to have a powerful influence on the attitudes developed by children. In turn these will be affected by the relationships between members of staff and between the staff and the school head. Children of primary-school age are still immature; they are still liable to feelings of insecurity, to unassimilated love and hate, and to aggressive impulses. Hence it is essential that the aims of the school as expressed through the attitude of all members of staff should be consistent and

---

1. The methods sketched above have been advocated and practised for many years by educators of the active school in Europe and America, and a considerable literature exists, as well as a good deal of specially prepared material and textbooks.

calculable. This does not imply that the head should impose his ideas *ex cathedra;* but that the staff should, through free discussion among themselves, arrive at agreement and work together as a team. It is particularly essential that children should not pass from a class in which they are taught by one method into another where the approach is entirely different. Differences, of course, there will be; and children can and do adapt themselves to adult inconsistencies; they learn to be one person at home and another at school; they learn to respond to Miss Y in one fashion and to Mr. X in another. This kind of adaptation is necessary at certain stages, since the adult in a modern society moves in a number of mutually inconsistent worlds; for the child under the age of 10 however, markedly abrupt changes in the attitudes and expectations of adults can delay if not inhibit his learning and be destructive of his security and provocative of aggression either turning outward to the environment or inward to himself.

During pre-adolescent years, under an apparently calm exterior in most cases and within a fairly stable pattern of adaptation, the process of building up an idea of one's self in relation to others is proceeding. It is largely from the attitudes of others, parents, teachers and other children, that this sentiment of the self is developed. Lacking any objective criteria for self-evaluation, children are dependent upon what they think others wish them to be or suggest that they are. Hence markedly divergent attitudes among members of staff or conflict between school and home are likely to be reflected in incompatibilities in the child's own idea of himself and may even provoke emotional crises which issue in a disturbance of behaviour. Children learn not merely from what they imagine others think of them and wish them to be but considerably also from the implications of the behaviour of others as they see it.

Most parents and teachers for example at one time or another complain of children's manners—forgetting how much these are dependent upon the kind of examples which they themselves set in a number of subtle contexts. All young children are learning how to behave, how to make and maintain contact with others, age equals or older; all have periods of imperfect adjustment and of covert or overt hostility, anxiety or insecurity; many of the things which they are expected to do—wash their hands, hang up their clothes, say 'please', 'thank you', 'sorry'—even at the age of 8 or 9 are far from automatic habits and are not clearly accepted as spontaneous desires. When they themselves are treated by adults with discourtesy or when they see that grown-ups do not perform the tasks which are enjoined upon them, such examples reinforce their own unsocialized impulses. If the adult is one with whom, out of fear or love, their identification is close, then the example of that person's behaviour is the more striking.

95

The same is true where more powerful impulses are involved. Children who are themselves the victims of adult hostility or aggression at home or at school (whether this expresses itself as corporal punishment or as unkind sarcasm) are liable to be more aggressive than they would be naturally. This is most noticeable and direct in young children, who will smack other children if they themselves are smacked, and who will—like an animal—bite or kick or scratch, if they have been physically hurt. In older children such aggression is more subtle in its manifestation. It not infrequently results in a servility towards adults and a bullying attitude towards smaller and weaker children or cruelty to animals. Much of the decline of bullying in schools can probably be attributed to gentler and less hostile relationships between adults and children.

MORAL EDUCATION, HABIT AND SENTIMENT

The moral education of children is not something that can be treated apart from normal growth and education. Ultimately, morality rests in a series of generalized attitudes and of daily habits which are continuous with and form part of the whole system of personality. Many of what seem to be moral decisions in the lives of adults are in fact the almost automatic result of deeply ingrained habitual responses, though of course, if challenged, the intelligent adult can usually produce the principle upon which the habit has been built or inculcated in him. A man does not steal money which he finds on someone else's desk, not, usually, because in each instance he makes a fully conscious moral decision to resist the temptation to do so, but because he has been taught not to steal and his response has become habitual.

It is frequently not realized how specific and unorganized such moral habits may be. For example, while most European societies inculcate habits of kindness to dogs, cats and other domestic animals, they may sanction considerable cruelty in the hunting of foxes or rabbits. The same man who is horrified if his dog or horse is wantonly hurt, will lay a spring trap for wild animals. One cannot therefore suppose that his kindness to domestic animals springs from an organized and conscious attitude of kindness to animals in general, but at best from a partial sentiment of kindness to specific animals or from habits of response which have not been organized into a sentiment of any complexity. Much the same will be found if we consider honesty. Adults who would not steal a penny from another person, will cheat a railway or bus company or the tax authority of their country.

Such unorganized habits of moral response not infrequently are the result of an education (at home and at school) which in childhood insists, probably rightly, on the importance of habit formation, giving only such explanation of principles as the child can grasp in terms more or less concrete and tied to particular situations; but which fails later to lead the adolescent to refer particular instances to more general principles and thus enlarge and make conscious the intellectual content. Some of the disorganization however is due to fundamental theological and philosophical differences as to the source of moral principles and as to what man is, where he came from and what is his final end.

Ideally the moral nature should rest in a series of sentiments—deeply ingrained attitudes organized into a series of intellectually comprehended principles—from which, whenever the individual is faced with a moral decision for which habitual responses are inadequate, he should be able to decide on right moral conduct, and carry it through. The formation of such sentiments in any fully developed and comprehensive way does not take place much before adolescence, partly because of the immaturity of intelligence and partly because of insufficiently generalized experience. Prior to adolescence, notions of right and wrong are more or less arbitrary reflections of parental attitudes, of the teaching and examples of other adults and of the social sanctions of the contemporary groups in which the child lives. Frequently one finds among children a dual morality—that which more or less reflects the demands of the adult world and that which has evolved in their own age group with notions of schoolboy honour and a united front against teachers and parents.

Often the child is aware that the demands made upon him by his parents and teachers differ from those to which they themselves conform.[1] For example, thoughtfulness for others, politeness and

---

1. In a comment on this passage in particular and on the whole of this section in general experts consulted by the Catholic Education Council, United Kingdom, write: 'This [i.e. discrepancies in the behaviour of parents and teachers] is always a difficult situation and can only be met, at least as far as the school is concerned, by proper teaching of moral principles. Not all will agree that this can be done, nor will there be agreement about how it should be done, but the following extract will give some indication of the Catholic approach: "From this it follows that the forming of the Christian conscience of a child or youth consists, before all else, in enlightening their minds regarding the will of Christ, His law, and His way, and also in acting on their inner self, in so far as this can be done from without, in order to bring it to the free and constant carrying out of the divine will. This is the highest duty of education".' (Pius XII broadcast message on 'The Christian Conscience as an Object of Education', 23 March 1952: *Catholic Documents* vol. VIII, Salesian Press, London.) They also comment concerning the reason behind moral behaviour: 'It is I suppose possible to teach children to behave socially without any reference to God and our duties towards Him, but if a child asks why one should behave socially, it is surely difficult to give him a satisfactory answer merely on the principles of a non-religious deontology . . . One can teach children to do what is right for love of God. The principle of morality then is no mere categorical imperative but a strong and vivid love for the person of Christ.'

With some slight differences this probably represents the position of most religious groups. In the text however an effort has been made to present as fairly as possible the psychological and technical considerations of which any particular conception of moral training would have to take account. Necessarily this is incomplete since, ultimately, while moral education must take account of psychological principles and of the intellectual and emotional reactions of children and adolescents, the content and inspiration of that education will be drawn from the moral, philosophic and religious belief of the educators, parents and teachers.

consideration should be based on a general sentiment of respect for human beings as such. Children are often obliged to be polite to their elders; but they are not in their turn treated with politeness by teachers or parents. From such a situation they are likely to derive the notion, usually implicit, that you have to be polite to the strong and that you may be rude to the weak. Similarly children are expected to be truthful and may be punished for lying; if they then find that their parents or teachers do not always tell them the truth—for example in response to questions about sex—they learn that apparently there are times when lies may be told. Examples might be multiplied of the way in which adults are apt to apply to children demands in the moral field with which they themselves do not conform, and thus to sanction the attitude that there may be a gap between moral professions and practice.

Much the same psychological conditions apply in the moral education of children as apply in their intellectual formation. We must expect notions of right and wrong to be crude and unorganizedatfirst and for the growth in integration and generalization to be slow. This implies that circumstances must be manipulated so that the demands made on children to conform and to resist temptation are nicely graded to provoke effort but also to ensure success, and the reward of praise. For example it is better not to expose young children to the temptation of stealing jam and sweets at an age when they cannot be expected to foresee consequences other than immediate ones. Similarly the teacher who places great store on success as measured by the number of sums right, or who punishes children who fail in a test, is likely in fact to provoke his pupils to cheat if they can. They may, and frequently do, arrive at the conclusion that it is being found out that matters, not the act itself, and that, while it is teacher's job to prevent their copying from each other, if the end is to gain a sufficiency of marks to avoid being punished, then cheating is perfectly legitimate.

SCALE OF VALUES

It is salutary for teacher and parent alike sometimes to take stock of the scale of values which, by their sanctions and prohibitions, they impose upon children; and thence to ask themselves, whether in fact they are not unintentionally inducing guilt, and anxiety, of a maladjusted kind, through the child's conscious or unconscious interpretation of their actions. If for example, dirty hands or bad table manners meet with the same apparent threat of loss of love or of punishment as theft or lying or unkindness to others, children may well be confused.

Adults, too, sometimes fail to recognize those aspects of behaviour which are parts of the developmental process and which the child himself, at the stage in which he is, cannot avoid. They may not, for example, understand that the fantasy story of the young child is the projection of his fears or his wishes and punish it as a lie. Thus not only do they not help the child adapt to reality but they teach him to associate imagination with guilt. They may react with shocked horror to his natural curiosity about sex or to his experimentation with 'naughty' words, instead of responding to the first as a legitimate inquiry and to the second as a phase through which most children pass with little lasting harm if adults gently discourage it. This does not of course mean that children should not meet with reproof for actions which are naughty or wrong in the adult sense, but that the grown-up should try to understand the child's point of view and, if he is in fact imposing a more adult standard, explain why such things are wrong in terms which the child can understand at his stage of growth.

Children are easily made to feel guilty and anxious, even in late childhood; they readily accept what to us is an isolated condemnation of some particular action of theirs, as an outright rejection of all that they believe or fear themselves to be. They recognize in themselves and in their contemporaries, impulses to lie, to steal, to be aggressive, to be 'naughty', to be interested in forbidden things, and they are liable to react strongly in fear against such powerful feelings of badness. If adult authority is suddenly withdrawn and they are left responsible for themselves, the system of punishments which they suggest for each other is likely to be savage—a reflection of their own fear and guilt, and need for external deterrents which their growth and upbringing have led them hitherto to identify with the wholly 'good' authority figures of parent or teacher. If the adults with whom they have had to do have never let it appear that they too have 'bad' impulses, and that they have learned to accept and deal with such, both in themselves and in children, then the discrepancy between the child's knowledge of himself as he is and his lesire to identify himself with his picture of the perfect adult, is too great to be accepted without severe anxiety.

CONFLICT OF VALUES

Most children, sometimes at considerable cost, manage to digest this anxiety; and to the outward observer pass through middle childhood satisfactorily. Where however there is considerable discrepancy between the values emphasized by the home and by the school, or where either is in conflict with the surrounding community—as for example occurs in some minority religious or cultural groups—the strains may become very great and seriously prejudice future development. Such a situation demands considerable skill in its handling either by parents or by teachers, so that the children can, as concretely as possible, come to understand and accept such differences. In general, parents and teachers alike usually find it easier to denounce aggressively, patterns of behaviour and schemes of values which are not their own, and, consciously or otherwise, they try to win the child to their own side. If however, instead, they try to help him to understand that there can be genuine and sincere differences of opinion, they give the first example of tolerance in their own reactions and at the same time reduce very considerably the strain which a conflict of loyalties may well be imposing on him.

RELIGIOUS EDUCATION

Such conflicts and indeed the whole progress of the child's moral development may be deeply affected by his religious education. The European community presents many divergencies of principle and of practice in this difficult matter. There is first the long tradition associating education with the various religious bodies—the Catholic, Lutheran, Calvinist, Anglican and many other Christian churches— and the strong if not entirely predominant influence of the Christian tradition on European culture. But since the Renaissance at least, and probably before, there is also the tradition of secular humanism. Few European communities are without religious or cultural minorities; most present the picture of many and deep divergencies of faith

Such variety presents an opportunity and a threat. The opportunity lies in that the existence of different ways of regarding life may be used to call forth that humility in faith which is the root of truly liberal attitudes. Children may be taught that these differences are not necessarily inferiorities, and that the fact that another group thinks or believes differently, is not a cause for alarm.

In most European countries, religious toleration is guaranteed by the State, though in many, tensions among religious and lay groups are marked and result in overt and subtle forms of discrimination. The healthy mental development of the young child may be greatly prejudiced by these tensions if they result in active proselytizing or if they arouse his anxiety. The danger of conflict is particularly great where home and school differ in their attitudes to religion. Such difficulty can be most readily avoided where provision is made within the educational system for a genuinely free choice of school; and where, if the State schools are undenominational or even neutralist, the religious communities are permitted, within the safeguard of a minimum educational efficiency, to develop their own concepts of education.[1] However, we know too little about the impact of religious teaching and religious attitudes upon the development of the personality of pre-adolescents to be anything but cautious over method and content. Such research as exists has been either hostile or partisan. What does seem to be important is that the problems of moral and spiritual education should rather be studied in terms of the happiness and responsiveness of the child at the stage of development in which he is, than in terms of educational methods and adult religious attitudes in their mature form. Children take their moral, spiritual and social values from the people they love and who love them, first at home and then at school and in the community. Love, in the everyday sense of the word, should be the basis of all human relations in education and from it springs a sensitivity to all other spiritual values. Some aspects of ritual, the archaic formulations of dogma, not a few of the Bible stories, especially of the Old Testament, may, either because of their content or because they lend themselves to misunderstanding in the immature mind, seem to be a denial of love, and thus increase rather than diminish tensions. Where prohibitions of natural impulses are allied to religious sanctions in a harsh and joyless way, a strongly pervasive feeling of guilt may be built in the child's mind from which he can never free himself or only by a complete denial of faith. On the other hand, while the actual words of any ritual may be completely misunderstood or garbled, it is by

---

1. On this whole subject M. R. Gal writes (private communication):

'Le système de l'enseignement public français présente une solution différente de celles qui ont été envisagées. En effet, cet enseignement ne sépare pas les jeunesses en écoles confessionnelles ou autres, mais est arrivé, après un long passé de luttes, à grouper dans la même école des enfants appartenant aux familles spirituelles les plus diverses: catholiques, protestants, libres penseurs, athées, etc. . . . De même y enseignent côte à côte des maîtres libres penseurs, athées, communistes, catholiques, israélites, etc. . . . La condition imposée à tous est de respecter la pensée de chacun et d'assurer la libre détermination des individus dans les domaines qui ne touchent pas directement à la science proprement dite. Et l'on peut dire que cette liberté et ce respect sont assurés par un personnel qui est à la fois très fier de sa liberté et très soucieux du respect de la liberté personnelle. Historiquement, quand on sait l'arrière-plan historique de luttes pour s'emparer de l'école et s'assurer la direction des esprits que la France a connu, et quand on connaît les traces qui peuvent en subsister encore dans certaines régions, on ne peut s'empêcher de considérer cet accord comme un véritable miracle. L'avantage de cette organisation scolaire, c'est qu'on fait vivre ensemble des enfants et des jeunes gens qui trouvent là l'occasion de se comprendre, de s'apprécier, d'affronter peu à peu leurs opinions à celles des autres. L'inconvénient est que, pédagogiquement, la neutralité peut conduire à éviter tous les problèmes brûlants sur lesquels il n'existe pas d'accord entre les hommes ainsi que les problèmes actuels qui sont pourtant ceux à l'occasion desquels peut le mieux se former la raison contre les passions et les entraînements grégaires. Personnellement, je crois que ce défaut peut être évité, à condition que le maître reste toujours lui-même objectif et compréhensif et, qu'enseignant selon les méthodes actives, il se préoccupe beaucoup moins d'apporter à ses élèves des solutions toutes faites, que l'art de reconnaître et cerner les problèmes, et surtout les attitudes de compréhension, de tolérance et d'amour, propres à permettre à chacun de les aborder et de les résoudre humainement.

'La neutralité n'est pas l'indifférence ou le scepticisme ou l'ignorance de certains problèmes, elle peut fort bien s'allier avec le respect dû aux personnes et à la liberté individuelle d'engagement.'

no means certain that children do not get some support, comfort, and joy from the ritual itself. Hymns, poems, music and such seem to evoke a response which may be far removed from their actual content. On teacher and parent alike, whatever their religious conviction or lack of conviction, devolves the task of seeing that religious teaching does not so greatly increase tensions within the child that they become harmful to the healthy development of his personality and that at the same time they do not, by their very anxiety to protect him from opinions with which they do not concur, shut him off from the immense area of human cultural and spiritual experience which religion has meant in the development of Western civilization.[1]

HETEROGENEITY OF CULTURE: A CHALLENGE

The child's mental and emotional development of which his moral growth is an integral part, is affected by all that happens to him at home, at school, in the playground, or in the streets and fields. His world cannot be fragmented without danger to the unity of his development: a separation between instruction and education, between home experience and school experience, between intellectual education and moral training is artificial and frequently adverse in its effects. The task of the adults who deal with him is complex; they represent authority, they offer objects of identification, they give security and acceptance, they proffer experience and stimulate effort. Children are liable to develop exaggerated ideas of the goodness of the adult, especially the teacher, in each of these parts; or they may, as frequently happens in late childhood, turn away somewhat from adults and find refuge in a world of concrete experience, seeming almost to postpone consideration of the grown-up world in favour of a simpler more extraverted and primitive society of contemporaries. If teacher and parent are tolerant, understanding and above all able to maintain an accepting affection for the children in their charge, they can help to interpret and give unity to the child's worlds and to the diversity which is characteristic of modern cultures. Thus they help to prepare for an enrichment and deepening of the personality in adolescence. The challenge of contemporary life to the educator is that while its lack of coherence, its tensions and its threats constitute a graver menace to the personal security and mental health of its participants than some at least of the more coherent societies of the

---

1. So little is known about the development of moral and religious thought and attitudes in children that it is worthwhile underlining here the need for developmental studies of children in different circumstances and concurrent practical research into methods of religious education. An excellent study of a group of Catholic adolescents is: L. Guittard, *L'évolution religieuse des adolescents*. Paris, Ed. Spes, 1954.

past, its heterogeneity of demands and possibilities offers scope for the widest variety of healthy personal development and the full realization of individual endowment.

BIBLIOGRAPHY

AGAZZI, A. *Panorama della pedagogia d'oggi.* Brescia, La Scuola, 1948. 124 p.

BOWLEY, A. H. & TOWNROE, M. *The spiritual development of the child.* Edinburgh & London, Livingstone, 1953. 84 p.

BUHNEMANN, H. *Die Selbstbildungsmittel der neuen Schule.* Lübeck, Wullenwever, 1949. 116 p.

CASTIELLO, J. *A humane psychology of education.* London, Sheed & Ward, 1938. 254 p.

CENTRE D'ÉDUCATION CONTEMPORAINE. *Cadres nouveaux, méthodes nouvelles.* Paris, Les Presses de l'Ile de France, 1947. 94 p.

CHATELAIN, F. *Les principes de l'éducation nouvelle.* Paris, Les Presses de l'Ile de France, 1951. 47 p.

CODIGNOLA, E. & CODIGNOLA, A. M. *La scuola-città Pestalozzi.* Firenze, Scuola-città Pestalozzi, 1951. 78 p.

——. *Maestri e problemi dell' educazione moderna.* Firenze, La Nuova Italia, 1951. 292 p.

COUSINET, R. *L'éducation nouvelle: actualités pédagogiques.* Neuchâtel et Paris, Delachaux & Niestlé, 1951. 162 p.

CUNNINGHAM, W. F. *Pivotal problems of education. An introduction to the Christian philosophy of education.* New York, Macmillan, 1940. 588 p.

DANIEL, M. V. *Activity in the primary school.* Oxford, B. Blackwell, 1948. 310 p.

DURAND, S. M. *Pour ou contre l'éducation nouvelle; essai de synthèse pédagogique.* Bruges, Desclée de Brouwer, 1951. 203 p.

ELMGREN, J. *School and psychology.* Stockholm, Esselte, 1952. 342 p.

ENGEL, P. *Pädagogisch-psychologische Gestaltung des Elementarunterrichts.* Mains/Rhein, Kirchheim, 1949. 175 p.

FLEMING, C. M. *Individual work in primary schools.* London, Harrap, 1934. 153 p.

GABERT, E. *Die Strafe in der Selbsterziehung und in der Erziehung des Kindes.* Stuttgart, Verlag Freies Geistesleben, 1951. 120 p.

GAUDIA, Z. "Het schoolkind", in Rutten, F. J. Th. *Jaren der Jeugd,* vol. II. Heemstede, De Toorts, 1952

GREAT BRITAIN. MINISTRY OF EDUCATION. *Seven to eleven; your children at school.* London, HMSO, 1949. 36 p.

GUILLAUME, P. *La formation des habitudes.* Paris, Alcan, 1936. 206 p.

HÄBERLIN, P. *Möglichkeiten und Grenzen der Erziehung.* Zürich, Schweizer Spiegelverlag, 1936. 139 p.

HECKER, W. "Über die sittliche Entwicklung von Schulkindern und Frühjugendlichen", in: Früger F. & Volkett, H. *Experimentelle Kinderpsychologie.* München, 1937.

HOURD, M. *Some emotional aspects of learning.* London, Heinemann, 1951. 82 p.

JONASSON, M. *Athöfn og Uppeldi.* Reykjavik, Hlaobuo. 1947.

JOTTERAND, R., ULDRY, R., BEGUIN, M., CHAPUIS, A., BÖLSTERLI, E. *Problèmes scolaires.* Neuchâtel, Delacheux & Niestlé, 1952. 56 p.

Lexikon der Pädagogik, vol. III. Bern, A. Francke, 1952. XIV + 624 p. E. Claparède, p. 89; R. Cousinet, p. 99; O. Decroly, p. 103; J. Dewey, p. 106; R. Dottrens, p. 112; A. Ferrière, p. 135; C. Freinet, p. 147; H. Wallon, p. 471; C. Washburne, p. 472.

Lustenberger, W. *Gemeinschaftliche geistige Schularbeit Entwicklung und Theorie Abhandlung.* Luzern, H. Studer, 1949. 95 p.

Magister (pseud). *Verso la scuola integrale.* Brescia, La Scuola. 228 p.

Meylan, L. *Pour une école de la personne.* Lausanne, Payot, 1942. 96 p.

Ministry of Education. *Seven to eleven: your children at school.* London, HMSO, 1949. 36 p.

Nunn, T. P. *Education, its data and first principles.* 3rd ed. London, E. Arnold, 1945. 283 p.

Parkhurst, H. *Education on the Dalton plan.* New York, Dutton, 1922. 278 p.

——. *Exploring the child's world.* New York, Appleton-Century-Crofts, 1951. 290 p.

Read, H. *Education through art.* London, Faber & Faber, 1943 320 p

Rossello, P. *Allons-nous vers une école d'action, de raison ou de passion?* Genève, Port Noir 6, 1944. 28 p

Schenk-Danzinger, L. *Entwicklungstests für das Schulalter 5-11 Jahre.* Pädagogisch-psychologische Arbeiten. Wien, Verlag für Jugend und Volk, 1953.

Seiwald, E. *Neue Gesichtspunkte für eine demokratische Schule und Bildungsreform in Österreich.* Klagenfurt, K. Dürrschmid, 1948. 78 p.

Slade, P. *Child drama.* London, University of London Press, 1954. 379 p.

Springer, J. *Schöpferischer Anfangsunterricht.* 3rd ed. Worms, Verlag E. Wunderlich, 1951. 360 p.

Stead, H. G. *Education of a community, today and tomorrow.* London, University of London Press, 1942. 165 p.

Strebel, G. *Das Wesen der Schulreife und ihre Erfassung.* Solothurn, St. Antoniusverlag, 1946. 124 p.

Vermeylen, G. *Les sanctions et l'éducation, leur légitimité, leurs modes et leurs résultats.* Bruxelles, Jean Vromans.

Warr, E. B. *Social experience in the junior school.* London, Methuen, 1951. 118 p.

Wettig, L. *Das Problem der Strafe in der Erziehung.* Ravensburg, O. Maier, 1949. 45 p.

Wössner, G. *Lernen und Lehren auf der Stufe der Volkschule.* Stuttgart, Klett, 1948. 255 p.

Ziegfeld, E. (ed.) *Education and art.* Paris, Unesco, 1953. 130 p.

——. *Art et éducation.* Paris, Unesco, 1954. 144 p.

CHAPTER V

SOME SPECIAL PROBLEMS OF THE PRIMARY SCHOOL[1]

THE INTER-DEPENDENCE OF THE INTELLECTUAL AND EMOTIONAL LIFE

The primary school years from about 6 to 11 or 12 are a period of transition, development and organization not only in the intellectual life but in the social and emotional growth of children. Indeed the demonstration of the close interdependence and interaction of these aspects of personality is perhaps the major contribution which the biological and dynamic psychologists have made to education.[2] Learning in the strictly educational sense will not proceed satisfactorily if the child's emotional life is disturbed; conversely the development of personality may be fostered or checked by the way in which a child is able to respond intellectually to the demands made by the school. Hence both mental health and intellectual progress depend upon the way in which the school adapts itself to the developmental level of its pupils, and while not abandoning its demands, adjusts those demands to processes of growth and maturation.

THE EMOTIONAL PROBLEMS OF FIRST ENTRY TO SCHOOL

In this adjustment, the child's first experience of primary school may be crucial. In most European countries, compulsory schooling begins at the age of 6,[3] and since the majority of children have not previously attended nursery schools or kindergartens, this may be their first contact with a school of any kind, the first time they have found themselves in a group of age mates supervised by one adult only.

At this age children are neither quite like the kindergarten child whose principal means of learning is symbolic play, nor the fully-fledged

---

1. Much of this chapter is based on working papers prepared for the conference by I. Rother, Pädagogische Hochschule, Celle, German Federal Republic ('Teaching the Basic Educational Skills') and by H. Aebli (previously cited), and upon the deliberations of Working Group I ('Pre-School and Early Childhood Education') of the conference.
2. This idea was implicit in the work of British psychologists from Hume onwards and notably in that of the biological school—Spencer, Darwin, Sully, Hobhouse and McDougall.
3. Exceptions are: the United Kingdom (age 5); Bulgaria, Denmark, Finland, The Netherlands, Poland, Portugal, Sweden, Yugoslavia (age 7).

primary child who is eager to acquire skills and build up a world of causal relationships. Emotionally they have not achieved detachment from fantasy and a purely hedonistic or pleasure-pain attitude nor have they markedly progressed towards a close and real acceptance of the world and people as they are. Their personal, social, independence is precarious, and though at times they may show considerable realism in their understanding of others, adults and contemporaries, they still revert frequently to subjective projections of their own fantasies. Their behaviour may show surprising swings from one extreme to the other, particularly in such things as the habits of cleanliness imposed by earlier training. Adjustments are less stable and fixed than most parents and teachers realize; and children of 5 or 6 are only provisionally and transitorily oriented in their world.

This first entry to school, to a world which is more specific in its demands and more impersonal than home, is likely, even for children with no unusual difficulties in development, to be provocative temporarily at least of mild anxiety and insecurity. It is by no means unusual, for example, to find a breakdown in what seemed well established habits. Some children show difficulties in sleeping or eating or even a reversion to bed-wetting and temper tantrums; others seem to become particularly vulnerable to minor ailments, coughs and colds, stomach upsets, bouts of sickness. Most show considerable fatigue. Almost all betray their immaturity and their anxiety by projecting on to the teacher, much in the same fashion as younger children in the nursery school, their attitudes to their own parents. They 'love' and 'hate' them in a fashion which usually seems exaggerated, and which may arouse the jealousy or hostility of those parents who are themselves more or less immature. For children who have not successfully detached themselves from mother at the normal 6-year-old level, or who for any reason are nervous or insecure, the new circumstances may prove to be so severely disturbing as to be intolerable, a disturbance which is likely to be reflected in their whole ability to respond to the intellectual demands made upon them.

INTELLECTUAL DEVELOPMENTS

The stage of fragile and delicate adjustment which coincides with entry to school is accompanied by a transition in the intellectual life closely dependent upon it. Many research workers have noted that the early primary school years are marked by a change from numerical, spatial and physical concepts that are rigid, inconsistent, seizing only the exterior aspect of things, to concepts and operations that are more generalized, mobile and consistent and that allow objective apprehension of reality.

The pre-school child apprehends and interprets objects and events very subjectively, in close dependence on his personal interests. For example young children define objects in terms of the activity which they allow ('a puddle is to step in'). As they approach the age of 7 years however they tend to define an object in terms of the sphere to which it belongs; and from then onward, begin to name distinctive features showing thereby that they apprehend things as they are, and can adopt objective criteria.[1] In his studies of child thought, Piaget[2] notes that during the period between 6 and 8 years of age, the logical structure of the fundamental concepts and mental operations pertaining to number, physical quantities, movement and space undergo a marked change. Concepts and operations that had previously depended on the perceptual configuration and were subject to all the illusions suggested by their superficial aspect (apparent variability of physical quantities, errors in comparing distances and movements, etc.) were found to acquire constancy, coherence and reversibility at the age of about 7 years. While the child was not yet capable of carrying out thought processes based on mere assumptions and hypotheses, he could reason logically if confronted with concrete materials or when remembering them. Authors affiliated with the school of gestalt psychology have put the matter in another and complementary form. They note that during middle childhood, a transition from syncretic to more analytic apprehension of data takes place.[3]

INDIVIDUAL DIFFERENCES

These related processes of socio-emotional and of intellectual growth in young children are profoundly and indistinguishably affected by genetic and environmental factors. The intellectual changes referred to above, for example, will proceed more or less rapidly according to the child's level of innate intelligence which sets an upper limit to his potentialities and to the speed of his growth. On the other hand there are considerable differences in temperamental endowment which alone would make for differences in the child's capacity to adapt to social demands. If in addition his previous circumstances have not met

1. C. Bühler, loc. cit., following Binet, in whose scale for the measurement of intelligence, definitions of objects formed a considerable feature and who distinguished several levels of development in interpretation.
2. J. Piaget and A. Szeminska, *La genèse du nombre chez l'enfant*. Neuchâtel, Delachaux & Niestlé, 1941; J. Piaget and B. Inhelder, *Le développement des quantités chez l'enfant*. Neuchâtel, Delachaux & Niestlé, 1941; J. Piaget, *Le développement de la notion de temps chez l'enfant*. Paris, Presses universitaires de France, 1946; J. Piaget and B. Inhelder, *La géométrie spontanée de l'enfant*. Paris, Presses universitaires de France, 1948.
3. H. Werner, *Comparative Psychology of Mental Development* (rev. ed.). Chicago, Follett, 1948; H. Wallon, *Les origines de la pensée chez l'enfant*. Paris, Presses universitaires de France, 1945. (2 vols.)

his fundamental needs then he will not have travelled far enough along the road towards emotional freedom, without which he cannot achieve an adequate conceptual development. Environment too plays a direct part in his intellectual growth. Children for example who, at home, have watched or helped mother with the cooking, who have weighed, measured and counted are likely to have had the opportunity to develop rudimentary number concepts. Similarly, children from environments relatively unfavourable in other respects, from their early experience in for example buying food at the local shop, have a marked and realistic knowledge of money values denied to the more sheltered. Those who come from families where parents talk intelligently to their children, where stories are told or read, and where their attempts to express themselves verbally have been fostered, are likely to be advanced in their vocabulary and in their readiness to use and understand words on which much of their subsequent educational progress will depend. Examples of these kinds might be multiplied to show, in practical terms, that no two children at the beginning of their primary school career will be at the same stage of development. Indeed since they have not yet been submitted to the uniform influence of schooling, children of 6 or 7 are perhaps more heterogeneous than at any other stage except very early adolescence.

CRITERIA OF READINESS FOR SCHOOL

It is not surprising therefore that attempts have been made to assess children's readiness for entry to primary school. Among these, the studies of Danzinger[1] and the Viennese child psychologists are significant. Basing her work on individual case studies, Danzinger suggested as essential: a certain level of intellectual development; an ability to engage in purposive work; some sense of duty and capacity to respond to set tasks, to concentrate, persevere and resist distraction; and the power to participate in collective activities and to respond to suggestions and tasks given, not to the child personally, but to the class as a whole.

On these and similar criteria, school readiness tests have been devised, but, in practice, they have rarely been applied except experimentally. To be scientifically validated, a test which attempts to measure readiness in terms of scores or standards, demands a set of fixed criteria. This might well lead to certain more or less standardized and rigid demands on the part of the school itself. The use of such a test mechanically by those who do not fully understand both the psychological and

1. L. Danzinger, 'Der Schulreifetest', *Wiener Arb. z. päd. Psychol.* 1933, no. 9. See also C. Bühler, op. cit. and full bibliography of French and German literature in Strebel, *Das Wesen der Schulreife und ihre Erfassung.* Solothurn, St. Antonius, 1946.

educational considerations involved, tends to lead to the blind accept-ance of a *status quo* and is therefore to be discouraged. Where, however, such instruments are used by those skilled in their interpretation and who have a clinical psychological training, they can lead to a closer examination of the demands made by the schools and to an attempt to adapt them more closely to the psychology of children. Danzinger's work has drawn attention to the fact that the expectations current in the State primary schools of Europe, evolving as they have from a combination of experience and more or less arbitrary standards, do not generally reflect the known realities of child development. If, however, these expectations are accepted by teachers as indicative and are modified to meet the great variations among children, they may do little harm. Unfortunately many school systems have rigid pro-grammes and syllabuses, laid down by a central authority, which, by attempting to force all children forward at the same pace make failure for many inevitable. Such failure in the initial stage of learning is likely to thwart the development of objectivity and abstractness of thought and to inhibit the growing purposiveness which should ac-company it.

THE RECEPTION CLASS

A sounder way of ensuring a successful adaptation to school life and to the more formal demands of primary curricula is to adapt the first years of school to the great heterogeneity of the children it receives. In some countries this is achieved by establishing a special infants' school or by a reception class in charge of a teacher alive to the needs of children at the age of 6 or 7. Such a class has no arbitrary programme but caters for many levels of emotional and intellectual growth, con-tinuing many of the symbolic play ways of learning of the nursery school and at the same time giving opportunities for the acquisition of skills in a steadily more systematic manner. In such a class it is possible to accustom children gradually to the disciplinary and organizational necessities of classroom teaching with large numbers—to sitting at desks, to habits of orderliness, to waiting one's turn to speak and the like, which often come so hard.

If such classes are kept small and remain with the same adult for a year or two, then as she progressively comes to know her pupils, the teacher can herself assess their readiness for formal learning. She can estimate how far a child has formed elementary concepts of number and knows that, for example, however grouped, five blocks are always five. She can gauge the child's comprehension of spoken language, the range of his vocabulary and the development of perceptual ability to the point where he can embark on learning to read. So too her day-today observations will indicate to her the growth of purposiveness, concentration and capacity to respond to set tasks in the members of her class. She can adjust her programme accordingly. One kind of child, however, is peculiarily liable to escape the understanding even of the experienced teacher unless her attention has been specially drawn to him. The very shy boy or girl who gives no overt trouble, often suffers severely in his first class. He is likely to remain mute, to join in no activities, and his very shyness may mask his real ability. Teachers sometimes regard such children as dull or lazy and other children tease them, thus adding to the difficulty of adjustment they are experiencing. The reception class teacher should never ask such shy children questions they cannot answer, but should try to engage them in some small activity and praise them privately for any progress they make. Other children may be asked, discreetly and obliquely, to help. For example when the child is out of the room, his fellows could be asked what he likes playing at and be encouraged to think why he doesn't play with them. Some child will probably say: 'Perhaps he is afraid of us . . .' and the group as a whole will join in to find a solution.

PREPARATION FOR ENTRY TO SCHOOL

Though the teacher is there to ease and assist the child's development from infancy to stable happy childhood, bridging procedures, though important, are secondary to a sound upbringing. The child's self-confidence, his attitudes to things, to grown-ups and to other children have been built up from earliest years. If he has already attended a nursery school he should have had, particularly in his last year, experiences which are similar in nature to those of the first primary school year. Provided there is no abrupt change of method between the nursery school or kindergarten class and that of the primary school, the transition is likely to be smooth and adjustment easy. Where, however, the nursery school is free and active and the primary school rigid and repressive, difficulties are almost bound to occur. It is of the utmost importance that the nursery school teachers and those of the reception class in the primary school should meet and agree on an approximation of methods, which though it may mean compromise for both, cannot but be of assistance to their pupils.

The majority of children, who do not attend nursery schools or kindergartens, need to be prepared by their parents and to be handled with care and insight by the teacher. As with younger children entering nursery school, it is ideal if parents and teacher can meet sometime before the child enters school, and if the child can himself visit the school in company with his mother. If, as is common in small, tightly knit communities, there are older children close at hand who attend the same school, a skilful mother can increase her child's confidence by enlisting their help to reassure him. The teacher, either through speaking to them individually or by means of a meeting with the mothers and fathers of new children, can help the family to understand and tolerate the difficulties of behaviour which may occur, especially towards the end of the school week—the reluctance to go to school, or the sudden, almost compulsive secrecy, and independence which their child may show. If contacts with the family begin soon enough and the teacher possesses the tact, skill and knowledge, she may be able to influence the early upbringing of her pupils so that they get the opportunities of social and intellectual development which facilitate later educational growth.

It may be agreed that most children apparently survive the experience of a plunge into more or less formal schooling with very little help from parent or teacher. Human material is, indeed, remarkably resilient and, at greater or lesser personal cost, children do make an adaptation. However the proportions of partial or total failure to make satisfactory educational progress which are revealed by the studies undertaken in European schools and which are probably more universal than most administrators and educators realize, should give us pause. We cannot afford to ignore the possibility that the child's whole attitude to himself and to others may be adversely affected by his early school experiences or the likelihood that some will develop a lasting distaste for school. On the other hand, properly handled by parents and teachers who are aware of the profoundly disturbing nature of the abrupt change involved, first entry to school may contribute greatly to the child's knowledge of himself and of others, of his own capacities and limitations, and to his ability confidently to enter novel situations later on.

RETARDATION AND BACKWARDNESS

One of the results of too abrupt a plunge into formal learning, of arbitrarily imposed standards and particularly of premature formal teaching of reading and number, is the prevalence of retardation and backwardness in primary schools. This matter, which hitherto has received too little attention from psychologists and educators,[1] is of crucial importance, affecting a much larger number of children than is generally realized.

The pioneer work of Binet and Simon in France and of Burt[2] in

---

1. Even though research work on readiness for school began at least 40 years ago with W. M. Winch, *When should a Child Begin School?* Baltimore, Warwick and York, 1911, and the research of Valentine's students published in *The Forum of Education*, 1925 ff.
2. A. Binet, 'Le développement de l'intelligence chez les enfants', *L'année psychologique*, 14, 1-94, 1908; C. Burt, 'The Relations of Educational Abilities', *Brit. Journ. Ed. Psych.* vol. IX, pt. 1, 1939.

England, drew attention to the fact that educability has a large innate, genetic component and that children's ability to learn shows marked variation. There are some children therefore who by reason of markedly low intelligence cannot maintain the same pace of learning as their contemporaries. Most European school systems recognize this by the provision of special schools or classes for children whose intelligence is markedly subnormal[1] though not as yet in sufficient numbers. Repeated testing of population samples indicate that about 1½ to 2 per cent of children are so markedly subnormal that they fail conspicuously to follow the curriculum considered suitable for the normal child.

THE DULL

The dull, however, are very much more numerous. If we take as a borderline an I.Q. of 85—that is a level of development in sheer all-round capacity to learn (not standard of attainment) which is 85 per cent or less than that of the average child of the same chronological age—then we should expect to find in any unselected age group of children about 12 to 13 per cent who are, while not markedly subnormal (i.e. not below I.Q. 70), unable to keep up with their better endowed fellows. It is important here to realize that rates of growth in ability are roughly proportional to the innate degree of that ability —that is to say that brighter children mature intellectually faster and duller children slower than the average. Hence the dull child—even if he works up to the limit of his capacity—is likely in the course of the five or six years of his primary schooling to fall further and further behind his abler contemporaries.

Few European countries recognize in their primary educational systems that the dull need a programme more closely adapted to their slower development. Indeed the age grade system which is nearly universal, in so far as it sets up standards more or less based upon the capacities of children of average ability, dooms the dull to increasing failure as they go through school. One would expect, for example, the child with an intelligence quotient of 80 to be working at the age of 10 at the level of children two years younger than he is. One would expect such children, in fact, to complete no more than five or six of the nine years of compulsory schooling. Few exact statistics are available from the schools of Europe showing the chronological ages of children actually working in the various age grade levels of primary schools. A very

---

1. In terms of standardized, individual intelligence tests with a mean and standard deviation of approximately 100 and 15 points respectively (e.g. the various Binet derivatives), the borderline of subnormality requiring special provision is usually taken to be an intelligence quotient of 70.

detailed Belgian study[1] however reveals that the proportions of children backward by one year or more in Belgian schools in 1951 were as follows: second year (age 7), 22.1 per cent; third year (age 8), 25.9 per cent; fourth year (age 9), 32.3 per cent; fifth year (age 10), 40.2 per cent; sixth year (age 11), 41.3 per cent.[2] From these figures—which are probably typical[3] of Europe—we may infer that failure (i.e. inability to conform to the standards set by the school programme) is more widespread than would be expected from the known proportions of the dull.

RETARDATION AN ARTEFACT?

The reasons for this are complex. In the first place if, for example, at the end of each school year 70 per cent of children in each age group are promoted to the next grade, then by the end of the sixth year not more than 16 per cent of children will have passed normally from grade to grade without doubling a class. Thus some backwardness may be an artefact of the age grade promotion system itself, especially

1. Hotyat et al. 'The Instruction, Education and Mental Health of Belgian Children and Adolescents'; a report prepared by the Centre de Recherches of the Institut Supérieur de Pédagogie du Hainaut, published in La revue pédagogique, Brussels, 27th year, no. 9, Nov. 1953, et seq. The figures cited above are based on information collected by school inspectors from all the schools, subsidized by the Primary Education Administration, in the Flemish, mixed and French-speaking areas. They do not include data for the approximately 7½ per cent of the school population in the preparatory sections of lycées, athenées and intermediate schools, etc. A similar study was made for the Paris region (Enfance, no. 1, 1948, no. 5, 1953) and for Lyons (Enfance, no. 3, 1949). The figures for retardation obtained correspond closely with Belgian figures.
2. Hotyat states that the final figure (41.3 per cent, sixth year) is smaller than it otherwise would be because of the numbers of retarded children who leave before the sixth year.
3. The Belgian study is one of the few comprehensive and exact ones available from postwar Europe, but similar trends are disclosed in figures supplied by R. Dottrens for Geneva in 1954—children backward by one year or more: second year (age 7-8), 20 per cent boys, 14 per cent girls; third year (8-9), 22 per cent boys, 16 per cent girls; fourth year (9-10), 30 per cent boys, 22 per cent girls; fifth year (10-11), 30 per cent boys, 22 per cent girls; sixth year (11-12), 35 per cent boys, 27 per cent girls. Allowing for the probable postwar trend to improvement and for the fact that education in Geneva was not so severely disturbed as in Belgium during the war, these figures are remarkably comparable. Figures from Holland supplied by J. A. Verlinden indicate much the same thing, though not comparably presented. For example, in 1947 of the total generation entering the first year class, 58 per cent (55 per cent boys and 62 per cent girls) reached the sixth grade without retardation and the over-all figures for retardation are approximately 30 per cent for boys and 25 per cent for girls (Centraal Bureau voor de Statistiek. De ontwikkeling van het onderwijs in Nederland. Utrecht 1953). Some 11 per cent of children do not reach the sixth class before the end of compulsory schooling, 2 per cent leave for special education, 2 per cent for other reasons. Figures of the numbers of children in each grade from Portugal and Italy suggest the same kind of tendency: e.g., in Portugal (1951-52 figures), 45 per cent of pupils in Grade I (7-year-olds) are above the age of 7; in Grade II (8-year level), 60 per cent are above the age of 8; in Grade III (9-year level), 65 per cent are above the age of 9, and in Grade IV (10-year level), 66 per cent are above the age of 10 years. In Italy (1950-51 figures) there are 1,068,847 children in the first grade as compared with 716,190 in the fifth, a sharp decline occurring after the third year. From the sixth year the proportions in attendance fall sharply (sixth year 339,354; seventh year 220,824; eighth year 158,426) indicating that many children (as many as 60 per cent) leave school without passing beyond the fifth grade—i.e. the 11 to 12-year level.

113

if the thresholds of promotion are arbitrarily and unobjectively fixed. Actually it seems from the Belgian figures that the promotion rate is rather more favourable[1] since Hotyat and his colleagues find (1951) that approximately 50 per cent of pupils complete the cycle of six primary years without remaining more than one year in the same class, but, significantly, they point out that the proportion of failures is highest in the first year.[2] An examination of the Belgian figures for 1938, 1945 and 1951 for two main school districts[3] indicated a deterioration of the situation as a result of the second world war and a steady recovery since, though it seems that the consequences of the war may still be exerting an influence on children born in 1941 and earlier.[4]

BRITISH STUDIES

More light on the matter is thrown by studies of a rather different type which have been made in Great Britain since Burt began his inquiries as psychologist to the London County Council in 1913. For more than two decades now promotion according to standards or grades has ceased to be a feature of English primary education. Children pass from class to class with their age mates, though in many schools there is a system of streaming and of special classes by means of which children of similar age are grouped in classes very roughly homogeneous in ability. As a consequence English work on the problems of backwardness and retardation is expressed in terms rather of educational and mental ages[5] or quotients than in terms of age-grade placement.

Investigation has tended to concentrate mainly upon the basic

---

1. About 89 per cent on the average. In Holland the figure seems to be about 91 to 92 per cent in 1952 as compared with 87 to 89 per cent in 1947.
2. loc. cit. sup. a situation shown in the Dutch but not in the Genevan figures.
3. loc. cit. sup. This seems likely to be a general phenomenon in the belligerent countries—see under 'Broad Social Causes' in this chapter—and is supported by the Dutch figures.
4. In France since 1952 the situation has also sensibly improved at least in the first school year—though it is difficult to distinguish the real improvement from the effects of increased promotions due to the influence of an increased birthrate. This again draws attention to the possibly artificial nature of some 'retardation'.
5. Educational ages and mental ages are units of measurement based upon the mean performance, on standardized and objective tests, of an unselected sample of children of a given chronological age. For example if a sufficiently large and representative group of children aged between 6 years 6 months and 7 years 6 months achieved an average score of 9 points, on a test of reading comprehension, then a child (whatever his chronological age) who scored 9 points on the same test would be said to have an educational age for reading comprehension of 7. Most English tests of attainment and many tests of verbal and non-verbal ability are scaled in this way (e.g. C. Burt, *Mental and Scholastic Tests*. London, King & Co., 1921; E. and F. Schonell, *Diagnostic and Attainment Testing*. Edinburgh, Oliver & Boyd, 1950; P. E. Vernon, *A Graded Word Recognition Test*. Scottish Council for Educational Research; M. E. Hill, *The Southend Arithmetic Tests*. London, Harrap, 1944). The method has certain disadvantages for scientific purposes, particularly because tests purporting to measure the same ability or attainment

skills of reading, spelling, arithmetic and written composition, and on the relationship between a child's level of attainment and his general ability, though the correlation between general ability, as measured either by group or individual tests, and attainment in the basic skills is by no means perfect,[1] the correspondence between school performance and intelligence is sufficiently close to enable us to estimate approximately how many children are likely, because of inferior ability, necessarily to be backward educationally. Burt[2] suggested that any child whose attainments at the age of 10 are equal or inferior to those of the average child of 8½ should be considered backward and in need of special help. This gives us as a rough borderline an educational quotient of 85. If we assume that innate ability sets limits on the child's power to learn at least up to the age of 11 or 12, then children whose intelligence quotients are inferior to 85 will in most cases also be backward educationally. We should expect some 10 to 12 per cent of children inevitably to be backward at the chronological age of 10, solely because of a lower than average ability.

THE UNDER-USE OF ABILITY

Prior to the second world war, repeated testings of groups of children in primary schools revealed that between 13 and 15 per cent of children in English schools were backward. This suggests that there was a small

---

may differ in their factor content as well as in their score distributions, and because mental growth whether in general ability or educational attainment is probably parabolic rather than linear. Thus 'mental ages' on different tests do not necessarily mean the same thing psychologically and the units of growth in mental age are not equivalent. This should lead to considerable caution in the interpretation of results, though not to an abandonment of the principle of comparing the performance of a given child with the mean performance of an unselected sample of contemporaries. On the whole problem of objective testing see Appendix I A.

1. Correlation ratios vary between r = +0.5 and r = +0.9. It is essential to be clear as to exactly what a correlation between a test of intelligence and an educational test really means. Theoretically a test of educable capacity or intelligence should measure potentiality of a (probably) innate kind. There will of course be factors in the subject and in the test which will make it an imperfect measure and reduce its validity as a test of the ability concerned. The score on an educational test however is more complex. A child's reading attainment is a function of his intelligence, any special intellectual abilities involved in learning, and of his opportunities to learn, as well as of his motivation to do so. If a group of children could be found who differed only in innate capacity but who did not differ on the kind and length of teaching they had experienced, we might be able to estimate more closely the relationship between intelligence and the acquisition of educational skills. Our correlations between scores on tests of intelligence and scores on tests in, say, reading or arithmetic, are likely to be reduced considerably by the fact that the samples on which they are based consist of children who have had, for example, teaching of differing degrees of suitability and effectiveness. It seems arguable that given identical conditions of prior experience and of methods of teaching, the correlation between intelligence and the acquisition of educational skills would be much closer than is usually indicated by empirical studies.

2. C. Burt, *The Backward Child*. London, University of London Press, 1937; *Mental and Scholastic Tests*. London, P. B. King and Co., 1923.

proportion[1] of children—between 2 and 4 per cent—whose back-wardness may probably be attributed to causes other than that of markedly lower than average ability, that is they were retarded.[2] When however the actual conditions of backward groups were closely investigated[3] it was found that nearly half the children were in fact achieving even less than might be expected of their limited ability and that some 15 per cent of them were of normal or even of superior ability.[4] In such groups therefore we may expect retardation to be a phenomenon not confined to any particular intellectual level.

The effects of the world war of 1939-45, with its disruption of education and general disturbance of the social and emotional security in which children lived are clearly reflected in a striking increase in retardation. The British Ministry of Education organized the testing of the reading ability of large and representative samples of children in 1948.[5] Accepting a borderline for backwardness somewhat lower than that adopted by most other authorities,[6] the investigators found that 30.1 per cent of 15-year-old children, and 20.5 per cent of 11-year-old children were backward or worse. These figures indicate a substantial increase in the proportion of retarded children, especially among those whose whole primary schooling took place during the

---

1. It could be argued that this discrepancy is a statistical artefact due to the imperfect correlation between tests of intelligence and tests of reading. Moreover the correlation between such tests is not strictly linear. However it is comparatively rare to find children whose attainment level exceeds their intelligence level and the arguments advanced in the footnote to p. 115 of this chapter apply; that is that the regression of tests of intelligence on tests of attainment is, at least in part, a function of genuine, that is not artificial, elements in the educational experience of children.

2. English usage in this field of research and practice reserves the term 'retardation' for that condition in which educational achievement is 85 per cent or less of that to be expected from the level of innate ability. This is an important distinction which should be borne in mind in what follows. A child whose educational age is $8\frac{1}{2}$ years and whose chronological age is 10 years is *backward*. If his mental age is 10 years, then he is *backward and retarded*; if however he has a mental age of $8\frac{1}{2}$, though he is backward he is nevertheless making the most of a limited ability and is not retarded. Similarly a child of 10 years old with a mental age of 13 years who is working at the level of an average 11-year-old, though he may appear to the teacher to be advanced by one year is in fact retarded. His attainment level is less than 85 per cent of that to be expected from his superior ability.

3. C. Burt, *The Backward Child*. loc. cit.; R. H. Adams, 'An Investigation into Backwardness in Arithmetic in the Junior School', M.A. thesis, University of London, 1940; G. Sleight, 'The Diagnosis and Treatment of the Dull and Backward Child', Ph.D. thesis, London, 1952; F. J. Schonell, *Backwardness in the Basic Subjects*. Edinburgh, Oliver & Boyd, 1942.

4. Hotyat's investigation in 1951-52 of 107 children in Charleroi who were in classes corresponding to age levels two or more years younger, showed a similar figure: 10 per cent had I.Q.s (T. and M.) between 100 and 90; and 61 per cent between 90 and 70. Adjusting his borderline of I.Q. 90 to meet the English one of I.Q. 85, his figure would slightly *exceed* 15 per cent.

5. Ministry of Education. *Reading Ability* (Pamphlet no. 18). HMSO, 1950.

6. The convention before the 1939-45 war was to accept an educational ratio of 85; the ministry survey accepted a borderline reading age of 8.8 years for 11-year-old pupils and of 12 years for 15-year-old pupils, i.e. a quotient of 80.

war. Current inquiries[1] suggest that with a return to more normal conditions in the schools, there is a return also to proportions of backwardness nearer to the prewar figure of 15 per cent. The problem of retardation, of the under-use of ability, is not however confined to the backward group. Wall,[2] in 1949 and 1950, investigating attainments in arithmetic, reading and spelling in a sample of some 1,500 8-year-old children in 15 junior schools, found that among children of ability superior to the average, more than half were two years retarded in reading comprehension, one-third two years retarded in arithmetic, and three-quarters, two years or more retarded in spelling as compared with their mental ages. Retardation among children of superior intelligence is apt to escape the attention of the teacher since such children, mentally sometimes two or three years ahead of their contemporaries, frequently achieve an average performance which passes muster.

BROAD SOCIAL CAUSES

The general increase in backwardness over the prewar figures shown in the figures from Belgium and Great Britain, reflects in the main the effects of the wholesale disturbance of children's lives wrought by war and doubtless is matched by similar increases in most of the countries in Europe. The amount of underfunctioning among children of supernormal ability revealed by the English study, is probably not specific to English schools. A similar situation might well be found wherever large classes impose mass teaching, with what this implies in disciplinary methods, and cause teachers to sacrifice the needs of the abler children by concentrating upon the progress of the average. These broad causes have clearly broad remedies; the restoration of more stable and normal conditions in the schools and in the community is already decreasing the number of backward children; the practical recognition of individual differences by an increase in individualized assignments and of the kind of group work suggested in Chapter IV would allow abler children to proceed more nearly at their own pace instead of keeping them in lock-step with their contemporaries. A further possible cause is more difficult to assess. There is evidence that some of the *élan* of popular education has been lost and that, particularly where reading is concerned, many children do not receive the necessary environ-

1. The whole matter of reading difficulty has attracted a great deal of attention in the United Kingdom since the end of the war and a great many studies and surveys have been published. See references in the article cited p. 116 footnote 5, and studies published in the *British Journal of Educational Psychology* and *The Times Educational Supplement* from 1945 onwards.
2. 'Problems and Methods of Dealing with Retardation in Junior Schools', British Association, Birmingham 1950. See also, ibid., 'Le retard scolaire en Grande-Bretagne', *Enfance* vol. VII, no. 4, 1954.

mental motivation to read.[1] This is a factor deserving more attention from psychologists, educators and sociologists than it at present receives and one which, if recognized, might lead to a considerable revision of our practical educational aims.

INDIVIDUAL CASES

Even however when such broad causes have been allowed for, there remains a hard core of children, representing the whole range of ability, who are underfunctioning for a combination of reasons which can only be estimated by a careful individual clinical study. Most investigators are agreed that in any one case the causes are multiple, combining in different ways in different children. It is clear however that failure to learn nearly always has emotional connotations. Social, physical, and physiological factors, unless they are very extreme,[2] though they may sometimes slow down a child's progress, are not insuperable obstacles unless they reverberate in his emotional life. Not infrequently retardation is the symptom of a series of adverse attitudes, habits and maladjustments in the entire social and emotional development of the child which find their roots in experiences in the family or in the early years of school.[3] Furthermore we are beginning to see that retardation, either as a symptom of deeper disturbances or directly by what it may mean in terms of wasted talent and lowered morale, is related to many cases of adolescent and adult breakdown and delinquency.[4] As such it is worthy of the attention of research workers in every country in Europe.[5]

1. W. D. Wall, 'The Backward Adult', pts. I and II, *Journal of Army Education* vol. XXII, no. 4, 1948, and vol. XXIII, no. 1, 1949. In a private communication Hotyat writes (my translation): 'Teachers in urban and industrial areas in my country [Belgium] complain that they have no longer the same prestige in the eyes of parents as they used to have. Most parents, they say, are indifferent to the teachers' remarks or advice and care less about the education of their children.'
2. See for example: M. McMeeken, *Ocular Dominance in Relation to Developmental Aphasia*. London, Univ. of London Press, 1939; B. Hallgren, *Specific Dyslexia*. Copenhagen, Enjar Munksgaard, 1950; 'Apprentissage de la lecture et ses troubles', special number, *Enfance* vol. IV, no. 5, 1951; G. de Gillet, 'Dépistage des défauts oculaires ou anomalies visuelles retardant l'apprentissage de la lecture', mémoire de licence, Louvain, 1950.
3. C. A. Mace and P. E. Vernon (editors), *Current Trends in British Psychology*. London, Methuen, 1952, p. 67-9; M. E. Highfield, *The Young School Failure*. Edinburgh, Oliver & Boyd, 1949.
4. See for example: C. Burt, *The Young Delinquent*. 4th ed. London, Univ. of London Press. 1944; E. Norwood-East, *The Adolescent Criminal*. London, Churchill, 1942; W. D. Wall, 'Reading Backwardness among Men in the Army', pts. I and II, *Brit. Journ. Ed. Psych.* vol. XV, pt. I, 1945 and vol. XVI, pt. III, 1946.
5. Research work into retardation and into the reasons for doubling classes is now proceeding in Austria (Tyrol—Miss E. Cleef), in the German Federal Republic (Mr. Frommberger, Bielefeld), and in Belgium and France (under the joint aegis of the Institut supérieur de pédagogie du Hainaut and the Laboratoire de psycho-biologie de l'enfant, Paris). The latter research which involves a long-term study of large samples of children in both countries from the time they enter primary schools seems likely to produce considerable evidence of the ways different factors interact to cause retardation, and of the circumstances in which, in spite of adverse factors, children do not become retarded.

REMEDIES

The school, especially in the early years, is the first line of defence against backwardness and retardation. It is most likely to succeed upon the basis of constructive mental health work applied to the education of all children, supplemented by some special remedial work where this proves necessary.[1] By a sensitive knowledge of his pupils, by close co-operation with parents, by the adaptation of method to differing capacities and above all by the quality of the human relationships he builds up, the teacher can play a key part in such constructive work, even where the earlier circumstances of the child's life have been adverse and even where the social milieu is unfavourable.

Unhappily in many schools in Europe the formal teaching of reading and arithmetic begins before the child has achieved the necessary physiological and mental maturity to start with a fair prospect of continuing success. In the eyes of parents, children, and teachers alike, the acquisition of the basic skills ranks as the major task of the primary schoolchild; and failure is immediately apparent to the child himself and usually to his parents who read into it misgivings prompted and intensified by their own anxieties. Hence there is the tendency, always a danger to good education, to attempt to start too early, to go too fast and to devote so much time and energy to formal teaching that little is left for other activities, which would both develop the child's expanding curiosity about his world and help him to increase his stability and self-confidence which lie at the root of his power to learn.

CRITICAL PERIODS

Recent research tends to indicate that for each child, whatever the method used and whatever the prior preparation, there is a stage at which he is insufficiently mature to learn certain techniques. Time spent in trying prematurely to teach him is not merely wasteful, but the resulting failure builds up in him adverse attitudes and actually delays subsequent learning. Similarly it seems, though this is not so certain, that there may be critical periods at which learning of particular skills or processes takes place more readily and surely than later. Such critical periods are difficult to determine with precision since, whilst ultimately dependent upon a general maturation which varies greatly from individual to individual, they are much affected by prior experience and environmental stimulation which are only partly under the control of the school.

---

1. For methods and organization see C. Burt, *The Backward Child*, loc. cit.; F. J. Schonell, *Backwardness in the Basic Subjects*, Edinburgh, Oliver and Boyd, 1942; F. J. Schonell and W. D. Wall, 'The Remedial Education Centre', *Educational Review* vol. II, pt. I, 1949; L. B. Birch, 'The Improvement of Reading Ability', *Brit. Journ. Ed. Psych.* vol. XX, pt. 2, 1950.

READING READINESS

This is well illustrated by the studies of reading readiness, the upshot of which is that learning to read depends upon a sufficient level of general intellectual development, a physical and physiological maturation which makes possible the fine perceptual discriminations on which the deciphering of print depends, and a growth in personality such that the child wishes to learn and has sufficient emotional energy to devote himself to the task. Learning to read moreover in part depends upon the child's own spoken vocabulary, which in turn largely reflects environmental stimulus. Other things being equal, the child from the well-to-do home is likely to be advanced by as much as two years in his verbal development at the age of 6 as compared with his contemporary from a poorer environment; he is thus not faced with the double task of acquiring the concepts and of learning how to read the words in which they are embodied.

Much attention has been devoted to physical and physiological defects—for example cross-laterality, visual and auditory weaknesses— as causative factors in reading difficulties. Such weaknesses may call for special attention, and if neglected, operate as severe handicaps. Many more children are found to have weaknesses in visual and auditory perception, independent of sensory defects; indeed up to the age of 7, confusions between the letters b/d, p/q, m/n and the like are rather the rule than the exception.[1] In themselves however neither sensory defects nor weaknesses in visual and auditory perception will prevent learning to read if the child is well motivated and well taught.

It seems probable that the main factor is that of personal development. Intelligence and physiological maturation set downward limits below which teaching is likely to be ineffective; but the decisive factors, given adequate intellectual maturation, seem to be orectic and to be a reflection of the child's whole prior developmental experience, and in particular of the stimulus which his environment has given him. If home and nursery school have satisfied his needs; if he is, at his level, stable, confident and enterprising, then he will welcome the challenge of new and difficult tasks.

If however his verbal experience has been limited or if he is manifestly unable to tolerate failure, the wise teacher will postpone formal teaching in favour of activities aimed at enlarging his experience and building up a sense of security. Such aspects of maturation cannot be mechanically determined or assessed by tests; only by careful study and understanding of each individual child with all his idiosyncrasies of ability, experience and development, can the teacher in fact adjust the programme to the widely differing capacities which will character-

1. F. J. Schonell, *Backwardness in the Basic Subjects*, op. cit.

ize a group of 40 or more children at the outset of their school career. At what age, then, may we expect that the child who is developing normally will begin to learn to read? Most American authors agree that a *mental* age of 6½ years is optimal for the conditions prevailing in their country. Gates,[1] while agreeing with this, notes that modifications of reading material and teaching method make an earlier start possible. Taylor, studying Scottish children[2] indicates that they may profitably start reading as early as 5 if, but only if, words of very simple structure and expressing a very limited range of ideas are used.[3] There seems however no reason to suppose that anything is lost by a later start;[4] much harm however may be done by a premature beginning which increases the chances of failure among those of an insufficient maturity. It is thus of the utmost importance to the healthy mental growth of children that, for each language and for each culture area, efforts should be made to determine the optimal mental age at which to begin the teaching of reading. Since however this is in part dependent upon method and materials, and in part upon the personal development of each pupil, more attention should be paid, in the training of teachers for primary schools, to the methods of teaching reading and to ways of assessing children's readiness to learn.[5]

ARITHMETIC

Even more than in the teaching of reading, teachers (and the framers of curricula) tend to go too far and too fast in pushing children to learn arithmetic. The ability to handle numbers in the abstract form of figures and to comprehend such processes as multiplication and division, depends upon the acquisition of concepts of quantity, size, extension and the like through repeated concrete experience.[6] It depends too upon a gestalt of experiential and emotional factors similar to those involved in learning to read.

1. A. I. Gates, 'The Necessary Mental Age for Beginning Reading', *El. Sch. J.*, 1937, 37, p. 497-508.
2. C. D. Taylor, 'The Effect of Training on Reading Readiness', *Studies in Reading* vol. II. Ed. by Scottish Council for Research in Education. London, University of London Press, 1950, p. 63-80.
3. This research work is valid only for English-speaking children learning to read English. Languages like Italian, French or Spanish for example, where the spelling is more nearly phonetic *may* be easier and permit an earlier start if materials and methods are suitably chosen.
4. D. E. M. Gardner, *Testing Results in the Infant School*. London, Methuen, 1942.
5. There are many valuable exposés of teaching method. The most recent is that prepared by W. S. Gray: *Preliminary Survey on Methods of Teaching Reading and Writing (Educational Studies and Documents)*. Paris, Unesco, 1953, 2 vols.
6. Scottish Council for Research in Education, *The Early Development of Number Concepts*. London, University of London Press, 1942; J. Piaget and A. Szeminska, *La genèse du nombre chez l'enfant*, op. cit.; R. Buyse, *Etudes et recherches louvainistes sur le calcul élémentaire*. Congrès International de Santander (R. Buyse, University of Louvain).

Where such concepts are inadequately formed or where the concrete experience is lacking, arithmetic very readily appears an incomprehensible puzzle around which children build up feelings of inferiority. The results of their efforts are so clearly right or wrong that failure is immediately apparent. Moreover an imperfect mastery of one basic process may entirely prevent subsequent progress. Hence it is of vital importance educationally that each stage of teaching and each new process should be introduced only when it is clear that the ability to understand and to learn is mature enough to give the best chance of success.[1]

Under the chairmanship of C. Washburne, a committee of seven educationalists carried out a large-scale experiment in the United States of America, designed to determine the optimal placement of practically all processes involved in primary and early secondary school mathematics. Washburne himself however points out that results for grades higher than the first depend more on the previous mastery of operations that enter into the new topic than on the mental age reached by the pupil. They are therefore not directly applicable to school systems where different sequences of subject matter are followed and where general levels of scholastic attainment differ from those in the United States. The one or the other condition probably obtains in most European countries. Reference here therefore will be made only to the age of the learning of the basic addition and subtraction facts, since these affect the age at which formal instruction in arithmetic can usefully begin. According to Washburne, these operations can be successfully learned at a *mental* age of 7 or 8 years,[2] a finding in accordance with Piaget's discovery that it is only between 6 years and 6 months, and 7 years and 8 months,[3] that the child acquires the notion of invariable quantities of discrete units. Before that age, the normal (i.e. not superior) child will believe that 'there are more pennies' or that 'there are less pennies' according to their being spread out or put together on the table, even if he has counted them. It is obvious that under these circumstances, understanding of arithmetic operations is impossible and that memorized number com-

1. This, it will be observed, is only a special case of the need for security or confidence.
2. C. Washburne, 'Grade-placement of Arithmetic Topics', *National Society for the Study of Education, 29th Yearbook.* 1930, Bloomington, Ill., Public School Publishing Co., 1930, p. 641-70; C. Washburne, 'The Work of the Committee of Seven on Grade-placement in Arithmetic', *National Society for the study of Education, 83th Yearbook*, part I. 1939, Bloomington, Ill., Public School Publishing Co., 1939, p. 299-324. Some of Washburne's findings have been questioned on methodological grounds by Curr (W. Curr, 'Placement of Topics in Arithmetic', in: Scottish Council for Research in Education, *Studies in Arithmetic*, vol. II. London, University of London Press, 1941, p. 183-218). Any student of age placement should familiarize himself with Curr's analysis of the methodological problems involved in this kind of investigation.
3. J. Piaget and A. Szeminska, *La genèse du nombre chez l'enfant.* loc. cit., p. 33-48; J. Piaget, *La psychologie de l'intelligence.* Paris, Armand Collin, 1947, p. 167.

binations remain mere vocal reflexes.[1] Washburne also showed, and subsequent inquiries have confirmed, that while there is a minimum mental age below which a notion will not be comprehended however presented, the method of presentation profoundly affects the age at which learning can successfully take place.

Only too frequently failure is induced in children by the teacher not drawing a distinction in his method of presentation between the logical structure of a subject, process or technique and the psychological mode in which it is taught. This distinction is at the root of successful pedagogic method and deserves more attention—particularly in the teaching of arithmetic—than it usually gets. When we speak of such arithmetical notions as simple common fractions or the inclination of a slope, we refer only to their logical structure. A fraction can be used concretely by handling sticks and surfaces or it can be expressed by symbols and handled representatively (abstractly). Similarly the inclination of a slope can be conceived as its steepness as experienced when one climbs it; it can be appreciated perceptively when looked at from the side; or it can be expressed as a ratio between the vertical and horizontal distances of two points.

Thus almost any given notion, process or operation found in the primary school curriculum can be dealt with concretely (by actual perception or by real action or experience) or symbolically or abstractly, and in a more or less generalized way. These are psychological dimensions. Moreover the context in which the latter occur will determine the amount of energy which the child will bring to their handling. If a given notion, operation, or technique is seen by the child to be of immediate interest and value to him, and if it is dealt with by the teacher in a more concrete and particular way, then it can be acquired both more surely and at an earlier age than if it is unrelated to his interests and presented in a symbolical, abstract or generalized way. Thus though logically the 'content' may be the same, psychologically very different processes are involved.

In many if not most countries in Europe, teachers and parents alike are reluctant to postpone the beginnings of formal teaching of reading, arithmetic and written composition even by as little as six months. In some countries indeed the tendency is noticeable for parents to enter children in primary schools if possible before the minimum compulsory age;[2] others[3] well provided with nursery schools have had to forbid

---

1. For a penetrating monograph on the development of arithmetical thinking during first grade, see also: W. Oehl, 'Psychologische Untersuchungen über Zahlendenken und Rechnen bei Schulanfängern', *Zeitschr. f. ang. Psychol.* 1935, 49, p. 305-51. The concept of 'vocal reflexes' ('*réflexes relatifs au maniement des symboles*') has recently been proposed by H. Aebli in *Didactique psychologique*. loc. cit.
2. e.g. Belgium.
3. e.g. Belgium, France.

the teaching of reading and number in such schools. In many communities parents insist upon homework being set and exercise pressure on the primary school to force children forward as rapidly as possible. Where two systems of education exist side by side in competition for pupils, such pressure is liable to be very marked and difficult for the teachers to resist.

There is little doubt that many of the objections to the idea of making education more child-centred and of adapting it more nearly to the conclusions of an increasing body of research in child development, are motivated, in parents and teachers alike, by a genuine if perhaps mistaken anxiety for the child's good.[1] Education and educationists are rightly conservative and well-tried methods should not be lightly abandoned. On the other hand it is as well to consider carefully whether, in order to ensure the best possible future for children, we are not submitting them to such heavy present disadvantages that we defeat our own ends.

PREDICTIVE AND COMPETITIVE EXAMINATIONS[2]

One of the major external causes of anxiety in parents and teachers and therefore of pressure on children is that in most European countries, after five or six years of primary education, the choice between the various forms of secondary education is determined by some kind of selection process, usually an examination. Some children, as a rule the least able intellectually, continue with studies similar to those of the primary school; others enter various technical or prevocational courses; and a smaller group passes into some form of academic education which may be the only way of entry to a university or to a profession. The guidance of children between these different forms of secondary education has always presented a problem. Sometimes the simple but undemocratic expedient of charging relatively high fees for some of the courses is the favoured way. Other systems have a sufficiently generous provision to allow parents and children a free choice between secondary schools. The method of economic selection results in a very considerable waste of talent among those children whose parents cannot or will not pay fees. On the other hand, unrestricted entry leads to a number of children entering schools for which they are intellectually

---

1. See for example: C. Brogan, 'The Decline and Fall of State Education', *Daily Telegraph*, 16 Dec. 1952.
2. Much of what follows is based on a working paper, 'External Examinations in the Educational System' prepared for the conference by E. A. Peel, University of Birmingham England.

unfitted and therefore to a very considerable rate of failure and premature school leaving.[1]

More usually children have been allowed to enter secondary schools, whether academic or technical, only after passing some kind of examination, set by the school itself, by the responsible local authority or by the State. Partly because of the apparent economic or social value of particular forms of education, partly because of the prestige of particular schools, parents and teachers have attempted to ensure that a child shall gain entry irrespective of whether the particular form of education provided is the one best suited to his aptitudes and interests. Where—as for example in England or in France—one form of education demanding a relatively high level of academic ability enjoys a social prestige and at the same time offers insufficient places for all the children whose parents wish them to enter, there is a tendency to prepare children intensively for the entrance examination almost from the outset of their schooling.

In most European countries the examination tends to be based upon some or all of the primary school syllabus. Most, for example Austria, Britain, Denmark, Norway examine solely or mainly the standard of attainment in the mother tongue and in arithmetic. Others, notably Belgium, Holland and Italy[2] bring other subjects into the examination, particularly geography and history. Clearly the form of the examination and its content will affect the primary school curriculum; in so far as it is competitive, it may lead both to cramming and overwork for the children and to a concentration by teachers on the teaching of those subjects chosen by the examiners at the expense of activities equally valuable but not examined.

Beside the possibility of a distortion or cramping of the primary school syllabus, there is also the danger that the natural eagerness of parents and teachers to do their best for their children will result in a period of mounting anxiety as the examination approaches. There is evidence that many children, whatever the form taken by the examination, experience emotional stress as the result of which they fail to do themselves justice; others, straining their ability to the utmost and nevertheless failing, develop apathy and a sense of inferiority which pursues them throughout the rest, at least of their school, life; yet others, carefully and expertly coached, pass the examination only to

---

1. C. Burt, 'Ability and Income', *Brit. Journ. Ed. Psych.* vol. XIII, pt. 2, 1943. Burt's estimate was that some 40 per cent of able children failed to get a suitable education because of their parents inability to pay fees. Since 1944 secondary education in the U.K. is free in the State-maintained schools. See Chapter VII, and notes.
2. In Italy the child at the end of his primary course, normally at the age of 10 or 11, undergoes a relatively simple oral and written examination for entry to a three-year 'middle school' *(scuola media)*. Only at the end of the middle school, and on the basis of a more difficult examination, is selection made for secondary education proper. Children who do not sit for the examination for the middle school continue their studies in trade, industrial, or agricultural schools.

find that they have entered a form of education for which they are not genuinely suitable.

It is easier to criticize current examinations for entry to secondary education than it is to suggest remedies. The effects of such examinations on primary schools and upon children, parents and teachers are closely related to social attitudes in the community, to the amount and types of education offered at the secondary stage, to the effectiveness of the examination itself and to the means used to decide in doubtful cases. Where, as exists almost nowhere in Europe, all forms of secondary education enjoy an equal prestige and are equally accessible to all children irrespective of economic or social factors, the problem is at its simplest—that of devising some series of tests, measures or observations which will enable us to guide each child to that form of education best suited to him. Even here however many problems arise. Such guidance depends upon the reliability and validity of the instruments —examinations, tests, interviews, or records—used to predict how children will develop. In most school systems, for sound educational and administrative reasons most children make the change from primary to secondary education between the ages of 11 and 13 (even earlier in some countries, e.g. 10 in Lausanne, Switzerland); guidance or selection operates at the threshold of adolescence which will bring about a profound change in the emotional, social and intellectual life. Thus prediction is perforce made at a period when many factors combine to make it difficult.

Research over the past 15 years in Belgium,[1] Holland,[2] Norway,[3] Sweden[4] and the United Kingdom[5] has indicated that *standardized*

1. A. Van Waeyenberghe, 'Une batterie de tests d'instruction pour l'orientation scolaire', *R. belge de Ps. Ped.* Brussels, 1947; 'La valeur prognostique d'un test de connaissance appliqué à l'entrée de l'enseignement moyen', *R. belge Ps. Ped.* Brussels, 1950; M. Schlepens, 'Intelligentiemeting en Schooluitslagen', *Persoon en Gemeenschap.* Antwerp, 1947, I, 2, 6.
2. Nutsseminarium voor Paedagogiek aan de Universiteit van Amsterdam, 1945-52.
3. J. Sandven, *Opptakinga til den högre skolen.* Oslo, 1949; O. Sundet, *Eksamen og skolearbeid.* Oslo, Cappelen, 1945.
4. S. Arvidson, *Skolreformen.* Lund, Gleerup, 1948; S. Hallgren, *Grupptestning.* Stockholm, Hugo Gebers, 1943; Sweden: Ecklesiastikdepartementet, *Sambandet mellan folkskola och högre skola.* Stockholm, 1944 (Statens offentliga utredningar, 1944: 21); T. Husen, *Testresultatens prognosvärde.* Stockholm, H. Gebers, 1950; F. Wigforss, *The Entrance Examination in View of Later School Performance.* Stockholm, Norstedts, 1937.
5. The British work is too extensive to be quoted in detail. The reader is referred to the following which cover the principal researches which have been made and each of which has an extensive bibliography: C. Burt, W. P. Alexander, V. J. Moore, E. J. C. Bradford, J. J. B. Dempster, E. A. Peel, C. M. Lambert, A. Rodger, 'Symposium on the Selection of Pupils for Different Types of Secondary Schools', *Brit. Journ. Ed. Psych.* 1947-50; W. McClelland, *Selection for Secondary Education.* Scottish Council for Research in Education, London, Univ. of London Press, 1942; National Union of Teachers, *Transfer from Primary to Secondary School.* London, Evans Bros., 1949; A. F. Watts and P. Slater, Nat. Found. for Ed. Research, *The Allocation of Primary School Leavers to Courses of Secondary Education.* London, 1950. A good deal of research and writing on educational and vocational guidance (particularly the latter) has gone on in Italy since 1932. Currently there is talk of creating official centres of research and training, see M. Ponzo, 'Nell'attesa dei provvedimenti legislativi sull' orientamento professionale nella scuola', *Rivista di Psicologia.* 1950.

objective tests of general intelligence, arithmetic and the native language predict, better than anything else[1] success in academic education as shown in the results of public examinations held three or five years later. Less research has been undertaken on the prediction of success in technical education but the conclusions are similar and suggest that the addition of tests of special abilities (e.g. spatial tests) improves the predictive power.[2]

Nevertheless, though such objective tests have high reliability and predictive value they are not entirely satisfactory alone. Mistakes and misplacements occur for a variety of reasons. It has been justly agreed that passing an examination like the English school leaving certificate, the French *baccalauréat* or the Swedish *matriculation* is by no means the sole criterion of profit even from academic education. Moreover, though we may guide a number of children into a form of schooling which is entirely suitable for them, we are by no means sure that among those excluded there are not some or many who could equally well profit from it. Indeed however reliable and predictive an examination may be, and wherever the borderline for success or failure be drawn, the group just above and just below the critical score covers so small a range of difference that a distinction between near failure and near success can only arbitrarily be made. This is the strongest argument for careful individual study of the borderline group by a trained psychologist or by a team consisting of teachers and psychologists. Similarly it has been argued, particularly on the basis of the clinical study of children who fail at the secondary stage, that while the intellectual component of success can be predicted with fair accuracy and failures due to sheer lack of ability can be eliminated, there remains the whole problem of the child's temperamental, emotional and social adaptation to the particular demands of secondary education. For example, the unstable child may in fact achieve his full possibilities under the stimulus of an examination lasting a few hours but be unable to sustain academic studies pursued over five years. So too the willingness of the home both financially and morally to support a boy or girl in studies outside the experience of the parents, and the nature and bent of the child's interests, immediately and potentially, are important factors which escape the examiner's probe.

It is doubtless for these reasons that attempts have been made to supplement the results of the examination in various ways or to delay the irrevocable decision as to a particular form of secondary education as long as possible. Some school systems rely on internal examina-

---

1. The coefficients of correlation, corrected for selection, are of the order $r = +.84$.
2. E. A. Peel, 'Selection for Technical Education', *Educational Review* June 1952; E. J. G. Bradford, 'Selection for Technical Education' parts I and II, *Brit. Journ. Ed. Psych.*, vol. XVI, parts 2 and 3, 1946.

tions set by the primary schools,[1] others supplement examinations, whether of the traditional kind or of the more reliable objective kind, by the judgments of teachers expressed through cumulative school records or resulting from a period of observation.[2] Yet others have an elaborate procedure of interviews especially for the borderline group. Some make the choice irrevocably when the child is 10 or 11; others interpose a more or less non-selective middle school[3] between the primary course and the secondary course proper. Few indeed have been able to go as far as to have a common secondary school for at least the first three or four years within which by a process of continuous guidance, rather than by examination, children may find the type of education best suited to their abilities, aptitudes and interests as they declare themselves in adolescence.[4] The solutions found by a particular country will always be in terms of the kind and extent of secondary education available, the length of the period of compulsory schooling, and the degree of enlightenment of public opinion, particularly among parents, teachers and educational administrators.

From the viewpoint of the primary school, and particularly from that of the mental health of the majority of children, any method of selection should fulfil certain criteria. If an examination be used, it should not impose on the primary school a syllabus or a method alien to the needs of children between the ages of 6 and 11 to 13. This suggests that any guidance procedure should test the child's ability to think in various ways—numerically, verbally and the like—rather than his mastery of more than an essential minimum of facts. Such an examination should be reliable—it should give consistent results no matter who marks it—and should be predictive of success in the future.

Few of the traditional examinations in use in European schools fulfil these criteria though efforts have been made with some success to increase the reliability of the marking of examinations which depend on essay-type answers. On the other hand the objective standardized test fails to test such things as the ability to synthesize knowledge or to write with sustained coherence in the native tongue. Nor are we without evidence that, where objective tests are used, children are effectively coached in doing them.[5]

No examination by itself is infallible. Hence the guidance procedure

---

1. Belgium, Italy.
2. For example Austria, Denmark, Germany, Holland and parts of the United Kindgom.
3. For example Austria, Belgium, Denmark, Italy (see note 2, p. 125). The French system treats the first three years of the secondary course as a *cycle d'orientation*.
4. This solution is practised in various forms in Australia, New Zealand, the United States of America, and has its advocates in the United Kingdom and elsewhere. One must however recognize that the comprehensive, or multilateral school has practical disadvantages and has not only a certain psychological *raison d'être* but also social and political implications. Many of the arguments for and against this particular solution, though dressed in psychological terms, are in fact based upon particular social philosophies.
5. P. E. Vernon, 'Intelligence Testing', I and II, *Times Ed. Suppt.* 25 Jan. and 1 Feb. 1952.

needs to take into account the child's previous career, his present interests and degree of emotional development, and the possibility of subsequent change. Cumulative school records, the judgment of the teachers who know the child well and the possibility of transfer later from one type of education to the other must all be included. By no means least in importance is the consideration that no method of selection or guidance, however efficient, absolves the secondary school from adapting its curriculum and method to the pupils it receives.

Ultimately, provided the procedures are as objective, fair and as valid as possible, the effect on children of selection at the end of the primary school career depends 'much more upon the attitudes of parents and teachers than upon the nature or timing of the examination. If parents and teachers can be brought to see where the child's best interests lie and to conceive of the examination and the associated techniques as a means of guidance rather than of competitive selection, there will be less anxiety at home, less pressure on children at school, and less feeling of frustration or failure if a particular pupil does not enter a particular kind of school. The achievement of this is partly a matter of adequacy of provision of the various types of post-primary education, especially in terms of those factors like laboratories, buildings, facilities for sport and the like which are the outward trappings of esteem. Partly it is a matter of public education, of explaining to parents only too ready to believe that if their goose is not a swan it can at least be disguised as one, the plain facts of individual differences and the importance of not pushing a child into a form of education for which he is unfitted. Beyond these however, lies the strongest factor of all, a social problem which the educator alone cannot solve. Educational selection and guidance in almost every European country implies also vocational guidance; the value, in economic terms or in prestige placed by a society on particular classes of vocation, does much to determine the regard in which schools whose pupils go on to these vocations, are held. Such values may or may not be wrong, but the over-emphasis on some of them which characterizes almost every European country certainly is one of the most potent, if least calculable and measurable, forces which prevent education from really matching the needs of developing children and adolescents.

CONSTRUCTIVE MENTAL HEALTH IN THE PRIMARY SCHOOL

Throughout this chapter, stress has been laid largely upon the more obvious ways in which our European primary schools are imposing upon children needless stresses which individual parents and teachers are often powerless to alter or even to control. It will be argued that none of the difficulties discussed in the present chapter is new and that, in the past, the pressures have been even greater and the large majority of children have passed through their primary schooling relatively unscathed. We may admit that this is largely true; backwardness and retardation, for example, are only seen to be problems when in fact we begin to evaluate the results of education or when—as during the recent war—the educational levels of a large number of adults are tested on their enlistment into the army.[1] Disquiet about the effects upon children and upon the primary school syllabus of selection at the age of 11 or 12 for various forms of secondary education only came to a head in England with the institution of universal and free secondary education. Since the war, however, almost every country in Europe has shown itself uneasy about some aspects of its educational system as is evidenced by the volume of new legislation and of expert reports since 1945.

The school is, after the home, the most important single shaper of the child's personality. As such, its part cannot be merely to avoid needless difficulties for its pupils; it has, or should have, a positive and constructive part to play in the healthy mental and emotional development of all children. This does not mean necessarily that the school should preach a particular social philosophy or that it should do more than provide the stimulus to and the opportunity for the fullest possible realization of individual potentialities within a social framework; but the need and potentialities of each child are different; and there cannot be, without loss, a complete standardization of curriculum and of method, a kind of blind mass teaching.[2]

Yet this in fact is what most schools in Europe are forced to provide. The class of some forty, fifty or even more children in a room crammed with serried rows of desks, makes individual attention difficult if not impossible; and it forbids all but the most limited activity on the part of the pupils. Such overcrowding is often at its worst where the need for the most enlightened methods is greatest—in the dingy slum areas of large towns. A second major problem is that of the official syllabus often laid down by the central authority and given greater force in the teacher's eyes by the competitive examinations for secondary school entrance. In many countries, recent reforms and directives have tended to make the primary syllabus more permissive; nevertheless our

---

1. Repeated testings of recruits to the British Army reveal that between 1 and 2 per cent of adult men are to all intents and purposes illiterate and a further 20 to 25 per cent so backward in reading that only the simplest forms of printed material are comprehensible to them. See also the very similar figures for the Belgian Army (1.31 per cent illiterate): L. Delys, 'La mesure de l'enseignement primaire', *Revue des sciences pédagogiques*. Brussels, 1948. The various publications of the examiners of recruits into the Swiss Army do not state figures for illiteracy as such but give, on the other hand, valuable qualitative analyses of the knowledge of such things as history, geography, politics, shown by these recruits. See, for example, M. F. Burki, *Rapport sur les examens civiques des recrues en 1948; rapport sur les examens pédagogiques des recrues*. 1949, 1950, etc.

2. D. MacDonald, 'Culture ou masse', *Diogène* no. 3, July 1953, p. 3-30.

ideas on curriculum have remained substantially unchanged since the nineteenth century. New subjects have been added; little has been dropped. In many countries the syllabus is so crowded that children from the age of 6 onwards have an hour or more's homework to do at night in addition to a school day of six hours or more.

The results of all this are seen in a primary school programme in which the formal elements of reading, writing and arithmetic predominate, where music, creative work, dramatics, and even physical education are regarded as 'frills', secondary to the grim purpose of ensuring by hook or by crook that most children attain a standard level of literacy and ability to calculate mechanically and are equipped with a body of more or less arbitrarily selected knowledge. The fact that, with traditional methods and traditional curricula, so much time is spent in achieving this purpose and with a success which is not unqualified,[1] is the strongest of all arguments in favour of continued practical research work into the psychology of teaching method and of the basic subjects. Verbal self-expression, oral and written, reading and calculation are all essential skills and, given time, it is certainly within the power of all but a very few children to acquire them; but they are not the only means of culture nor the sole skills of value to modern man; and they can be bought too early at too high a price. More and more the evolution of our industrialized civilization is thrusting on teachers the duty of consciously analysing the needs of the local and wider community and its children and of adapting their curricula to supply the stimulus and experience which may be lacking in the homes or in the streets. The greater the stresses imposed upon children, the greater is their need for play by means of which they can come to grips with their problems and solve them. Free dramatic work, drawing and painting, mime, discussion, music—none of these are luxuries in the primary school, except perhaps to children whose home background is rich in possibilities of a similar kind. They are essential to healthy growth. Not only can such activities form the basis of an insight into great cultural media, but, for those who need it, they give an outlet through which children themselves may work through their own emotional problems. Education in Europe regarded as the transmission of a minimum culture is relatively efficient; regarded as a way by which children are prepared emotionally for the enjoyment of a full and happy adult life it still has far to go.

---

1. Vernon (private communication) writes: 'There is strong evidence of most loss after leaving [school] in the most drilled subjects: arithmetic and spelling.'

EDUCATION AND MENTAL HEALTH

BIBLIOGRAPHY

I. THE FIRST YEAR AT SCHOOL

BRUCKL, H. *Der Gesamtunterricht im 1. Schuljahr.* 4 Aufl. München, Oldenbourg, 1949. 159 p.

COPEI, FR. *Der fruchtbare Moment im Bildungsprozess.* 2 Aufl. Heidelberg, Quelle & Meyer, 1950. 134 p.

JUNGE, E. *Vom Kleinkind zum Schulkind.* Iena, Aderhold, 1943. 76 p.

KOLLER, E. *Der neue Weg im ersten Rechenunterricht.* München, Ehrenwirth, 1948. 268 p.

MAZZA, M. *Il metodo naturale nella classe: leggere, scrivere, esprimersi.* Brescia, La Scuola, 1949. 207 p.

NIEGL, A. & SCHÜLLER, M. "Zur Sorge um einen guten Schulstart", *Pädagogische Mitteilungen.* Wien, Bundesministerium für Unterricht, 1952, no. 1, p. 1.

"La liaison des méthodes à l'école maternelle et à l'école primaire", *Cahiers de pédagogie moderne pour l'enseignement du premier degré.* No. 6. Paris, Bourrelier, 1939. 118 p.

SCHAAP, J. E. *Van kleuter tot schoolkind.* 3e dr. Groningen, Wolters, 1953. 40 p.

II. RETARDATION AND BACKWARDNESS

BODIN, P. *L'adaptation de l'enfant au milieu scolaire.* Paris, Presses universitaires de France, 1945. 146 p.

BÖKE, W. "Über Rückständigkeit im Schreiben und Lesen", *Westermanns Pädagogische Beiträge.* Braunschweig, Sept. 1951.

BUCK, J. M. DE. *Pourquoi vous résigner aux échecs scolaires?* Paris, Desclée de Brouwer, 1948. 215 p.

BURT, C. & LEWIS, B. "Teaching backward readers", *British journal of educational psychology.* London, 1946, vol. 16, p. 116-32.

HENNIG, H. "Zur Frage der Sitzenbleiber in der Volksschule", *Zeitschrift für pädagogische Psychologie und Jugendkunde.* Berlin, 1937, vol. 38.

HILL, M. E. *The education of backward children.* London, Harrap, 1938. 174 p.

INSTITUT SUPÉRIEUR DE PÉDAGOGIE DE HAINAUT. *Rapport sur le niveau d'instruction primaire des enfants du Hainaut en juin 1946.* Morlanwelz, 1947. 292 p.

KELLMER-PRINGLE, M. L. "Social maturity and social competence", *Educational Review.* Birmingham, 1951, no. 3, p. 113-28, 183-95.

KERN, A. *Sitzenbleiberelend und Schulreife.* Freiburg i. B., Herder, 1951. 133 p.

LEWIS, M. M. *The importance of illiteracy.* London, Harrap, 1953, 188 p.

LONDON HEAD TEACHERS' ASSOCIATION. *Memorandum on the attainments of the average entrant to secondary modern schools.* London, 1950.

MIDDLESBOROUGH HEAD TEACHERS' ASSOCIATION. *A survey of reading ability.* Middlesborough Education Committee, 1952.

ROBIN, G. *Les difficultés scolaires chez l'enfant et leur traitement.* Paris, Presses universitaires de France, 1953. 138 p.

SCHONELL, F. J. *Diagnosis of individual difficulties in arithmetic.* Edinburgh, Oliver & Boyd, 1937. 126 p.

TRAMER, M. *Schülernöte.* Basel, B. Schwabe, 1951. 160 p.

SOME SPECIAL PROBLEMS OF THE PRIMARY SCHOOL

III. SELECTION FOR SECONDARY EDUCATION

BROUWER, W. H. *Selectie en schoolsucces (Mededelingen van het Nutsseminarium voor paedagogiek aan de Universiteit van Amsterdam, no. 50)*. Groningen, Wolters, 1951. 91 p.

GAL, R. *L'orientation scolaire*. Paris, Presses universitaires de France, 1946. 148 p.

Intelligence testing; its use in selection for secondary education. London, Times Publ. Co., 1952. 32 p.

OATES, D. W. *New secondary schools and the selection of their pupils*. London, Harrap, 1945. 60 p.

Toelating tot en selectie op de middelbare school. Den Haag, Christelijk Paedagogisch Studiecentrum.

WATTS, A. F., PIDGEON, D. A. & YATES, A. *Secondary school entrance examinations*. London, Newnes Educational Publ., 1952. 78 p.

WIGFORSS, A. *A paper on the awarding of marks and certificates in the primary school and the possibility of normalizing the awards*. Stockholm, P. A. Norstedt & Söners, 1941. 152 p.

IV. PSYCHOLOGY OF THE BASIC SUBJECTS

Reading, Writing, Spelling

ARISTIZABAL, E. *Détermination expérimentale du vocabulaire écrit pour servir de base l'enseignement de l'orthographe à l'école primaire*. Louvain, Laboratoire de didactique expérimentale du professeur R. Buyse, 1938.

BERTHOLD. "Vom Schreiben in der Schule", *Pädagogische Beiträge*. Sept. 1951, Braunschweig.

BOSCH, B. *Grundlagen des Erstleseunterrichts*. 2 Aufl. Düsseldorf, Verlag Der Pflug, 1949. 157 p.

CALIEWAERT, H. *L'écriture rationnelle*. Bruxelles, Office de publicité, 1942. 48 p.

DOTTRENS, R. & MARGAIRAZ, E. *L'apprentissage de la lecture par la méthode globale*. 3e éd. Neuchâtel, Delachaux et Niestlé, 1947. 113 p.

EGGERMONT, P. A., OVERBEEKE, P. F. & VELDE, I. VAN DER. *Het taalonderwijs in de hogere klassen*. Groningen, Wolters, 2 vols.

JAHN, R. *Sprachelehre im Unterricht der Muttersprache*. Düsseldorf, Pädagogischer Verlag Schwann, 1950. 78 p.

KERN, A. & E. *Lesen und Lesenlernen*. 3 Aufl. Freiburg, Herder, 1952. 177 p.

KRANENDONK, M. G. & VELDE, I. VAN DER. *Het Taalonderwijs in de laagste twee klassen*. 3e dr. Groningen, Wolters, 1946. 48 p.

MINISTÈRE DE L'INSTRUCTION PUBLIQUE, DIRECTION DE L'ENSEIGNEMENT PRIMAIRE. *L'enseignement de la lecture*. Bruxelles, Moniteur Belge, 1951. 113 p.

OLSEN, W. C. *This is reading*. Washington, Association for Childhood Education International, 1949. 40 p.

PIRENNE, A. *Programme d'orthographe d'usage pour les écoles primaires*. Namur, La Procure, 1949.

PRÖVE, H. *Der Muttersprachliche Unterricht in der Volksschule*. Stuttgart, Klett, 1950. 171 p.

RICHARDSON, M. *Writing and writing patterns*. London, University of London Press, 1949. 7 parts.

EDUCATION AND MENTAL HEALTH

ROE, F. *Fundamental reading.* London, University of London Press, 1948. 4 vols.
SCOTTISH COUNCIL FOR RESEARCH IN EDUCATION. *Studies in reading.* London, University of London Press, 1950. vols. I & II.
UNESCO-BIE. *L'enseignement de la lecture.* Paris, Genève, 1949. Publ. no. 112. 148 p.
UNESCO-IBE. *The teaching of reading.* Paris, Geneva, 1949. Publ. no. 113. 137 p.
WENZ, G. *Der Weg zum selbständigen Schreiben.* Stuttgart, Loewe, 1950. 96 p.
WENZ, G. & PFIZENMAYER, O. *Der Weg zum selbständigen Lesen.* Stuttgart, Loewe, 1949. 31 p.

Arithmetic

BALLARD, P. B. *Teaching the essentials of arithmetic.* London, University of London Press, 1928. 284 p.
BREIDENBACH, W. *Rechnen in der Volksschule.* 2 Aufl. Hannover, Wissenschaftliche Verlagsanstalt, 1949. 141 p.
COMMISSION CONSULTATIVE UNIVERSITAIRE DE PÉDAGOGIE. *La division écrite des nombres entiers et ses difficultés.* Bruxelles, Ministère de l'instruction Publique, 1953. 64 p.
SCOTTISH COUNCIL FOR RESEARCH IN EDUCATION. *Studies in arithmetic.* London, University of London Press, 1939, 1941. vols. I & II.
TIMMER, J. K. & TURKSTRA, H. *Het rekenonderwijs in de laagste twee klassen.* Groningen, J. B. Wolters, 1952.
——. *Het rekenonderwijs in de hogere leerjaren.* Groningen, J. B. Wolters, 1952.
UNESCO-BIE. *L'initiation mathématique à l'école primaire.* Paris & Genève, 1950. Publ. no. 120. 272 p.
UNESCO-IBE. *Introduction to mathematics in primary schools.* Paris & Geneva, 1950. Publ. no. 121. 247 p.

General

CONSULTATIVE COMMITTEE ON THE PRIMARY SCHOOL. *Report.* London, HMSO, 1931.
FLEMING, C. M. *Research and the basic curriculum.* 2nd ed. London, University of London Press, 1952. 130 p.
Lexikon der Pädagogik, vol. III. Bern, A. Francke, 1952. xiv + 624 p. J. Piaget, p. 361.
PLANCHARD, E. *La pédagogie scolaire contemporaine.* Tournai, Casterman, 1948. 378 p.

134

CHAPTER VI

GROWTH IN ADOLESCENCE [1]

EARLY CHILDHOOD AND ADOLESCENCE

It is sometimes argued that in the first three to five years of his life, the child's whole outlook, attitudes, temperament and the like are moulded irrevocably for good or ill and that, subsequently, little can be done to modify or change the course of development. This pessimistic doctrine may be true where the young child experiences severe adverse situations or fails to achieve a sufficient measure of security at this early stage of development to enable him to go successfully forward to the next. The physical and psychological needs of young children are rarely if ever completely denied by normal parents and situations which are in the psychological sense, damaging, are abnormal. The principal criticism to be made is that some parents do not fully satisfy their children's emotional needs.

Later in life, however, the period of adolescence presents a phase where the growing human being is equally in a state of emotional sensitivity and equally confronted with a rapid succession of new demands. This second period offers great possibilities, if they are used aright, both for setting straight difficulties arising from earlier faulty development and for a constructive attempt to help young people to achieve not merely emotional balance but the fullest flowering of personality. The broad foundations may be laid in infancy, but adolescence, as it is experienced by contemporary boys and girls, is critical for the development of the entire superstructure of character.

Unlike early infancy however, adolescence is much more a social or even a socio-economic phenomenon than it is a biological one. Its needs are more complex and variable and there are no obvious and general patterns of response sanctioned by experience and custom. Many of the characteristics of boys and girls between say 12 or 13 and 18 or 19, though they seem typical of the period are in fact reflections of attitudes and expectations on the part of parents and community. Very little was heard of adolescence, as a period of storm

---

1. This chapter is very largely based upon the discussions of Group III.

and stress for example, until the nineteenth century when it became a favourite theme with romantic novelists and diarists; and in many primitive tribes the transition from boy or girlhood to adult status is abrupt. It is, in very many respects in Europe, the creation of an advanced civilization which progressively prolongs the period of the child's dependence and sets, between the world of childhood and that of adult privilege, power, and responsibility, not the bourne which a brief initiation ceremony overleaps but a no-man's land of six or more years.

PHYSICAL AND PHYSIOLOGICAL CHANGES

This is not to say that there is no biological or maturational basis. There are all the visible and invisible physical and physiological changes that precede, accompany and follow the onset of puberty, the biological end of which is the attainment of physical adulthood and the power to reproduce the species. There are the considerable acceleration and variability in physical growth, the changes in glandular balance, the development of secondary sex characteristics, the dramatic onset of menstruation in girls, the slower but no less marked signs of puberty in boys, the increase in physical strength, the maturation of sheer intellectual power almost to its maximum. It is probable that, in any social situation, such changes would lead to a modification of the emotional life and that the strengthening and canalization of the sex impulses would have repercussions on other instinctive tendencies. In the complex and constantly changing social situation in which the boy or girl growing up in a European town or city finds himself, however, the physical phenomena of puberty, and the more or less inevitable changes in the emotional life, have for the individual, the family and his society, a psychological significance which transcends the aspect of pure biological maturation.

It is perhaps herein that resides the principal difference between early childhood and the period of the teens. In childhood the physiological stages—weaning, crawling, walking, rapid growth physically and mentally and the like—dominate and largely dictate the responses and pressures of the environment. The child is, for the first two or three years at least, more or less unique; he is the only one of his kind in his group and his life does not greatly impinge upon that of his contemporaries. The adult world, and particularly his mother, is prepared to make concessions and to adjust the rhythm of the family's life to his needs. The physiological development of the adolescent proceeds side by side with a series of changes in his social life which, if at all, are only roughly adjusted to his growth and are the consequence rather of his age than of his maturity. He is not unique; he is one of a group, at least outside his home; and concessions to his needs are much less obviously necessary. At the same time, both because of the differences between individuals in such things as the age of onset of puberty, the irregularity of its physiological effects, and the variety of family attitudes towards pubescent and pubertal children, and because of the changeableness within boys and girls themselves, each adolescent child finds himself in a group of chronological contemporaries whose physical and psychological levels of maturity make them even more heterogeneous in certain respects than a group of 4-year-olds in a nursery school. Moreover, whereas with the young child, physical, intellectual and social maturation bear a fairly close temporal relationship to each other, many adolescents show strikingly divergent levels of growth in these three spheres. Such discrepancies are likely to be particularly marked among the most able and the least able groups, but at one time or another in the teens characterize all but a few children.

Fundamentally however the psychological phenomena of adolescence are similar to those of young childhood and this for reasons of the same order. In each we find the child attempting to gain security in a series of novel situations, reacting with fear, aggression or withdrawal to new and not fully understood threats and frustrations; in each there is the inexorable drive forward to new integrations, to meet new demands, and to leave a previous hardly won security. In each there is the threat of loss of love and the thrust towards a reality which, because of inexperience, is not understood and therefore is at times feared and rejected; in each there is found the delicate balance between maturational factors and environmental pressures, between what growth brings inevitably and what society imposes and expects. The difference lies in that adolescents are faced with an apparent variety of choice of solutions to their problems, have already certain habitual modes of response which they have either to modify or abandon, and have also a greater potential insight into the situations in which they find themselves.

THE DEVELOPMENTAL TASKS OF ADOLESCENCE

The education of boys and girls between 12 and 18 if it is not to hinder development and still more if it is constructively to contribute to healthier emotional growth, must seize the chances offered by the psychological adjustments of the teens. This implies a clear perception of and differentiation between the inevitable results of the growth processes and the products of interaction with the environment. It implies too that the educator should be aware of the tasks, the psychological goals which every young person has to' achieve for himself before adulthood, and of the possibilities offered by the child's intensified emotional sensitivity of setting right previous maladjustments.

The central fact of adolescence is the achievement of physiological sex maturity. It is probable that the increased energy of the sex drive itself (in both sexes) at least in the early stages, reinforces aggressiveness and accounts in some measure for the unruliness, difficult behaviour and even delinquency which is a marked feature of the period between 12 and 15. All societies tend to delay and regulate heterosexual activities; but while sex gratification may be discouraged or prohibited, the achievement of physical maturity is not delayed. Hence one of the major developmental problems for the young, often vexed by distorted attitudes acquired in childhood and by the fears and inhibition of adults, is that of acquiring a fully adjusted sexual self, able to accept and control one of the most powerful of all the drives of the personality and, at a later stage, to form a close attachment to a member of the opposite sex.

The strengthened aggressiveness coupled with increased physical strength and maturity, enhances the thrust towards independence. In some respects adolescence is a second weaning, a more complex and difficult detachment from emotional, intellectual and economic dependence upon the family. Apart altogether from the attainment of vocational independence, itself a process made difficult by modern conditions, the growing boy and girl have to win an emotional and intellectual independence of those who have formerly largely shielded and protected them. Parents and teachers frequently are reluctant to accept this need to wean oneself from the safety of the emotional and intellectual domination of others and fail to understand that the sometimes crude self-sufficiency, even conceit, of adolescence, is an essential stage in growth. Where the mother, father, teacher, youth club leader or any other adult, seek to buttress their own security by the dependence and uncritical love of the young, they are apt to resist the child's need to detach himself. The consequences of such adult resistance may be disastrous; either the child's dependency is asserted and he never becomes psychologically mature; or the severance is a painful revolt, wounding to both child and adult.

INTERESTS

This second weaning is accompanied and coloured by the emergence of a variety of new interests and sometimes by a striking expansion of the intellectual horizon. But while it is not difficult to determine a broad, relatively calculable, and homogeneous pattern of interests in boys and girls up to the age of 11 or 12, investigations into the interests of adolescents have led to markedly conflicting results.[1] Many researches insist upon the relative permanence and as many upon the relative transience of interests in the teens. Some at least of this divergence of result is due to differing definitions of what psychologically constitutes an interest. If we define it specifically as the desire to perform some particular activity—for example collecting stamps or reading romantic novels—then changeability is a marked feature of much adolescent interest. If, however, we attempt to relate the interests pursued by individual boys and girls to certain more fundamental needs and drives, it will be found that while the expression changes, the ends sought tend to remain more constant.[2] Moreover, in different adolescents, apparently similar activities subserve very different ends. An unusual interest—for example in Egyptology—may be the result of a desire to be different, to assert oneself and to shine in a field in which there is no competition; it may be the result of identification with an admired adult and put on with as much intention to imitate as a hair style; or it may be a genuine expression of an emotional-intellectual curiosity about the past. Similarly the marked increase in reading which is characteristic of many adolescents, especially girls and the highly intelligent, may be genuinely intellectual, may be a search for information about the new and subtle world of human relations, or may be a means of retreat into fantasy. It is probable that with different young people and with the same individual at different times many motives operate in the same apparent interest and conversely many interests may subserve a similar need.

Those who wish to help adolescents grow up healthily should understand the psychological functions both of manifest interests and of their apparent instability in the teens. Any attempt simply to follow the expressed interests of youths and to adapt a curriculum to specific activities as they appear would be doomed to frustration and failure; on the other hand, if the interests of adolescents are seen as what they are—temporary solutions to conflicts, means of gaining knowledge or outward expressions of dominant and more or less permanent trends of the growing personality—then they not only should but can validly be met by the school and the home.

---

1. See for example: W. Dennis, in *Manual of Child Psychology*. Ed. Carmichael. London, Chapman & Hall, 1946; C. L. Fleming, *Adolescence: Its Social Psychology*. London, Routledge, 1948; D. Fryer, 'Predicting Abilities from Interests', *J. App. Psych.* vol. IX; Lehman and Witty, 'One More Study of the Permanence of Interests', *J. Ed. Psych.* vol. XXII, pt. 7, 1931.

2. See W. D. Wall, *The Adolescent Child*. London, Methuen, 1948, p. 101-19. Adolescents try out their possibilities in many directions, led in their choice of activity partly by their own desires and partly by the opportunities offered by the environment. The success or failure attending these efforts determines those interests which endure and those which fade.

EXPLORATION

There are, to help us in this, certain generalizations which may safely be made. Most adolescents are interested in exploring, to the confines, their own developing powers—they need to test the limits of their physical endurance, to pursue an impulse of thought to its dangerous conclusion, to experiment with the shocking and the unconventional, and to know excess. It is for this reason that young people so often upset their elders by the violence of their extremes of laziness and of activity, of conformity and antinomianism. Just as the child tries to find security by seeing how far he can go in disobedience, so the adolescent more subtly tries to find categoric imperatives in his world and to learn more of his own capacities and limitations; and just as the child's confidence can be undermined by fears instilled by adults, by over-protection and by not allowing him to learn by his own experience, so adolescents may be deprived of security by a world which protects them from challenge and therefore from real knowledge of success and failure. The ambitions, daydreams, the impatience and pride of the young, like the wishful fantasy of infancy, have to be brought to terms with reality; and this transition is a personal individual affair which adults can foster or hinder but which each youth must ultimately achieve alone.

SELF-AWARENESS

The increasing awareness of self and of others which is a marked feature of growth in adolescence gives rise to a marked interest in human relationships—as experienced in the family circle, among friends, through books and the cinema.[1] The primary school child has roughly two worlds, his home and his school. He recognizes himself as one of a group of age mates with a general group relationship to adults and as a person within the specific family pattern. The youth however is more mobile than the child; he forms part of many groups apart from home and school. His own heightened emotionality and

1. See N. D. Dodman, 'The Cinema Attendance of Adolescents', *Proceedings of the Brit. Assoc.* Sept. 1948; 'The Adolescent and the Cinema', *Education*, November 1948; B. Gray, 'Enfants et adolescents devant les films', *Revue internationale de filmologie* no. 4, 1954; 'The Social Effects of the Films', *Sociological Review* vol. XLIII, sec. 7, 1950; B. Kesterton, 'The Recreational Cinema and the Adolescent', Ph.D. thesis, University of Birmingham, 1945; The *Payne Fund Studies*. New York, Macmillan, 1935 onwards; W. A. Simson, 'The Social and Emotional Effects of the Cinema', *Proceedings of the Brit. Assoc. 1948*; H. Storck, *The Entertainment Film for Juvenile Audiences*. Paris. Unesco, 1950; W. D. Wall, 'The Adolescent and The Cinema', *Educational Review* vol. I, no. 1, October 1948 and no. 2, February 1949; 'L'adolescent et le cinéma', *Revue internationale de filmologie*. 1950; W. D. Wall and W. A. Simson, 'The Emotional Responses of Adolescent Groups to Certain Films', *Brit. Journ. Ed. Psych.* vol. XX, pt. III, November 1950; 'The Effects of Cinema Attendance on the Behaviour of Adolescents as seen by their Contemporaries', *Brit. Journ. Ed. Psych.* vol. XIX, pt. I, Feb. 1949; W. D. Wall and E. M. Smith, 'The Film Choices of Adolescents', *Brit. Journ. Ed. Psych.* vol. XIX, pt. II, June 1949.

consciousness of himself makes him sensitive to the varying opinions of others as they seem to be expressed in their reactions towards him; he becomes aware of differing family patterns and attitudes; and above all he discovers the range of nuance that exists in personal social relationships.

The home and the school can feed and shape this by a tolerant understanding of the experimental behaviour to which it leads; by deliberately helping the boy or girl to acquire acceptable patterns of social behaviour through a variety of experience, and by using the resources of history and literature to throw light upon human values, motives and ideals. One of the major criticisms that can be made of most secondary schools and of many families in every country of Europe is that, making no provision for the social education of the young, they leave it to the cinema to become, by default almost the sole means by which boys and girls can learn how to behave, to dress, to open and conduct a conversation and the like. A purely intellectual formation at school and an uncertain series of family patterns at home is insufficient for the guidance of the adolescent. Many schools and parents fail to use the theatre, the cinema and the rich variety of real social activities which could be made possible, as a means of providing the growing child with a multiplicity of roles which he can play and through them of educating the personality and the moral character. Serious and sympathetic discussion, on the adolescent's own level, of the behaviour patterns and values exhibited by the films he sees, by the books he reads, and by the group with which he meets, discussion without dogmatism or condemnation, in which the adult puts his experience objectively at the service of the young and, while not protecting them from the mistakes that we all must make, in which he clearly shows that he accepts a certain responsibility for preventing really destructive consequences, is one means by which teachers and other mature people can constructively contribute to the mental health of the growing generation. The club leader or teacher who can adopt an attitude of calm acceptance of them as people in their own right, who can respect their opinions even though disagreeing with them, and who is on sufficiently good terms with himself to be able to be objective towards others, can play a major part in helping boys and girls to a full healthy psychological development. Every child in adolescence confronts problems, which he is reluctant to discuss with parents with whom he has been and is still closely involved. Through the small informal discussion group, through impromptu dramatics which allow role playing, through creative work which makes demands upon time, energy and the capacity for sacrifice, the skilful adult can lead adolescents to know and understand themselves. Such a task requires an insight into the real problems of growth— problems of sex, of relationships to others, of family discipline of the impact of social norms and expectations—a willingness to listen and a genuine affection, without sentimentality and without condemnation.

SELF-DISCIPLINE

Example and experience too are of the utmost importance. Tolerance, courtesy, security in social relationships, respect for the personality of others, healthy attitudes towards the opposite sex, are not learned by precepts alone, by verbal instruction or even through books and other cultural media. A school or home which is organized on repressive principles, in which children have no rights and are subject only to a web of compulsions, paves the way for that conflict of the generations which is a marked feature of some European societies. Conversely the home and the school which progressively grant the young more and more responsibility for their own actions—even at the expense of some trouble over unfulfilled tasks and insouciant neglect; in which compulsion springs obviously from the needs of the social group and from clearly understood ethical principles and not from the egotism and power of the adult; in which consequences of wrong actions, are seen to be not punishments arbitrarily inflicted but the direct result of the actions themselves or of the violation of agreed moral principles; such an environment is likely to foster independence and to give the growing child a trust in the world of adults towards which he is moving. Essentially the social task of the school in the second decade is, by acceptance of the facts and stresses of adolescent growth, by the respect shown by the staff for the personality of every child, and by helping adolescents to be aware of the variety of social experience, to manifest to each pupil his own worth, to draw out from him a contribution to the general good, and to help him to interpret the increasing complexity of his relations to others. Where the young feel themselves to be needed and to be accepted as partners in their own education and upbringing, there is no conflict of the generations. Where techniques of behaviour in a variety of situations are learned from adults who practise what they preach and are prepared to accept the clumsiness of early attempts for what it is, there may well be awkwardness and self-consciousness, but there is no hostility. In this connexion it is difficult to overestimate the importance to young people of school societies run mainly by themselves, of youth clubs, of the right to invite one's friends home and to accept the responsibility for entertaining them, of being called into the family councils over such topics as where to go for holidays and of being given steadily more and more responsibility for others younger than themselves, for fulfilling obligations such as homework, the control and payment of money and the ordering of their own leisure time.

THE RE-ESTABLISHMENT OF EMOTIONAL CONTROL

Development in the social adjustment of adolescents does not proceed in isolation or independently; it is a facet of the development of a whole personality. The key to the understanding of adolescence lies in a just estimation of how from a combination of causes, some biological and many environmental, the whole balance and patterning of character is changed. This is not to say that new impulses, powers, or characteristics suddenly appear; the weight of evidence is against this; but that the strength and direction of the fundamental drives and their relation to each other is altered. Almost certainly under any circumstances there is some quickening of general emotional responsiveness around puberty, but this is greatly increased by the environmental provocations from which no child entirely escapes. Such a strengthening and quickening of the emotionality means that many of the controls and inhibitions developed in childhood prove too weak; hence one may find marked irregularity and even tempestuousness of behaviour in contrast to the relative peacefulness of the normally developed 10 or 11-year-old child. One at least of the tasks of the second decade is the re-establishment of controls and inhibitions and the growth of the ability to interpose increasing delay between the stimulus to emotion and the overt response.

ALTRUISM

If it were only this, adolescence would not have such great significance for the mental health of society as it has. In fact however the period of adolescence should mark the transition in each individual boy or girl from the relatively simple, more or less crudely egotistic personality of the child to the adult character which, while of necessity having itself as a reference point, achieves some liberation from egotism and is able to think and to act altruistically. Impulses of altruism seem to be an essential component of the sex drive and of maternal feeling, though their strength, especially in relation to submissiveness and aggression, varies considerably among individuals; moreover the conventions and cultural regulations of every society sophisticate all human attitudes from the outset. The unselfishness of the young child is nearly always in relation to adult approval[1] either present or anticipated. The self-sacrifice of which adults are capable, whilst indeed it has frequently or even usually, childish components, may be qualitatively different.

---

1. J. Piaget, *The Moral Judgement of the Child*. London, K. Paul, 1932. See also E. McCaulay and H. Watkins, 'An Investigation into the Development of the Moral Conceptions of Children', *Forum of Education* vol. IV, nos. 1 and 2, 1924.

Not merely is the mature adult able to delay a response and to interpose judgment; he should also be able to be aware of himself with some measure of detachment, and refer his judgment and action to a set of principles. Thus one of the signs of psychological maturity is that ego-reference is not exclusive and that the adult can contemplate himself in the same light as he contemplates others; he is capable of a genuine altruism; because he can evaluate himself with some charity and impartiality, he is able truly to sympathize with orders; not dependent upon them for affection and support, not hostile to them because they represent a threat, not afraid because they exhibit characteristics he fears in himself, the value he places on others, his likings and affections are related to reality. Just as the young child has to come from the world of the magical wish into the world of impersonal causal relationships, the adolescent has to move from a world of emotionally toned ego-reference to the acceptance of himself and of others as they really are.

THE ROLE OF ADULTS

This supreme task begun in the second decade is only more or less successfully accomplished by the majority. It is a process which continues long beyond the period of the teens—at least to the point where a new family is founded and the *egoisme à deux* of heterosexual affection dissolves into a wider affection for children and, at its most mature, for mankind. Parents, teachers, youth leaders, older men and women who come into contact with the young, socially or at work, all have a fundamentally important part to play; on what they say and do, and still more upon his callow interpretation of the meanings implied in adult behaviour, the youth builds up an idea of himself in relation to others, and spurred by growing consciousness of his own motives, he increasingly interprets the motives of adults, matching them with his widening vision of life and learning from the discrepancies in his search for a new level of security. If for any reason, any of the fundamental needs of the growing child are not met—the need to be needed by others, the need for increasing independence, the need to achieve adequate adjustment to the opposite sex, the need to rethink the cherished beliefs of one's elders—a full integration of the personality is delayed, distorted or even rendered impossible. If the adult world denies or seems to deny these needs, imposing frustrations without at the same time offering alternative outlets or sublimations, it not only delays development but risks turning the whole course of it awry.'

Even in favourable circumstances, most parents are nearing middle age when their children reach mid-adolescence, and in ageing societies like those of western Europe, the discrepancy between generations is normally greater. Not infrequently adults find it difficult or distressing to recall what they themselves were like and felt at 14 or 15, and fail to understand that the formulae applied to them when young are not necessarily those most appropriate to the changed circumstances in which their children have grown up. Unhappily many parents have not themselves successfully passed through adolescence. They see the growing beauty of the girl, the increasing strength of the boy, the intellectual challenge that maturing intelligence brings, as threats to their privilege and authority, a cause of jealousy, or a reminder of hopes and ambitions that time has defeated.

This may be clearly illustrated in the results of a faulty sex education. Because of their own fears and wrong attitudes, many parents and teachers maintain a conspiracy of silence in this matter; some even treat it as filthy and obscene, sternly condemning or even punishing the normal manifestations of interest in childhood; others separate the physical, emotional, and intellectual aspects of sex or, in the case of girls, strive to protect their innocence by representing men as brutal cruel animals who desire only one thing from a woman. Children who have been brought up in this way may react with grave and destructive anxiety to the physical phenomena of puberty and regard their natural impulses towards the opposite sex as guilty, something of which to be ashamed and to conceal. Thus not only do they fail to pass through the phase of harmless flirtation by means of which each sex comes more fully and truly to know the other, but the very feelings of guilt increase their insecurity in heterosexual relationships later. Marriage is liable to be based not upon the more or less realistic valuing of another as a person, but viewed as an acceptable way of gratifying a guilty appetite. Alternatively where the fear of heterosexual impulses is very great, the child may permanently seek safety in an attachment to one of the same sex. Such attachments, normal in the early stages of adolescence and essential in the rich opportunity they give through close friendship of exploring the personality of another, become regressive when they are a substitute for a genuinely erotic attachment to a husband or wife.

Not so strikingly adverse but even more pervasive are adults' attitudes to the growing boy or girl's need to find a self by playing a variety of parts. Young children imitate striking figures in their environment; they *are* the policeman, milkman or postman. The same process of empathy, of trying to feel like someone else and so gain understanding, is at work in the teens, though with an increasing subtlety of identification. The 14 or 15-year-old tries on, as it were, a great variety of attitudes and behaviour, often in an exaggerated way because of his inexperience. In much the same way as a 2 or 3-year-old child, he wishes to test the limits of the world. He imagines himself powerful and explores the extent of his power, mentally, physically and socially; he imitates a favourite film star, a prestige figure in the world of sport, a teacher, or an older companion or some character in a favourite book. Such experiments are signs, not of extravagance or loss of individuality, but of the striving to shape one's self acceptably, to achieve independence and to find out something more about the world on the threshold of which one stands.

Few parents or teachers realize the fears and anxieties which may beset growing adolescents. They are not normally the imaginative or concrete physical terrors of childhood—of going to bed in the dark or jumping from high places. They are fears of 'loss of control' of powerful emotions, of the physical signs of growth which may be temporarily unequal; they are social anxieties about how to behave, about what others will think, about what one is going to do to earn a living, about whether marriage will be possible; they are uncertainties about what adults expect from one, about one's capacities, and about the future generally.

A sympathetic insight into such problems coupled with a reasonable objectivity and freedom from undue involvement or anxiety are the essential equipment for all who have to do with boys and girls in the second decade. Unhappily adults and, in particular teachers and most parents, are even more ignorant in this than in other fields of child development. The young not infrequently complain of a lack of understanding, of a world which ignores or flatly denies their needs, which at one moment treats them as children and the next demands adult behaviour; adults are irritated at the incomprehensible, wayward behaviour of the young, at their instability of mood, their enthusiasm and cynicism, their energy and lassitude, and at their extravagant and callow emotional behaviour. A more imaginative handling of the education of adolescents and a clearer comprehension of the close relationship between social patterns of expectation and of frustration and the behaviour of adolescents, would do much to diminish the tensions and the 'conflict of the generations' which are marked features of some European cultures.

PHILOSOPHY OF LIFE

Closely related to the preceding aspects of growth, indeed dependent upon them is the attempt—from identification with striking figures in the environment, from literature and talk, from questions posed to adults, from the teachings of religion, or philosophy or politics—to construct an interpretive view of what life means. The boy or girl wishes to know who he is, how he is related to his own past and to the future of which he becomes increasingly aware; and he strives to build into a coherent scheme the moral habits and opinions formed in his childhood. Characteristically, among the more intelligent at least, adolescence is the period of 'turning the world upside down', of self dedication to a cause or an idea, political or social, of religious conversion, of the attempt to generalize specific truths and to form from them a philosophy of life. At its least developed, this phase is marked by a passive acceptance of what are thought to be the values of adult society, an often cynically exaggerated caricature; at the best, phases of ambition amd self-abnegation, often curiously mingled with extreme intolerance, give place to an increasingly consistent and altruistic idealism which may be the leit-motif of the whole adult life.

The quality, content and the degree of conscious understanding implied in this master sentiment will depend ultimately upon the individual's capacity for introspection, and his ability intellectually to understand and develop abstract conceptions. Its content however will be markedly affected by the type and level of interests he pursues, by his apprehension of the principles behind moral habits earlier acquired, by the interpretations placed on his own and the behaviour of others by adults and by the values and ideals with which his own society presents him overtly or by implication.

The integration of such a master sentiment into his whole emotional life is a slow and often difficult process and it is important to realize that with different adolescents and at different times the process may proceed smoothly or by sudden bounds. Experience and research combine however to suggest that the insecurity, tension, heightened consciousness and emotionality of adolescence make the period pre-eminently that of conversion—conversion which in the past, because of a coherence of belief, generally took a religious form.[1] Such conversions although often they may seem dramatic have frequently a long period of incubation and may be followed by crises of doubt or of protective cynicism. The growing child may seem to be vacillating from one extreme to another and be obsessed with feelings of guilt at his own defections or arrogant in a new security. Sarcasm, irony or angry argument from adults, especially parents, is likely to provoke stubborn opposition. The wisest course is that of sympathetic detachment which unobtrusively makes other viewpoints available to the groping mind of the boy or girl and which above everything reassures them that, whatever happens, there is no risk of loss of affection and support.

A philosophy or an interpretation can of course be imposed temporarily at least, on some, if not all adolescents. The danger to mentally healthy development, a danger to which girls seem more liable than boys, is when, in however good a cause, an adult uses the emotional

---

1. E. D. Starbuck, *The Psychology of Religion*. London, W. Scott, 1901; R. H. Thouless, *Introduction to the Psychology of Religion*. Cambridge, The University Press, 1923; L. S. Hollingworth, *The Psychology of the Adolescent*. New York, King, 1930, p. 188.

lability and tension of the adolescent to provoke a 'conversion' which is thus the result more of temporary insecurity and unbalance than of any genuinely integrated conviction. Certain systems of education have exploited this tendency by continuous indoctrination coupled with a dominant leadership. Coherent social and educational pressure, possible in totalitarian régimes of all types, gives a kind of security which is deeply seductive in adolescence when so much else seems dangerously uncertain. This pressure may be intensified by covert or overt implications of superiority to others. Racialism and hostility to other groups—for example Jews, Negroes or another nation—are particularly effective means of raising aggression and of enhancing the feeling of superiority and belongingness. The disturbed, the unsatisfied, the maladjusted and the unstable are particularly prone to see in authoritarian philosophies, the refuge of casting the burden of decision—and of guilt—upon others. Mentally healthy adolescents also search for a philosophy which will integrate their own lives and may for a time accept such solutions as a respite, to be followed by crises of doubt and rejection until finally they incorporate a sounder conception into their personal philosophy. The situation is much more serious when, after a distorted development in childhood, adolescents find refuge from deep emotional disturbance in blind obedience to a dictatorship which exploits their almost morbid need to be needed. Such dictatorships may be exerted in many ways, not merely politically. Teachers, parents, club leaders may exert a dictatorship over the young, unconsciously seeking in their devotion a satisfaction for themselves. It is for this reason that authoritarian adults and those whose own immaturity leads them to seek authority over others, should be dissuaded from taking up employment which gives them influence with young people. In parts of Europe even now there are groups of youths living in societies shaken by the results of the war, without a clear future before them and whose insecurities make them an easy prey to anyone offering the spurious certainty of authority and of an uncritically accepted doctrine. It is clear that such groups constitute a grave problem not only to themselves but to society, a problem which depends for its solution only partly upon changes in the external circumstances of life. Adolescents such as these, even more than others, need help in understanding themselves and in changing their personal attitudes. The kind of integration which a creed imposed from without might give to such maladjusted and unsatisfied young people—however worthy such a creed might be—is no substitute for genuine mental health which is essentially an internally developed integration founded on a philosophy or a religious faith won through living.

RELIGION[1]

In most modern communities the primacy of the religious interpretation of life has been challenged even if religion is not ignored or abandoned, and the adolescent is faced with a bewildering choice. Instead of having the alternative of faith or unbelief, of acceptance or rejection and the security of a generally accepted pattern of behaviour derived from a religiously sanctioned ethical code, he now has to choose for himself, and often indeed to hew out anew a set of principles for his own life. It is this absence of an accepted framework, and the consequent difficulty of the search for an interpretation of life, that makes adolescence an even more critical period for the individual and more fraught with consequences for the mental health of society in the contemporary world than it was, say, half a century ago

The task of helping the growing boy or girl to interpret his world cannot be left to chance without serious risk—risks of exploitation by the interested or of the kind of drifting indifference which marks many even of the most intelligent of contemporary youth. One of the more urgent tasks for research is that of examining how the home, the community and the school may best aid the young to achieve for themselves a coherent scheme of values.[2] Clearly the school cannot be indifferent. Education cannot avoid the fundamental human problems without falling into a narrowly utilitarian or purely intellectual approach to studies.

On the other hand, while seductive, dogmatism—secular or religious —may provoke a catastrophic revolt or a thoughtless acceptance. The challenge of modern times is that of helping youth uncynically to appreciate and respect the many honest differences of opinion and faith in every community. Such an acceptance is by no means incompatible with a personal belief, but it is slow to acquire and, in helping the young to a philosophy of their own, the teacher must exercise restraint and objectivity. This does not mean that he should not state his own opinions, it means that he must be honest and just to the beliefs of others.

In Europe, the most marked religious influence in the flowering of culture, and the strongest contemporary one, is Christianity; and as

---

1. The paragraphs are based on the paper cited in the footnote p. 151 and that presented by *Pax Romana*, 'The Religious and Moral Education of Children'. See also: The Committee on Religion and Education, *The Relation of Religion to Public Education, the Basic Principles*. American Council on Education Studies, series I, no. 26, Washington, 1947; and G. Delcuve, S.J., 'Ecole d'état et formation chrétienne, aperçu d'ensemble', *Lumen Vitae*. vol. 1, 1950. See also Chapter IV.

2. See *The Year Book of Education, 1951*. University of London Institute of Education and Evans Bros. Ltd., London, 1951, which gives a series of penetrating studies of this problem from many points of view. Particularly valuable and illuminating is the introductory essay 'Education and Morals' by the editors J. R. Lauwerys and N. Hans.

such it cannot be left out of account in education, and particularly in the education of adolescents. This applies whether the child belongs to a religious community or whether he comes from the large proportion of families in some countries which though nominally perhaps Christian are not believers. In this the task of the denominational school seems clear enough; through its organization, staffing and curriculum, it will offer (and not impose) a particular way of life and a particular interpretation of human experience whether this be history or literature or science. If however it does this in an exclusive fashion without attempting to show its pupils that other ways of life exist, it may prepare the way for intolerance, or defeat its own ends by provoking the thoughtful youth to revolt. And some young people will ask questions about the formal instruction they receive; there may be disturbance in adolescence if instruction in dogma is not fused with a way of life to which young people can give their allegiance. The secular school has a somewhat different and in many ways more difficult task, which, unhappily in some communities it is forced by old bitternesses to leave at best only partially fulfilled. Apart from itself reflecting in its staffing organization and curriculum, the best humanistic values and personal relationships existent in its own culture, it should deal fairly with the meaning and contribution of religion to human development both in the past and in the contemporary world. It can thus help adolescents to understand and sympathize with varieties of belief and unbelief and lead them to an appreciation of differences in the forms of faith and to a suspension of unbelief.[1]

The moral and spiritual education of the young cannot however be confined simply to teaching about religion or even to the fostering of more or less isolated spiritual experiences. With the majority of adolescents, the home, the school and the community must go further.

Men of good will of all persuasions would agree that in all those fields which deal with moral and spiritual values adolescents need help to reconcile a genuine humanism which asserts the worth of the individual with the technological, scientific and empirical spirit underlying our material civilization and which, at its worst, tends to depersonalize existence. The danger of some forms of secular education, is that in their scrupulous neutrality they ignore or deliberately avoid discussion of spiritual values and genuine humanism and thus intensify the materialistic and depersonalizing influences. The danger

---

1. In this general connexion, it is well to emphasize that one at least of the roots of anti-Semitism is to be found in the way in which the teaching of biblical and post-biblical history is often handled. There is a danger that the child may gather the idea that the Jews are for ever outcast. This danger is obvious for example in the presentation of the life of Christ, in which the horror felt at the persecutors is particularly liable to be transferred to Jews in general, including contemporaries (see 'The Ten Points of Seelisberg', Recommendations of the Interconfessional Conference, 1947, cited in J. Isaac, 'Les bases de l'antisémitisme chrétien', *Christianisme social*, March-April 1948).

of some religious education is that it adds to the moral conflicts of adolescence, that it stultifies thought by dogma or that, by its insistence on exclusive possession of the truth, it implies if it does not overtly preach, hostility to other beliefs.[1] The question of the relation between religious and scientific experience—though different people may give different answers—cannot be avoided without risking a philosophical dichotomy which may affect the personality.

Unhappily religious education often has been given negatively and in association with a general education of an authoritarian and rigid type, or as a means of inculcating and supporting a morality which to the young appears to be chiefly repressive. Similarly the concepts of Christianity—that of the Incarnation for example—may be so presented as to appear as an outmoded mythology which the adolescent rejects later along with all its spiritual content. Even prayer and the sacraments are sometimes so treated that they seem to be magic rites, or they lead to a fixation at an immature level, to neurotic fears and scruples, or to egocentric and fetishistic attachment. However, none of these dangers is inherent in religious education as such, and, though different in form, similar disadvantages exist wherever education is made the plaything of sectarianism, prejudice or politics and where the free development of the personality of each child is sacrificed to ulterior motives.

The critical modern problem, and one to which research has as yet provided no answer, is that of how, in a society so little unified in its beliefs, adolescents may best be helped to achieve and integrate their own lives and to acquire a conscious morality and an ethic, liberal, disinterested and based on a genuine inner love for others. It seems likely that to this problem there is now no universal or ready-made solution, and that the best we can do is, according to our sincerely held convictions, to make it possible for each growing youth to work out slowly his own personal faith.

---

1. We may cite here a significant and valuable paragraph from a working paper prepared for the Conference by the Medico-Social and Psycho-Pedagogic Commission of the International Catholic Child Bureau on 'The Influence for Good or Evil of Religious Education on the Child's Mental Health'. This states that 'from the truly Christian standpoint, religious training is synonymous with progressive liberation and is normally imbibed in an atmosphere of happiness. But this freedom is an internal value; the human personality becomes free by degrees as the organic, biological and even psychological elements that constitute it become integrated. Accordingly mental health is more than the absence of mental illnes; it is a positive reality, completely attained by humanity when it aspires towards good and surpasses itself by virtue of a strength that corresponds to its natural aptitudes, but elevates them to the plane of the divine'.

BIBLIOGRAPHY

BOVET, P. "Pédagogie religieuse et éducation fonctionnelle", *Revue de théologie et de philosophie* no. 124. Lausanne, La Concorde, 1942. 14 p.

BREUER, J. M. *Bases de l'éducation traditionnelle nationale.* Jerusalem, 1945.

CHAMBRE, P. *La famille et l'école devant le problème de l'éducation sexuelle.* Paris, Fédération Nationale des Associations de Parents d'Elèves des Lycées et Collèges, 1948. 200 p.

CONGRES INTERNATIONAL DES ÉCOLES DE SERVICE SOCIAL. *L'adolescence de l'après-guerre et ses problèmes.* Paris, Les Éditions Sociales Françaises, 1948.

DEBESSE, M. *L'adolescence.* Paris, Presses universitaires de France, 1942. 120 p.

———. *La crise d'originalité juvénile.* Paris, Alcan, 1936. 435 p.

FAUVILLE, A. *Eléments de psychologie de l'enfant et de l'adolescent.* Louvain, Nauwelaerts & Paris, Vrin, 1948. 172 p.

FERRIERE, A. *Adolescence et école active.* Neuchâtel, Delachaux et Niestlé, 1932.

———. *Education religieuse et psychologie de l'inconscient.* Genève, Labor & Fides, 1950. 141 p.

FLEMING, C. M. *Studies in the social psychology of adolescence.* London, Routledge & K. Paul, 1951. 266 p.

GONCALVES VIANA, M. *Psicologia do adolescent.* Porto, Editorial Domingos Barreira. Biblioteca de Cultura Portuguesa, no. 6. 299 p.

GREAT BRITAIN. MINISTRY OF EDUCATION. *Youth's opportunity—further education in county college* (pamphlet no. 3). London, HMSO, 1946. 54 p.

HORWITZ, S. L. *Sefer Ha-dath we-hachinnuch.* New York, 1927.

HOVRE, F. DE. *Ensayo de filosofía pedagógica.* 2ª ed. Madrid, Ediciones Fax, 1941. 356 p.

HUSÉN, T. *Begåvning och miljö.* 2uppl. Stockholm, Hugo Geber, 1951. 196 p.

IOVETZ-TERESCHENKO. *Friendship-love in adolescence.* London, Allen & Unwin, 1936. 393 p.

KONFERENZ SCHWEIZERISCHER GYMNASIALREKTOREN. *Die philosophischen und religiösen Grundlagen des schweizerischen Gymnasiums.* Aarau, Sauerländer, 1941. 90 p.

LANGEVELD, M. J. *Inleiding tot de studie der paedagogische psychologie van de middelbare schooljeugd.* Groningen, Wolters, 1947. 468 p.

MORGAN. *Young citizen.* Penguin, 1943.

MUCHOW, H. H. *Flegeljahre: Beiträge zur Psychologie und Pädagogik der "Vorpubertät".* Ravensburg, Maier, 1950.

MUNK, E. *Probleme der jüdischen Jugenderziehung.* Frankfurt, Judentum & Unwelt. 1933.

PARTRIDGE, E. D. *The social psychology of adolescence.* New York, Prentice Hall, 1939. 361 p.

PHILLIPPS, M. *The education of the emotions through sentiment development.* London, Allen & Unwin, 1937. 318 p.

REEVES, M. *Growing up in a modern society.* London, University of London Press, 1946. 126 p.

RIMBAUD, J. *L'éducation, direction de la croissance.* Paris, Aubier, Editions Montaigne, 1946. 476 p.

RUDIN, J. *Der Erlebnisdrang.* Luzern, Verlag des Instituts für Heilpädagogik, 1942. 142 p.

SCHNEIDER, E. *Psychologie der Jugendzeit.* Bern, Francke, 1948. 302 p.

SCHWEINGRUBER, E. *Pubertät.* Zürich, Gotthelf-Verlag, 1951. 248 p.

SPRANGER, E. *Psychologie des Jugendalters.* Leipzig, Quelle & Meyer, 1929. 364 p.

STERN, E. *Jugendpsychologie.* Breslau, F. Hirt, 1923. 98 p.

UHER, J. *Středoškolský student a jeho svět.* Praha, 1939. 459 p.

WHEELER, O. A. *The adventure of youth.* London, University of London Press, 1945. 212 p.

WOLMAN, B. *Ha-chofesch we-hamaschmaôth be-chinnuch.* Tel Aviv, 1951.

WOLMAN, P. *Lebajôth ha-humanism be-chinnuch uwe-safruth.* Jerusalem, Yavneh, 1948.

ZILLIG, M. *Psychologie des Jungmädchens.* Heidelberg, Quelle & Meyer, 1949. 132 p.

THE SCHOOL AND THE ADOLESCENT [1]

INTELLECTUAL DEVELOPMENT

The changes in the emotional and social life of young people described in the previous chapter have been dealt with in some detail since the circumstances in which young people grow up greatly modify the nature and direction of the development of personality and character during the adolescent period. The cognitive aspects of growth however are less directly amenable to environmental influences, though both socially and educationally of fundamental importance.

Since the pioneer work of Galton, Binet, Meumann and Stanley Hall, research has told us much of the growth and differentiation of ability in childhood and puberty. It seems likely that innate general all-round intellectual efficiency continues to mature at least until the age of 14 to 15. Thus the range of differences noticeable in the primary school becomes wider, and, when growth is at its maximum, the gap between the very dull and the very bright may be as much as 10 or 11 years of mental maturity.[2]

What is technically called intelligence, however, is not a purely additive or quantitative characteristic, as one can see when closely watching the intellectual growth of a child. A sometimes quite small increment in measurable ability will bring into the child's range the possibility to achieve a whole series of intellectual feats. For example it seems that from the mental age of 13 there may be marked and quite sudden increase in the ability to understand cartoons, allegories, parables and double meanings generally; the full understanding of abstract terms such as 'kindness', 'justice', 'charity' and the like does not come until the mental age of 14 has been attained.

The rate of growth in innate ability however decelerates markedly in the second decade and, particularly towards the age of 14 or 15, the increments may be quantitatively small; but the period from 15 on-

---

1. This chapter is based largely upon the deliberation of Groups II and III of the conference and upon working papers specially prepared by R. Gal, 'The French Effort to Adapt Education to Modern Needs', by H. Aebli (previously cited) and by P. E. Vernon on 'The Assessment and Objective Testing of Children'.
2. See Appendix I B.

wards is remarkable for the possibilities that it opens, to the more able children at least, of a high intellectual culture. This may be looked at in another way; in social rather than individual terms, it seems likely that the relation between an individual's innate capacity and his potential contribution to society is expressed not by a straight line but by a J-curve, that is that small increments in ability may mean increasingly greater qualitative and propably quantitative social output.[1]

INTELLIGENCE AND PERSONALITY

Differences in ability however have another effect, which becomes steadily more noticeable in the teens. There is no correlation between intellectual and emotional development as such, but, almost from birth, the child's ability to learn desirable responses is conditioned by his power to analyse the factors in a given situation. Later, the sublimation of the energies of an instinctive drive into channels satisfactory to the individual and acceptable to society will be accomplished at different levels and with differing degrees of success by children of different capacities. The increased emotional tension of adolescence, the greater complexity of the situations in which the child finds himself, the very novelty of many of them, and the lack of habitual techniques, puts a greater strain on the adaptive power of the intelligence. The development of an adequate sentiment of the self, the acquisition of moral sentiments—as distinct from more or less blind habits—and their expression in conduct, the whole process of personal integration and control, will to a very large extent depend upon the power of intelligent discrimination, upon appraisal of all the factors in a given situation and on foresight in predicting consequences.

This does not mean that high intelligence necessarily implies a high level of moral and personal development; it does imply that inborn ability may set limits to the kind of personal development possible and determine, for example, the balance between moral habit and moral choice in behaviour. Hence education must adapt itself to real capacity, not only in the intellectual demands which it makes but also in respect to moral education. With the ablest and the least able children the problem at adolescence is, seen in its most critical form, that of discrepancies in physical, emotional and intellectual development which impose strains of differing kinds on the child's adaptive powers.[2] Two facts of contemporary society must lead us to question whether great success has attended our efforts hitherto to educate these two groups. The majority of delinquents and of criminals come, not from

1. C. Burt, 'Ability and Income', loc. cit.
2. For a fuller discussion of this see: L. M. Terman, *Genetic Studies of Genius*. Stanford, University Press, vols. I-IV, 1925 ff.; W. D. Wall, op. cit., especially chap. V.

the markedly subnormal group, but from those with intelligence quotients between 70 and 95.[1] Conversely it is noticeable that many men
and women of high ability and extensive education, in all countries
of Europe, fail through defects of personality, to achieve the level
they might, and many others regard their gifts more as a means of
personal advancement than as an obligation to make a greater contribution to society than their less fortunate fellows.

SPECIAL ABILITIES

Increase in the power of the intelligence is accompanied by a differentiation of cognitive capacities. Modern research indicates that there are
abilities which are to some extent independent of general all-round
capacity, and that these become of more marked educational and
vocational significance in the second decade. It seems that success in
any intellectual task, such for example as the solution of a mathematical
problem, depends upon the g or general factor of ability plus one or
more of these special or group aptitudes. So far, psychologists have with
some certainty[2] identified verbal aptitude (v) consisting of two sub-
abilities verbal-literary and verbal-linguistic; number or arithmetic
aptitude (n), which also has sub-abilities and enters into operations
involving the manipulation of figures; spatial perception (k), which is
involved in comparative judgments of areas, shapes and patterns;
mechanical aptitude (m), called forth by the understanding and construction of mechanisms; musical aptitude; manual dexterity; and one
or two others of less clear educational or vocational significance.[3] The
rate at which these group abilities mature, the degree to which they
are possessed by individuals and the ways in which they may combine
with general ability, with the effects of interest, temperament and
training, show wide variation. English[4] research suggests that at the
age of 8 or 9—with the exception of a very few precocious mathemati-
cians or musicians—general ability is about seven times as important
as number ability and over 20 times as important as manual dexterity
in educational success. In early puberty, around the age of 13, special
or group abilities become much more prominent; general intelligence
is however still three times as important as verbal ability in school
success, twice as important as number ability and just over four times
as important as manual aptitude.[5] Later still in adolescence, it seems,

1. C. Burt, *The Young Delinquent*. 4th ed., London, University of London Press, 1944.
2. See Appendix I D.
3. See Appendix I D.
4. With some variation as to the balance between g and group factors, one might expect a similar
   picture from educational systems other than the English. It would be of value and interest if
   parallel investigations were carried out in schools in different countries.
5. C. Burt, 'The Education of the Young Adolescent', *Brit. Journ. Ed. Psych.* vol. XIII, pt. 3, 1943.

it may be possible to distinguish mental types of a more complex kind made up of constellations of capacities and emotionally toned dispositions.[1]

DIFFERENTIATION OF PROVISION

In every country in Europe, the education of children after the age of 11 or 12 takes some account both of this differentiation in ability and of the apparent needs of society. Most, in the past 30 years, have developed a system for children, up to the end at least of the compulsory period, whereby there are two or three main types of school or course: an academic secondary course concentrating in the main upon the subjects considered necessary for entry to the universities or learned professions;[2] a course which gives an education with a commercial or technical bias but which is pre-vocational rather than vocational in character;[3] and a course continuing and extending the work of the primary school.[4] More recently it has been recognized that guidance between the types of school or course in fact implies vocational guidance of a broad kind and that at the age of 11 or 12 children are too young for an irrevocable decision to be taken. Hence the first two or three postprimary years (from 11 or 12 to 14 or 15) are regarded in many countries as a period of choice[5] and decision is postponed to the second half of the teens. In some countries[6] the period of orientation is spent by all or most children in a middle school during or at the end of which a choice of more specialized education is made; in others, where no organized middle school exists, more or less of provision is made for individual children to change from one type of course to another. Technical and vocational education properly so termed is in most countries postponed until at least the age of 13 or 14,[7] and in some (e.g. Denmark) to as late as 18.

Clearly the organization of secondary education is to some extent conditioned by the length of the compulsory school period. A secondary course of less than three years is of dubious value and most educators urge the need for four or five full-time years. On the other hand,

1. P. E. Vernon, 'The Educational Abilities of Training College Students', *Brit. Journ. Ed. Psych.* vol. IX, pt. 3, 1939.
2. cf. the grammar schools (U.K.), *oppiloulu* (Finland), *lycée* (France), *lycée, collège* or *athénée* (Belgium), *gymnasium* (Holland).
3. cf. Belgium, Denmark, Finland, France, Holland, Italy, Portugal, Sweden.
4. cf. *examens frei Mellenskole* (Denmark); *cours complémentaires* (France, Luxembourg); the advanced elementary schools (Holland); the secondary modern school (U.K.).
5. In French parlance, *cycle d'orientation* covering the first three secondary years followed by the *cycle de détermination*.
6. e.g. Denmark, Finland, Italy, Sweden.
7. e.g. Finland, France, Luxembourg, Portugal, Sweden, U.K. In Belgium and in Italy however it may begin as early as 11 or 12. Where this is the case, the programmes of the first years are pre-technical and largely devoted to a continued general education with a slight vocational bias.

psychologically speaking, secondary education might be considered as education for adolescents, and if we take the age of onset of puberty as a criterion of adolescence, should not begin much before the age of 12 or even 13,[1] which would extend the upper limit of full-time school to the age of 17 or 18 at least. Few European countries have been able, for reasons of cost and manpower, to extend the period of full-time schooling for all children beyond the age of 15. In Europe generally not many more than 25 per cent of all young people between the ages of 14 and 18 are in full-time education, though there are very wide variations both between countries and between age-groups. For example, of 15 to 16-year-olds in six industrialized countries[2] some 30 per cent are at school, but the proportion in different countries may be as high as 50 per cent, as in Belgium or Holland, or as low as 25 per cent or thereabouts, as in the United Kingdom. In the older groups the variation between countries is even greater—from as few as 2 per cent to as many as 25 or even 30 per cent.

It is however of importance to note that, especially in those countries where only a relatively small proportion of older adolescents continue in full-time education, there has been recently a considerable extension of optional or compulsory part-time education[3] and vocational training and a wider provision of evening schools and of apprenticeship schemes which include a considerable educational element.

It thus seems that contemporary society has come to accept that the entire period of adolescence—and not just merely the first few years— should be considered as a period predominantly of guided growth, even though in fact for most children the earning life begins around the age of 15, that is before the age at which full mental and physical maturity is attained.

Moreover through a variety of provision, it seems that secondary education in almost every country in Europe is beginning both to meet the range of differentiation of ability which marks intellectual growth in the second decade and to respond to industry's hungry demand for skilled workmen and technicians.

---

1. The English independent school system (as distinct from the State schools) has a preference for 13 to 14 as the age of admission to a five-year course. The medieval universities, which in many ways discharged the task now fulfilled in the upper forms of academic secondary schools, admitted their students at the age of 14 to 16.

2. Belgium, France, Italy, Holland, Sweden, United Kingdom (Great Britain and Wales). The figures cited above are rough approximations only, based upon the data given in the *World Handbook of Educational Organization and Statistics*. Paris, Unesco, 1952.

3. Twice in recent history compulsory part-time education to the age of 16 or 18 has received the sanction of law in the United Kingdom (Fisher Education Act, 1918, and the Education Act of 1944), but economic difficulties have forbidden implementation. On a voluntary basis however the movement has grown to the point where rather less than 20 per cent of young people in industry are released by their employers for day continuation classes either of a general educational nature or, more usually, of a technical or craft training kind.—*Times Ed. Suppt.* 11 Dec. 1953. In France the Loi Astier (1919) made apprenticeship and continued education compulsory for all children under 18 not attending full-time schools. This law is applied at least in the cities, though it is more difficult to enforce in rural areas.

THE FUNCTION OF SECONDARY EDUCATION

Before, however, we accept the contemporary structure of secondary education as completely adequate, it is as well to examine the part which the school is called upon to play in adolescent development. For the young child, the family circle is the most important influence in personal development, particularly in the growth of feelings of security. In adolescence normally the influence of the parents declines and the child emancipates himself from dependence upon his family. Other adults with whom he is not so closely identified affectively become of increasing importance. By its coincidence with the crucial developments outlined in the previous chapter, by the actual strains which it may impose, and because of a change in the influence and role of the family, the school as a human community assumes for good or ill a different and greater significance in the second decade than in the first.

The psychological progress of the young child is conditioned markedly by biological maturation; in the second decade, while sheer maturation cannot be neglected as a factor, it is secondary to the impact of the environment, especially of social attitudes and expectations. Thus apart from the necessity to meet differing levels of sheer educable capacity and the growth of special abilities, the post-primary school has, psychologically speaking, both a greater liberty than the primary school and a greater responsibility towards the individual pupil and towards the society in which he will take his place as an adult.

The problem confronting contemporary education, and particularly secondary education is that of facilitating the best possible adaptation of each individual to a society which, by its very richness of possibilities, by the very inco-ordination and discrepancy of its development is potentially more productive of strain and maladjustment than simpler and more coherent ones. It is rarely realized that, even within one national group, there is now an immense range of difference in evolution as well as in trend; and that while economically and socially there appears to be a levelling process at work, individual and group differences in the comprehension and acceptance of the ideas on which our culture rests are perhaps greater than ever before. As Jung wisely remarked, with the decay of the ethical uniformity imposed by organized religion, man 'has lost the protection of the ecclesiastical walls carefully erected and reinforced since Roman days and, on account of that loss, has approached the zone of world destroying and world creating fire'.[1]

The increased complexity of possibilities and determining factors

---

1. *Psychology and Religion*. London, Oxford University Press, 1938.

has rendered more necessary, and at the same time more difficult, the extension of secondary education to a larger and larger proportion of children in the course of the present century. Whatever the political outlook, or religious faith, whatever the social group or regional or national affiliation, primary schools in Europe have curricula containing much the same formal elements, pursued with similar educational aims in view, shared by the bulk of the population and roughly in step with children's physical and mental growth. Education for adolescents is marked by a variety of aims and curricula; it is in many respects a patched-up edifice in the construction of which historical factors and notions derived from economic arguments, social privilege, political and social philosophies, have all played and continue to play unco-ordinated and frequently illogical parts.

This very width of the possible choices raises an extremely anxious question for those who see in the development of western European society an increasing incoherence. If, after some stage of middle childhood, we offer many educational alternatives, do we not artificially create divisions between those who have pursued different studies, and often in different kinds of schools? Do we not, instead of enriching the participation of more and more children in cultural life, in fact fragment the culture itself by developing more or less autonomous groups cut off from other differently educated ones and only superficially held together by a 'culture' which has ceased to exist as a unity?

The economic organization of our society aggravates this problem. Industrialization, whether applied to the factory or the farm, implies specializations of two kinds. It demands a small number of highly qualified technicians, research workers and the like, and at the same time, by the breaking down of complex processes into small, specialized, easily learned, repetitive units, tends for the majority to rob work of challenge, of interest and of creative value. At both extremes it may tend to narrow the area of effective cultural and social participation either between groups or among individuals; and by educating men to be highly trained instruments or by failing to relate their education to the fact that they may well be hands that guide machines, perhaps we rob them, not only of responsibility for the task on which they are engaged, but of responsibility for themselves as thinking and rounded human beings with a duty towards the whole of their society. It is possible that a rising standard of material life exacts as its price a lack of individual satisfaction in work; that, as a consequence of an increasing awareness of not being really necessary, many men and women lose the capacity for fullness of living; and that the result is not revolt, but a malaise which expresses its hopelessness in all kinds of more or less psychosomatic disturbance. Certainly the incidence of neurotically determined illness in industry seems to suggest

160

something of this kind,[1] as does the decline in such symptoms when a great war places clearly and simply before the eyes of each person his value in the struggle of the group to survive.

EDUCATION AND THE CULTURAL CONTEXT

It has been fashionable to assert that education should be child-centred. In the face of considerations such as those outlined above, this position cannot, in its extreme form, be maintained in the education of adolescents. More and more, in the second decade, the school must look towards adult life and towards the society into which its pupils have been born. On the other- hand a schooling directed solely or even mainly to adaptation to things as they are, would, particularly for the majority, reduce itself to the narrowest vocational training and social indoctrination, coupled perhaps with some attempt at imparting a certain prophylactic 'culture' to fill in an otherwise empty leisure. Secondary education, whilst adapting itself to the needs and potentialities of each child, and consciously taking account of the cultural context from which its pupils come, has the task of preparing its pupils for a society changing more radically than ever before. Thus though the school continues to be, as it has been, society's instrument for the transmission and preservation of culture, it has also dynamically and consciously to help shape the future.

Such a conception, fully implemented, demands from the administrator, the teacher and the parent a deeper insight into contemporary life and its implications and a greater willingness to experiment than has hitherto been shown by most school systems. There is a strong tendency to be conservative; to assume that the circumstances in which one grew up oneself will in essence continue; and that traditional educational means are as suitable in the present as they were in the past. Conservatism as opposed to feckless innovation is no bad thing in education; but it can become a dead hand when it confuses educational values—such for example as a genuine spirit of scientific inquiry or an informed curiosity—with particular and cherished curricula or with notions such as would divorce education from contemporary relevance.

SECONDARY EDUCATION AND MENTAL HEALTH

The relations between education, the values of society, and the psychology of the individual have been insisted upon, since it is only by

1. M. Smith, *Introduction to Industrial Psychology*. London, University of London Press, 1943; M. Culpin and M. Smith, *The Nervous Temperament in Industry*. Industrial Health Research Board, pamphlet no. 61, HMSO, London, 1930.

fully understanding their interdependence that the problem of healthy mental development in adolescence can be solved. We meet here the age-old crux. An individual can obtain in many ways, a level of emotional stability and security which leaves him free to use his intellect and his energy on external problems; freedom from neurotic anxiety and fear can be achieved in societies having widely differing political, ethical and social systems. In this sense mental health is a purely psychological conception without ethical reference. But adaptation implies reaction to the strains imposed by living in a group as well as a controlled constellation of drives and attitudes in the individual. The pressures and strains of any group take on values of a moral, social, ethical, religious or political kind—conformity is 'good', non-conformity is 'bad'. Thus, whereas physical health may be considered in non-ethical terms, mental health is essentially a socio-psychological concept and tends to take on as many meanings as there are different philosophic contexts.[1]

Because of its coincidence with the growth and differentiation of personality described in Chapter VI, the secondary school has a great responsibility for the mentally healthy development of adolescents—a responsibility which it cannot discharge by concentrating upon a purely intellectual formation. Its syllabus, its methods and its organization must take account of the striving of its pupils to achieve vocational, social, sexual and philosophic selves, of the stresses and anxieties which growing up in a modern world impose on young people, and of the need which, in varying degrees, they all experience to arrive at an interpretation of the world and of life. This is an aim which can be compassed by a variety of means; it is not bound up with any particular syllabus, or educational conception. The key to success is an appreciation of the fact that a school or a class is a system of human relationships within which each person, pupil or teacher, has a part to play which influences himself and all the others. The teacher cannot withdraw himself and be content indifferently to present a body of facts and ensure that they are learned; he is there to select the experiences presented, to guide and stimulate his pupils in their acquisition, and above all to help them to interpret for themselves the increasingly complex world which opens out. The acquisition of culture is the work of a lifetime and is not purely or even

---

1. It is possibly a lack of awareness of this which has led to some confusion in the mental health movement itself and to attacks upon it from various interested quarters. In so far as it is a body of techniques without content, mental health work can seem to be neutral; in fact the application of these techniques to human beings in any particular society at once involves certain, not by any means always explicit, assumptions on the part of the worker and the client. For example, an individual identified with and secure in a totalitarian regime, rooted in a group loyalty to a State-centred ethic and turning his aggression against another group could be said to be mentally healthy, though the group to which he belongs would not be so as a group. Criticism of such an adjustment must be made upon ethical and moral grounds, rather than on psychological ones.

primarily an intellectual· process; five years of secondary education can at best provide pupils with the eagerness and the ability to acquire it. In this the genuineness of the teacher's own culture—as distinct from his learning—is the most important factor.

CURRICULUM[1]

If the secondary syllabus is conceived from the point of view of adolescent needs and of the society into which they will enter, it becomes clear that areas of culture and modes of thinking are more important than subjects, however hallowed by time and custom these may be. The division of knowledge into 'disciplines' is artificial and corresponds neither to the realities of human psychology nor to the actualities of life itself. At least up to the age of 16, children should be mastering increasingly more complex modes of thought and action rather than acquiring knowledge, for example, of physics or chemistry or literature as such. Broadly one may state that there are a number of kinds of thinking which are of relevance to modern man and which, in their most fully developed form, are a dynamic combination of intellectual techniques, acquired knowledge and emotional dispositions or attitudes.

There is first the whole field of human interrelationships, which may express themselves in love, in friendship, in partial social groupings of many types and for many purposes, in systematized interrelationships of a political or other kind within groups or between groups. Here the disciplines of literature, poetry, history, geography, economics, political science, philosophy and psychology all have a contribution to make in different ways, at different periods of growth and at different levels for children of varying ability; but the ordered corpus of knowledge which each subject represents will not of itself bring about that understanding of oneself and others which is at the basis of a genuine humanism. If consciously the teacher helps his pupils to perceive the relevance of geography or history to his own life and society, to what happens in the street and in the playground; if the dramatic interplay of character on the stage is interpreted in terms of the adolescent's own experience in the family or among his companions; then there is a chance that instead of being inert knowledge about things, it will become actively formative and cultural.[2]

Complementary to a knowledge of oneself and others is a knowledge of the physical world, its system of causal relationships, and the

---

1. For a fuller discussion of the points treated here see: *Interim Report of the Council for Curriculum Reform.* London, University of London Press, 1945; *General Education in a Free Society.* Report by the Harvard Committee, Harvard, Harvard University Press, 1945, and a series of articles by E. B. Castle (U.K.), M. Sire (France) and D. Goldschmidt (German Federal Republic), *Times Ed. Suppt.* 6, 13, 20 and 27 November 1953.

2. See work by Ojemann described in Chapter XI, p. 294.

numerical and quantitative bases upon which our knowledge rests. This however does not imply the teaching of physics, chemistry, mathematics, biology and the like as such, as independently coherent systems of facts. Rather it implies that through experimentation, observation and deduction the scientific approach to phenomena and to evidence should be developed. To modern man the ability to think objectively, to weigh and balance evidence, to interpret and apply general laws is of greater importance than knowledge of specific physical and chemical facts. Applied science in any field is too complex for many to master it at the highest level; it is of importance however that all men should have sufficient insight into scientific thinking to combat gross superstition on the one hand and not to be overawed by the superstition of technology on the other. Again we must note that it is not the structure or content of the syllabus which will achieve this, but the ability of the teacher to use the disciplines involved to create attitudes and skills in his pupils rather than knowledge.

Creation and self-expression are closely interwoven with modes of thinking and interpretation; and are, not infrequently, the most neglected aspect of secondary education. Almost the only channel officially allowed to children in many schools is the written word—and then only as a means of regurgitation of what has been taught. The arts of creative speech and writing, of externalization of thought and imagination through letters, verse-writing, story-telling, conversation, spontaneous drama, debate and discussion are not cultivated, though they are in fact within the scope of most adolescents and of increasing importance in our culture. The non-verbal media of expression are frequently even more neglected; music, drawing, painting, craftwork in varied materials, are either banished by the more 'serious' tasks of preparing for academic examinations or grudgingly allowed an inferior place in the curriculum. Yet as means of outlet for emotional drives, as means of ingress to the riches of past and contemporary culture, and as ways by which the child may acquire techniques of lasting service and interests of permanent value to himself as an adult, all forms of expressive art should form a cardinal part of the secondary syllabus. In many ways creative work performs for the adolescent and the adult the same essential psychological function as play for the child. To deny creativity is in fact to court maladjustment.[1] Because of the forces which work so strongly towards the depersonalization of daily

---

1. For a fuller discussion of the role and methods of education in the visual arts see: E. Ziegfield (ed.), *Education and Art*. Paris, Unesco, 1953, and also the recommendations of the IBE Conference on Public Education, July 1950, *Collected Recommendations 1934-1950*. Paris, Unesco, Geneva, IBE, 1951. In a series of articles (*Rapprochements*, Brussels, 1945, nos. 3, 4, 5 and 6, 'Pour une reconstruction démocratique de notre enseignement populaire') Hotyat suggests that, in view of the increasing specialization of interests in adolescence, a choice of creative activities could be offered from which the pupil could choose and which he would pursue in sufficient depth to acquire a genuine means of creative leisure occupation.

life, the release and shaping of creativity in each individual is of even greater importance to mental health now than it has ever been. Unhappily, just as one finds in young children that inability to play is a serious symptom of emotional disturbance and regression, so one finds that the damming up of creative expression in adolescence and its practical absence from the lives of many adults is at once an effect and a cause of many of the psychological ills from which individuals and society appear to be suffering.[1] It is perhaps not without significance that a decline in spontaneous creativity has accompanied the universalization of education in Europe, and that with the increasing mechanization of work, passive amusement has taken the place of active cultural participation.

There is nothing strikingly revolutionary in the suggestions that the curriculum and method of the secondary school should aim at developing the modes of thinking required to comprehend the contemporary world, should actively assist each adolescent to develop himself, and should impart that true culture which consists in active participation and expression as well as in knowledge. Nor does it imply a particular curriculum. The means whereby such aims may be achieved must of necessity vary widely with differences in level of ability, in age and in the social environment of the pupils. The current administrative arrangements whereby children in early adolescence are guided among a variety of academic and pre-vocational courses provide the basis for differentiation according to ability and interest; the danger which is apparent in every educational system in Europe is that syllabuses are conceived more in terms of knowledge to be acquired by the pupils than in terms of the development of thought and expression and of harmonious personal development. The postponement of instruction in specific disciplines in favour of a continuation of a more general education, of course, presents administrative difficulties and demands teachers rather differently trained and prepared than is usual at present. We may question however whether the thorough and systematic study of any discipline as such—e.g. physics or history—is strictly necessary for any but those who will go on to universities.

This is not to advocate the lowering or abandonment of standards of scholarship, of rigour and exactitude of thought. One at least of the objects of education should be to give the intellectual security which comes from a relization of the power and limitations of one's own intelligence. Just as adolescents need to explore the confines of their physical endurance and learn from it a wise judgment of their capacities so the pursuit of knowledge in depth gives a basis from which

---

1. It is of interest to note here the effective use which has been made of craft and art work—particularly of drawing, painting and clay modelling—in the treatment of adolescent and adult neurosis and of, 'occupational therapy' in the rehabilitation of physically handicapped or hospitalized adults.

to develop humility where knowledge is lacking. On the other hand, a specialization which is premature, or which insists more on the acquisition of facts than on the perception and generalization of relationships, within the specialization itself, between branches of knowledge, or on their application to life, is likely to give a false confidence and to decrease the possibilities of contact with others differently formed.

LIBERAL AND VOCATIONAL EDUCATION

Here perhaps it is of value to remark that the conventional distinction between a liberal and a vocational education is largely false since it does not correspond to contemporary social reality. Usually identified with a classical curriculum and 'the pursuit of learning for its own sake', a liberal education was originally conceived as appropriate to a leisured class, in contrast to the trade training of the artisan; at times it almost seems that practical *in*utility was the criterion upon which the entry of a study to the liberal curriculum was determined. When however one considers closely the academic education given in the majority of grammar schools, *lycées, gymnasia, collèges* and the like, it is clear that it is as vocational in direction as any other. The obtaining of the *baccalauréat*, the matriculation or the *maturitas* is an essentially vocational objective, since the entry to particular careers (and the social status they confer) depends upon the appropriate certificate. Even at the university level the exclusion from the syllabus of subjects of direct commercial or industrial utility does not make studies liberal —especially when chances of employment depend upon the results of an examination. Thus the detailed study of Molière, Shakespeare, Dante or Homer may in fact be the narrowest and least liberal of occupations if its sole object is—as is only too often the case—the passing of a test of factual knowledge. Consider for example the prefabricated critical opinions which adorn many of the school texts in which these authors are presented to adolescents. Conversely a practical, theoretical and aesthetic study of black-smithery or of the design and construction of bridges may be broadly educative, cultural and liberal. The pedant and the narrow technician are closely similar products; each reflects the effects of an exclusive concentration upon forms rather than upon principles, upon content rather than upon relationships—in short, upon training instead of education.

EARLY ADOLESCENCE A PERIOD OF DIFFERENTIATION

Our knowledge of the way in which intelligence, special abilities and interests grow and differentiate in adolescence, as well as the needs of a highly technical society, dictate a considerable variety of courses at the secondary stage and, between 12 or 13 and 20 or 21 (or even later), an increasing measure of specialization. Up to the age of 15 or 16 at least, however, there should be little or no stress on skills or knowledge of a purely vocational bearing, though practical work, and even direct industrial or commercial experience may have immense educational value, for the increasing contact it gives with reality. The orientation of studies in this first period should be in terms of wide occupational categories and determined by levels of ability and the constellation of aptitudes and interests revealed as adolescence progresses. At this early stage the syllabuses of the various courses offered and, even more particularly the educational methods employed, should emphasize the triple aims of understanding of human relationships, comprehension of scientific causality, and capacity for a variety of verbal and non-verbal communication and expression. Moreover, since assessments of ability and aptitude, however scientifically made in the early adolescent years, are liable to a considerable margin of error, and since a community of education is one of the best means of ensuring common understanding between groups, an effort should be made to have a basic curriculum shared by all schools, even though such a curriculum be treated at very different levels of abstractness-concreteness. Transfer from course to course and from school to school according to need and development would thus be easier.

VOCATIONAL SPECIALIZATION

Only in the second half of the teens is it psychologically sound to consider a more or less irrevocable vocational commitment for children, and even then only in terms of broad categories of occupation and in clear relation to the child's capacities. Here we may note that human occupations may be graded, roughly it is true, in terms of the intellectual demands which they make, the special training and experience they require and—to a very much lower degree than is usually thought —the special cognitive or psycho-physical abilities needed for success. Vocational guidance of a general kind can be given fairly easily, especially if contra-indications of a physical or emotional type are carefully weighed; but it remains true that it is easier to select those required for a specific job than it is to determine the specific job for which any given person is suited. Moreover the skills and techniques required by a job and the personal adjustment necessary to adaptation to work are best acquired in the work situation. Thus for the majority of children in the second half of adolescence, education, while occupationally biased and providing the wider technical training necessary, should merely complement the daily work in factory, office or farm.[1] Its principal task is to assist in adjustment to working life and to continue to help the young develop and formulate their understanding of the world in which they live. In view of the occupational instability which is characteristic of the period,[2] some at least of which is probably necessary to a satisfying adjustment later, the continuity of educational influence and particularly of wise guidance, both personal and in terms of vocational aptitudes, especially for the less able group, is the more necessary.

Such a conception of continued part-time education is scarcely anywhere fully realized in Europe,[3] and many, if not the majority, of children leave school at a critical period of physical, mental and social growth to plunge into working life without skilled and sympathetic guidance of any kind even in the first year of earning life.[4] Even where, through day time release or at evening classes, training is provided, it is frequently narrowly technical and devoid of humanistic content. Moreover the least able 25 per cent of children are those who in many ways are in most need of guidance and who are most usually abandoned to their own devices from the age of 14 or 15 onwards. The only directing influences are chance initiation into industry at

---

1. See C. Stimson, *Education after School*. London, Routledge and K. Paul, 1948, which gives an account of research work on the life and educational needs of young adolescents in an English industrial town. Also: M. Reeves, *Growing up in a Modern Society*. London, University of London Press, 1946; P. Jephcott, *Girls Growing up*. London, Faber & Faber, 1942; *Rising Twenty*. London, Faber & Faber, 1948.

2. A study made in Leeds in 1938 (W. Raphaël, 'An Inquiry into Labour Turnover in the Leeds District', *Occupational Psychology* vol. XII, London, 1938) revealed that the percentage of boys leaving their jobs within one year was 26 as compared with 9 per cent of men over 18, and the percentage of girls 48 as compared with 30 per cent for women.

3. One of the most interesting attempts to smooth the transition from school to work seems to be the Maison de l'apprenti at Verviers, Belgium. The establishment is managed jointly by representatives of the employers' federation and the trade unions. It accepts adolescent boys and girls at the age of 14 and their course of apprenticeship at the centre lasts one year. It trains young people for the various specialized branches of the cloth trade in the district; this is work generally demanding manual skill acquired by systematic practice rather than theoretical knowledge. The eight-hour day is divided equally between trade instruction and general education. Although apprentices are made to work according to a set method, the prevailing atmosphere and conditions are those of a workshop. The general education is on broad lines; it includes judicious physical training, instruction centred upon the trade, and civic instruction aimed at developing in the apprentice a keen sense of responsibility and a liberal, tolerant outlook. Pupils are guided between specialities on the basis of psycho-physical tests and other data.

   Certain factories in many countries too have schemes of supervision whereby young workers are put into the charge of experienced 'guardians' who try to gain their confidence and help them to adjust to the new life. In the United Kingdom a scheme of county colleges for young people from 15 to 18 has been conceived and written into the Education Act of 1944 but has not yet been put into operation (see *Youth's Opportunity*, Ministry of Education [U.K.] pamphlet no. 3, London, HMSO, 1945). Certain towns—the best known of which are Rugby, Bourneville and Birmingham—instituted in the early 1920s schemes of more or less universal and compulsory or voluntary, part-time day continued education with excellent results (see P. I. Kitchen, *From Learning to Earning*. London, Faber & Faber, 1944).

4. In one Scottish town for example, at the age of 17, one in four boys was still in a stop-gap job with no idea of what his life work is to be.—T. Ferguson and J. Cunnison, *The Young Wage Earner*. Oxford, Oxford University Press, 1952.

the hands of workmates, more or less of parental direction, and perhaps the youth club or youth organization.[1]

ACADEMIC SECONDARY EDUCATION

It might seem that those adolescents who remain to the age of 16 or older in the more academic courses (grammar schools, *lycées*, *gymnasia*, *collèges* and the like) fare better than the majority of their contemporaries. They at least have the opportunity of studies without too heavy a commercial, technical or industrial pressure, and the chance to remain in full-time schooling at least until the age of 18 or 19, and in some countries even longer. The proportion of such children in most countries of Europe varies between 15 and 40 per cent of the age group, and of those who commence the courses between the ages of 11 and 13 or 14 by no means all continue beyond the end of the period of compulsory school attendance. If we adopt the stricter criterion of success in final examinations of a level to admit to university studies, it seems that only some 10 per cent of children in most countries 'profit' by academic education. This however needs qualification. Many children leave such schools for economic reasons; probably many enter who have not sufficient ability to profit from the particular kind of education given. There are, it is true, values in this kind of education other than that of gaining a qualification at a particular level and these can be realized even by those who are not academically gifted if neither parents nor school put too much stress upon the passing of examinations. Nevertheless the figures from a number of European countries cited in Appendix II suggest that we are faced with a situation of considerable waste on the one hand of talent and on the other of teaching. Those children who enter an academic course pressed by the overvaluation which parents and employers place on a particular certificate and who fail to win through to the end, find themselves in a situation of intolerable failure and frustration which will leave its mark throughout life. On the other hand it has been suggested[2] that as many

---

1. In England it is on the whole the most necessitous group which does not belong to youth organizations or attend day or evening classes. L. J. Barnes (*Youth Service in an English County* King George's Jubilee Trust, 1945) found that a maximum of 56 per cent of boys and 46 per cent of girls were members of a youth club. The figures are now probably lower; and are certainly lower elsewhere in Europe.

2. In a working paper submitted by J. Maxwell to a Working Party (Unesco 1954) on the 'Relation between Fertility of Different Groups and Development of Intelligence in New Generations', it is stated that in Scotland of 8,000 children annually who could successfully complete a full academic education only about 4,000 do so. C. Burt, 'Ability and Income' loc. cit., reached much the same conclusion about English prewar education. The position since the 1944 Act has probably changed in State-controlled secondary education. A. Girard, in 'L'orientation et la sélection des enfants d'âge scolaire dans le département de la Seine', *Population* vol. 8, no. 4, 1953, p. 649-72, points out that social factors are more important than intelligence in determining what children from working-class families do after the age of compulsory education,

as a quarter or more of the most able do not get the chance of an education which would ensure their fullest intellectual development.

This situation, if it is at all general, may be the more serious since the academic courses tend to attract the children of superior ability. Until comparatively recently the academic school was synonymous with secondary education; and its tradition was one of a 'liberal' education based on the humanities and evolved in classical and medieval times on social and economic assumptions which no longer hold good even for a small proportion of the population. Its impulse was often that of training the scholar-gentleman or the clerk. It was not devoid of democratic and popular components; the history of the great charity schools and of the wandering scholars of the medieval universities contradicts such a thesis; but it was essentially distinct from the growth of technical, vocational and pre-vocational training, and from the popular education movement which took its roots largely in such social and political thinking as lay behind certain of the statutes of Henry VIII and Elizabeth in sixteenth century England, the statements of Luther in 1524, Calvin's embodiment of universal compulsory education in the constitution of the ecclesiastical state of Geneva in 1542, and the Prussian education law of 1717.

Recent educational history, correlated with the democratization of western European society and the increasing appreciation that social differences do not inevitably correspond to differences of ability, has shown a diminution of the discontinuity between elementary or primary education and secondary education. The process has been hastened by political aspirations, and, as the result of two great wars, particularly the last, has gathered increasing impetus. In no country in western Europe can it be said however that 'vertical' divisions in education no longer exist; on the other hand, almost every major State has since 1945 adopted or reaffirmed the principle of equality of educational opportunity irrespective of social or economic status, religion or politics, and has applied this by instituting a considerable expansion and differentiation of education at the secondary level. Nevertheless, by reason of its social prestige and apparent economic value, the concept of a classical education, or at least of an academic and highly verbal one, has been and still largely is identified in the public mind with secondary education. Obscurely at work too is the belief that education can create ability and that particular kinds of education will create particular kinds of ability. Hence equality of opportunity is confounded with the idea of intellectual egalitarianism;[1]

---

1. The reasons for this cannot be fully discussed here. Clearly however it is related to the old idea that the mind consists of a number of faculties which can be trained and developed by particular disciplines and become universally serviceable (see Appendix IC). If we add to this the confusion whereby the humanitarian and philosophic doctrine that all human beings are equally valuable and have equal social and political rights is held to imply the scientific corollary of equality of innate endowment, it is easy to see how many nineteenth century reformers and

and the initial political impulse is to extend to all the academic classical education hitherto reserved for a privileged few.

Until relatively recently the curriculum of the grammar school, *lyceum*, *gymnasium* or high school has been exclusively dominated, in most European countries, by the requirements of the examination for university entrance—the matriculation, *baccalauréat*, *maturitas*—in spite of the fact that only between 2 and 5 per cent of any age-group eventually graduate from a university. Its basis has been the study of the classics and mathematics. Conservatively, syllabuses have been widened in the past 50 years[1] to include more 'modern' subjects, particularly of course the biological in addition to the physical sciences,[2] and the exclusive concentration upon academic standards, upon verbal learning in the dead languages and upon the acquisition of facts, has been tempered by the addition of manual and artistic activities,[3] and in some countries and schools, by a move in favour of active rather than didactic methods of teaching (e.g. the *Classes nouvelles* in France). In many countries,[4] either generally or as more or less isolated experiments, attempts have been made to develop, within the framework of such schools, courses in which modern languages, and even commercial subjects, have been offered as alternatives to the classical curriculum. In not a few, a modification of the entry demands of universities, and a consequently greater variety of alternative combinations of subjects offered at the matriculation stage, has led to a considerable development of higher studies in the modern field.

Clearly, academic education as at present conceived in Europe,

some twentieth century political theorists are led to welcome the doctrine that all differences in ability are solely the product of environment. In fact according to Vernon it seems that 64 per cent of the variance of I.Q. may be attributed to heredity, 16 per cent to differences of environment, 3 per cent to differences within families and 17 per cent to interaction between heredity and environment (see P. E. Vernon, 'The Quality of the Population', *Brit. Journ. Ed. Psych.* vol. 20. pt. II, 1950. See also Appendix IB). Nevertheless it may be agreed that there are possible sources of error in such calculations which it is difficult to avoid and that figures such as those of Vernon are open to misinterpretation. In the actual state of our knowledge, the problem is difficult to resolve with certainty. Some research workers maintain that the influence of heredity and of environment are not additive and that the possible variations in the impact of the environment are infinite in regard to the common basis of nature. It is realized how often the wish is father of the thought and how a politically attractive hypothesis or a philosophic or ethical concept may slip into the acceptance as a 'fact' of something which should be submitted to exact research. The extreme environmentalist theory is in the forefront of some educational apologetics based on political premises though little evidence other than circularity of argument is adduced in its support. For a typical exposé: see B. Simon, *Intelligence Testing and the Comprehensive School*. London, Lawrence and Wishart, 1954.
1. It was not until 1861 that the University of Cambridge granted a degree in science.
2. See *The Teaching of Natural Sciences in Secondary Schools; Fifteenth International Conference on Public Education*. Paris, Unesco; Geneva, IBE. In French education, the biological sciences preceded chemistry and physics, which were considered unprofitable for children under the age of 14. For a review of the history of science teaching in England, see Sir G. Savage, 'Presidential Address to the Science Masters' Association', *The School Science Review* vol. XXXIV, no. 124, June 1953.
3. The recommendation of the IBE Conference on Public Education, July 1950 (*Collected Recommendations 1934-1950*. Paris, Unesco; Geneva, IBE) is of particular relevance here.
4. e.g. Belgium, France, Holland (the high school and *lyceum*), Italy, Sweden, U.K.

whether it is biased towards the classical curriculum, towards the exact and natural sciences, or towards modern studies, is essentially an education for the most intelligent and verbal section of the school population. If the figures given in Appendix II are an indication, perhaps only some 10 or 15 per cent of children have the capacity, the qualities of personality, and the social circumstances necessary to meet the intellectual demands made and the methods employed at present by such schools. In view of the known relation between intelligence and socio-economic group[1] and between socio-economic group and parental ambitions for children, it is not surprising to find that such schools cater essentially for the middle classes. Even where, as in the United Kingdom since 1945, the entry to such schools has been in terms of intelligence and attainment at the age of 11, it is still essentially adapted to the middle classes.[2] If as in most European countries a fee is charged for tuition and entry is not fully selective on purely intellectual grounds, it is likely that the middle-class element will be even more heavily predominant.[3]

CONFLICT

A consideration of these facts gives rise to important questions of relevance to the mental hygiene of adolescents and of society. The academic secondary school, access to which has been made more and more open to all classes, has been and still is one of the most important instruments in social mobility. The intelligent child of a manual worker, for example, gaining entry to such a school and obtaining a bursary to help his parents to maintain him, has been able later to join the salaried middle-classes; and the tendency in all countries of western Europe has been to make the process easier, and actively to encourage such recruitment. On the other hand, the tradition of the education given, the back-

1. See C. Burt, 'Ability and Income', loc. cit.; J. L. Gray and P. Moshinsky, 'Ability and Opportunity in English Education' in L. Hogben (ed.) *Political Arithmetic*. London, 1938; Q. McNemar, *The Revision of the Stanford Binet Scale*. New York, Houghton Mifflin, 1942. It should be noted that while differences in mean I.Q. can be demonstrated between groups of children coming from different socio-economic backgrounds, the variation of I.Q. within each group means that there is great overlap. Moreover, while, for example, the percentage of highly intelligent children coming from professional families is higher than from the families of unskilled manual workers, owing to the relative size of the social groups, the absolute numbers may be very different.
2. A. H. Halsey and L. Gardner, 'Selection for Secondary Education and Achievement in Four Grammar Schools', *Brit. Journ. of Soc.* vol. IV, no. 1, March 1953.
3. In 1953—54 in France, for example, of pupils in the *6ème classe classique* of the *enseignement publique du 2ème degré*, 56 per cent came from the families of civil servants, proprietors of commercial enterprises and members of the liberal professions, as compared with 36 per cent from the families of industrial workers, artisans, farm labourers and employees. A similar situation holds in Italy, where 48.2 per cent of the pupils in the *Scuole medie superiori*, come from the families of superior State employees, professional men, owners of businesses, rentiers, etc.—Commissione Nazionale d'inchiestei, *La Reforma della scuola*. Rome. IPDS, 1950.

ground of most of the teachers themselves, the implications of the curriculum and of the atmosphere of the school are frequently different from the values of working-class societies. Thus whereas for the middle-class child, home and school may be more or less in accord, for the child of a labouring family there may be a considerable conflict.

This may be translated into a variety of tensions. In such a school the adolescent from a working-class family finds himself different from most of his natural companions who live near his home and who may start their earning life whilst he has still many years of study and dependance in front of him. His need to be quiet and to read may be impossible to satisfy because of lack of space in the home or be irritating to parents who equate work with the labour of the hands; he may be forced to acquire two fashions of speech and behaviour, one for school and one for home, to avoid criticism or ridicule in either place. On the other hand, the driving ambition of his parents that he should make the most of his opportunities, their over-valuation of the kind of education which he is receiving, and his own sense of the sacrifices necessary to maintain him at school, may make him unduly anxious over the possibilities of failure. As mid-adolescence approaches and many of his contemporaries leave school for work, such conflicts are likely to reach their maximum and undoubtedly in part account for the wastage and for the relatively high failure rate in academic schools.

Children whose parents have themselves been educated in academic schools find the position easier in most respects—provided that they are sufficiently intelligent to meet the demands of the curriculum. For those whose abilities are moderate, but who because an academic education is the only one possible without loss of prestige, are forced for five or more years steadily to fail in an unsuitable school, the situation is indeed unhappy.

Both these causes of maladjustment—social and intellectual—are probably commoner in academic education than is supposed. From the incomplete figures given in Appendix II, it would not be rash to estimate the proportion of children affected by them as being at least one third and probably more if we include those who, persisting to the end of the course, may be said rather to survive their education than to profit by it. Where the staff of a school consider it to be their sole duty to dispense an intellectual culture, to enforce a verbal learning and to hold aloof from the personal lives of their pupils, it is likely that serious and lasting damage is being done to a considerable proportion of the pupils. Much could be done by the schools themselves, without abandoning traditional values and standards, to mitigate their impact. Through close contact with parents, careful appraisal of individual capacity and a modification of method and attitude, such schools can, even within the harsh limits imposed by external examinations, and by archaic syllabuses, go a long way towards helping their pupils to

173

interpret for themselves and adapt to the demands made by this form of education. Even so it is probable that for all but the most able children there is need for considerable reform of the academic curriculum itself, which over the past century has steadily become more and more charged with casual accretions, until it presents, not a coherent and relevant picture of culture, but a patchwork of factual disciplines to be studied in haste. In such circumstances the efforts of the teacher are inevitably limited by the conditions imposed upon the schools by educational authorities, by examining bodies, by the fears and ambitions of parents and by a public opinion which is generally insufficiently informed.[1] By no means all teachers would agree that the academic curriculum should be adapted to differences in the ability and socioemotional circumstances of pupils—even of those of above average intelligence. They are inclined to regard the education itself as selective and formative; and point to the undoubted successes as evidence that rigorous intellectual discipline, and stringent demands upon intelligence and industry from the earliest years, are essentials to culture and scholarship. They look upon themselves as guardians of such standards and, reasoning from their own academic success, insist on the rigid application of these standards to all children who enter an academic course.

. Such a viewpoint has something to be said in its favour; there certainly is a group of highly intelligent adolescents for whom scholarship, in its stringent sense, is the most valuable form of education. In the early years however, and up to the age of 14 or 15 or even older, it is doubtful whether the emphasis should be as exclusively upon memory and verbalization as is usual. That many able children do well after an intensively academic education does not prove such an education to be the best they might have had. The one-sidedness and even creative sterility of many intellectuals (to say nothing of their tendency towards obsessional neurosis) is in part an indictment of the kind of education they have received.

A BROADER ALLOCATION OF TALENT?

The problem is of still wider importance to society and to the individual. Because of the social and economic prestige of academic education, there is tendency in all European countries for the abler children, irrespective of their interests, special capacities and ultimate vocational aims, to enter such courses rather than those oriented towards a more scientific, commercial or industrial culture. In general, the mean in-

---

1. Perhaps the most significant attempt to meet this problem by allowing the schools freedom to educate is the highly successful 'Eight Year Study' undertaken in America. See J. Hemming, *Teach Them to Live*. London, Heinemann, 1948.

telligence level of pupils (though of course with some overlap) drops, as does the length of time spent in full-time education, from the classical to the scientific, from the scientific to the technical and from the technical to the trade or commercial courses. Moreover since a school tends roughly to adjust its level of expectations to the calibre of the abler half of its pupils, the standards of attainment in these various courses tend to differ.

Inherently however there is no reason why technological or commercial studies, for example, should not have aspects to challenge the intelligence of the ablest adolescent. In fact industry and commerce themselves call for men and women of outstanding capacities in the purely intellectual sense. If we accept the conception of the aims of secondary education outlined earlier in the present chapter, a truly general culture could be achieved within many curricular combinations, Differentiation would then be in terms of intellectual maturity and capacity *within* particular forms of curriculum rather than between schools or courses.

Such a principle could not be applied rigidly; there are studies which only the ablest can pursue just as there are types of training within the compass of the dullest which hold no challenge for adolescents of more intelligence. It would mean for example that the classical-humanistic education (though not necessarily that part or level leading to university entrance) would be open to children of more nearly average ability, not as poor relations, but in their own right; and that, in technical and commercial schools, there would be scope for boys and girls of the highest ability not as tritons misplaced among the minnows and often marking time to keep pace with the average, but as a group for whom progress could be more rapid and teaching more abstract and scholarly. Such a redistribution of talent among forms of education would correspond more nearly to the structure of contemporary society with its increasing demand for intelligent leadership in commerce and industry and its proportional decline in the numbers of those who enter the 'learned' professions. Academic education, in spite of the modifications which it has undergone in the past 50 years, reflects a particular set of cultural assumptions, of immense value to society, but not of universal contemporary significance. As yet, even in highly industrialized countries, a scientific or commercial humanism has hardly developed; it is unlikely to do so, as long as the education of the most able children makes no attempt to face the technical, economic, social and human problems which will form the framework of their adult lives.

It would be absurd to say that the redistribution of ability among types of education and the equality of esteem which it implies, could be achieved overnight by a stroke of the administrator's pen. The reorganization of secondary education in England after 1944 attempted to achieve not only equality of educational opportunity but parity of esteem among the three types of school envisaged—secondary grammar, secondary technical, and secondary modern. But the esteem in which a school or a kind of education is held depends upon the social valuation of the jobs to which most of its pupils go, and upon the successes which its pupils achieve. Schools which receive a high proportion of the highly intelligent are likely to produce more 'successes' and to enjoy a correspondingly higher place in public esteem. Physical amenities in terms of equipment, playing fields, buildings, play a secondary part. Thus real freedom of choice between kinds of education is likely to follow only from a complex series of changes in which a change in public opinion, and in the prestige values attached to particular types of employment, play a considerable part. As such, while administration can facilitate the change, it is on the educator that the main task of shaping public thinking will fall.

In the current developments of secondary education in Europe we can perceive the beginnings of such a change. Many academic schools —influenced by a growing liberality in the demands made by external examining bodies—offer a range of alternatives in the scientific, linguistic, commercial and economic fields. Not a few countries have established technical and commercial education at all levels on an administrative parity with other forms. Some countries, notably the United Kingdom, are experimenting with comprehensive secondary schools which accept children of all levels of ability and with multilateral schools which, for a particular level of intelligence, offer courses equal in their academic demands but of widely differing orientation. Different class attitudes and prejudices for and against particular kinds of curriculum and marked differences in environmental stimulation, especially within the family circle and extending from birth, operate, however, not only to impede broad educational progress but to make it difficult for particular children to follow the kind of education best fitted to their capacities.

GUIDANCE

Wise educational guidance, at least from the age of 11 onwards, is of the essence of a constructive education for adolescents; but it must be guidance conceived in terms much broader than currently in use. Guidance of a rough kind is inherent in any system which provides alternatives; what is more, since particular curricula lead to particular certificates which are themselves required for entry to many occupations, the choice of a course or school implies crude vocational choice. In point of fact, in most countries, the process is not one of guidance— that is of the study of the individual and the choice of the most suitable education for him—but of selection, that is that certain more or less arbitrary demands are set up to which the child must conform, and such standards are set in terms mainly of intelligence and verbal development. Guidance of the kind which allows education to play a constructive part in the healthy mental and emotional development of adolescents implies much more than this. It cannot be a snapshot based alone upon a battery of cognitive tests, nor can it be solely the intuitive judgment even of an experienced teacher. Adolescents change and develop, especially in the first half of the teens and especially in the patterning of those emotional drives which lie at the basis of interests and aptitudes. Moreover at different stages of growth, environmental influences have varying degrees of importance in shaping the intellectual life. Hence guidance must be cumulative and continuous, and at the same time must take account of temperamental, personal, familial and environmental factors as well as of such more readily measureable variables as intelligence, special ability and declared interests. Moreover, those who undertake such guidance must also accept the responsibility for interpreting their study to the family, to the adolescent himself and to the school, and must thus fulfil a dynamic as well as a diagnostic role—endeavouring actively to bring about the best possible adjustment between parental attitudes, the child's capacities, and the legitimate demands of education.

Finally we must revert to the role of the school in adolescence as the interpreter to boys and girls of the world into which they are growing. Culture will at best be only superficially acquired if the deep needs of the personality are not met. However a school is organized, and however much it may seek to confine itself to the cultivation of the intellect or to the training of the hands, it cannot avoid a powerful influence on the emotional life of its pupils. It is a system of human relationships, and it cannot but be personal. The school which tries to sterilize relationships between teacher and taught or which confines itself to the group instruction of a class, may apparently succeed if the home life and social activities of its pupils are rich, varied and coherent. Even in ideal circumstances such an educational method is likely to enforce an unhappy division between the intellectual and emotional life; at its worst, the indifference or even hostility towards the pupil which it seems to imply, the constant disciplinary effort it necessitates, and the aridity of content or treatment to which it tends, evoke fearful or passive acceptance whilst in school, and the absorption of emotional energy in daydreams or in an unguided or partial struggle of the child himself to attain a balanced maturity. For increasingly many adolescents, the school is the only means through which they may begin to acquire the deeper emotional education which will shape the whole of their adult character. The trusted teacher, who is sensitively aware of the needs of his pupils, can, both in the classroom and outside school hours through clubs, societies, hobbies and other varied activities, do much to help the young find for themselves the answers to the many questions which vex their growing minds; and by helping his pupils to meet their developmental needs, to accept emotionally the world in which they live, to solve or to hold temporarily in suspense the problems with which their own growth confronts them, he can in fact liberate their energy and justify in their eyes the value of the studies which he advocates.

BIBLIOGRAPHY

I. PHILOSOPHY, CURRICULA AND METHODS

BOALT, G. *Skolutbildning och skolresultat.* Stockholm, 1947.

BOSSHART, E. *Erziehung zur Persönlichkeit auf der Grundlage von Wesen und Würde des Menschen.* Zürich, Rascher Verlag, 1951. 240 p.

CASTIELLO, J. *Geistesformung. Beiträge zur experimentellen Erforschung der formalen Bildung.* Bonn, Dümmlers Verlag, 1934. 142 p.

CHATELAIN, F. & COUSINET, R. *L'état présent de l'éducation nouvelle.* Paris, Les Presses d'Ile de France, 1953. 40 p.

CONFÉRENCE DES DIRECTEURS DE GYMNASES SUISSES. *Le gymnase suisse. Problèmes actuels.* Fribourg, Imp. Saint-Paul, 1949. 83 p.

CRAECKER, R. DE. *Les enfants intellectuellement doués.* Paris, Presses universitaires de France, 1951. 138 p.

DAVIES. H. *The boys' grammar school to-day and to-morrow.* London, Methuen, 1945. 142 p.

DOBINSON, C. H. *Education in a changing world.* Oxford, Clarendon Press, 1951. 145 p.

DOTTRENS, R. *Notre enseignement secondaire.* Genève, 1938. 100 p.

EARLE, F. M. *Reconstruction in the secondary school.* London, University of London Press, 1944. 188 p.

ETHERINGTON, T. H. *In and out of school.* London, Pitman, 1950. 98 p.

FERRIÈRE, A. *Le progrès spirituel.* Genève, Forum, 1927. 359 p.

——. *Der Primat des Geistes als Grundlage der aufbauenden Erziehung.* Langensalza, J. Beltz, 1932. 260 p.

FISCHER, H. *Zwei Bücher über die innere Gestalt des schweizerischen Gymnasium. Beilage zum Jahresbericht des Städtischen Gymnasiums.* Biel, 1940. 234 p.

FUETER, E. "Das Studium generale", *Schweizerische Hochschulzeitung.* Zürich, Verlag Leemann, nos. 4, 5, 1952.

GARCIA HOZ, V. *Cuestiones de filosofía de la educación.* Madrid, Consejo Superior de Investigaciones Científicas, Instituto de Pedagogía San José de Calasanz, 1952. 144 p.

Genetic studies of genius. Stanford, Stanford University Press, 1925-47. 4 vols.

Grammar school sixth forms. London, Times Publishing Co., 1949. 18 p.

GREENOUGH, A. *The educational needs of the 14-15 group.* London, John Heritage, The Unicorn Press, 1938. 182 p.

GREENOUGH, A. & CROFTS, F. A. *Theory and practice in the new secondary schools.* London, University of London Press, 1949. 132 p.

HAPPOLD, F. C. *Citizens in the making.* London, Christophers, 1935. 146 p.

——. *The English subjects synthesis.* London, Christophers, 1951. 126 p.

HEMMING, J. *Social studies in secondary schools.* London, Longmans Green. 176 p.

HYLLA, E. *Vergleichende Leistungsmessung im 4. und 5. Schuljahr.* München, Oldenbourg, 1949. 79 p.

INTERNATIONAL BUREAU OF EDUCATION. *Equality of opportunity for secondary education.* Geneva, 1946. Publ. no. 96. 126 p.

——. *L'égalité d'accès à l'enseignement du second degré.* Genève, 1946, Publ. no. 92. 124 p.

JAOUEN, J. *La formation sociale dans l'enseignement secondaire.* Juvisy, Editions du Cerf, 1932.

JAMES, E. *Education and leadership.* London, Harrap, 1951. 112 p.

MALLINSON, V. *The adolescent at school.* London, William Heinemann Ltd., 1949. 165 p.

MARITAIN, J. *Education at the crossroads.* Newhaven, Connecticut, Yale University Press, 1943. 120 p.

MEYLAN, L. *Les humanités et la personne.* 2ᵉ éd., Neuchâtel & Paris, Delachaux & Niestlé, 1944. 270 p.

——. *Sélection ou culture?* Lausanne, Payot, 1942. 24 p.

MINISTÈRE DE L'ÉDUCATION NATIONALE. *Les classes d'orientation.* Paris, Centre national de documentation pédagogique, 1938. 114 p.

NEUBAUER, V. E. *Die Persönlichkeit des Hochschülers.* Innsbruck, Wien, München, Tyrolia-Verlag, 1951. 151 p.

OZOUF, M. *Documents officiels: Le nouveau statut des lycées et collèges.* Paris, F. Nathan, 1942. 326 p.

PAYOT, J. *La faillite de l'enseignement.* Paris, Alcan, 1937. 60 p.

ROMANINI, L. *Il movimento pedagogico all'estero.* Brescia, La Scuola, 1951. vols. I & II.

The problems of secondary education today (University of London Institute of Education, Studies in Education, no. 6). London, Evans Brothers. 153 p.

THOMPSON, D. & REEVES, J. *The quality of education.* London, Müller, 1947. 232 p.

VALITUTTI, S. *La scuola e il problema sociale.* Città di Castello Il Solco, 1946. 110 p.

VERNIERS, L. *La rénovation de l'école (Equilibres: Cahiers périodiques, 3ᵉ série, no. 4).* Bruxelles, 1936. 88 p.

VIAL, F. *Trois siècles d'histoire de l'enseignement secondaire.* Paris, Delagrave, 1936. 288 p.

WARNER, W. L., HAVIGHURST, R. J. & LOEB, M. B. *Who shall be educated? The challenge of unequal opportunities.* London, K. Paul, Trench, Trubner, 1946. 180 p.

WENKE, H. *Wissenschaft und Erziehung.* Heidelberg, Quelle & Meyer, 1952. 206 p.

WURTENBERG, G. *Existenz und Erziehung.* Düsseldorf, Schwann, 1949. 222 p.

II. VOCATIONAL EDUCATION

L'adolescence ouvrière; conférences du service social. Paris, Editions sociales françaises, 1939.

CECH, F. *Zur Neugestaltung der österreichischen Berufsschule.* Wien, Österreichischer Bundesverlag, 1950. 124 p.

CHRISTIANS. "Les conditions actuelles du travail des jeunes de moins de 18 ans", *Revue française du travail.* Paris, Ministère du Travail, no. 1, 1953. p. 68-85.

CHRISTIANS, "Prévention et dépistage dans les milieux du travail", *Sauvegarde de l'enfance.* Paris, Mars-avril 1952. p. 262-93.

CONFÉRENCE INTERNATIONALE DU TRAVAIL. 24e session. *Enseignement technique et professionnel et apprentissage.* Genève, 1938. 252 p.

DOBINSON, C. H. *Technical education for adolescents.* London, Harrap, 1951. 123 p.

GRAEMIGER, S. *Erziehung zum Beruf. Erziehung im Beruf.* Basel, Helbing & Lichtenhahn, 1945. 62 p.

HOLTROP, W. F. *Vocational education in the Netherlands.* Berkeley & Los Angeles, University of California Press, 1951. 158 p.

INTERNATIONAL LABOUR OFFICE. *Technical and vocational education and apprenticeship. International Labour Conference, 1939. Twenty-fifth session.* Geneva. ILO. 251 p.

——. *Enseignement technique et professionnel et apprentissage. Conférence internationale du travail, 1939. Vingt-cinquième session.* Genève, BIT. 263 p.

JAHODA, G. "Adolescent attitudes to starting work", *Occupational psychology* T. 23. London, National Institute of Industrial Psychology, 1949.

MALLART, J. *La enseñanza profesional en España.* Madrid, Chambre de l'Industrie, 1944.

MATAGNE, L. & VERCLEYEN, J. *Enseignement professionnel et apprentissage.* Bruxelles, Centrale du PES de Belgique, 1938. 122 p.

MATRAY, F. *Pédagogie de l'enseignement technique.* Paris, Presses universitaires de France, 1952. 147 p.

NAVILLE, P. *La formation professionnelle et l'école.* Paris, Presses universitaires de France, 1948. 134 p.

PETERS, I. O. *Relèvement social et prospérité économique par l'éducation et la formation professionnelle de la classe ouvrière.* Bruxelles, Erasme, 1947. 96 p.

Probleme des beruflichen Bildungswesens. Stuttgart, Verlag Reinhold A. Müller, 1951. 143 p.

REUCHLIN, "Étude sur l'inadaptation à l'apprentissage", *Travail humain.* Paris, Presses universitaires de France, no. 1-2, 1950.

UNGDOMSKOMMISSIONEN. *Ungdommen og Arbejdslivet.* København, Schultz, 1952. 194 p.

VOGEL, V. DE. *Le préapprentissage et l'admission des enfants de 12 à 14 ans dans l'enseignement professionnel.* Ligue de l'enseignement de Bruxelles, 1935.

VYSNEPOL'SKIJ, I. *Iz opyta vospitatelnoi raboty v spezialnykh remeslennykh outchilischakh.* Moskva, Union des travaux scientifico-pédagogiques, 1950. 58 p.

Young workers and their education. London, British Association for Commercial and Industrial Education, 1943. 40 p.

CHAPTER VIII

SOME SPECIAL PROBLEMS OF SECONDARY EDUCATION

THE FIRST YEAR OF SECONDARY EDUCATION

For most children in Europe, the age of 11 or 12 brings a change of school. Their primary course is finished and they begin the three or more years of secondary education. For some, it is true, this next period is simply a continuation, perhaps at a higher level, of the same kind of work as they have earlier experienced; for many however it represents a complete change.

The school which they now begin to attend may be more distant from their home than the primary school; they may be separated from the friends of their childhood; instead of being among the oldest and strongest of their group, they become the youngest and newest; from being under the charge of one familiar teacher, they come daily under the care of many, with none of whom they form a close link. The discontinuities of method, differences of expectations by the school, and the challenge of beginning many new studies, may be even greater than a simple change of district or of school would indicate.

Probably no child meets such a change without some misgiving and without temporarily experiencing strain. Even the well-balanced outgoing 11 or 12-year-old will be bewildered and feel himself insecure. A few begin by rejecting the new situation entirely. Those children who, driven by the ambitions of teacher and parent, have had a hard task to gain admission to the academic school and for whom entry comes at the end of a more or less lengthy period of mounting anxiety may find the transition particularly difficult. On the other hand, those who have failed to gain admission to the kind of education for which their parents were ambitious, may find in the new school a confirmation of their sense of failure, of not being able to meet the expectations of their family.

All such periods of transition may be critical for children. The first weeks or even days in the secondary school are important for the attitudes towards the next few years of work, and the intelligent, sensitive teacher has a considerable part to play in making the change

---

1. This chapter is based upon the work of Group II and Group III of the conference.

a stimulating and not a depressing one—especially for those children who labour under a sense of failure through not having gained entry to some other school. In the case of those who have scrambled through the entry examination after a period of cramming and pressure, the teacher's task may be yet more delicate—that of adapting initial academic demands to the child's real ability and of allowing for a considerable and persistent fatigue induced by the previous driving.

In not a few European countries, entry to post-primary education is determined less by examinations than by parents' capacity to pay fees or by family tradition and choice. The first year at the new school then tends to become the selecting period during which the pupil has to show whether or not he can adapt to the new demands. For the period of anxiety which precedes a competitive examination is substituted a trial period, which may be no less anxious and perhaps longer in duration.[1]

Helping the child to adjust to school in the first year is not however solely the responsibility of the school. The family has its part to play in aiding the child to understand and adapt. Few families are equipped to do this alone, and close co-operation between parents and teachers is as essential at this as at previous periods. Ideally, before the new term begins, a personal contact should be established between the school staff and the parents of newcomers. The staff should be at pains to inform parents of the aims of the school and to seek their co-operation in such practical matters as the provision of suitable clothing, the supervision of homework, discipline and the like. From the first, such contacts should aim to reduce the anxieties of parents, and to bring them to accept more objectively their own children as individuals in their own right. This is particularly important where the intelligent child is the victim of parental aspirations or unsatisfied desires, or where the child's ability is mediocre and parental disappointment is manifest.

THE MULTIPLICITY OF SPECIALISTS

Children's adjustment to the secondary school is made more difficult because the curriculum is usually divided among many teachers. There are the specialists of the mother tongue, of foreign languages, of history, geography, science, mathematics and other subjects—so many in fact

---

1. Of 1,000 consecutive cases referred to the psychological service of the Lycée Claude Bernard, Paris, 12.3 per cent were of I.Q. 95 or lower, and a further 31.6 per cent between 95 and 105. Even setting fairly low the level of innate ability necessary to profit from an academic course, this represents a considerable number of children foredoomed to failure. 'Psychological Problems of Adolescence', report specially prepared for the conference by G. Mauco, educational director of the Centre Psycho-pédagogique Claude Bernard, Paris. This report has been published, see Appendix IVD.

that in the course of one day a pupil may meet a different teacher every 45 minutes, and no one of them more than five times in the course of a week. Each of these teachers will have his own demands to make, each will have contacts with upwards of 200 different pupils in the course of his work; there is no one person to whom the child can turn; and if, as is usual at this stage of education, the school is a large one containing many hundreds of pupils up to the age of 18 or 19, it may seem a huge unfriendly place where no one really has the time to think of the child as a child. For a boy or girl coming from a primary school where for most of the day he was with one teacher, the impersonal kaleidoscope of teachers and subjects in the new school, and his own desperate wish to establish himself in the new world, may be a severe ordeal; if to this is added the transition from a school close to home in a small village where everyone knows you, to a school in a town which involves a journey, a meal away from home, and a considerable lengthening of the day, then the task of unassisted adjustment is for some children insurmountable.

Some specialization of teacher and subject at the secondary stage is certainly necessary and becomes increasingly so towards the middle and end of the course. It is also true that the initial stages of teaching, for example, the rudiments of a foreign language require great skill and insight such as the specialist, adequately trained, may be expected to have. On the other hand, the multiplication of specialist teachers easily leads to a fragmentation of knowledge, to a lack of co-ordination between subjects, to impersonality and, to what is perhaps worst of all, a series of competing and unco-ordinated demands on children. This is nowhere more plainly seen than in the teaching of the mother tongue, which, because it is the vehicle for all education, is in fact taught by every member of staff. Some teachers will allow incomplete sentences, errors of grammar and spelling, inelegancies of phraseology and the like to pass, provided the matter is good; others insist upon a form of presentation—for example of the results of practical work in science—which is stereotyped and in fact beyond the immediate capacity of the pupil except as an acquired trick; and meanwhile the teacher of the mother tongue himself may be trying to teach the same pupils to master the sincere and accurate expression of their thoughts. Sometimes it happens, in large schools with complicated timetables and several specialists for each subject, that subdivision is carried to the point where different closely related aspects of the same subject— for example arithmetic and algebra or language and literature—are taught by different specialists; and the consequent differences within the same subject field produce additional confusions.

Differences in methods of control, in discipline, in the standards applied to the pupil's efforts, in the kind of behaviour insisted upon, even in modes of address from child to teacher are perhaps even more common and more bewildering. One member of staff may be aloof, sarcastic and exacting, another just but stern, a third repressive, a fourth friendly and permissive and another weak and vacillating.

It may be admitted that complete coherence between subjects and teachers even in the first years of secondary education is probably unattainable. Moreover some variety of approach and difference of attitude if not too extreme is of value. Ultimately children and adolescents have to learn to move freely and to adapt in many groups and to conform to a range of different and sometimes incompatible demands. The years between 12 and 15 or 16 however are a period of delicate adjustments, of considerable emotional flux and a time at which a growing consciousness of self in its many aspects, coupled with great inexperience, make each child particularly malleable and vulnerable. A school system which leaves the child unaided in an impersonal world of specialists is, at best, not assisting healthy social, emotional and intellectual growth; at worst it is contributing to the incoherence of view which marks many young people.

THE FORM-MASTER OR MISTRESS

Many European schools, particularly the academic ones which tend to have an older tradition and a more lavish pupil-teacher ratio, have adopted the expedient of the form-master or form-mistress, at least for the first few years, and often throughout the whole secondary course. It frequently happens however that this means no more than that a subject specialist is allotted to each form and, in addition to his speciality, perhaps teaches one other minor subject. Outside this, his part is often confined to calling the daily register, making out the periodic reports and perhaps seeing to it that the classroom does not become too untidy. His knowledge of the 30 or more pupils for which he is supposedly responsible will scarcely be more intimate than if he merely lectured to them on history or mathematics, and left it at that.

If the form teacher system is to contribute constructively to the adjustment and development of children at the secondary stage it must be based upon a conception of the teacher as a tutor responsible for all aspects of the child's development. The first charge on his time and energy should be that of getting intimately to know each of his pupils and building up between himself and them an atmosphere of trust and confidence. He should be the principal contact between the school and the parents and, within the limits imposed by the organization—which desirably should be flexible and supple—should be responsible for all the academic work of those under his care, acting in this respect as a kind of general supervisor. This does not mean that he should teach all the subjects of the curriculum; it does mean however that, in consultation with the subject specialists, he should plan the year's work, reconciling competing demands, especially in the amount of homework to be set; and trying to bring about some uniformity of approach and consistency of discipline among his colleagues. For all general matters affecting the child's life at school he alone should be responsible and should, as it were, occupy a half-way position between the adult friend and the aloof pedagogue. It is to such a person that the child should naturally turn when he finds himself in difficulties whether in his work or in his general life; and to the form-master the rest of the staff should refer the human problems which all teachers encounter in the classes they teach.

If the form-master is to discharge such a tutorial task adequately he should have contact with his pupils, in their first years at least, for half the week and for some time every day. Thus he should be responsible for the teaching of two or three of the major subjects of the time-table. In addition it is desirable that he should have one period a week during which, while the form is perhaps doing supervised preparation, he can work with individual pupils. If he is to make a fruitful contact with parents he will need, as well, some time during which he can make an occasional visit to a child's home or discuss a pupil's progress with his parents.[1]

Such a task probably demands a special training, certainly special personal qualities, and a different attitude towards the needs of young adolescents than is customary in the more traditional schools. Yet if the high percentage of failure and partial failure at the secondary stage[2] for intellectual, social and emotional reasons is to be reduced,

---

1. In the *Classes nouvelles* in France this system has been cautiously developed with great success—especially in the diminution of maladjustment and failure. The form-master or form-mistress system is of course well known in many countries. Often however it is an administrative expedient rather than a measure aimed at the better adjustment of the pupils. Only rarely is the form-master fully responsible for the human aspects of his class, and still more rarely is he or she trained, not as a subject specialist, but as an educator whose first job is to help adolescents to learn and to grow. So long as a high degree of specialization is the sole means of gaining a post on the staff of an academic school, and so long as many specialists receive little or no teacher-training, the chances of developing such a system will be smaller than they need be. Subject specialists are in general easier to find than good teachers!

2. A survey of a sample of 100,000 primary school children in France revealed that, from the age of 10 to 13, only 57 to 65 per cent of the pupils graded as normal intellectually were normally successful at school, while 30 to 37 per cent found their work difficult, and 4 to 6 per cent were doing badly.—*Le niveau intellectuel des enfants d'âge scolaire*, G. Heuyer, H. Piéron, Mme. H. Piéron et A. Sauvy, Paris, Presses universitaires de France, 1950. On the other hand, in an article published in *Enfance* (no. 5, 1952) on 'La répartition des écoliers parisiens', Zazzo suggests (p. 409) that 50 per cent of the pupils arrive in the class preparing for the *baccalauréat* (first part) with at least one year of retardation, and 56 per cent in the *classe de philosophie*. Similarly in the primary schools nearly 50 per cent of children repeat one class on the average. The five years of primary education are achieved in six years by 50 per cent of children.

In the Italian *liceo classico*, 33.2 per cent of pupils repeat at least one class, in the *liceo scientifico*, 31.9 per cent. In the *scuole secondari inferiori e superiori* together, 56.2 per cent of pupils repeat a

it can only be by the early detection and skilful handling of difficulties. It is often not realized how childlike young adolescents are, even to the age of 16 and older, how much they need the understanding and sympathy of an admired but relatively detached adult, and how greatly the form-teacher who knows them objectively and unsentimentally may help them to a smooth, effective development. Only if there is some member of staff whose business it is to know the child out of school will the sometimes vital piece of information be forthcoming which enables the staff to understand the waywardness and difficulties which crop up in the growth of every boy and girl.

No matter how excellent the form-teacher may be, however, he cannot work without his colleagues; nor can they retreat into their specialities and dissociate themselves from the whole atmosphere of the school in which they teach. Ideally, a school staff should be a team, not as so frequently is the case, an agglomerate; it should be united by certain commonly agreed and accepted educational ideas and aims.

These will not be achieved in thought nor applied in action if each staff member considers that his responsibility ends with the teaching of his own subject in isolation from the work of his colleagues. Clearly, the teachers should meet frequently to agree not merely upon the general principles which govern their work and dominate the atmosphere of the school, but upon such practical matters as the system of rewards and sanctions which they propose to apply, upon the degree of participation by the pupils in framing and carrying out the rules of the school, upon the amount of homework to be set, upon the organization of the timetable, upon subject co-ordination and on how the newcomers to the school shall be aided to adjust themselves to the new environment.

Most important of all perhaps is the systematic pooling of knowledge gained by each member of staff about individual children. What usually happens is that children who present difficulties—usually disciplinary problems—and those who are outstanding, are casually discussed in the staff room at breaks. The rest are neglected. Opinions are expressed but never recorded, and markedly unobjective and even

---

whole year or have to repeat at least one subject; only 15.7 per cent are considered to be good.— *La riforma della scuola.* loc. cit., p. 225-6.

An analysis of figures from Holland for all types of secondary school, 1946-50 (data supplied by J. A. A. Verlinden, Ministry of Education, Holland) indicate that, of the pupils *still* at school, 67 per cent after one year, 48 per cent after two years, 35 per cent after three years and 25 per cent after four years have passed normally from class to class without retardation. After four years the mean percentage of those who remain who are one or two years retarded in their studies is 33 per cent. The precise figures vary from one type of school to another, being highest both for repeating and for non-repeating pupils in the *gymnasium* and *lycée*.

It will be recalled, from Appendix II, that 25 to 27 per cent of pupils in one of the *collèges classiques* in Switzerland failed in one way or another, and that in 1942-45 only 47 per cent were continuing their studies normally.

erroneous judgments upon a few individuals are built up which, in all their partiality or injustice, pursue certain children throughout their school lives. Not infrequently for the want of a careful study of all the factors, both in and out of school, a child who begins with a mild and easily solved difficulty becomes, through sheer neglect, a problem for the psychological centre or child guidance clinic.[1] Maladjustment to school, though it may not be a frequent direct cause, is often a contributory factor in delinquency; it certainly is a symptom which calls for investigation and for preventive action as early as possible.

As most secondary schools are at present organized and, it must be said, in view of deficiencies in the training of teachers (particularly of subject specialists, many of whom have not been trained at all beyond their specialization), a complete and detailed case study of every pupil is probably impossible.[2] What can be done however is systematically and regularly to consider whether each pupil's progress and adjustment are satisfactory or whether further investigation and probably some help are needed. This cannot be achieved by hurried consultations at the end of the term, nor by the periodic entry of marks in a weekly or fortnightly report book for parents. Indeed the weekly or fortnightly report book becomes for many children a recurrent anxiety; the causes for their failure or success are unintelligible to them or to their parents; and what is well meant by the staff as a stimulus to effort not infrequently becomes a nightmare or is met by sullen indifference. It is essential that the school in its contacts with the home should estimate the effect of its reports on parents and on children and, while not shirking the truth, should see that they play a constructive part in development.

A sound method of organization is to discuss thoroughly a small number of children each week—say, five or six at most—as a matter of routine, seeing to it that each child is considered at least once a term. Those who seem to present special problems should be considered more frequently and be the subject of special study and of special reports. In the markedly difficult cases, where no skilled outside help is available, it should be made possible for a member of staff to get into close, friendly and helpful contact with the child's family and to discuss with them ways of helping in what is after all a joint task. Records of such discussions kept cumulatively throughout the child's school career provide not only a valuable means of helping and guiding each pupil, but a realistic and effective way of making each member of staff more aware of the orectic factors in educational progress and

---

1. Of the 1,000 cases of failure studied by the Centre Psycho-pédagogique Claude Bernard (Paris, France) (working paper previously cited), 56.1 per cent were considered of an intelligence level sufficient to achieve the course satisfactorily.
2. In 13 of the *athénées* in Belgium, this is possible since each has a *centre médico-psychopédagogique* as part of its organization.

of developing common educational ideas. Indeed a school staff is more likely to reach a common understanding and to develop a coherent educational policy on the basis of the systematic study of practical problems and of individual children than in any other way.

Studies of individual children and attempts to aid their growth and adjustment are improved if use is made of a commonly accepted rating scale or analytic study chart as described in Appendix IA. Such devices however rely for their value upon a willingness continually to improve and systematize one's insight into the problems of growth, and a genuine liking for young people. Unfortunately there is in some schools a latent hostility or indifference to the pupils embodied in the very methods and atmosphere, expressing itself in repressive discipline and a collective attitude of rejection towards those who fail to meet the arbitrary standards set. In many others there is a simple and convenient unawareness of the fact that learning is not solely a matter of intelligence and the will to learn; that it is a global process in which the whole personality of the child is engaged.

FATIGUE, OVERWORK, HOMEWORK, LEISURE

This very interrelatedness of the various aspects of the pupil's life should lead to a careful consideration of the nature and balance of the school day, especially in terms of the strains, physical, mental and emotional of adolescent growth. In most countries the length of the school day, including short breaks between lessons and the midday interval, is some seven or more hours on each of five days of the week. In addition, at least at the secondary stage—and often from the age of 6 or 7—children are expected to do from one to two hours of home-work each night.[1] Thus the minimum length of the working week is likely to be 35 to 40 hours; and at some stages it amounts to as much as 60 hours or even more. If, as is the case in many schools, the in-struction is didactic, the content formal, a child of 12 or 13 may be expected to sit still and listen attentively for hours on end.[2] Few adult intellectual workers would have the fortitude, will-power and atten-tion-span to tolerate a régime of this type for 30 or more weeks in a year.

---

1. Some countries have forbidden, at least until the age of 13, the traditional type of homework and substituted for it supervised group or individual work either of preparation or application, together with work of a less formal kind which the child prepares at home. This matter has been closely considered in Belgium, see Circular of 9 October 1948 (Ministère de l'Instruction Publique, 'Instructions provisoires concernant la réforme de l'enseignement moyen—Généra-lités. Document A 4'): a similar idea underlies the *travaux dirigés* of the *classes nouvelles* in France, which occupy 5 hours of a week of some 30 hours. (*Nouveaux horaires et programmes de l'enseignement du second degré*, 6th ed., Paris, Vuibert, 1952.)
2. With only two hours a week of physical education and the opportunities of movement provided by between-lesson breaks and the lunch interval.

The fact that many if not most adolescents survive this does not argue that it is good or the best. No serious research has been done to determine the optimal length of a lesson period, the appropriate balance between study, reproductive and creative activities in the school day, the most efficient use of time for preparation and individual learning, or even the simple incidence of physical and mental fatigue among children of different ages under different educational conditions.[1]

A number of things however are fairly certain. Adolescents need rest as well as activity; they need leisure and solitude to dispose of as they will, even in idleness, as well as periods of exacting and disciplined work, individual and collective. Learning proceeds best when interest provides a driving motive, but at the same time children have to learn that there are, in everything worth while, long periods of hard and often apparently unrewarding work which only the value of the hoped-for results can compensate. A legitimate criticism of secondary education is that it tends to confine its attention to the child at school and accept no responsibility for the balance of his life. Thus both in and out of school these truths are ignored. Not infrequently, as well as his school work and preparation, a pupil receives privately special coaching for some weaker subject, learns a further language, attends music lessons and is a member of one or many organizations. All his leisure is directed and organized for him, and he—or more usually she—may have, in addition, considerable home duties. It is true that holidays provide a period of blessed relaxation; but there is a growing tendency, for social reasons, for more and more young people to attend holiday camps of various kinds where again their leisure is organized and directed and where the stress is upon collective activity rather than upon the exploitation and development of individual resources. So too, few schools study the balance between the more usual learning and reproductive aspects of education and creative activities—of all the varied kinds, verbal, musical, manual, social—in the lives of their pupils. Many include periods of 'art', music and woodwork in their curricula, it is true; but such activities are regarded as frills and are often the first victims of overcrowding in the timetable or shortage of staff or of money; at best, not being important examination subjects, they are likely to be relegated to a place of secondary consideration. An analysis of published programmes and other data available which give sufficient detail as to time allowances for the various subjects of

---

1. One should mention here the Harvard-Florence research project, which represents an important initiative in the thorough study of fatigue among *primary* school children in four schools in the Italian city. Two of the schools are traditional in their methods, two are 'active', and the study, extending over a number of years, is aimed at throwing light both on the effects of differential feeding and on the effects of different methods of teaching. There does not appear to have been a scientific study of the problem of 'overwork' in school since A. Binet and V. Henri, *La fatigue intellectuelle*. Paris, Schleicher Frères, 1898.

the secondary curriculum indicates that on a week of 30 to 35 hours, drawing, music and manual work occupy at most four hours (of which two or three may be optional). Frequently drawing is the sole non-academic outlet for creative work, and even this disappears at the end of the third or fourth year. A glance at the syllabuses for drawing indicates that, so far from being creative, in most cases they consist largely of studies of plants (not always alive!—often merely drawings or photographs), of simple objects, copies of the antique, exercises in perspective and the like. By contrast, the *classes nouvelles* in France have a much more liberal provision, amounting in the first and second secondary school years to $6\frac{1}{2}$ hours with a further two hours of local study; in the third and fourth years this may amount to as much as $10\frac{1}{2}$ hours by the choice of certain options, but does not in any case fall below $4\frac{1}{2}$.[1]

Creative activity is not however confined to the arts and crafts; it can form a part, and should be an essential part, of the humanities, and particularly of the teaching of the mother tongue; nor are mathematics and the sciences, even in the elementary stages, devoid of creative possibilities. Many of the emotional changes of adolescence stir the young to construct and to create as well as to investigate and to know. That these desires can be powerful motives which will make necessary drudgery worth while is often ignored; there seems to be implicit in many of our methods the idea that drudgery is a good thing in itself, that it has more disciplinary value if no reason can be adduced for it; instead of meeting the intelligent demand that the utility—though not necessarily the immediate utility—of studies should be manifest, adults generally allow the intelligent adolescent to believe that much of the curriculum has been framed in a silent conspiracy to keep him at unrewarding labour.

It would be foolish to suggest that at 13 or 14, or even at 16 or 17, young people are sufficiently mature to order their own education entirely, to choose what they will or will not do, or even to work steadily at difficult tasks without some (decreasing) measure of adult-imposed discipline. The discipline of scholarship however is ultimately self-imposed like any other; and undertaken for good reasons. Adolescents have the right to know why, and increasingly to develop into a situation where, external compulsion being absent, their success or failure depends upon their own exertions.

In these matters as in others, individual teachers or even a school

1. *Nouveaux horaires et programmes de l'enseignement du second degré.* 6th ed., Paris, Vuibert, 1952. *Piano di studi per la scuola media inferiore.* Rome, Signorelli, 1949. Ministère de l'instruction publique (Belgium), *Horaires et programmes des troisièmes,* n.d. *Svensk Författningssamling,* 1950, no. 60, 13 March 1950. *Kungl. Maj: ts Kungörelse angående timplaner för rikets allmänna läroverk* (Timetables for the State secondary schools). E. Hylla and W. L. Wrinkle, *Die Schulen in West Europa,* Bad Nauheim, Christian, 1953.

staff cannot act alone. The child's academic life must be related to his home life and to his leisure, as well as there being balance and co-ordination within school hours. Where the balance between work and leisure, between self-determination and discipline, between the acquisition of facts and techniques and creative activity, between group and individual work and between social life and solitude is concerned, no universal prescription can be made. For example, in an economically well-to-do district where the majority of children come from cultured homes, allowing plenty of freedom and rich in creative outlets for pupils, adolescents can properly benefit from a curriculum which emphasizes the more formal aspects of education. On the other hand, if pupils come from homes with few facilities for quiet work and only a tenuous cultural stimulus, then the school may have to undertake, both in normal school hours and outside the class, a programme of freer and more creative activities. In any case the curriculum of schools cannot be stereotyped; the staff must become aware of all the influences in the lives of their pupils and, by co-operation with the parents, by out-of-school activities, by the provision of facilities if necessary for supervised preparation, see to it that so far as is humanly possible their pupils get what they need for a rich and varied development. Only when schools, particularly at the secondary stage, recognize in practice that a part at least of their task is to supplement, where that is necessary, deficiencies in the family and general environment, will we realize true equality of educational opportunity, and give every child the right to the full development of his personality.

This is not a plea that the teacher should interfere endlessly in the private lives of his pupils; nor that he should try to take over the task of the parents; still less that he should be invested with dictatorial powers in any direction whatsoever. It is a suggestion that the education of an adolescent is a global process and should be recognized as such. The professional educator has the task of understanding the whole needs of his pupils and of winning the co-operation of the family in what is a joint task. Unless educators themselves are sensitively aware of all the factors involved and unless they are prepared to set their own curricula and methods in order, they are unlikely to eliminate the some 30 per cent or more of wastage and failure at the secondary stage; nor, unless they stand for some coherent educational ideal, are they likely either to gain the willing co-operation of their pupils or the fruitful relationship with parents which can enrich the contribution of the school to the community.

EXAMINATIONS[1]

A major obstacle in the way of a smooth development of education at the secondary stage, so that it can meet the needs both of individual pupils and of a changing society, is the system of examinations which is in force in most European countries. The studies set on foot by the International Examinations Inquiry[2] between 1932 and 1938 drew attention to the many defects in the examinations themselves, as reliable assessments of attainment, as comprehensive measures of the results of education and as predictors of future success, even in the relatively narrow field of university education. A more serious criticism is that although examinations are generally supposed to *follow* a syllabus, they tend to determine it and to restrict curricula, homework, pupils and teachers; all that is not examinable may be ignored or find only a second place. Similarly, the teacher is tempted to concentrate upon facts and their retention at the expense of wider objectives; and, complementarily, to concentrate his attention upon the abler pupils leaving those who are less likely to pass to get on as they may.

Since the International Examinations Enquiry there has been a great deal of research into the techniques of examining and a considerable improvement in the objectivity and reliability of the papers set by most official examining bodies in European countries.[3] Research is tending to show too how far such examinations can be regarded as predictive of success in the future.[4] With many imperfections, some of which are unavoidable, modern examinations have given more weight

---

1. What follows is based largely upon a paper prepared for the conference on 'External Examinations in the Educational System' by E. A. Peel (U.K.).
2. International Examinations Inquiry (Carnegie Corporation and Foundation, and Teachers' College, Columbia University): P. Monroe (ed.), *Conference on Examinations—III*. New York Teachers' College, Columbia, 1939; P. Hartog and E. C. Rhodes, *An Examination of Examinations*. London, Macmillan & Co., 1936; P. Hartog, E. C. Rhodes and C. Burt, *The Marks of Examiners*. London, Macmillan & Co, 1936; C. W. Valentine, *The Reliability of Examinations*. London, University of London Press, 1932; M. Sadler, et al., *Essays on Examinations*. London, 1936. See also *The School and Examination System of Finland*. Helsinki, 1939 (cited Chap. VII). The Finland Examinations Inquiry: *The Matriculation Examination in Finland*. Helsinki Suomalaisen Kirjallisuuden Seuran Kirjapainon Oy, 1940; C. W. Valentine, *Examinations and the Examinee*. Birmingham, The Birmingham Printers, 1938.
3. e.g. P. Hartog, et al., *The Marking of English Essays*. London, University of London Press, 1936; P. B. Ballard, *The New Examiner*. University of London Press, London, 1923; G. H. Thompson and S. Bailes, 'The Reliability of Essay Marks', *Forum of Education*. 1926; B. M. D. Cast, 'The Efficiency of Different Methods of Marking English Composition', *Brit. Journ. Ed. Psych.* vol. IX pt. 3, vol. X, pt. 1; R. L. Morrison and P. E. Vernon, 'A New Method of Marking English Composition', *Brit. Journ. Ed. Psych.* vol. XI, pt. 11.
4. e.g. E. M. Williams, 'The Value of Higher School Certificate Results in Predicting Performance in First-Year University Examinations', *Brit. Journ. Ed. Psych.* vol. XX, pt. 2, 1950; R. R. Dale, 'Prognostic Value of the University Entrance Examination', *Brit. Journ. Ed. Psych.* vol. XXII, pt. 2, 1952; H. Himmelweit, 'Student Selection', *Brit. Journ. Soc.* Dec. 1950, Mar. 1951; Scottish Council for Research in Education, *Prognostic Value of University Entrance Examination in Scotland*. London, University of London Press, 1937; A. Van Waeyenberghe, 'Quelle est la valeur prédictive d'un test de connaissance appliqué à l'entrée de l'enseignement moyen?', *R. belge de ps. péd.* Brussels, 1951.

to truly educational progress rather than simply to the reproduction of facts.[1],[2]

Nevertheless, for many reasons, which have little to do with the techniques of examining and are to some extent beyond the direct control of schools, educational authorities and examining bodies, examinations continue to exert a cramping influence on secondary education, and particularly upon the academic school.

Much of the problem lies in a confusion of aims, between the examination as an indicator of suitability to enter a university or a course of higher professional training and a certificate which attempts to give an evaluation of the benefit which a child has received from his four, five or more years of secondary studies. In every European country the various professional bodies have tended, since the middle of the nineteenth century, to set up more and more stringent standards both of professional training and of requirements for entry upon training. What is worse is that each body, going ahead in its own way according to educational theories uncontrolled by investigation, has laid down demands in terms of subjects to be studied, standards to be attained, or even syllabuses to be followed.[3] This has led to a chaos of competing demands on the schools and to a situation in which the ablest pupils, presenting themselves for a number of competitive examinations on different syllabuses are in serious danger of overwork and failure and of a fantastic dissipation of effort. Attempts to introduce one examination for university entrance or entrance to a course of equivalent professional training and to have, for other pupils who are not going on to specialized studies, some kind of more general certificate, have resulted in the one regarded as the higher of the two—usually the university entrance—being universally demanded for purposes far outside its relevance, and, on the part of universities and professional groups, in an insistence upon a graded indication of passes, credits and honours. Thus, not merely does the certificate of proficiency—which is usually more liberal in its conception—become a lower (instead of a different) qualification, but the competitive element of the examination is seriously and sometimes disastrously emphasized.

Although examinations are open to these and other serious criticisms, the consensus of educational opinion is that examinations at the conclusion of a course have value to pupils, teachers and to the community at large. They give a clear-cut aim and provide stimulus to effort, as

---

1. See for example the various reports of the Secondary Schools Examination Council (United Kingdom, Ministry of Education).
2. Since 1946, reform of the secondary school examination system has been under study or carried through in Austria, Belgium, Denmark, Finland, France, Italy, Spain, Sweden, United Kingdom, Yugoslavia.
3. For example the Ministry of Education (United Kingdom) found it necessary to publish details of the requirements for entry to various professions: *Professional Bodies Requirements in terms of the General Certificate of Education*. HMSO, 1950.

well as a mark of attainment. Properly constructed, and set by a body external to the schools, they have an impartiality and objectivity which commend them to all concerned and enable schools to compare their achievements, in certain directions at least. Probably industry and commerce could not dispense with certificates nationally accepted and awarded by responsible bodies such as the universities. Not so clear is the value of such tests as sole criteria for entry to universities and to courses of professional training; here some kind of internal assessment made by the school and taking account not only of knowledge but of qualities of industry, personality, character and the more subtle aspects of vocational aptitude is clearly necessary. Such an assessment, made jointly between the schools and the universities or professional bodies concerned, seems both to leave the schools more freedom and to result in a more satisfactory selection. Such an idea lies behind the internal *Abitur* of Germany and the *maturité* of Switzerland.[1]

School-leaving examinations and tests for entry to universities, however, still leave much to be desired. Since the war, many countries have endeavoured to give greater flexibility in the requirements and thus greater liberty both of choice of subject and syllabus and of combinations of options. Almost universally the primacy, or even uniqueness, of the classical languages-mathematics combination has been abandoned. In France, for example, a reform is proposed which would allow *baccalauréats* of *sciences humaines et économiques* and of *enseignement moderne* as well as the various classical combinations. In the United Kingdom the idea of compulsory combinations of subjects which have to be taken together at one and the same time has been abandoned in favour of a universal school-leaving certificate which will bear details of the subjects in which passes at ordinary and advanced levels have been attained. There is too a growing tendency to allow schools to offer syllabuses of their own choosing, as, for example, is done in Belgium, Italy and the United Kingdom.

---

1. And, of course, the assessments made by the schools of the Eight-Year Study in America. The intention is that fitness for university entrance should be judged on the school work of the year preceding university entrance, upon a series of examinations held at different times during the year, as well as upon the examination for the *maturité* itself, which comes at the end of the year. This examination, which is partly oral, is an internal one. Such a system has many advantages over that of a single external examination, which comes as the culmination of a course and which alone determines entry. Yet it is far from perfect, and probably does not give enough weight to qualities of personality, nor to the changes in character, interests and outlook which take place in mid or late adolescence.

Recent experiments in the selection of students for dentistry, teaching, medicine and other university schools by methods which include standardized tests of reasoning, intelligence, tests of interests, carefully planned interviews, the use of teacher's assessments and the like, have given promising results. In view of the fact that university entrance is in fact vocational guidance for the most able and, ultimately, the most potentially influential section of the community, it would seem worth while to encourage bold experiment over the next years. (See G. E. R. Burroughs, 'The Selection of Students for Teaching', Ph.D. thesis, 1951, University of Birmingham Library; H. Himmelweit, 'Student Selection', *Br. Journ. of Soc.* Dec. 1950-March 1951; E. A. Peel and B. G. R. Moore, 'Selection for Dentistry', *Occupational Psychology*, 1951, and *Conference of British Universities on Student Selection*, 1952).

It remains however to educate public opinion both inside and outside the teaching profession to the point where destructive elements of competition are eliminated from examinations, and where due weight in the final assessment of a child's school progress is given to the many important aspects of education and personality which escape the examiner's probe. However liberal an examination may be and however well conceived, it will continue to exert an evil influence on education and militate against the mental health of pupils so long as passing or failing in the critical test is regarded as the most important fact of a child's career. The anxieties of parents and teachers readily project themselves on to children; and boys and girls between the ages of 15 and 17 or 18 are ill equipped psychologically to withstand the anxieties of adults or to see themselves objectively. If adult opinion can be brought to consider examinations as a means of further guidance, as a form of assessment rather than as a competitive hurdle, and if every effort is made to put such an evaluation in a framework which does objective justice to all the other aspects of development, then their value can be retained without the destructive consequences which have inspired attacks on the system itself over the past 20 years.

COMPETITION

The roots of many of the difficulties attributed to external examinations go however much deeper into the whole educational system. Often from the moment of entry to the secondary school, the child is thrown into a highly individualistic and competitive system, ruled by marks, by subject and form positions, and by the results of periodic examinations inside the school. His achievement is evaluated, not in terms of his own efforts, and not with the aim of showing him where and how he can improve, but in terms of comparison with his fellows. Moreover the marks which are awarded, however conscientious the teacher, are liable to be impressionistic, unreliable and frequently meaningless even for comparative purposes.[1] Such a system inevitably

---

1. It is instructive for the teacher, with the aid of an elementary handbook of statistics (for example A. Garrett, *Statistics in Psychology and Education*. London, Longmans Green & Co., 1942) to calculate the mean and dispersion (s.d.) of the marks awarded by himself and his colleagues. He will note (a) a wide fluctuation in the means for different subjects; (b) a marked variation in the range of marks awarded and in the curves of distribution which they give. If he goes further and examines the way in which different sets of marks contribute to a final aggregate score and determine a general class position, he will find that the more widely dispersed a series of marks, the greater is their contribution to the final order based on the aggregate. It will be seen that where pupils are 'guided' into different forms on the basis of aggregate marks on end-of-term examinations (as often happens), certain subjects—e.g. mathematics or courses where the marks are widely dispersed—have a prevalent effect and gain a weighting which has nothing inherently to do with the importance of the subject itself. Most of the difficulty lies in a misconception of measurement in education. There is a tendency to believe that 6 out of 10 means something of absolute value, and that it always means the same; and to forget that, whereas a centimetre or an inch can be precisely defined in terms of a fixed and universal

emphasizes egocentric attitudes and leads to cheating—the only form of co-operation allowed—especially where parents and teachers set great store upon success as measured by marks. In any class run on such a competitive system, there are always the same four or five pupils in the lead; the rest, knowing that they cannot beat the abler ones, content themselves with a more moderate effort or become discouraged. If, in addition, the parents in their anxiety or pride continually threaten or complain about low marks or make them the basis of rewards and punishments at home, the consequences for the adolescent may be serious, not only in his attitude to school work, but in his growing concept of himself as a person. The greatest of all spurs to effort is success; competitive systems in schools grant absolute success only to the few ablest, and deny it to the many, except at rare and capricious intervals.

A system of marks too is liable to fail to emphasize the right elements in progress. Adolescents have few standards by which to measure themselves and their progress save the opinion of their teachers; and under normal circumstances, most pupils try to do what they conceive their teacher expects them to do. Thus, for example, if the reproduction of facts and dates in a history test is awarded high marks, it is upon facts and dates that the pupil will concentrate; if grammatical correctness, spelling and punctuation alone are sanctioned by high marks, the pupils will neglect other aspects of work in the mother tongue. A system of competitive marking easily tends to foster uniformity and emphasis on more or less formalistic elements at the expense of more subtle qualitative excellences, and genuine diversity of approach on the part of the pupils.

The argument for marks is of course that they give pupil and teacher alike a measure of progress and act as a spur to effort. Periodic evaluation of achievement is stimulating and necessary—just as the swimmer glances over his shoulder to encourage himself by a sight of the distance covered. These objectives however can be compassed by a system whereby effort and attainment are separately assessed and compared, not as between pupils, but by comparison with each pupil's own previous levels. Clearly this involves a more detailed knowledge of each pupil and a greater insight into the efforts he makes than are required by an arbitrary competitive system of marking. It involves, for example, the attempt by the teacher from time to time to review

standard, a mark for mathematics or history or drawing or composition is fixed against nothing better than a momentary judgment of what is good, moderate or bad. To give educational measurements a degree of objectivity it is necessary (a) to be sure that the test would be reliable, i.e. always give the same result if similarly applied; and (b) to have its results graduated in terms of a definable group—for example a sample of children of a given age under given circumstances. In the usual classroom circumstance neither of these conditions is even approximately fulfilled (see also Appendix IA). Cf. O. Decroly and R. Buyse, *Introduction à la pédagogie quantitative*. Brussels, Lamertin, 1925; G. Mialaret, *L'éducateur et la méthode des tests*. Paris, Ed. du Scarabée, 1953.

with each child the good qualities and the weak spots in his current work in a particular subject, and the attempt to bring him to see where improvements can be made and where greater effort is required. It implies a somewhat different method of reporting to parents on progress, and of bringing them to forego or at least to understand the element of spurious accuracy in numerical marks. It does not necessitate the abandonment of external standards as levels to be attained. Properly handled, with the clear aim in view of encouraging the pupil to compete with himself, it can show him his progress towards these levels, confirming his confidence at each stop, and helping him clearly to see the relationship between ability, effort and success. The analogy with sports is relevant here; the boy and girl can see how progressively they can come to jump further or higher and run faster; they can compare their successes with previous ones and with a goal clearly set and, up to a point, they can improve with sustained effort in training. Only rarely is success invested by parents and teachers with heavy emotional significance, and everyone understands that for reasons of physical difference there are inevitable differences in achievement.

DISCIPLINE

Such a system of self-comparison in terms of effort and previous achievement is unlikely to succeed in a school where the authority is adult-imposed and more or less arbitrary. It is closely bound up with the whole atmosphere in which adolescents are educated, and depends for its effectiveness not only upon the school, but upon the co-operation of the home. Boys and girls between 11 or 12 and 16 or 17 are liable from time to time to be turbulent, wayward, aggressive and unreliable; this is not only a normal aspect of growth, but probably essential to the whole complex process of constructing an independent self. It is in many ways easier to stem this self-assertion, and keep it within bounds comfortable to the adult, by more or less rigid repression; and where such repression is not hostile or sadistic it probably does little harm. On the other hand it is not constructive; it does not emphasize or foster the growth of self-discipline and self-control and is liable, by repressing the often crude attempts at self-assertion, to hinder the growth of independence of spirit and thought. Furthermore, by failing to give graduated responsibility, it encourages the attitude that you only do those things which others in authority oblige you to do, and that you don't work unless you are watched. In such an atmosphere it is easy to see how antagonism to authority is transferred into a general antagonism to everything authority seems to want, good or bad.

On the other hand, the weight of too much liberty can be a heavy burden on the immature personality. Adolescents readily recognize that there are some things they have to be made to do, temporarily at least; and if there are no imperatives in their lives, they will become anxious and uneasy, reproaching the adult for not being sufficiently firm. If the school staff is animated by the twin ideas of respect for the growing personalities of their pupils and of the need progressively to transfer to adolescents themselves responsibilities, first for their own work and conduct and then for the conduct of others younger than themselves, the school can build up in each child a genuine discipline and genuine social attitudes.

In practice, how far this can be realized will depend upon the pupils' previous educational experience, upon attitudes to authority built up in the primary school, and upon the atmosphere of the homes from which the children come. Within such limitations, however, the staff can determine the minimum rules which have to be imposed by authority for the good of the whole school community. These will be found to be fewer than is usually supposed; and, what is more, readily explicable and acceptable to the pupils. Beyond these few rules, lies what might be more properly termed the morality of human relationships—consideration for others, courtesy, honesty, reliability—and of personal discipline. By a process of discussion, trial and error, and common agreement between staff and pupils, either through form or school councils or more informally, pupils can be brought actively to sustain a code to the framing of which they themselves have contributed.

Such a system of government by participation is the very image of democracy; it revolutionizes adult-child relationships in that the adult is himself seen to be bound by the rules which all accept, and the child is obliged to think and to take increasing responsibilities. At the same time due weight is given to superior experience and judgment. The difficulty arises that, being experimental and progressive rather than static and adult-imposed, this type of discipline demands from the staff, not only a real insight into and nice judgment of the psychological growth of their pupils, but patience with immaturity, and a personal security such that they can allow the young to learn by experience.

Essentially, though more subtly, the same principles apply as in the education of very young children. The growing human being learns not through precepts enforced by others, but by success and failure. The task of the experienced adult is to allow his charges to proceed to the very edge of danger and to intervene only to prevent catastrophe. Discipline in adolescence can be over-protective, permitting no experiments and warding off all dangers; it can also be so free that it gives no protection against real dangers which the young are not equipped to meet. The difficulty lies in that, whereas for the young child the dangers being mainly physical are easy for grown-ups to assess, the adult judges the adolescent's less tangible world in terms of his own fears, anxieties and conflicts.

CORPORAL PUNISHMENT

It need perhaps hardly be pointed out that, under a system of discipline based upon fostering success, upon mutual respect and understanding between staff and pupils and upon progressive self-discipline there is no place for corporal punishment. Nevertheless, in view of the opinions held by many practising teachers,[1] a word must be said. It is probable that for most normal children and young adolescent boys, corporal punishment, sparingly and humanely used, has little direct and obvious adverse psychological effect. In many cases it may seem to achieve its object and act as a quick, safe deterrent to breaches of discipline; and many a child given the choice between a punishment which keeps him in from the sunshine and play for several hours and a short sharp experience of pain would choose the latter. The effects of any form of punishment on children and adolescents depend however much more upon the nature of the adult-child relationship than upon the form of punishment used; and more lasting damage may be done by the hostility which underlies sarcasm than by a beating administered by a teacher or parent whose affection is never in doubt.

In certain cases, however, particularly among adolescents, the effect is seriously adverse; it may arouse sado-masochistic feelings either in the victim or in the spectators. Where physical punishment is used by a teacher who is himself neurotic there may be real brutality, and there is certainly a grave risk that the fear instilled, the spectacle of naked adult aggression, and the half-delighted, half-terrified enjoyment of the class will result in some at least of them developing masochistic fantasies of a seriously abnormal kind. It must be emphasized that the emotional life of the growing boy or girl in the pubertal period is in a state of precarious balance and the intricate relationship between aggression and sexual feelings is easily and lastingly disturbed. The narcissism of the pubertal girl may be even more profoundly vulnerable to physical punishment than that of the boy; and both sexes can be deeply injured in their development by pain inflicted by an adult of the opposite sex. Moreover a careful examination of the records of any school which uses corporal punishment freely will show that there are a few children who are continually the victims; and that they seem to become hardened to it, even deriving a certain satisfaction from the admiration of their companions. Close study of such children frequently reveals a degree of maladjustment in their home or school lives which warrants rather help in the solution of their difficulties than continual and increasingly ineffectual punishment.

It is noticeable that, with the decline of physical punishment both

---

1. M. E. Highfield and A. Pinsent, *A Survey of Rewards and Punishments in Schools*. National Foundation for Educational Research. London, Newnes & Co. Ltd., 1952.

in the home and in the school of recent years, there has been a corresponding decline in bullying and fighting among children and adolescents. It is also worth comment that in the Hitler education system, deliberate steps were taken in schools, colleges and universities to reintroduce all forms of interpersonal physical violence as a means of enhancing aggressiveness.[1] Thus, one of the principal arguments against corporal punishment at home or at school is not that it may do harm to a few more or less unbalanced children, adolescents, or adults, serious as this may be for the individual or for the society, but that it encourages crude aggressivity and sanctions a kind of relationship between human beings which is the very denial of respect. The fact that many children have been used to being struck by their parents is no argument that the school itself should countenance the sanction of physical force. Family discipline is quite different in its psychological effects from school discipline. The parent-child relationship is normally more emotionally charged than the teacher-child relationship and, where a child has developed normally, is a much more secure one in which elements of affection, acceptance, aggression and the like are held in a state of intense dynamic interaction. Often the pupil-teacher relationship is impersonal until punishment is inflicted; the punishing teacher does not play the same part as an accepting and loving adult as does the father or mother; and is apt to be regarded simply as hostile and hateful or as impersonal and unjust. A situation in which children have experienced considerable physical punishment at home makes more difficult the task of developing a constructive discipline at school; it also makes it more necessary; and lays upon the school staff the obligation to bring the parents as far as possible to understand and to co-operate.[2]

Corporal punishment is, it should be noted, only a special case of punishment in general. Ideally a constructive education at home and in school should be able to dispense entirely with punishments other than those which are seen by the offender himself to be the direct and necessary consequences of wrong actions, and from which all element of adult revenge or arbitrariness is removed. Such a perfect system can rarely be developed, even in a school which enjoys the full understanding of its community and it must be admitted that in the adult world there are strong personal and arbitrary elements in the sanctions which are applied. On the other hand, in many classrooms punishments are inflicted more to assuage the outraged dignity of the teacher than for any other reason, or they exist as a threat to maintain an obedience which a more skilful appeal to interest would bring of itself.

---

1. See G. A. Ziemer, *Education for Death*. London, Oxford University Press, 1941.
2. Countries in which corporal punishment has been forbidden in schools do not have noticeably more disciplinary or other troubles as a consequence (e.g. Belgium, France, Switzerland [Canton de Genève]).

Children, and still more adolescents, are quick to detect and resent elements of hostility and injustice in the discipline under which they live, to take advantage of different standards and to meet mere repression with numerous expedients of deceit, covert revolt and a primitive code of solidarity against grown-ups. If education is to be constructive, the accent should be placed upon positive things, on success, the value of an honest attempt, and of the effort to contribute to the well-being of others. Ways of satisfactory behaviour should be pointed out, without preaching; and punishment should be used sparingly, always with scrupulous justice and always accompanied by an attempt to get the offender to see that it is a necessary consequence of his actions. More and more the sanctions used should derive their force from public opinion and less and less from the personal authority of the teacher.

The kind of discipline developed by a school will, by its direct effects upon individual pupils and by its covert implications in terms of human values and human relationships, affect the adolescent's attitudes to himself, to others and to the community in which he lives. Thus while the content of the curriculum may be said to contribute to his understanding of the world into which he is going, the framework of his daily life and personal relationships with contemporaries, juniors and adults directly shapes and colours his consciousness of himself. These two cannot and indeed should not be separated and the teaching staff, through example as well as through deliberately pointing out the bearing of their studies on life, have a responsibility helping to bring about a coherence and integration between them.

SEX EDUCATION

Nowhere is this more clearly necessary than in the field of sex development. In the course of adolescence boys and girls have to make the transition from a more or less egocentric proto-sexuality[1] to a fully developed hetero-sexuality which in the completest sense is capable of love and marriage. In modern societies, sex is even more heavily regulated than aggression and is surrounded by numberless taboos, many of them markedly unhealthy. Moreover social and economic factors combine more and more to postpone marriage, whilst the glossy magazines, the hoardings, the cinema and many other uncontrolled influences combine to stimulate adolescent eroticism.

Sex education goes on from earliest childhood and it is upon the interpretation of relationships between his mother and father, between himself and them and his brothers and sisters, that a child builds up

---

1. The term is Thouless's: see *General and Social Psychology*. Cambridge, University Tutorial Press, 1937, p. 171 ff.

the fundamental attitudes on which his subsequent adjustments will be based. So too the attitudes, expressed and unexpressed, shown by his mother and father towards the body and bodily functions, the way in which his innocent questions about birth, the role of the father and the mother in conception and the like are met, and the constructions he puts on casual remarks—all these will operate to colour his thinking and reverie at adolescence when the increased energy of the sex drive and the physical changes of puberty direct attention to what is after all one of the most essential and powerful of human motive forces.

Ideally the physiological facts of sex are best acquired slowly through free and frank replies to the normal questions of childhood, supplemented by experience with living things and the more systematic study of the reproductive system in the course of general science or biology courses. In this way, before adolescence charges the whole atmosphere with emotion, the facts are known and assimilated. Puberty however brings other problems on which growing boys and girls need information and reassurance, which they can best get from their parents; they need to know something of the changes to be expected in themselves, to have their minds freed from anxiety and guilt over such things as menstruation, nocturnal emissions, and erotic dreams; to be aware that they are not alone in undergoing such changes; and to learn to respect and understand their own bodies. Much adolescent depression, difficult behaviour, lassitude, preoccupation and unwillingness to work can be traced to conflicts and anxiety over sex developments which could be relieved by a timely word from a respected and trusted adult. In not a few cases—especially where the conflicts are aggravated by unwise warnings of disease and insanity—adolescent suicides can be traced to a fearful ignorance of the most elementary facts or to the fantastic half-information that circulates among children.[1]

Partly because of their own ignorance, fear, and wrong attitudes, many parents find it difficult or impossible to enlighten their own children; some, though increasingly few, confound ignorance with innocence and, maintaining the conspiracy of silence, prepare the way for what may well be a devastating shock later, especially for girls at marriage. In such circumstances, by agreement with the parents, it may fall to the school to undertake this aspect of the sex education of its pupils and, in a number of countries, this is the official recommendation.[2] This throws on the teacher, the priest, the psychologist or the doctor the responsibility to question his own attitudes, to come to terms

1. It should be remembered that some kind of sex enlightenment (usually inaccurate and often accompanied by sniggering guilt) is received by most children before the age of 12—see L. S. Hollingworth in *Handbook of Child Psychology*. Ed. Murchison, Massachusetts, 1933; Partridge, *The Social Psychology of Adolescence*. New York, Prentice Hall, 1939; and N. Carnivet, 'Enquête sur l'initiation sexuelle', *Archives de psychologie*, vol. XXIII, no. 91, Jan. 1932.

2. See for example *Sex Education in Schools and Youth Organizations* (Ministry of Education pamphlet no. 119), HMSO, 1943.

with his own conflicts in the sexual sphere, and, on the basis of a warm relationship between himself and the class or individual child, to deal sincerely and frankly with the matter. Where staff-pupil relationships are indifferent or hostile, the attempt by the teacher or even by an expert outsider at this aspect of sex education is likely to fail or even to do damage. A matter so intimately woven into the lives of the young can be tolerated only where questions can be freely posed and answers honestly given. None but those adults who have come to terms with their own sexual lives, who are free from fear or jealousy of the young and who have experienced fulfilment in marriage and parenthood are likely to be able to deal objectively yet intimately with the sex problems of adolescents.

The provision of objective information and the relief of anxiety how-ever are only one aspect of a proper education of the sexual self; and if it is given in such a way as to ignore the essentially personal, spiritual aspects of human love, then it may do as much harm as good by con-niving at a divorce between physiology and the emotional life. Essen-tially, sex education is a preparation for marriage and for the whole graded texture of relationships between men and women. Thus the teaching of religion, history and literature, particularly the novel, poetry and drama, have an immense contribution to make in the hands of a teacher who is sensitive enough, both in his choice of texts and in his questions and comments, to meet the half-formulated inquiries of his class, and to allow them at times, without real or implied criticism of their callow judgments, to discuss personal issues in the light of the views of life expressed by great writers. Much too can be done by a sane, uncensorious but mature, discussion of the experiences which adolescents have at the cinema; rather than ignoring the screen or condemning it as though it were a somewhat shameful activity, the wise teacher will attempt to guide, refine and make critical the taste of his pupils; and will use the vivid contemporary experience as a supplement to the education of the classroom. In this way, the elements of the false, selfish or purely sensual in human relationships can be seen for what they are and the noble and unselfish be accentuated; and adolescents can be helped to find the distinction between the fantasy, displaced values, and shoddiness which mark some screen romance (as they do some literature) and the more realistic and healthy relation-ships upon which genuine happiness is founded.

CRUSHES AND HERO WORSHIP

Literature however is life at one remove; and in adolescence boys and girls pass through many phases of partial growth which affect their ultimate sex development on the socio-emotional side. These too

203

require wise handling by parents and by teachers. Many adolescents form deep and passionate friendships in which some of the elements of adult love are found—possessiveness, intense admiration, the desire to imitate and always to be together, susceptibility to hurt, slavish devotion and intense anguished jealousy. To grown-ups such friendships may seem ludicrous—a legitimate target for jokes and witticisms; they may even provoke parental jealousy and become the centre of angry scenes and recriminations. Where, as is often the case, they occur between an older and a younger boy, the fear of homosexuality may lead to attempts at separating the two. Boys are inclined too to hero worship, in a more or less distant way, an admired teacher, scoutmaster, club leader, priest, or even a less immediate personality in the world of sport or the stage. Sometimes a guide troop or a girls' school is completely disorganized by a series of 'crushes' or 'pashes' on members of the staff; there will be slavish service, the bringing of flowers, lying in wait for a sight of the beloved object on the way to and from school and sometimes more extravagant manifestations of a deeply emotional attachment. Again, overtly or unconsciously, to the adult observer there seems to be a homosexual element in such affairs; and a frequent reaction is one of horror which creates an atmosphere of guilt.

Few normally developing boys and girls in our civilization escape these intense experiences entirely, and they seem to serve an essential purpose in the transition from child to adult emotionality. In the early stages of development in the teens, the heterosexual feelings may be so intense as to provoke fear and the desire to seek a love object which is 'safe'; the intense friendship or the crush may provide a midway stage between complete emotional dependence on parents and emancipation to the point where adult love of a member of the opposite sex becomes possible. Whatever the ultimate psychological motive, and there are probably considerable differences from child to child, such experiences, by their very intensity, increase knowledge of oneself and of another. Stage by stage they move from emotional over-valuation to a more real appreciation unclouded by romantic exaggerations. In the process, they may be more or less painful and disturbing; but, by their very impermanence and experimental nature, they allow the exploration of deep emotion and close personal relationships as a preparation for a more genuine, less selfish and blind love in young adulthood.

Danger only arises when one of the parties is abnormal, maladjusted or unsatisfied. There is the possibility that a homosexual fixation may result or a serious sexual shock may occur if a young boy is seduced by an older homosexual man or by a senior boy who has homosexual leanings. Even however when such a seduction occurs, if the victim is himself secure and even moderately well adjusted, he is likely to pass through it with little ultimate damage—provided his parents or any other adults who may become involved treat the matter with skill and restraint, rather than, in their horror, piling up guilt and fear in the child's mind. The single sex boarding school is, of course, peculiarly liable to give rise to such problems; but a sensible and understanding watchfulness on the part of a staff who are themselves mentally healthy, and who do not read into the actions and feelings of adolescents more than is really there, is the best preventive measure. Adolescents who are living a full, interesting and satisfying life are in little danger of developing sexual abnormalities.

The risk of overt homosexuality is less with the adolescent girl, even in the environment of a segregated boarding school. The danger and the potentialities inherent in the 'crush' or 'pash' are however much greater. Everything depends upon the maturity of the adult concerned and upon the reactions of other members of the school staff and parents. If the youth club leader, the guide captain or the teacher is herself immature and frustrated, she may batten upon the callow adulation and, by encouraging it for her own satisfaction, gain an ascendancy over the pupil, lasting well beyond what is normal or desirable. Alternatively, the passionate adoration offered may provoke anxiety or self-protective hostility, either in its object or in the staff generally; the attachment is cruelly rebuffed or even bitterly condemned, arousing in the child painful feelings of being involuntarily silly or even wicked in spite of oneself. Parents too not infrequently complicate the situation; seeing their child devoted to a stranger, they react with angry or ironic jealousy and possessiveness. When once such manifestations of adolescent 'love' can be accepted for what indeed they are, a transitional and probably necessary phase of growth, teacher and parent alike can make constructive use of them as a means of education in human relationships which will contribute to happy sexual adjustment later. The fierce jealousy and possessiveness of such a 'crush', its disorganizing effect upon the adolescent's life, the bitterness and the joy it brings and the over-valuation of the beloved object, even the final waning and disillusionment, all have value in organizing the sentiments of the adolescent girl and in bringing her step by step nearer to a true, unpossessive love for and valuation of another, which is the basis of a successful relationship in marriage. Outside the intense emotional life of the family, such an emotional possession may be her sole experience of the intimacy of love before she has her first heterosexual love affair.

CO-EDUCATION

Crushes, pashes, and intense and passionate friendships are more common, last longer and are more potentially unhealthy in single-sex schools. Fortunately, most children who attend such schools come daily from families where there are children of the other sex and the segregation is far from complete in out-of-school hours. There is thus the chance that each sex will not build up false and romantic ideas of the other, nor that life in a bisexual world will be delayed until late in the teens. In the boarding school on the other hand segregation is likely to be complete.

There is little doubt that where the attitudes and traditions of the community favour it, the education of boys and girls together in the same school has much to commend it; it brings the sexes into a sane healthy relationship with each other throughout adolescence, encouraging ideas of equality, of mutual acceptance and of respect. To the boy, the girl is not a remote mysterious object; nor to the girl is a boy either a primitive beast or a romantic knight in shining armour. Co-education at least makes it possible for love, when it comes, to be founded on an appraisal of the opposite sex which is based upon a daily experience of growing up together, and of the real nature of the differences of emotional and physical organization between the sexes. A co-educational school also usually means a mixed staff with the chance which that gives of a social atmosphere in which masculine and feminine elements are balanced.

Where for any reason co-education is undesirable, it is usually possible to arrange, at least for the older pupils, mixed intellectual and social activities so that growing boys and girls work and play, compete and co-operate together, learning to recognize that difference of sex may well mean difference of capacity, of viewpoint, and of social role; but that it does not mean difference of humanity or of value. Innocence and romance are not killed by knowledge which is gained on the basis of respect for others; and nothing is more pitiful than the adolescent, boy or girl, who arrives on the threshold of adulthood full of sentimental illusions or fears of the opposite sex.

Much of the resistance to co-education comes from a deep-seated and often unconscious fear of precocious physical sex experience. It may be specially difficult for those single women teachers who feel frustration and anxiety in their own lives to refrain from carrying these over into their attitudes to their pupils. To the perfectly natural and transient flirtations of girls and boys, and even to the more serious and durable attractions, they may be tempted to react as if the worst was bound to happen. By numerous expedients they seek to turn aside the inevitable and even hold up to scorn or shame girls who are seen talking to boys. Thus they add, to what begins in all innocence, a flavour of the forbidden and even of the morally wicked. Adolescents who have developed soundly, who come from happy and united homes, and who are trusted with considerable personal liberty, do not as a rule carry their sexual experimentation too far; there is a kind of protective shyness which marks the teens, and if two young people in fact go astray the fault lies much more with their previous upbringing and with the attitudes of adults around them than it does with mere opportunity. Indeed an unemotional acceptance by adults of sex and of the interest of adolescents in each other, a sympathetic understanding of what calf-love means to the lover and a gentle insistence that all this is a normal part of life but that, like anything else, it is the better for self-restraint, is probably the surest prophylactic against premature physical experience. Prohibitions, segregation, angry sermons and the like may lead to concealment; they are likely to precipitate, rather than prevent, the undesirable consequences they seek to avoid.

A mentally healthy person accepts sex as an important part of life but not the whole of it; and attitudes towards the other sex which are founded upon a genuine understanding of and respect for the personality of the other are the only adequate basis for marriage. The development of such attitudes will be hindered or favoured by all those who have to do with the growing youth—by the parents in the pattern of intimate relations which they give, by the teachers, clergy and others who come into contact with boys and girls, and especially through their judgments on conduct, the example which they set, their willingness unemotionally to discuss the problems which vex the young and to abstain from hostile or damaging comment.

THE EDUCATION OF GIRLS

A word may perhaps be said in conclusion on the education of girls. The tradition of European education is essentially a tradition of the education of boys; female education having been in the past very largely a domestic apprenticeship, and the acquisition either of useful crafts or of accomplishments likely to attract a husband. The steady emancipation of women in the eighteenth and nineteenth centuries led to a demand for equality of educational opportunity, although even now there are, in most countries, fewer girls than boys pursuing academic courses and fewer women than men in the universities. In general, the studies pursued, the organization of the schools themselves, and even the methods of teaching, are closely modelled upon those considered appropriate for boys.

We may agree that demonstrable intellectual differences between the sexes are few and uncertain; we may also admit that differences of temperament, of interests, of the organization and direction and expression of aggressivity, of the structure of personality and the like between the sexes are probably largely the result of social pressures, and especially of the processes of identification by which each boy or girl adopts the sex role; and that therefore considerable changes could

207

be wrought by a change in the environment. Yet the fact remains that biological differences and especially the bearing and care of children make for differences in the social part to be played by the two sexes in adult life.

This should lead us to ask whether the education of girls, at least in adolescence, should so closely follow that of boys. Most schools, it is true, have special subjects reserved for boys or girls respectively—cookery, sewing and domestic science being regarded as girls' activities; and woodwork, gardening and the like as appropriate only to boys. In other than the academic schools, and especially in the more strictly vocational courses, there is of course even more differentiation and a closer adaptation of curricula to the apparent needs and interests of girls, most of whom however will become wives and mothers after a transition period in employment.

The academic school for girls, on the other hand, is frequently run on the tacit assumption that the intelligent girl must prepare herself to compete with men on their own ground and that, instead of joyfully accepting the fact that she is a woman she must regard it as an unjust handicap over which she must triumph. This at least in part contributes to the relatively lower marriage rate among the better educated and more intelligent women, with a consequent impoverishment not only of their own lives but of the whole community and its future children. The very fact that adolescent girls are taught by unmarried women, and that in many countries marriage debars a woman from teaching, further unbalances the atmosphere in which abler girls are educated and emphasizes the implied rejection of the feminine role. Co-education paradoxically tends to diminish this, since the difference in the approach of the two sexes to the same subject, especially to those subjects such as languages or literature which involve emotional and social elements, enhances the contribution of both; and, properly handled, can lead each to an appreciation of the other's viewpoint. Moreover, while segregation is necessary for certain activities, it need not be rigid for many of those things—such for example as cookery, woodwork, metalwork, embroidery—hitherto regarded as appropriate only to one sex.

But co-education does not solve the root problem of the education of women which is that of enhancing the specifically feminine contribution to the community and at the same time of developing a confidence in herself as a being different from man but neither superior nor inferior. The solution to this lies partly in a change in the entire structure of attitudes in our society; but, both in this process of change and in developing more surely and healthily the character of the wives and mothers of the future, our schools could do very much more than at present.

208

BIBLIOGRAPHY

ALLEN, A. B. & WILLIAMS, E. H. *The psychology of punishment*. London, Allman, 1936. 148 p.

ALLERS, R. *Sexualpädagogik; Grundlagen und Grundlinien*. Salzburg, Anton Puslet, 1934. 270 p.

ARATÓ, A. *L'enseignement secondaire des jeunes filles en Europe*. Bruxelles, Le Begue, 1934. 312 p.

BARBER, G. O. *School education in hygiene and sex*. Cambridge, Hueffer, 1936. 84 p.

BERGE, A. *L'éducation sexuelle et affective*. Paris, Editions du Scarabée, 1948. 172 p.

BIBBY, C. *Sex education*. London, Macmillan, 1944. 222 p.

BUREAU INTERNATIONAL D'ÉDUCATION. *L'admission aux écoles secondaires*. Genève, 1934. Publ. no. 34. 222 p.

CHAMBRE, P. *La famille et l'école devant le problème de l'éducation sexuelle*. Paris, Fédération nationale des associations de parents d'élèves des lycées et collèges, 1948. 200 p.

CORNIOLEY, H. *Das Schulkind ausserhalb der Schule*. Bern, Schuldirektion 1938.

CRICHTON-BROWNE, J. *Report on the alleged over-pressure of work in public elementary schools*. London, HMSO, 1884.

CROUZET, P. *Bachelières ou jeunes filles*. Toulouse et Paris, Privat-Didier, 1949. 328 p.

DOMS, F. P. "Recherches expérimentales sur la paresse des écoliers", *Revue de pédagogie*, Cahier VI. Bruxelles, 1938.

DURAND, S. M. *Education féminine. Chemins nouveaux*. Lyon, Les Editions de l'école et la famille, 1949. 288 p.

ERRANDONEA, I. *El plan de bachillerato actual*. Madrid, Razón y Fe, 1943. 98 p.

FOREL, O. *L'accord des sexes*. Paris, Payot, 1953.

FORSTER, A. *Das Gefahrenmoment in der Mädchenerziehung*. Luzern, Verlag des Instituts für Heilpädagogik, 1941. 140 p.

GONÇALVES VIANA, M. *Exames escolares e concursos*. Lisboa, Garcia & Carvalho, 1949. 141 p.

GRIFFITH, E. F. *Sex and citizenship*. 4th ed. London, Methuen, 1948. 224 p.

HAENSEL, L. *Die Jugend und die leibliche Liebe*. Innsbruck, Kerle. 1938.

HUBBACK, E. M. *Education for family life (Education paper, no. 4)*. London, British Social Hygiene Council. 20 p.

HUGUENIN, E. *La femme devant son destin*. Neuchâtel, La Baconnière, 1942. 190 p.

JUNG, C. G. *Psychologie und Erziehung*. Zürich, Rascher, 1946. 204 p.

KING, J. L. *Sex enlightenment and the catholic*. London, Burns, Oates & Washbourne, 1944. 68 p.

Les équipes de Saint-Joseph de Reims présentées par elles-mêmes. Reims, 1947. 78 p.

MESEGUER, P. *Aspectos técnico-administrativos del examen de bachillerato*. Madrid, Fax, 1945. 16 p.

MILLOT, A. *L'éducateur et l'action éducatrice*. Paris, Presses universitaires de France, 1941. 156 p.

MILNER, M. *The human problem in schools*. London, Methuen, 1938. 320 p.

MORGAN, A. E. *Youth services*. London, Longmans & Green, 1948. 40 p.

NATIONAL UNION OF TEACHERS. *Sex education in the schools*. London, 1947.

NEW EDUCATION FELLOWSHIP. *Examination tangle and the way out*. London, W. Rawson, 1935. 116 p.

RENAULT, J. *Nos adolescents.* Paris, Lethielleux, 1936. 142 p.

ROSSIER, J. *L'éducation sexuelle.* Genève, Impress, 1938. 14 p.

SHEARS, L. W. *The dynamics of leadership in mixed adolescent groups.* Thesis. London, University of London Institute of Education, Library, 1952.

SKINNER, J. W. *School stresses. The grammar school today and tomorrow.* London, The Epworth Press, 1949. 128 p.

STEPHANI-CHERBULIEZ, J. *Le sexe a ses raisons.* Ruschlikon-Zürich, A. Müller, 1946. 147 p.

CHAPTER IX

THE PROBLEMS OF SPECIAL GROUPS [1]

THE EDUCATION OF DEVIANT CHILDREN

The schools of a nation are necessarily normative and their avowed object is the education of the majority of children. More and more however, as has been noted earlier, the education given has been adapted to take account of individual differences among children and the consequent variety of needs presented even by an average group. There is however a degree of deviation—in intelligence, in sensory equipment, in physical tolerance or in emotional development—beyond which, with the best will in the world and the most skilful teaching, an ordinary class cannot adapt itself to differences without a grave sacrifice of efficiency and of the interests either of the 'normal' children or of the deviants. The limits of such tolerance will depend partly upon the flexibility of the school or class organization, upon the skill of the teacher, the size of the class and the availability of equipment. For example a highly trained and experienced teacher can so organize the activities of a group of 10 children as to give them a sound education even though their intelligence ranges from the markedly subnormal to near genius, and though several of them have physical or sensory handicaps. On the other hand, one blind child or one child with a severe personality difficulty might either disorganize the work of a class of 30 or 35 pupils or himself be neglected.

Most countries in Europe recognize that there are children for whom classes in the ordinary primary and secondary schools cannot provide efficient education. Hardly anywhere however is adequate provision made for all those who could profit by it; and in many countries, certain groups, with special needs, are not administratively recognized as such, and others receive no education or one not well adapted to them.

Progress has been, and still is, somewhat hampered by a confusion between medical and pseudo-medical classifications based upon symptoms and postulated causes and the kind of educational treatment which is needed by children with particular handicaps or potentialities.

---

1. This chapter is based on the deliberations of Group IV of the Conference.

It is for this reason that a classification based on educational needs is probably the best for children of school age. Here the postwar practice in the United Kingdom may be found to indicate a significant advance. Starting from the concept of the 1944 Education Act that all children have the right to be educated according to their age, ability and aptitude, the Ministry of Education has described as in need of special educational treatment all those children who cannot be educated in the ordinary schools—at least without special arrangements.[1] The education authorities are required by law to discover all such children of school age and to make suitable provision for them. Moreover parents have the right to bring their children, from the age of 2, to the attention of the education authorities, if they believe them to be handicapped in any way and to ask that adequate educational provision be made for them.

Such an arrangement carried fully to its conclusion stresses the variety and complexity of conditions which may make education in the ordinary school unsuitable for a given child. It draws attention to the interrelations of educational, psychological, medical and social factors, and to the need for an adequate examination which covers not merely physical or pseudo-physical factors but the whole child in his potentialities of adaptation, immediately to education and, later, to adult life. Correspondingly too, it should make for greater caution in recommending special measures to be taken, greater flexibility in educational provision, and a more cautious and provisional assignment of children to particular types of special school or class. Moreover, when emphasis is placed upon differentiation of educational needs, then procedures of legal certification—which has frequently come to mean total and irrevocable exclusion from the normal school system and in the eyes of parents and the community a shameful stigma—can be abandoned.

I. THE MENTALLY SUBNORMAL

IDIOTS AND IMBECILES

The most obvious deviation, and one of those earliest provided for, is that of markedly subnormal intelligence. The imbecile, and the idiot,

---

1. *Special Educational Treatment.* Ministry of Education pamphlet no. 5, HMSO, 1946. The categories outlined in this booklet are of course those mentioned in the Education Act of 1921 and the additional ones indicated in the Act of 1944. The Ministry's pamphlet enlarges in detail on what is now established by law.

whose potentiality for mental development is less than half that of the child of average ability, are often detected soon after birth or in the pre-school period. In all, such children amount to about three per thousand of the population, of whom a large proportion are in the true sense 'defective'; that is they are genuinely pathological cases of hereditary or environmentally caused defect. A few suffer from no demonstrable pathological disturbance and are the extreme of the normal curve of development of intelligence. With the exception of conditions caused by thyroid deficiency, little[1] can be done medically or otherwise to raise their level of potential ability. The problem is that of upbringing and education to enable them to make the best use of their very limited capacity. A very small proportion it is true are so feebly en-dowed, or so organically or emotionally disturbed, as to be incapable of forming even the most elementary type of habits, and the best that can be done for them is to provide a humane care to prevent damage to themselves or to others. The majority, however, can, in a very limited way, be taught to feed and clothe themselves under super-vision, to become to a moderate degree socialized, and even to under-take the simplest, most repetitive forms of occupation for the hands. They will never be self-supporting, and even in favourable cases will not surpass the attainment of the average child of 7; most will not learn to read even the simplest words or to make the simplest calcula-tions. Yet, there is evidence to show that many more are trainable than at present are trained. It is regrettable that, in many institutions for such children and adults, medical care and physical supervision are still all that is provided and that little or no skill or time is devoted to the systematic training which could in many cases markedly im-prove their lives.

MODERATELY AND MILDLY SUBNORMAL

Between children such as these and those whose intelligence allows them more or less readily to profit by ordinary schooling, there is an even larger group amounting to 2 or 3 per cent of the population who though capable of progress with specially adapted curricula, constitute a considerable social and educational problem, with which the ordinary teacher is not equipped to deal. For such children, whose intelligence level is between I.Q. 40 to 50[2] and I.Q. 60 to 70, special classes, schools

---

1. Attempts with varying and so far inconclusive results have been made to raise the intelligence of markedly subnormal children by the use of glutamic acid.
2. Below I.Q. 50 such children may be excluded in some countries (e.g. U.K.) from the education system proper and are placed in occupation centres (day care) or in institutions. The implied distinction is highly artificial, and such centres should be regarded as providing education and therefore forming part of the education system.

or institutions have been set up in most European countries.[1] Unfortunately however, by the very provision made for them, these pupils are often completely segregated from other children, sometimes wholly or partly from their parents[2] and even from freely mixing in the community. Equally with the more profoundly subnormal, they are still often labelled mentally *defective*. In by far the majority of cases no demonstrable physical or physiological pathology can be alleged as cause for their intellectual inferiority and in the present state of our knowledge they must be regarded merely as deviating below the average in ability in much the same way as highly able children deviate above the average—that is to say they are *subnormal* and not defective.[3] Such a distinction, though it may seem verbal, has important implications for the handling of such children. The very term 'defect' seems to imply medical treatment; whereas in most cases the main factor in helping such children to develop is a wisely adapted special education for themselves and a sound system of social and psychological help for their families. Such children occasionally are inferior physically and have need of special medical care: a few must of necessity pass much of their time in hospitals or institutions. For all, special educational arrangements should be made, and for most this is best given in schools or classes directly under the control of the education authorities. This is the more important since infrequent cases do occur of children who, apparently innately subnormal, improve in middle or late childhood to the point where a return to the ordinary class is justifiable.

THE DULL-NORMAL

The marked dullness of children whose mental potential is barely or less than two-thirds of the average usually leads to their detection at least before the end of the primary school period; yet there remains a group numerically some four of five times larger, amounting to some

---

1. For example every town, and most of the large villages, in Holland has at least one special school provided by the State for children with I.Q.s under 80. A similar situation exists in the U.K. and Scotland. In the canton of Geneva there are 28 urban and 2 rural special classes. In France, for children between I.Q. 60 and I.Q. 87, there are some 1,300 special day classes, including 150 in the department of the Seine, with a total attendance of about 20,000. One thousand feeble-minded children are catered for in day centres which combine educational or vocational training with medical care. A further 10,000 children are cared for in residential, custodial establishments and psychiatric hospitals, and 7,000 in medico-pedagogic institutions (see also footnote 2 this page).
2. For example, an inquiry reported by the French Centre for Child Welfare to the International Child Welfare Congress at Zagreb, 1954, reports that, of 33 institutions for the mentally subnormal, 7 have no contact with the family. Of 31 medico-pedagogic institutions in the Paris region, 13 permit visits on a fixed day once a month, 10 on a fixed day several times a month, 2 when it suits the families, 1 has 'no rules', and 1 allows visits in certain cases only; 17 allow children to go home during the holidays, 2 on exceptional occasions, 5 regularly but for short stays, 10 for the whole of the school holidays.
3. The 'Sub-Cultural' group of Lewis. See Penrose (op. cit.), p. 45.

TABLE I. Estimated proportions of various grades of mentally subnormal children in the school population[1]

Degree of mental subnormality	Terms in current use	Approximate I.Q. level	Approx. percentage in population of school age
Severe subnormality	Idiot (English, French, American, German usage)	0-19	0.06
Moderate subnormality	Imbecile (English, American) Imbécile profond/léger (French) Imbezill (German)	20-49	0.24
			2.56
Mild subnormality	Feeble-minded (English) Moron (American) Débile profond (French) Debil (German)	50-69	2.26
Dull-Normal	Dull & Backward (English) Peu doué/débile léger (French) Unterbegabt (German)	70-85/90	10[2]

1. The designation adopted here is based upon that accepted by the Joint WHO/Unesco Expert Committee on *The Mentally Subnormal Child (WHO Technical Report Series*, no. 75). Geneva, 1954 (q.v.) with the addition of the dull-normal group.

The figures, as they relate to the first three categories are also taken from that report; but it should be noted that they are based upon those of L. S. Penrose (*The Biology of Mental Defect*. New York, Grune and Stratton, 1949) derived from the findings of the Wood report (*Report of the Mental Deficiency Committee*. 1929, pts. I-IV, HMSO, London), so far as it relates to children in the 10 to 14 age group, where the use of psychometric tests (notably the Binet and its derivatives) is most accurate. The somewhat lower figure arrived at by Burt (*The Subnormal Mind*) is probably nearer the true incidence. Hence the total figure (2.56 per cent), and the I.Q. indications must be regarded as approximations only. Obtained incidences vary according to the criteria adopted and to the effectiveness with which ascertainment of cases is carried out. Estimates from other countries than the U.K. have shown variations—between about 1 per cent and 5 per cent (Penrose, loc. cit., p. 21-2) of subnormality.

Reliance on such scales as the original Binet and its variants in estimating intellectual capacity can be criticized mainly on the grounds of their verbal-educational content. Current practice includes non-verbal scales in the assessment of intelligence. However it can validly be argued that, for children of school age, the verbal-educational content of the Binet derivatives is an essential element in an examination concerned with educability and educational guidance. From the educational viewpoint, it is less sound to give weight to social and emotional factors at this stage (as is often done) and to allow these to determine in borderline cases. The result of such practices, as Penrose has pointed out, is to turn the special school or class into a dumping ground for backward children, not necessarily of truly subnormal intellectual endowment, who because of their emotional difficulties are a nuisance in the ordinary class, and who should benefit from a different provision. This is not to say that social and emotional factors should not be considered. A stable child of relatively low I.Q.—say 68—can with the help of his parents and teacher hold his own in a class for the dull and backward; whereas an unstable one with an I.Q. of say 75 or 78 might be better off in a special school. Placement in all borderline cases should be made on the basis of a careful case study and in terms of a knowledge of the school proposed rather than of rigid classifications by any kind of criteria. If differentiation of provision is to achieve its end, it must be matched by careful appraisal of the educable capacity of the child and of the circumstances which will best bring it forth.

2. The figure given here is that arrived at by Burt as the result of his work in London and Birmingham between the wars (C. Burt, *The Subnormal Mind*. 2nd ed. University of London Press, London, 1937). Burt points out that in rural areas the figure is nearer to 20 per cent. The proportion of 10 per cent given here therefore must be regarded as conservative. The over-all figure is probably nearer 12 to 15 per cent.

10 or 15 per cent of the school population, for whom few European countries make any adequate special provision, and which contains those whose intelligence quotients range between 65 to 75 and 85 to 90 and whose dullness, in the early stages at least, is only apparent when they are carefully observed. Such children frequently pass undetected throughout the whole compulsory schooling period. They are slower to develop in almost everything; they may learn to read later than the average, or acquire only the more mechanical aspects of reading, lagging markedly behind in comprehension; they experience especial difficulty in problem arithmetic; the acquisition of social habits, particularly where these involve foresight of consequences, is slower and more difficult for them. As they go through school, even if they live up to their limited intelligence (which in point of fact few of them do), they tend to become more and more backward compared with others of their own age. For such children, education which makes no allowance for their more limited ability, particularly in a school which has a system of annual promotion by attainment[1] tends to be a period of continued failure, often of repeated punishment, of effort made without success and, rather sooner than later, abandoned as useless, of disappointment to themselves and of reproach from their teachers and parents. It is not surprising that there should be among such pupils many who develop behaviour and personality problems, who become aggressive and delinquent. Nor is it strange that in after life many of them are semi- or totally illiterate, unstable and even criminal or that they swell the ranks of the unemployed and unemployable, becoming a costly social liability instead of contributing, as they well can, to society and leading lives adjusted to their capacities.

THE HETEROGENEITY OF THE SUBNORMAL GROUP

It must not be assumed that these categories are anything but arbitrary, or that the lines of demarcation between them can be accurately determined either in terms of intelligence quotient or of any other criteria, educational, social or medical. In practice at each of the borderlines there are many children who should be assigned to one or the other category more in terms of the availability and flexibility of the provision made, than according to a fixed criterion. Practically indeed it seems that for children of school age the appropriate principle of guidance is that of suitability for different forms of educational provision; and, correspondingly, the provision of a considerable variety of types of class, school and method to meet the great individual

---

1. Promotion by age may, in a different way, be equally unfortunate. It means that the dull child has no time to learn at his own pace and is put into a new class to tackle new work before he has time to consolidate the old.

differences which lie behind the figures of the textbooks and statistical studies.

These differences are particularly marked among those usually called the high-grade mentally defective and the dull and backward. A closer examination of such groups of children when they are found in special schools and classes reveals that some are not, in the intellectual sense, dull at all.[1] There one may find children with more or less severe degrees of emotional disturbance who, because of their difficulties, are unable to concentrate, or are turned in upon themselves, unwilling or unable to speak, and who are severely retarded in their academic and social development. Others, perhaps because of early prolonged deprivation of emotional and intellectual stimulus, have not developed their capacities more than to a limited extent. Yet others, because of a marked instability or because of an abnormal lethargy, are unable to achieve more than a fraction of what their endowment should enable them to achieve. Where adequate psychological examinations have not been carried out, a large group will be found to be merely educationally backward, often as the accumulated result of periodic absences from school. There will be those who have specific cognitive difficulties—difficulties for example in the visual organization of space or in the auditory analysis of sound—which effectively prevent learning to read by conventional methods; others have a marked lack of development of cerebral dominance; or speech, visual or auditory defects[2] of a kind which escape all but the most competent physical or neurological diagnosis and which slow up or even prevent learning. A proportion because of cerebral damage at or before birth present the appearance of low-grade defect; have severe motor disturbance, spasticity or athetosis and many associated troubles, but yet have an intellectual capacity markedly above the average.[3] In a few cases, where highly specific difficulties in reading or in arithmetic exist

---

1. 'Special schools for mental defectives, instead of being training places for the intellectually backward, have tended to become dumping grounds for especially troublesome backward children together with those who are so obviously uneducable that their parents cannot reasonably object to their being removed from the ordinary classes.'—Penrose, op. cit. p., 19. (See footnote 1, p. 215).

2. High tone deafness, undetectable by the somewhat gross methods of diagnosing hearing loss in general use, may hinder or effectively prevent the development of intelligible speech. Such children are being more readily detected now by the use of pure tone audiometers, but cases are all too frequently still found of intelligent children labouring along among the dull or even markedly subnormal, consigned there on a superficial diagnosis which failed to detect high frequency loss. The testing of the special senses by the various psycho-physical methods now available is a skilled process requiring, with children at all events, a sound training in child psychology as well as a knowledge of physiology and of the instruments used.

3. A certain amount of significant research suggests that some disturbances of the visual field, of attention, of the finger and body schema, of apperception of sound sequences, of patterns, of rapid figure-ground discrimination during tachistoscopic presentation, of the ability to sort according either to logical or formal elements, etc., which are found either generally or selectively among groups with identifiable cortical damage, can also be shown to exist in children without

and hamper cumulatively general educational progress, one may suspect the existence of cerebral lesions undetectable as yet by neurological examination.

It is this variety of capacity and of difficulty that makes imperative a careful examination of any child thought to be subnormal. His life history, and particularly that of his speech and motor development, his social circumstances and family background must be studied; a careful series of physical, neurological and endocrinological tests may have to be made; and certainly a thorough psychological examination must be carried out before any attempt is made to forecast the child's future potentialities and consequently to decide upon a suitable education for him. It is only on such a basis—which implies close team work among psychologist, social worker, medical specialist and, for children of school age, the teacher—that a real appraisal of potentialities and handicaps can be made, and the vital distinction be drawn between subnormalities which are unalterable and those which may be improved by the appropriate remedial action. Moreover any decision taken should be provisional, and throughout the school period at all events be subject to periodic and unprejudiced review.

Similarity of causal type of subnormality or similarity of present level of intellectual functioning, however, do not necessarily imply similarity of educational treatment; and in this respect psychiatric labels and intelligence quotients have been misleading, especially when they have become the basis of rigid administrative or legal classifications. The very complexity of handicapping conditions, the very differences in each child's circumstances, in his prospects of development, and the uncertainty of prediction of the interplay of temperamental and social factors with intellectual ability, should lead both to discriminating psychological examination and to a rich variety of educational provision, to facility of interchange between one special class or school and another and, where the occasion arises as it does commonly in the borderline cases of mild subnormality, from special class to the ordinary school.

---

any demonstrable neurological damage but who do present specific learning difficulties in arithmetic and reading. See: L. Bender, *Visuo-Motor Gestalt Test* (*Research Monograph* no. 3). New York, American Orthopsychiatric Association, 1938; E. A. Doll, W. M. Phelps and Melcher, *Mental Deficiency Due to Birth Injuries*. New York, Macmillan, 1932; E. Lord and L. Wood, 'Diagnostic Values in a Visuo-Motor Test', *Am. Journ. Orthopsychiatry* 1942; K. Goldstein and M. Scheerer, *Abstract and Concrete Behaviour* (*Psych. Monographs* vol. 53, no. 2), 1941; B. S. Kendall, 'A Note on the Relation of Retardation in Reading to Performance on a Memory for Designs Test', *J. Ed. Psych.* vol. 39, no. 6, 1948; A. A. Strauss and L. E. Lechtinen, *Psychopathology and Education of the Brain Injured Child*. New York, Grune and Stratton, 1950; A. A. Strauss and H. Werner, 'The Mental Organization of the Brain Injured Mentally Defective Child', *Am. Journ. Psychiatry* vol. 97, 1941; Dissertations by C. Monks and B. Ash, University of Birmingham Library, 1951.

EDUCATIONAL PROVISION

Most subnormal children will as adults live in the community. Hence, while they should not be put in competition with their abler contemporaries during their schooldays, neither should they be segregated from them unless it is absolutely essential. Certain very low-grade defectives are probably best housed in institutions, but before this step is taken a most careful exploration should be made of the possibilities of keeping the child in his own home under the affectionate care of his mother, at least during the first part of his childhood.[1] It is frequently not realized that where adequate social and economic assistance is available, this is not only sounder psychologically but cheaper in practice. In large towns the provision of small day-care centres grouping some 30 to 50 such children gives a respite to the family and provides for the child, under the skilled guidance of adequately trained teachers[2] a social training as well as means of occupation. Even the dullest child is susceptible to affection and individual care; no institution can provide the same continuity of emotional stimulus as is provided even by a moderately successful home; and there is little doubt that the care and affection of a mother provide the background for a genuine if circumscribed education for all but dangerously violent cases or the completely incapable idiots. What is important is that the family, and especially the mother, should be helped in what is after all a difficult and exacting task.

Those children who, while not deeply defective, cannot receive anything approaching a normal education—that is to say a few of the moderately and most of the mildly subnormal—are at present usually placed in day special schools. But it seems probable that at least for the relatively high grade and emotionally stable pupils among the mildly subnormal and certainly for the dull, the happiest solution is the special class attached to the ordinary school, provided it can be so handled that the needs of the subnormal neither unduly interfere with the smooth running of the rest of the school nor are unduly sacrificed to it. In this way some of the social stigma of subnormality may be avoided and subnormal and normal children can be brought into close and understanding contact instead of being segregated. It has the further advantage of allowing easily those members of the teaching

---

1. As is done in Holland, where only 6 per cent of children under I.Q. 80 are in residential institutions, and these only the low-grade or seriously complicated cases—and even many of these are placed with foster-parents near to the institution caring for them. The imbeciles normally attend either specialized day schools, or special classes attached to day schools for the less severely subnormal. (Report to Child Welfare Congress, Zagreb, 1954. Dutch Union for Maternity and Child Health and Dutch Union for Child Welfare.)
2. In some countries, centres of the type are provided not by the education, but the health authorities; and the staff consequently do not form part of the education service, having different (and unfortunately usually inferior) training, status and salary. Such centres exist for example in the U.K. and France.

219

staff specialized for the education of the subnormal to maintain a contact with the needs and capacities of normal pupils, as is being done with great success in many of the *classes de perfectionnement annexées aux écoles primaires et écoles autonomes de perfectionnement* in France and in a number of places, such as the city of Leicester, in the United Kingdom.

Many subnormal children, however, have associated difficulties and handicaps; frequently they cannot conform to the rhythm of the normal school day, need special physical treatment, speech training, psychological help and the like; some are markedly unstable and require constant supervision; others live in remote rural districts and cannot therefore attend day classes. For these, boarding accommodation is necessary in schools which have not only a qualified educational staff but sufficient domestic and auxiliary staff to assure a genuinely personal and homelike care. Where boarding schools are set up it is as well—both for the sake of the staff and of the children—to situate them near enough to a real community, a small town or village, so that they may live in contact with normal life and not become isolated. So too the school should make every effort to keep in close touch with the child's family, and as far as is practicable the child should return home for holidays.

THE EDUCATION OF THE DULL-NORMAL AND MILDLY SUBNORMAL

As can be seen from Table I (page 215) mentally subnormal children of all groups amount to about 2½ per cent of the population of school age. Few European countries as yet have made provision for the whole of this group, and most have special schools or classes for little more than half of those who need it. The dull-normal, who are four or five times as numerous [1] as the subnormal, are scarcely anywhere recognized as a considerable group for whom modification of the customary standards is necessary [2] and, where some more or less adequate provision is made, only too often no distinction is drawn between them and

1. In a country with a population of some 40 to 50 millions one would expect at least half a million of such children between the ages of 7 and 14.

2. In the United Kingdom all children whose educational attainment is less than 80 per cent of that to be expected of the average child of the same chronological age are considered to be 'educationally subnormal' and to need special educational provision. In the larger towns some 1 to 2 per cent of provision is made in special schools for the moderately and mildly subnormal; and in those primary and secondary modern schools where numbers permit, special classes are formed for the dull and backward. There are in addition in some towns special opportunity classes for children failing for reasons other than lack of intelligence. In Geneva, in addition to the schools or classes for the subnormal mentioned earlier (p. 214, note 1), similar provision in special classes of about twenty pupils is made for those children who have difficulty in following the normal programme. The experiment was also tried of a special class of children handicapped by speaking a foreign language or by periods of absence from school through illness. In some Dutch towns, State special schools have been started for those who, while not markedly or even mildly intellectually subnormal, have educational difficulties.

those whose relative educational failure is due to causes other than innately inferior educable capacity.

Dull children are not likely to attain the same standards as their better endowed contemporaries, and their rate of educational progress, even under favourable conditions, will be markedly slower. Attempts to force them to keep pace with the average meet with no success and result either in destroying completely their educational and personal morale, or in a range of more or less overtly aggressive attitudes which may lead to delinquency. When however such children are, from the earliest moment, put into the charge of a sympathetic teacher who understands both their limitations of learning capacity and the techniques essential to enable them to progress socially and educationally, all but those who have additional difficulties can be educated to become self-supporting and self-respecting citizens and to live well adjusted and satisfying lives.

The subnormal and the dull however have special needs, and make special demands upon the teacher's skill. Their most marked and general disability is in the verbal field and in all those operations which require abstract reasoning. Hence, in varying degrees according to an accurate assessment of their potentialities and to a continued and well informed study of their progress, the curriculum should be based upon concrete realizations, practical work, the development of manual skills, and upon increasing social independence. In the absence of specific disabilities, all the dull and most of the mildly subnormal can learn to read sufficiently to make limited use of notices, newspapers and even of simple books. The giving and receiving of change, the management of a family budget, calculations of wages, simple additions and subtractions of money, elementary calculations of space and volume such as are required in some semi-skilled and unskilled jobs are within the range of all but the least able[1] if they are taught concretely, slowly and with plenty of well motivated practice, in situations as near to those of real life as possible. While many if not most of such children, whether as adolescents or adults, are unlikely to grasp the abstract conceptions or to form the generalized moral notions which lie behind discriminating ethical or social behaviour, it is certainly possible to build up in them notions of right and wrong, of duty and of citizenship.

It should perhaps be emphasized that the curriculum and methods appropriate to the dull, and still more to the subnormal, are not to be regarded either as narrowly vocational or as a diluted version of the programme for average or superior children. A precocious vocational training—which is still considered appropriate for the mildly subnormal or the dull—neglects both the child's over-all needs and the

---

1. Few of those with I.Q.s below 60 can do much more than read simple sentences and undertake purely repetitive tasks.

facts of industrial employment. A subnormal or dull child who is taught a trade and nothing else may become proficient in the mechanical aspects but unable to adapt himself to change; with a variation in organization or machinery he finds himself unemployable without a further lengthy period of re-training. Indeed, for the subnormal, and probably for the dull, the period of general education, and consequently of wise and informed supervision, needs to be extended for at least one and preferably for two years beyond the normal termination of compulsory schooling. In this way such children can be helped over the early crises of adolescence before they have to fend for themselves; the extended period of schooling allows for their slower rate of learning and assimilation. Moreover many of the subnormal and all the dull are capable of enjoying many of the more purely cultural aspects of their education, music, art, dancing, acting, for example, as well as of receiving a training which enables them to satisfy creative urges through concrete expression in wood, metal, leather and the like. Similarly, even the mildly subnormal can grasp elementary notions of civic and political responsibility, can come to know their duties and rights as citizens and can be taught how to use the social and administrative machinery of their community, which exists to help and protect them. Only when such children have truly been educated as far as possible for the life which they will have to live as individual human beings is it legitimate to concentrate upon a purely vocational training; and even this should be much more than the inculcation of useful skills. Such children need skilled vocational guidance to make the best use of their capacities and a continued friendly supervision to integrate them into a working life which is stable and satisfying, and protected from exploitation or corruption.

The needs of the dull and the subnormal cannot adequately be met if they are educated in large groups. For the dull and the best of the mildly subnormal the maximum is 20 children with one specially trained teacher; and even then the success of the group depends upon a careful selection of the children so that they are relatively stable emotionally and free from complicating difficulties. For those whose level of intelligence is lower, that is for most of the mildly subnormal, or those whose subnormality is complicated by physical handicaps, by emotional disturbance or by specific psycho-physical defects, the class should be smaller, the methods more individualized, and the contact between teacher and pupil even closer and more continuous. The programme should be so arranged that the teacher has the time and the energy to come intimately to understand each pupil, and, preferably, he or she should remain with the group for considerably more than a year, taking within his province not merely their education in the narrow sense of intellectual and physical skills but their whole social development.

Such an education in small groups however should not entail continuous segregation from other children. Many of the activities of the school week are such that all children can join them; singing, music, much art and craft work, physical education and games, religious services, and the general social occasions in which a healthy school life abounds, all provide opportunities for the dull or mentally subnormal child to mix on terms of relative[1] equality with his comrades. Such a mixing, as well as minimizing any sense of inferiority, and even providing occasions when the dull child can outdo the abler, has an ulterior purpose. The mental health of the dull or subnormal adult depends in large measure on his ability to accept others and be accepted by them. Where a school places an accent upon differences between individuals without labelling them inferiorities or superiorities, and without either rejecting the dull or sentimentalizing over them, there is a good chance that most of its pupils will learn to draw the essential distinction between the value of a human being *per se*, and the variety of capacities which makes human groups unequal in their responsibilities and needs.

II. THE PHYSICALLY HANDICAPPED AND DELICATE[2]

HANDICAP AND GENERAL PSYCHOLOGICAL DEVELOPMENT

Children with physical handicaps, of greater or lesser severity, present educational and mental health problems of a different order from those of the mentally subnormal. Whilst of course physical handicap may be

---

1. The equality is certainly relative. Many dull and most even of the best mildly subnormal children are conspicuous for their want of muscular co-ordination and their slowness of reaction. It is, too, a fallacy to assume that duller children exceed the brighter in handwork. Where however the school staff are skilful in their handling both of the dull and of the normal children in the school, they can arrange occasions in which the special class can join in with the others or even 'show off' a carefully prepared superiority.

2. Here are included all those children whose physical handicap—crippling, rheumatism, diabetes, heart disease, tuberculosis, delicacy of constitution, etc., does not directly and necessarily affect their intellectual capacity or their psychological growth. It is well established however that among the subnormal in intelligence there is a higher proportion of children with various forms of physical handicap or constitutional inferiority than in better endowed groups and that conversely, among those who are handicapped or subnormal physically, while the whole range of intelligence is represented, there are more dull and mentally retarded children. Moreover one finds often severe emotional disturbances in such children, some, if not most, of which are probably secondary consequences of their handicap; but there are probably many more cases than is usually supposed—especially among diabetic, asthmatic, delicate and pathologically obese children—where the psychological disturbance and the physical disability are intimately interconnected and should be regarded as a psychosomatic syndrome. Little scientifically valid research exists as yet in the field of the psychology of the physically handicapped; but there is little doubt that, had we more exact knowledge, the whole education, upbringing and medical treatment of such children could be markedly improved.

associated with mental subnormality—and in certain types of case is frequently so—the majority of crippled and of delicate children are, in the purely intellectual sense, normal in their potentialities. Their physical conditions however may involve physiotherapy or other forms of remedial medical treatment, restrict or prohibit mobility, subject them to a régime or in some other way interrupt or make difficult their education in the ordinary school or class.

The obvious practical handicaps imposed by general delicateness of constitution or by a physical disability must not, however, lead us to neglect the more subtle and ultimately more important repercussions of the defect upon the child's whole psychological development. The importance of walking for emotional and intellectual development in the second year has only to be recalled to see that a crippled child dependent upon others for mobility may lose a vital stimulus to growth. Later, as he becomes aware of difference from others, and as progressively he lacks the confirmation of security that the ordinary child gains from physical achievement, his personality development may begin to deviate. Obscurely he may come to feel that his handicap is a punishment and develop a feeling of guilt; or he may become by turns aggressive against his environment or fearful of it in a vague, anxious way. Unless special arrangements are made for him, his schooling is likely to suffer from his inability to support the fatigue of a normal school day, from the interference of medical treatment, or from many short absences. Because of the attitudes of their parents, of other adults and even of their teachers, many physically handicapped or delicate children find refuge in their disability and use it as an excuse to avoid efforts which they can well perform. Thus, among the handicapped, one finds not a few who exploit their condition to reduce a parent or relative to a state of slavery, and who become parasitic on a community to which, with different handling, they could have made a contribution.

A POSITIVE APPROACH

The essential emphasis in the upbringing and education of the handicapped and delicate is upon what they *can* do; and upon providing them with the experience and stimulus to growth of which their condition would otherwise deprive them. Thus though the child who cannot walk, run and jump may be deprived both of the widening range of experience and of the praise which physical acquirements bring to the young, his life can be organized by an intelligent mother to give him similar experience and similar stimulus. Many such children in their young days undergo physical pain, or have to lie for long periods immobile staring at the ceiling or are taken off to hospital

and separated from their mothers. Clearly, for the efficient administration of medical treatment it is easier if the child can be handled as
if he were a physical organism without psychological reactions. In the
long run however, it may be better, for example, to delay an operation
until the child is able to support absence from his mother, or to submit
to the inconvenience of doing it at home rather than to straighten a
limb at the expense of severe psychological damage. Similarly, a child
should always be prepared for the experience of pain, be reassured that
it means neither punishment nor aggression; and where, as sometimes
happens, his movement has to be restricted almost completely, steps
should be taken to reduce to a minimum the emptiness of the hours,
and to see that as far as possible he has enriched opportunities later to
make up development. Moreover the limitations imposed by physical
treatment should be carefully examined in terms of their psychological
effect upon the child, and upon the attitudes of his family. It will often
be found that their rigour can be mitigated when understanding and
ingenuity are used, and that there are many ways in which handicapped children and their parents can be brought to concentrate upon
what can be achieved rather than upon the limitations imposed by
disability.

GUIDANCE AND EDUCATION

The psychological guidance of a physically handicapped child and of
his family is a delicate and skilled business. Medical skill has a major
contribution to make, but by no means the sole one; the future of the
child depends upon his achievement of personal, social, educational
and vocational adjustment at the highest possible level, and throughout
his growth he and his parents need well informed and sympathetic
help. This can only be given by those who, made aware of the inexorable limits imposed by the handicap, are equipped by their training to consider the child as a whole person with needs of the same order
as those of normal children and which, without risking permanent
psychological damage, cannot be long denied. The family caseworker,
the educational expert, and the psychologist have a contribution to
make, not only to the initial examination, but to the continuing supervision of such children. Indeed as the critical early phase of physical
treatment passes, it is the psychologist and the educator who should
accept the principal responsibility.

Convenience of medical and para-medical treatment and the heterogeneous nature of the difficulties of handicapped and delicate children,
have led to many of them being sent to special schools and to a prepond-
erance, at least for the severely handicapped, of hospital or boarding
school provision. In many cases this is unavoidable; but the grave

disadvantages for the child himself should not be overlooked. A boarding school tends to cut him off for considerable periods from his family; and by the very grouping of many handicapped children, isolates them from the community. Such children are likely to be fairly representative of the whole range of educational ability and of age, found in an ordinary school population; a group of some sixty or a hundred of them will thus have a variety of special needs for which, in spite of smaller classes, the special school cannot adequately provide. The tradition that all or most of such children need an education with a predominantly manual or vocational content dies hard, yet among them are a proportion for whom a more academic and intellectual education is a necessity and who can, properly handled, later enter professions for which their disability constitutes no particular handicap. Once again therefore it is necessary to emphasize that the decision to segregate a physically handicapped child from his normal fellows and from his family is not to be lightly taken and certainly not upon grounds of administrative convenience. Much more could and should be done to integrate such children into ordinary schools and classes and, where this is not possible, to bring the special school or class into a close functional relationship with the ordinary educational system of the district.

THE CEREBRALLY PALSIED CHILD

One group of the physically handicapped has recently come to be recognized as posing a special series of psychological and educational problems. A number of children as the result of intra-uterine degenerative and toxic factors, natal cerebral haemorrhage, asphyxia and the like, suffer cerebral lesions affecting the central nervous system. They frequently present the appearance both of deep mental defect and of severe physical handicap. Recent surveys[1] suggest that the incidence of all types of cerebral palsy in the United Kindgom is about one per thousand children from 0 to 16; and that, of these, the principal types are spastic[2] (about 80 per cent), the athetoid[3] (10 per cent), and those showing ataxias, tremors, rigidities and mixed symptoms (about 10 per cent).

1. P. Asher and F. E. Schonell, 'A Survey of 400 Cases of Cerebral Palsy in Childhood', *Arch. Dis. Child.* vol. 25, 1950; M. I. Dunsdon, *The Educability of the Cerebrally Palsied Child.* London, National Foundation for Educational Research, 1952.
2. A condition in which 'knife clasp' rigidity of muscles results in characteristic stiffness of movement and contractures producing deformity or in some cases an abnormal flaccidity of muscles. According to the number of limbs affected, the condition is called monoplegia, hemiplegia, quadriplegia and (where only the legs are affected) paraplegia. Other terms are used, but these seem to be becoming standard English and American practice.
3. These characteristically show uncontrolled writhing movements, particularly of the limbs, but often of facial and tongue muscles.

Any or all the motor functions are likely to be affected in a greater or lesser degree, some cases showing rigidity, flaccidity or athetosis of all four limbs, some of those on one side only. Many, especially among the athetoids, have difficulties in the innervation of the vocal organs such that they cannot learn, unaided, to speak; others have specific defects of hearing or vision. In the past many such children have been treated as idiots or imbeciles and have, for want of adequate physical and educational treatment, become hopelessly bedridden or institutionalized.

A more careful examination of the group reveals however that, while the cerebral lesions or arrested development in many cases affect intellectual development, and while rather more than half of all cerebrally palsied children are either mildly, moderately or severely subnormal, there exists a considerable group which, under favourable conditions, can be educated and for whom, by patient physiotherapy, speech therapy and other forms of physical treatment, very much can be done. Nor is the hopefulness of a case educationally solely limited by the degree of crippling. The assessment of the child's future prospects is complicated and must be based upon a full knowledge of the physical and social condition of the child, upon an estimate as accurate as possible of the mental level, and upon a careful qualitative analysis of intellectual functioning.[1] For no other group is the need for close understanding and team work between psychologist, specialized teacher, orthopaedic specialist, physiotherapist and speech therapist so clear— not only at the stage of initial examination, but continuously throughout childhood. The demands of physical, educational and psychological handling often compete; for example, it may be necessary for the progress of the physiotherapy that the child should be prevented from using his hand in a particular way although this movement is almost his sole means of communication for educational purposes; or it may be that some exhausting treatment is recommended just as the child has begun to master reading; or that physiotherapy or speech therapy are failing because of a psychological discontinuity or temperamental difficulty in the child himself which can only be detected and explained by the psychologist. In all such situations—and they abound in the education and training of the cerebrally palsied child—a decision must be arrived at in terms of the whole development and needs of the child and not in terms solely or predominantly of one speciality.

---

1. The assessment of the educability of a cerebrally palsied child calls for great skill and experience from the psychologist and at present we have no tests which are suitably adapted for use with children who often can indicate no more than a positive or negative response. The author remembers or e child of eight who could make practically no movement except with the toes of his left foot and with his eyes. Nevertheless, in a supine position he attempted and solved a series of performance tests at a level little below that to be expected of the average child of his own age. Another child, unable to speak or move his limbs, for over three hours, ingeniously using his forehead and nose, struggled successfully through certain tests of the Terman-Merrill and Weschler Bellevue scales and a series of supplementary performance tests, securing an (estimated) I.Q. of 140.

Attempts to educate such children are relatively recent, relatively few and, owing to the need of equipment, staff and accommodation, expensive. In the United Kingdom, some eight centres exist where education and physical treatment are combined and where children who are fairly certain to profit by the expensive and complex services given, are admitted. The most successful are special day schools[1] to which children from a wide geographical area are brought by car and ambulance and where the facilities for education and for physical treatment are centralized. Such day provision has the great advantage that direct and continuous contact is maintained with the home, and, by participating actively in the life of the school, the mothers and fathers are brought into partnership and can continue at home certain of the physical and educational activities necessary to their child's progress.[2]

CHILDREN WITH SENSORY HANDICAPS

In contrast with the relative novelty of provision for cerebrally palsied children, special education and training for blind children and for deaf children has a considerable history in Europe covering more than two centuries.[3] The handicap of blindness is obvious to the layman as is to a lesser extent the handicap of deafness and gross cases of either are usually detected at an early age. It is however only comparatively

---

1. For example The Carlson House School, Victoria Road, Harborne, Birmingham. Similar initiatives exist in Australia, and in the United States, where attention has been concentrated on the problem particularly since the success of Dr. Carlson, himself a spastic. It should be pointed out that there is no direct correlation between the extent of physical or sensory impairment and level of intelligence. Some very defective children have little physical involvement; some of the most highly intelligent are severe athetoids. A considerable proportion are so little handicapped physically or mentally that, with some degree of medical and psychological supervision, they can profitably attend ordinary or special schools with other children.

2. Much of the stimulus to provide education for cerebrally palsied children in England has come from a voluntary federation of parents and others interested in the problem—The British Association for the Welfare of Spastics—which publishes a journal and encourages medical, social, psychological and educational research.

3. Preoccupation with the care and protection of the blind and of the blinded is of course much older, and many occupations (begging, professional mourning, soothsaying, handmill grinding, music, etc.) were entirely or partially reserved for them in some countries of the ancient world. Many of the blind made efforts, not only to acquire culture themselves, but to educate fellow-sufferers, e.g. Didymas of Alexandria (fourth century) who taught with a carved wooden alphabet. The first school for the blind seems to have been established by Haüy (1745-1822) in France and was followed by that founded in Liverpool (U.K.) in 1790. Developments elsewhere in Europe followed within two decades. The education of the deaf preceded that of the blind by several centuries. It seems to be agreed that the first great teacher of the deaf was the Spanish Benedictine monk, Pedro Ponce de Leon (1520-84), and it was two Spaniards (Bolet of Madrid and Ramires de Carrion) who in the seventeenth century published the earliest textbooks on the education of the deaf. From Spain the inspiration came (through Kenelm Digby) to England and (through Jacob Pereire) to France. Towards the end of the eighteenth century, schools of considerable size were established in France (Abbé de l'Epée), Germany (Samuel Heinicke), and Britain (Thomas Braidwood). See: M. E. Frampton and H. G. Rowell (editors), *The Education of the Handicapped*. London, Harrap & Co., 1939, vol. 1.

recently that increasing knowledge of child development and specific research into the psychological problems posed by these handicaps have begun to lead in educational practice to an effective embodiment of the concept that a deaf or a blind child is first and foremost a *child*, whose normal development, prejudiced by sensory defect, must be ensured by educational means in the widest sense. That is to say that the currently accepted aim of education for the sensorially handicapped is to educate them to take their place as normally as possible, in the sighted and hearing world rather than to allow them to find their place solely in a closed and self-contained community of those similarly affected.

The psychology of the congenitally blind or deaf,[1] and, to an extent dependent upon the age at which they become so, of those who become blind or deaf, is essentially one of frustration and of deprivation, of the reaction of psychologically normal children to an environment made abnormal for them by their handicap. Hence, well informed handling in infancy and in the pre-school period, and an education based upon the attempt to capitalize the child's resources and to find substitutes for the experiences of which he is deprived, will enable him very largely to develop a healthy and well adjusted personality.[2] It would be foolish to contend that the blind or deaf child can become an adult who is socially, intellectually and economically as efficient as he could have been without his handicap; but a wise education can make the difference between a wholly or partially dependent, more or less maladjusted individual and one who is a happy and effective human being within the limits similar to those imposed on all of us by our temperamental and intellectual endowment.

Until comparatively recently, little attention has been given to the importance to the subsequent development of the handicapped child of the pre-school period; and consequently, of the guidance and help which should be given to his parents from the earliest possible moment. Without discriminating help the blind child is likely to suffer in a number of ways. His blindness prevents him from those social experiences—smiles, games of 'peep-bo' and the like—which supplement and subsequently take the place of physical handling as assurances of maternal love and as stimuli to development. He lacks the seeing element in the gestalt of visual-auditory-kinaesthetic associations which come from his exploration of his own body and of objects in his environment, and from play with adults and his own brothers and

---

1. Definitions of 'total' blindness and of 'total' deafness vary from country to country and tend to differ according to whether one is concerned with educating the child, applying some form of disability allowance or placing him in employment.

2. For a fuller treatment of this topic see: W. D. Wall, 'The Psychology of the Handicapped Child in Relation to his Family', *Child Welfare in Relation to the Family*. Geneva ,International Union fo r Child Welfare, 1955, p. 65-79.

sisters. His range of experience of objects upon which his early conceptualization, speech and intellectual development in part depend, is limited to those which come within the grasp of his hands. So too attitudes in his parents of over-protectiveness, excessive sympathy, covert or overt rejection, or even simple neglect, may early operate to colour his whole conception of himself and of society. Uninstructed, the parents are not likely to appreciate or compensate for these and similar cumulative psychological effects of blindness. It is small wonder that by school age, many blind children seem to be retarded in their mental and personal development, are often markedly insecure, and frequently have developed a number of mannerisms and stereotyped movements, some at least of which are strikingly similar to those exhibited by children early deprived of maternal care.

A child who is deaf may lack stimulus, intellectually and socially, in an even more serious way. Up to the end of the first year of life touch and vision are probably primary to general development; thereafter and, certainly from 18 months onwards, hearing and speech begin to play an increasingly important part in the organization of the intellectual, social and emotional life. The child who cannot hear the speech of others, and cannot hear the sounds he himself makes, does not learn to speak and may become mute. Lacking words, his conceptual growth is inhibited, delayed or turned awry; and his early social contacts are limited to the visual and tactile fields. Such children often appear to be dull or even markedly subnormal; and are treated accordingly. To the negativism, which is a normal phase of the two- to three-year-old, they may add a fiercely aggressive reaction to their frustrations and become tiresome problems. As in the case of the blind, the attitudes of parents and other adults, of older brothers and sisters, play a large—and often seriously adverse—part in the deaf child's personal development.

It sometimes happens, with the blind and with the deaf, that their early development is complicated by associated physical disabilities or by the psychological consequences of prolonged or painful medical treatment. Others, because of their need for special care, because of the inadequacy of their homes or through the death or illness of their mother, pass into institutions of one kind or another. Unless careful steps are taken to minimize the impact of such further interventions on the child's already difficult growth task, the results may well be so far-reaching as to be irreversible by subsequent educational or psychological handling.

Space does not permit a full treatment of the education of severely sensorially handicapped children, and the foregoing somewhat cursory and superficial analysis of the problems of the pre-school period has been made to draw attention to what is probably at present the most neglected aspect in work for such children. Most European countries have well developed schools and tried methods of teaching the blind and the deaf; ard in the last half-century there has been a growing amount of research and practical experiment directed to the improvement of educational methods in this highly complex field, to a greater stress upon the general social and emotional training of such children, and to the training of specialized teachers aware of all the problems involved. Yet it remains true to say that for want of the kind of help which parents need in aiding the development of their handicapped children, and for want of special nursery school provision for children from the ages of 2 or 3, much of the effort later put forth by the schools is frustrated. The work of the Ewings at Manchester for example has clearly demonstrated that under expert guidance parents can help their deaf children to begin to speak and to comprehend speech through lip-reading from before the age of 2,[1] and that children thus taught come to school, later, markedly advanced in their mental, social and linguistic development as compared with other deaf children. Similar research and controlled practical experiment are needed to improve the family education of the young blind child who is too often either left to the care of an uninstructed mother or prematurely removed to a residential nursery.[2]

In many if not most European countries, while the amount[3] of provision for blind and for deaf children of school age is relatively sufficient, the problems of partially sighted and hard-of-hearing children have not fully been met. The difficulties experienced by such children, especially in the early stages of education, may pass undetected or, when severe enough to attract attention, lead to their being grouped with the blind or the deaf. The best current practice indicates that teachers should be trained to detect and bring forward for specialized examination likely cases of visual defect and auditory loss, that periodic screenings of the school population should be made, and that, partly through special classes, partly through the use of sight-saving apparatus or hearing aids, and partly through the adaptation of methods in ordinary classes, most of such children can be helped. Again however, the emphasis must be placed on early detection and upon continued, specialized, psychological, educational and medical guidance for the child's family and for the school which receives him.

1. I. R. Ewing and A. W. G. Ewing, *Opportunity and the Deaf Child*. London, University of London Press, 1947; *The Handicap of Deafness*. London, 1938; *Speech and the Deaf Child*. Manchester, Manchester University Press, 1954.
2. Descriptions of techniques of parent guidance will be found in J. H. Levy, 'A Study of Parent Groups for Handicapped Children', *Exceptional Child*. 1952 vol. 19, pt. 1.
3. No one would suggest that the conception and quality of the education given is as high anywhere as it could be or that the quantity of research devoted to the educational and psychological problems of this group is sufficient. Indeed the psychology and education particularly of the blind child is one of the most neglected fields of research in the whole range of education.

CHILDREN WITH SPEECH DEFECTS

Apart from those children whose speech difficulties are associated with auditory defect or deafness or arise from various forms of cerebral palsy, including the genuinely aphasic, a few children from a miscellany of organic causes,[1] and many more, for psychological reasons, exhibit symptoms of speech disturbance—lisping, lalling, stuttering, rhinolalia, idioglossia, mutism and the like. Speech is an essential intellectual and social instrument; and it is deeply and intricately connected with the whole emotional life. Thus even though in rare cases a speech defect may have a purely organic origin, it very quickly acquires psychological meaning for the child and for his milieu and may, if neglected, become the crystallizing point of a profound personality disturbance, as well as an educational handicap of the first magnitude. Speech defects, notably stammering and stuttering, lisping and some forms of mutism, are however in most cases not organic in origin at all, but are the reflections of a disturbance in the whole emotional growth of the child. Early detection of anomalies of speech and an examination which differentiates causes and effects are thus an essential basis for remedial action. Detection must in the main come from parents and teachers, who see the child in his daily life. The examination and subsequent care of a child who is defective in speech is a matter for a team composed of psychologist, audiometrist, otolaryngologist, speech therapist, social worker and the child's teacher and able to call at need upon even more specialized diagnostic skills.

A growing practice in Europe is to set up for such children diagnostic and remedial speech clinics and to provide a certain number of special classes for the worst cases. Unfortunately, where such clinics exist outside the educational system or in the absence of adequate psychological services, speech therapy or surgical intervention is often unaccompanied by the attempt to readjust the child's whole emotional life and re-educate what is often an immature, disturbed or regressive personality. Frequently, too, where the speech defective attends an ordinary school and has to be absent from his class at regular intervals to attend the clinic, no attempt is made to see that he makes up what he has missed.[2]

---

1. e.g. cleft palate.
2. The result in later life of such a double neglect is illustrated by the two following cases of 18-year-olds. The first had twice been to hospital for operations to rectify a cleft palate and a hare-lip at the ages of 6 and 9; he had then attended a speech training clinic part-time for three years, finishing his educational career in a private school at 14. His speech was very blurred, and at 18 he had a pronounced personality difficulty (inferiority feelings, dependence, immaturity), partly centred on a still obvious hare-lip and cleft palate. Though slightly above average in intelligence, he was able to read no better than a 7-year-old child, and his occupation was the lowest and least skilled form of labouring. The second man, of similar age and of average ability, had so severe a stammer that he twisted his head down to his shoulder with

CHILDREN WITH MULTIPLE HANDICAPS

Except perhaps those children who are physically crippled without cerebral involvement, most handicapped pupils have more than óne defect. Usually however, they can be classified for administrative purposes and educated in terms of a major difficulty. Thus a mildly mentally subnormal or physically handicapped blind child is best educated in a school for blind children rather than in one for mentally subnormal or orthopaedic cases. Similarly children with cerebral palsy, which is often accompanied by crippling, by defects of vision, hearing and speech, as well as by anomalies in intellectual growth, are likely to fare better in a school or class staffed by those specially acquainted with the problems of cerebral palsy.

There exists however a hard core of cases in which it is difficult to say which handicap is paramount in educational importance. An extreme example, of course, is the deaf-blind child, who needs the help of specialized techniques derived both from work with the blind and from work with the deaf. Fortunately, relative to the numbers of the more or less uncomplicated cases of blindness, deafness, subnormality or crippling, complex cases of multiple handicap are few. In the past many of them have been considered ineducable, and even now one meets cases of children who have been passed as failures from one specialized school to the next before being finally excluded from the educational system entirely to pass their lives either in asylums or as a burden upon their family. As with all forms of handicap, a major factor in planning help for such children is the level of the child's innate ability. Roughly speaking, the greater the degree of handicap, the higher must be the child's ability in order to overcome the obstacles which his disability interposes in his educational development. To some considerable extent too this is true for those forms of physical treatment and re-education which depend upon intelligent co-operation. It has for example been found that markedly or severely handicapped cerebrally palsied children whose I.Q. is much below 85 do not respond sufficiently well to physiotherapy, speech therapy or special education as at present developed to justify the outlay of skill and money involved. On the other hand, a school which specializes in the education of blind children who are, most of them, physically and mentally handicapped to a marked degree, has had a striking success in training such children to be physically independent, personally and socially well adjusted and, in a few cases, in developing

---

the effort of speech. He was unable to read, even silently, as well as a child of 8. He had attended an ordinary school but for most of his career there, had spent half a day a week attending a speech training clinic. In this case a profound emotional disturbance was at the root of the speech defect; and he began to make progress both in speech and in reading when efforts were made to readjust his personal difficulties. (See W. D. Wall, 'Reading Backwardness among Men in the Army', loc. cit.)

something more than the rudiments of formal education.[1] A proportion of the pupils of this school do become at least partially self-supporting, although they belong to a group for which hitherto little could be done.

Such examples, and the apparent miracles wrought by the devotion, intuition and skill of teachers who undertake 'hopeless' cases of handicapped children, draw attention to two things of great importance to the mental health of the community. A handicapped person may be not only an economic and social liability both as a child and as an adult, but also the focus of severe emotional disturbance in his own family. In many cases, still, the only solution proposed to the second of these problems is that of removing the child completely from his own home and placing him in an institution. Indeed the suggestion is often heard and sometimes followed, that severely subnormal children should be separated from their mothers immediately after birth. It is however by no means sure that the mental health of the family or of the community is best served by shutting from sight all even of the most severely handicapped persons. Where adequate social, medical, and educational services are available to help the family in its task, and where from the earliest stages informed measures are taken to prevent psychological disturbance either in the child or in his family, and to promote the progressive social adaptation of the handicapped, many even of the most severe cases can continue to live, ultimately at far less social cost, with their parents, and some can gain a partial independence. The second important point to emphasize is that, whereas the prevention of many handicapping conditions is a matter particularly for the health services, the control of the personal and social consequences of a handicap from the earliest stages demands wise psychological, educational and social guidance and involves ultimately many services. Unfortunately research into the developmental psychology of the handicapped and into the special methods of educating the family and the child himself is in its infancy; it is under-financed and hindered in almost every country by inter-professional rivalries and by the watertight compartments which tend to grow up between social, medical and educational services.

---

1. Condover Hall Special School for the Multihandicapped Blind, Condover, near Shrewsbury, Shropshire, England. The majority of the children of this school have intelligence quotients below I.Q. 60, and a number are more or less severely crippled, though mobile. The school has a special unit devoted to the deaf-blind.

III. MALADJUSTED CHILDREN

THE NATURE OF MALADJUSTMENT

Physically handicapped or mentally subnormal children find adjustment to the normal world made difficult by particular—and usually
noticeable—limitations. School surveys show that there is a smaller
group of children physically and intellectually normal who, because
of inherent anomalies of temperament, marked emotional instability
or abnormal strength or weakness in one or other of the fundamental
psychological drives, are handicapped to the extent that their personal
development, even under favourable conditions and often from an
early age, is recognizably pathological. In addition there are some few
who have an organic pathology, the main outward symptoms of which
are emotional or behavioural—for example the unstable post-encephal-
itic, certain of the epileptic, some children with cerebral tumours,
children in whom a cerebral lesion gives rise to excessive activity and
the like—and a few psychotic children or children with a constellation
of peculiarities which suggest imminent psychosis, depressive, maniac,
or schizoid. Taken together, however, these children form only a frac-
tional part [1] of those who, temporarily or permanently, show signs of
maladjustment in the school period, or whose marked anomalies of
emotional growth in adolescence are reflected in delinquency, in
scholastic or vocational failure, or in marked deviations of personality
development.

It is possible that there are some situations which, without prior
distortion of development, can dramatically give rise to maladjustment
and neurosis. The sudden death of a beloved parent, the birth of a
younger brother or sister, a scene of adult violence, may, supervening
at a critical moment in psychological growth and without adequate
interpretation to the child, provoke serious emotional disturbance
which becomes apparent immediately and has reverberations subsequently. Demands made upon a child to adjust may be too great
either for his level of maturity or for his emotional force and instead
of moving forward to a new and acceptable integration of behaviour,
he may revert and remain fixed at an earlier level.

In any situation of difficulty or shock, the temptation is to retreat

---

1. Precise estimates are difficult to obtain because of differences of opinion as to what constitutes
an inherent anomaly of temperament or a clearly psychiatric illness in children. The experience
of child guidance centres and clinics in England however tends to suggest that only some 10 to
15 per cent at most of all cases referred fall into the group, and that if we take into account
all forms of maladjustment, major and minor, the proportion is very much lower still. (See
C. Burt. 'Symposium on Psychologists and Psychiatrists in the Child Guidance Service', *Brit.
Journ. Ed. Psych.* vol. XXIII, pt. 1, Feb. 1953.)

to a previously successful form of behaviour, and normal development in fact shows a series of advances and retreats, much like the waves of a rising tide. The important thing is that new and adaptive integrations should predominate and become steadily prepotent. The range of individual variation in adaptability is immense; what might be seriously damaging for one child leaves another more or less unruffled. Individual susceptibility to emotional shock is markedly influenced by constitutional factors, by all that has happened from the moment of birth, by the immediate situation, and by the interpretation which the child comes to put upon it.

It is therefore rarely possible in any given case to trace the source of maladjustment to any one incident; though a particular happening in a child's life may well have been the precipitating cause, or, unassimilated and unexplained, may have given rise to a series of fears, attitudes and expectations, which later develop into a neurosis or into a minor behaviour or attitudinal deviation. Most usually maladjustment is of slow growth, the result of a series of wrong turnings which progressively bring about a disequilibrium between the resources of an individual and the demands of his society. In all such cases the reaction of the individual begins by being normal and the abnormality is in the environment—that is, either the environment is frankly unsatisfactory and does not provide what a child needs for growth, or it makes demands which the child's stage of growth does not enable him to meet. An example of the first situation is that of parental friction—a classic 'cause' of maladjustment—in which the child's security is assailed by disunity between his parents, by divided loyalties and by fear of aggression. An example of the second is where the parents unite to exact standards of behaviour, manners at table, quietness in the house or tidiness, for example, which are quite beyond the child's power to accomplish. That in the one case the child should become anxious and endeavour to reinforce his security by clinging to his mother, and in the other should show lack of self-confidence or react by aggression, is perfectly normal. If, however, the situation provoking such reactions continues, the conflict aroused becomes interiorized and slowly becomes part of the child's whole unconscious life, affecting his personality; he makes a continued adjustment which reduces the immediate tension, but which—even when the provoking situation no longer exists—colours his subsequent emotional life and operates as a factor in determining the adjustments to future challenges.[1]

Between the extremes of a healthy and normal reaction against an environmental pressure which exceeds the power of adaptation of an otherwise satisfactorily developed child and the reaction which in itself is abnormal because a prior conflict situation has resulted in an im-

---

1. See Appendix III A and III B.

pairment of the capacity to adapt, all degrees and graduations of maladjustment exist. The reactions too of individual children vary in terms of their previous history, their temperamental endowment, and of the types of pressures to which they are subjected. For example, insecure children brought up in a fairly rigid and strict discipline are likely, turning in upon themselves, to become nervous and excessively well behaved; those who live in a society which is very permissive tend rather to become aggressive and turbulent, noisy and destructive. But these reactions are by no means invariable; there are, for example, many cases of children whose fierce aggression is a reaction against a discipline which they resent as unbridled power directed against them; and some, who seeing indifference or danger in an over-permissive world, react with intensified anxiety.

We may perhaps sum up by suggesting that a piece of behaviour should only be considered as abnormal if it tends to set up a barrier between the child and his group and to indicate a far-reaching system of disturbance or potential disturbance in his relationships with others. A child can only truly be said to be maladjusted when he is unable, to a noticeable and incapacitating extent, to enter freely into the life of his group and to meet the demands it makes on him in a way which the group itself finds acceptable.

CRITERIA OF MALADJUSTMENT

Much current discussion of the signs of maladjustment and many theoretical postulates as to causes are based upon studies carried out by those whose experience is confined to cases of clearly maladjusted children. Only too frequently such studies have been carried out in terms of certain theoretical assumptions which tend to determine the data sought and the interpretations offered. Moreover the social nature of any definition and therefore of any criteria of mental health and personal adjustment make comparisons from country to country or even from one social group to another somewhat precarious. Such studies as have been made on the basis of comparing abnormal groups with groups of normal children matched for such variables as socio-economic group, age, sex and level of intelligence, indicate that, whereas certain personal factors, signs of maladjustment and environmental influences, are significantly more frequent in various types of maladjusted group, they are not absent from the lives of otherwise normal children.[1]

---

1. Classic examples of the study by means of control groups of the complex of associated personal and social factors in school maladjustment and in delinquency are the two studies by Burt previously cited (*The Young Delinquent; The Backward Child*), and the more recent study by Burt and Howard cited in Appendix IIIA.

Moreover behaviour which at one age is normal may be a sign of maladjustment if it is persisted in when the child grows older. A good example of this is the temper tantrum, normal in the 2 to 3-year-old child, but, at least in its primitive form, a serious sign of maladjustment in a 10-year-old. Even here however, judgment is not simple. We lack objective norms of behaviour and social development[1] for normal children by which deviations may be judged; some groups accept behaviour from which, in other groups, the child is weaned; and within any one community—particularly for example in large towns—considerable variations in tolerance will be found from one social level to another.

In the lives of most children, who subsequently develop satisfactorily, there occur periods of considerable disturbance, which however pass without more direct psychological assistance than a school can give and simply, it seems, as the result of maturation.[2] In one of the rare studies of the development of normal children, Cummings found, in an unselected group of 239 children aged between 2 years and 7 years in three infant-nursery schools in Leicester, England, that on an average each child showed between two and three 'emotional symptoms'[3] and that none was entirely free. She found also that certain symptoms (e.g. frequency of micturition, specific fears) are less frequent in older children, whereas others, notably day-dreaming and lack of concentration, are more so. Following up the same children 6 to 18 months later, she found that there was a tendency for symptoms to fade with the lapse of time. This was marked only with these children who at the time of the original study were in the younger group.[4] For example, after 6 months, 55.5 per cent of the children aged originally between 2 and 5 had improved as compared with 18.3 per cent of those aged originally 5 to 8; after 18 months the proportions were respectively 86.6 per cent and 53.2 per cent. This seems to indicate that certain 'emotional symptoms' are normal to young children under 5 but tend

---

1. The Vineland Social Maturity Scale (E. A. Doll, *Manual*, Educational Test Bureau, Educational Publishers, Inc. 1947; 'The Vineland Social Maturity Scale', *Train. Sch. Bull.* vol. 32, 1935; 'A Preliminary Standardization of the Vineland Social Maturity Scale', *Am. Journ. Orthopsychiatry* vol. 6, 1936).

2. See C. W. Valentine, *The Difficult Child and the Problem of Discipline.* 5th ed., London, Methuen, 1950; *Abnormalities in Normal Children.* London, National Children's Home, s.d.

3. J. D. Cummings, 'The Incidence of Emotional Symptoms in School Children', *Brit. Journ. Ed. Psych.* vol. XIV, pt. 3, 1944. Cummings' list includes all those symptoms usually considered as possibly indicative of maladjustment and which can be observed in the classroom and playground. Those of most frequent occurrence were: excitability, restlessness (28.9 per cent); day-dreaming, lack of concentration, laziness (28.9 per cent); generalized anxiety, timidity and shyness (23.0 per cent); specific fears (22.2 per cent); bladder control, frequency of micturition (21.3 per cent); nervous habits (18.9 per cent); cruelty, aggression (15.1 per cent); speech difficulties (14.2 per cent); lack of appetite, food faddiness (11.3 per cent); babyish behaviour, frequent crying (11.3 per cent); lying, stealing (10.1 per cent).

4. J. D. Cummings, 'A Follow-up Study of Emotional Symptoms in School Children', *Brit. Journ. Ed. Psych.* vol. XVI, pt. III, Nov. 1946.

to be signs of a persisting disturbance if they occur in older children. In her group too were a number of children manifestly sufficiently disturbed to warrant further investigation and probably psychological help. Such children would be conventionally regarded as maladjusted; it is interesting to note that rather less than half improved more or less spontaneously in the 18-month period, while the remainder, though frequently showing later a different behaviour or attitude pattern, continued to be markedly unadjusted to school.

THE INCIDENCE OF MALADJUSTMENT

The difficulty of defining accurately what constitutes maladjustment, what is a sign of a transitory disequilibrium and what is sufficiently indicative of a serious disturbance to warrant intervention, special remedial action or removal to a special school or class, makes the estimation of the incidence of maladjustment hazardous. Until long-term follow-up studies of the emotional development of unselected samples of children from birth to maturity have been made, and until we are more fully aware of the outcome of apparent anomalies of behaviour or personality occurring at any age, we can proceed only empirically and with a rather more conservative humility than is customary in some quarters.[1]

Such evidence as there is, however, tends to indicate that both serious maladjustment and states of developmental difficulty are more common in children than is usually supposed. In estimating the need for provision of special classes and schools for maladjusted pupils, the British Ministry of Education cites the figure of about 1 per cent of the population of school age.[2] This however can be considered a conservative estimate made in terms of minimum administrative provision for special educational arrangements. There remains a much larger group of children who need some help themselves or whose teachers or parents may need advice. The numbers of these are difficult to estimate. In Table 2 are grouped eight estimates derived from studies in the United States, New Zealand, France and the United Kingdom, the general trend of which is to suggest that the proportion of seriously maladjusted children of school age is as high as 5 per cent and may be more, and that those for whom some help should be available represent 20 or even 25 per cent of the school-age population. In general, such estimates have been made to exclude those children whose sole symptom is educational retardation. It is found however that, while many maladjusted

---

1. The uncritical acceptance for example of certain doctrines—that children should not be repressed or that they should not be shown too much affection—has often provoked maladjustment rather than prevented it.

2. *Special Educational Treatment*. Ministry of Education pamphlet no. 5. HMSO, London, 1946.

TABLE 2. Comparative table of estimated incidence of maladjustment: eight investigations [1]

Investigator	Source of information	Date	Sample size	Age range	Showing some symptoms of maladjustment	Seriously maladjusted	Total
					%	%	%
Burt (U.K.)	Case study	1920 approx.	391	7-13	31.4[2]	4	35.4
Wickman (U.S.A.)	Teachers	1927	870	6-12	42	7	49.0
McFie (U.K)	Teachers	1934	697	12-14		46	46.0
Milner (U.K).	Teachers	1935	1 201[3]	10-16		17	17.0
Rogers (U.S.A.)	Various 'indices' including teachers' ratings	1940	1 524	6-12 approx.	30	12	42.0
New Zealand (N.Z.) Ed. Institute	Teachers checked by psychologists[4]	1948-49	2 363	5-14		7.6	7.6
Heuyer (France) et al.	Teachers	1944	95 237	6-13		28.6[5]	28.6
Ullmann (U.S.A.)	Teachers	1950	810	14	22	8	30.0

1. C. Burt, *The Backward Child*. 2nd ed., London, University of London Press, 1946; E. K. Wickman, *Children's Behaviour and Teachers' Attitudes*. New York, Commonwealth Fund, 1928; B. S. McFie, 'Behaviour and Personality Difficulties in School Children', *Brit. Journ. Ed. Psych.* vol. IV, pt. 1, 1934; M. Milner, *The Human Problem in Schools*. London, Methuen, 1938; C. R. Rogers, 'Mental Health Findings in Three Elementary Schools', *Ed. Research Bulletin* 21, 1942; *Emotional Maladjustment in New Zealand School Children*. New Zealand Educational Institute; G. Heuyer, H. Piéron et al, *Le niveau intellectuel des enfants d'âge scolaire*. Paris, Presses universitaires de France, 1950; C. A. Ullmann, *Identification of Maladjusted School Children* (*Public Health Monograph* no. 7), Washington, Government Printing Office, 1952.
   Of the 656 London schoolchildren studied by S. Isaacs and others (*The Cambridge Evacuation Survey*. London, Methuen & Co., 1941), 155 were referred to the Child Guidance Clinic (23.6 per cent), 13 per cent were in need of skilled help, and of these 4 per cent were cases of considerable severity. It will be observed that this group is rather special, since they were children abruptly removed from their homes in wartime and at a period of considerable general stress.
2. *The Backward Child*. p. 542. Burt gives figures for his control group of normal (i.e. not backward) children. This figure is the result of grouping various temperamental and emotional conditions. Burt points out that excitability (included in this figure—frequency for normals 9.7 per cent) is partly a characteristic of the social group from which these children were drawn.
3. Girls only. The investigation was carried out in five schools having a population drawn mainly from economically superior groups and having a progressive educational outlook.
4. Teacher's comments were checked by a committee of psychologists and doubtful cases ruthlessly eliminated. Only the results for urban populations are given as more comparable with those in the rest of the table.
5. This includes 24.7 per cent of children with personality difficulties and 3.9 per cent with speech difficulties.

children give very little sign in school of their difficulties, in some, educational retardation is itself one, if not the only, obvious sign of maladjustment; conversely, many children who become retarded in school develop difficulties of personality or of behaviour as a consequence of their lack of success. Moreover, maladjustment, though it may differ in its forms of expression, is as commonly found among dull and subnormal children as it is among those of normal or superior endowment. Hence between the various groups somewhat artificially separated in this chapter, there is probably considerable overlap; and the figures given should be considered also in relation to the proportions of scholastic failure in primary and secondary schools.

On the other hand, we should again emphasize that maladjustment is a relative concept; and that teachers and psychologists are likely to have different views. Teachers tend understandably to pick out those children who are difficult in class, usually because of bad behaviour, poor work, aggressiveness, and the like, and who are therefore maladjusted in that they fail to conform satisfactorily to the classroom situation. Many of such children, however, are passing through a phase of difficulty which is temporary and they readjust without help later. Some indeed may be reacting against the personality of the teacher, and the 'symptoms' pass when they move to another form; a proportion are difficult for causes of a transitory nature, outside the knowledge of the school. On the other hand, children whose behaviour is marked by excessive conformity, timidity, shyness or inhibition, may escape the teacher's notice or be regarded as model pupils. The psychologist, preoccupied with the whole long process of development and less personally involved with the children, considers maladjustment more in terms of its ultimate outcome in development than of its present convenience or inconvenience. Hence he is likely to discount irritating behaviour and to stress particularly any signs which suggest that the maladjustment shows itself, not merely in the classroom, but in the system of personal relationships with which the child is surrounded. Moreover he is likely to attempt the distinction between maladjustment which is an immediately unfavourable reaction to the environment and that which arises from a deviation in emotional growth in the past. The former can be met either by helping the child temporarily or by mitigating the pressure of the environment; the latter may entail a patient process of re-education.

PREVENTION AND REMEDY

It should be clear from the foregoing that much if not most maladjustment—that is to say, all which is in one way or another mainly the result of interaction with the environment—is preventable. The small group of children pathologically abnormal from birth or soon after can be helped (but probably not enabled to develop entirely satisfactorily) if they are recognized early enough and their parents assisted to adapt family upbringing to their special needs. So too children whose childhood is rendered abnormal by severely disturbing experiences and by their consequences—children who lose their mother in the first two years, or who spend long periods in hospital, for example —can, if measures are taken at once, be protected from the worst consequences of deprivation or shock.

Many personality deviations, behaviour and habit disorders and the like however arise from mistakes in parental upbringing, especially, but by no means exclusively, in the pre-school years; many too are the direct or indirect result of living conditions. Social action to improve physical living conditions, and particularly to remove the necessity for mothers of children under 3 to work for long hours outside their homes, will do much to improve matters especially if it is seconded by a practical and tactful education of parents so that, understanding the psychology of their children, they can within the restrictions imposed by urban life and the contemporary shortage of living space, satisfy their needs.

In childhood and adolescence the school as the sole institution which touches all children has a big part to play both in the prevention of maladjustment and in the cure of those whose development is awry. It is the task of the school to see that its demands for achievement and for adjustment are such as to be generally within the compass of its pupils' normal development, and to be ready to temper them considerably to individual variations in tolerance. Moreover the teacher should recognize that some children take longer than others to adapt or may need a little friendly help at a critical moment. This is particularly true in the first school year, at periods of transition, and whenever an examination or other testing period is imminent.

There is, however, a limit beyond which a teacher in an ordinary class cannot tolerate maladjustments shown, for example, in aggressive behaviour or markedly bad work; moreover those children whose maladjustment attracts little attention, the over-conscientious or markedly timid, may, though acceptable to the school as causing no trouble, need help beyond the power and the training of a teacher, preoccupied with 30 or 40 children, to give. Many such children can be helped by being put into a small group of 8 or 10 under a sympathetic, and preferably specially trained, teacher.[1] Such a group can be more tolerant and accepting of difficult behaviour, can give more creative and remedial outlets, and the teacher can build a closer, more personal contact

---

1. The London County Council has established a Problem Children Conference which considers children referred by schools, by the psychological service and by medical officers. It has established a number of small day classes which disturbed children attend for periods up to nine months or a year, and where they can be given special supervision and individual help.

with pupils and with parents. It has been shown that, with little if anything more than this, many children can be helped through a period of severe personality difficulties, until with increased age greater stability comes. In more serious cases and where the cause is clearly in the home, a period in such a class may support the child and prevent him from deteriorating whilst efforts are made to improve the family itself.

In some cases, the home circumstances are so bad and the pressures on the child so intense, that there is no alternative but, for a time at least, to send him to a residential school, or to place him in a hostel from which he can attend the ordinary school. The advantage of such a measure is that all the circumstances of the child's life can be controlled and the adults in his environment can adapt themselves to his needs whilst carrying out an intensive re-education. Unless however, at the same time, an attempt is made to remove those adverse factors in the child's home environment which lie at the root of his difficulty, his problems will arise again upon his return. The decision to remove a child from his home, though the temptation to do so is great when his troubles are clearly the result of parental mishandling, is not to be lightly made; moreover it should be regarded essentially as a short-term solution for all but those few cases where it is impossible to help the child and his family mutually to adjust. This solution of a short-term stay, arranged usually with the consent of the parents, but sometimes by order of a juvenile or other court, is now provided in a number of European countries, including Austria, France, Holland and the United Kingdom. In all these countries, however, emphasis is laid upon the exploration of alternatives such as boarding out, hostel care, keeping the child and family together under supervision, and upon vigorous social work with the family so as to prepare for the child's return if he is removed for a period.

THE CARDINAL IMPORTANCE OF THE ENVIRONMENT

It is important to emphasize, both in examining and in helping problem children, the social and environmental aspects of their difficulties, since it is mainly through the educative or re-educative quality of the environment that remedy must come. Many children, by the time they are referred to specialized psychological services, it is true, have so serious a disturbance and one which has continued for so long that they need psycho-therapy, special remedial education, or some other form of direct personal help. But even in such cases, the treatment of the child alone is rarely sufficient. Most maladjustment, unlike physical disease, is not a simple clinical entity referable to a direct physical cause which, once removed, leaves all as before; it is the result of a process

243

of multiple interacting factors which have modified, and continue indirectly to modify, the whole pattern of the child's social life as well as his emotional growth. Hence, while in many cases a relatively small change in the environment may be all that is necessary or possible, the child himself cannot be helped in isolation; home and school are both directly involved, and from the outset should be called into collaboration. It would seem that the weakness of much psychiatric and some psychological work in the past, its comparative inefficacy and the frequency with which an immediate improvement is followed by a relapse, may be traced to the fact that psycho-therapy has not been sustained by a close study and modification of the whole world in which the child lives and to which he has become maladjusted. It follows as a corollary that all those who have to do with a problem child are involved in the remedies and, while it may be necessary for the psychologist to take the lead in the examination of the child and in the co-ordination of measures to help him, the success of any attempt will depend upon the closest co-operation of all those—teachers, parents, doctors, psychologists, social-workers—who may be concerned.

Behaviour difficulties, habit disorders, scholastic failure, character or personality deviations, are always matters to be taken seriously— even though they may, in many cases, prove transitory. All children from time to time, and especially in early childhood and in early adolescence, display signs of maladjustment and disturbance, which indicate strains in their lives and are normal, even healthy, signs of growth. It is important that the teacher and the parent should recognize these for what they are and should have the understanding to help the young to confront their difficulties. Some, indeed much, maladjusted behaviour, may be due to weakness or fluctuation in home discipline and not to personality deviation in the child at all. The school can often best help such children by a constructive and consistent firmness. The difficulty is to distinguish those cases which demand such treatment from those which have need rather of a very permissive environment, or for skilled remedial work. On the teacher particularly falls the duty of calling in to his assistance expert psychological help when a child's difficulties persist and there is reason to suppose that something more than tolerance or firmness from the school is necessary. This expert help should be based upon a thorough study of the child in his family and in his school and, since the variety of the needs and difficulties of maladjusted children is great, should have a corresponding range and flexibility in the services at its disposal. Special remedial coaching, psycho-therapy, the small group or special class, the long or short-term residential school or hostel, social-work with the family— any or all of these may prove to be necessary; and there are few communities, even those of the largest size, which as yet have the trained specialist staff, a teaching service alert to the detection of maladjustment at its early stages, and an adequate range of the special educational provisions by means of which the problem of maladjustment can mainly be tackled.

HOMELESS CHILDREN

We may conclude this chapter by a brief discussion of certain special groups of children whose difficulties are closely related to those of the maladjusted and who may, in fact often do, fall into the maladjusted group. In any community there are some children—the number varying with social and economic conditions—who, because of death, desertion, illegitimacy, the inefficiency or cruelty of their parents, are deprived, often from an early age, of a normal life. The second world war rendered many children homeless. Its social consequences too precipitated a breakdown in the family lives of many more. Such children, orphaned actually or effectively, are in grave danger of serious and ultimately irreversible emotional damage unless they are cared for not only materially but psychologically. The classic solution has been, and still largely is in Europe, the large orphanage consisting of huge barrack-like buildings constructed in an age when to be poor was almost a crime and benevolence exacted the tribute of dutiful gratitude. In many such institutions, children are all dressed alike, have little or no personal property, are herded together in large dormitories, and looked after or rather guarded by an untrained staff, whose major object is to impose a discipline sufficiently firm to prevent trouble. Not infrequently orphanages of this type accommodate several hundred children from birth until 14 or 16, have their own schools and workshops, and enter into little or no contact with the outside world.

In view of what is now known of child development and of the importance to growth of the affection shown by parents and particularly by the mother in the early years, it is small wonder that many children from such institutions seem mentally dull, are apathetic or aggressive and sometimes delinquent or markedly abnormal. A growing realization of the fact that a child without a normal and satisfactory home life is a serious present and future problem not only to his own mental health but for the mental and social hygiene of society, is leading to many experiments and to many reforms aimed at providing for such children the emotional stimuli which they would otherwise lack. The ideal solutions, where social circumstances permit, are adoption or foster-home placement.[1] Even in those countries where such solutions

---

1. This is the solution strongly advocated and practised in the United Kingdom, which since the war has set up a special service of children's officers, whose task it is to guard the interests of all homeless children and of those declared in need of care and protection by the courts.

are practicable, they do not meet the whole problem, and measures have to be taken to group many such children in communities or orphanages. Here, success or failure depends upon organization and upon the quality and training of the staff. Ideally, such communities should be organized to give to their children the nearest possible approach to a normal family life. Instead of being large and barrack-like, the buildings should be small and scattered, resembling ordinary houses as closely as possible, with small groups of children of all ages living under the care of a 'mother' and 'father'. The children should have property of their own, a measure of privacy, should have the same variety of dress as other children, and above all should be able to develop a permanent affective link with their substitute parents, secure in the knowledge that love and protection will not fail them. This, with considerable variations, is the solution which has grown up in many countries in Europe, notably in France,[1] in response to the needs of multitudes of children whose lives were broken by the war. It has its disadvantages. The 'families' are much larger than normal. What is more they are constantly renewed, and the 'parents' may not be able to continue to provide a home for the older adolescents and young adults. There is too, always the element of relative impermanence in the 'parents', and the tendency for the work to attract those who themselves are abnormal or maladjusted.[2] It is however coming to be realized that such communities are an essential part of provision for homeless and abandoned children and that therefore adequate standards of employment, selection and training of staff should be applied to ensure that children, who—for no fault of theirs—are the victims of our social order, shall be given the chance of a normal and satisfactory development.

DELINQUENCY

Much has been written and much disquiet expressed on the subject of juvenile delinquency and since the end of the war almost every country

---

See report of *The Care of Children Committee*. London, HMSO, 1946. Adoption and foster-home placement have their dangers, and the disposal of any child should only be made after careful study of all the circumstances involved: see *Mental Health Aspects of Adoption* (WHO *Technical Report Series* no. 70). Geneva, WHO, 1953.

1. In France there are some 250 homes for children grouped under an Association nationale des communautés d'enfants. Among these are a number which were set up specially for children made homeless by the second world war. Since then, there has been a marked increase, mainly in Europe, in communities which base themselves, not on the old concept of impersonal charity and physical care, but upon the attempt to meet basic psychological needs. The formulae adopted vary, but the end is the same—that of providing for each child a close affective link with mother and father substitutes. See the *Bulletin* of the International Federation of Children's Communities, and T. Brosse, *War-Handicapped Children*. Paris, Unesco, 1949, *Vagrant Children*. Paris, Unesco, 1951; *Les maisons d'enfants*. Paris, Presses universitaires de France, 1951.

2. W. D. Wall, *Bulletin* no. 4 of the International Federation of Children's Communities, 1953.

has reported an increase in the numbers of young people—particularly boys—brought before the courts. According to statistics from the United Kingdom, for example, there was in 1948 a rise of 25 per cent on the previous year.[1] If we compare the postwar incidence of delinquency with the prewar incidence,[2] we find that the proportion of boys between 8 and 14 found guilty of indictable offences has increased by half, and of those between 14 and 17 by one-third. For girls, the incidence in both groups has nearly doubled. It seems that now one may expect between one and two boys in a hundred and between one and two girls in a thousand (most in the 14 to 17 age group) to be convicted of an indictable offence.[3] Some of this increase is undoubtedly factitious. It reflects more adequate detection and recording of offences and the creation of new offences through the restrictions and temptations of life in a period of scarcity and disturbance. Some of it reflects the impact of war and its consequences on the early lives of children now become adolescent—the absence of fathers in the services and the anxieties and disturbances of the whole social atmosphere during and succeeding hostilities.

Delinquency, however, is a legal rather than a psychological concept, and a close investigation of delinquent groups shows that they belong in the main to the maladjusted. Thus the delinquency figures are in part at least an index to the phenomena discussed earlier in this chapter and are related closely to the estimates of major and minor maladjustment given in Table 2. There are some few children and adolescents, it is true, who break the law because they are conforming to the behaviour of an anti-social group. Within their immediate environment they are adjusted, but they have acquired attitudes and habits which bring them into conflict with the law. Delinquents of this kind tend to become fewer with the improvement of education, with the extension of welfare and other services, and with the clearing of slum areas in which adult criminal groups tend to congregate. For the rest, it seems that the delinquent act is but one of a series of symptoms of widespread developmental disturbance for which the causes are the familiar ones of emotional upset and psycho-neurosis—defective home discipline and defective home relationships, the weakness or strength of specific instincts, the effects on the child of intellectual disabilities for which his

1. This and subsequent figures are from the Joint Circular from the Home Office and the Ministry of Education, *Juvenile Delinquency*. Cir. 265/1953, 20 July. (U.K.).

2. Based upon the incidence per 100,000 of the population of boys and girls of the same age in the 8 to 14 group and in the 14 to 17 group, and comparing the average of the years 1938-39 with the average for the years 1945-49 inclusive.

3. Figures from France are slightly different from those for the U.K. Since 1949 there has been a decline in the number found guilty, though the figure is still higher than that for before the war. Moreover, the decline in delinquency among girls is greater than that among boys. The French figures confirm a tendency for there to be relatively more (detected) delinquencies in the 16 to 18 than in the 13 to 16 age groups. See Ministère de la justice, Direction de l'éducation surveillée *Rapport annuel à M. le Garde des Sceaux. 1953*. Melun, Imprimerie administrative, 1954.

247

education has made insufficient allowance, various detrimental influences in the immediate environment, and the like. Although delinquencies occur in middle and late childhood, adolescence is the period when, for most delinquents, the first clash with the law takes place. In part it may be traced to the general intensification and instability of the emotional life, and especially to the upsurge of aggression characteristic of the period. In part it is because adolescence coincides with such new factors in the youth's life as leaving school and beginning work, and, whereas the misdemeanours of a child are likely to be infringements of the rules of the school, those of the young bring him up against the laws of society.

Essentially, the problems of prevention and remedy are the same as for maladjustment—the improvement of those social, economic and psychological conditions which weaken the educative role of the family, the early detection of deviations in development, whether they result from hereditary or from environmental causes, and the attempt—through remedial education, through aid to the parents, through psychotherapy, through special schools or classes—to set the child on the right path.

A special word should perhaps be said about the part of the school in this. Many delinquents and many adult criminals are intellectually dull, educationally backward, and sometimes illiterate, with few legitimate interests to occupy their hands and minds; many of those who are not markedly subnormal in their intellectual ability are yet found to be retarded educationally. Not all dull or subnormal children become delinquent; nor do the maladjusted or retarded; nevertheless, schools which make no provision to help those who fall behind for any reason offer little satisfaction to a considerable group of children from among whom many delinquents are recruited. One at least of the preventive measures comparatively ready to hand is the opportunity or remedial group for the child who is noticeably failing, and the special class or school for the clearly subnormal.[1]

IV. CONCLUSION

No country in Europe has solved all the problems presented by the various groups of exceptional children. Specialized services for the ascertainment, examination and supervision of such children are but imperfectly developed; only here and there can be found an adequate

---

1. For a fuller treatment of this point, see W. D. Wall. 'The Educational Aspects of Delinquency', *International Review of Education* vol. I, no. 4, Oct. 1955.

training for the teachers on whom falls the main responsibility for helping those who for physical, social or psychological reasons deviate markedly in their educational needs from the average; and, except perhaps in the field of the education of the deaf or the blind and to some extent of the markedly subnormal, research has only begun to sift out the educational and psychological methods by which we may hope eventually to reduce the human, economic and social toll exacted by all forms of handicap.

Improved maternity and child welfare services, the prevention and control of such diseases as syphilis, meningitis, measles, scarlet fever and whooping cough have done much to diminish the numbers of blind, deaf, mentally subnormal and crippled children. We may expect that earlier detection of subnormalities, even mild ones, will, if appropriate measures are taken, reduce the effects upon children of a handicap which cannot be cured. Where, as in some intellectual subnormality, in educational retardation and in most maladjustment, the causes are largely environmental, we may expect that an increased general awareness of the dynamics of child development would both reduce the incidence and lead to the application of remedies in early stages when success is most easy and most likely to be achieved.

That the problems of the dull, the retarded and backward, the maladjusted and delinquent are urgent, is evidenced by the figures. If we accept the most conservative estimates[1] and allow for a measure of overlapping between groups, it seems likely that no less than one child in five or six needs some kind of special educational or psychological help if he is to stand a fair chance of satisfactory and happy growth and if he is not to act as a brake upon other children in the normal class. For the majority of such exceptional children the best solution is the special class in the ordinary school under a properly trained teacher and supported by a psychological service. Such classes however must be small and freed from the exigencies of rigid timetables and examinations. So far as is practicable too they should be specialized and not group a miscellaneous body of children, some dull, some markedly subnormal mentally and some retarded or maladjusted. This may mean, in all but the largest schools, that the children of the special class are drawn from a wider area than the rest of the school population, and that different schools have classes attached to them of different types. It should also mean that measures are taken to mix whenever possible the children from the special class into the activities of the others and to see to it that whereas both groups will be aware of differences, a common sympathy and understanding grows up. In certain cases, as has been done in the *Sonder Kindergarten* school in Vienna, classes of different types of handicapped children, blind, deaf,

---

1. See Chapter V, p. 112-17, Chapter IX, p. 240 and Appendix II.

crippled and mentally subnormal may be grouped together with some classes of children in no way handicapped, into one school and at points in their education suited to it, handicapped and unhandicapped children share the same curriculum and teacher.

Whatever the arrangement for exceptional children which has to be made on grounds of practical expediency, however, certain basic principles should never be lost sight of nor should their fulfilment be needlessly interfered with. No matter what the nature of his difficulty, physical, mental, emotional or social, the handicapped child is first and foremost a child with psychological needs like those of any other. He needs affection and security, he needs emotional and intellectual stimulus, he needs to assert his independence, to learn, and to pass through the successive stages of physical and emotional growth. His handicap is an obstacle to smooth progress; it may set limits to his possibilities; but it does not make him essentially different from his more fortunate fellows. Thus whatever is done for him, medically, socially, or educationally, must be conceived and evaluated in the light both of his immediate need as a growing human being and of its ultimate bearing upon his adjustment and happiness as an adult living as far as possible in the world of ordinary people. It often happens that a measure is taken—for example an operation or removal to a residential school or home—which inevitably involves psychological repercussions in the child or a further deprivation. Any serious step of this kind, however, should only be decided upon when all the factors have been considered by those competent to assess their impact upon the child's total development and where any such intervention is unavoidable, no effort should be spared to minimize or compensate for the damage or deprivation which results. This implies a close study of all aspects of the child's life and the co-operation of all those who have to do with him, parents, teachers, social worker, medical officer and psychologist. It is only upon genuine team work and the pooling of knowledge of the tangibles and intangibles of growth, of the mental and physical factors in development, that wise decisions as to the care and welfare of exceptional children can be taken and implemented.

BIBLIOGRAPHY

ABRAMSON, J. *L'enfant et l'adolescent instables*. Paris, Alcan, 1940. 390 p.

AICHHORN, A. *Verwahrloste Jugend*. Bern, Huber, 1951. 212 p.

——. *Wayward youth*. London, Imago Publishing, 1951. 236 p.

ALBASTRO, A. & SIDLAUSKAITE, A. "Nuove ricerche sui fanciulli instabili", *Vita e Pensiero* vol. III. Milano, Universita Cattolica del S. Cuore, 1944. 202 p.

ALBO MARTI, E. *Estadística de los factores influyentes en el extravió de los menores ingresados en 1944 en la acción tutelar reformadora permanente del Tribunal tutelar de Barcelona*. Barcelona, Sociedad Anónima Horta de Impresiones y Ediciones, 1945. 80 p.

ALLERS, R. *Heilerziehung bei Abwegigkeit des Charakters*. Einsiedeln-Köln, Benziger, 1937.

ASPERGER, H. *Heilpädagogik*. Wien, Springer, 1952. 280 p.

BAZELEY, E. T. *Homer Lane and the little commonwealth*. 2nd ed. London, Allen & Unwin, Heinemann, 1948. 200 p.

BENJAMIN, E. et al. *Lehrbuch der Psychopathologie des Kindesalters*. Zürich, Leipzig, Rotapfelverlag, 1938. 382 p.

BENO, N., BERSOT, H. & BOVET, L. *Les enfants nerveux*. Neuchâtel & Paris, Delachaux & Niestlé, 1946. 186 p.

BURT, C. *The causes and treatment of backwardness*. London, National Children's Home. 144 p.

CARR-SAUNDERS, A. M., MANNHEIM, H. & RHODES, E. C. *Young offenders*. Cambridge, University Press, 1943. 168 p.

CHAZAL, J. *L'enfance délinquante*. Paris, Presses universitaires de France, 1953. 119 p.

CLARKE, J. S. *Disabled citizens*. London, Allen & Unwin, 1951. 238 p.

CREMIEUX, A., SCHACHTER, M. & COTTE, S. *L'enfant devenu délinquant*. Marseille, Comité de l'enfance déficiente, 1945. 176 p.

DESCOEUDRES, A. *L'éducation des enfants arriérés, ses principes, ses méthodes. Applications à tous les enfants anormaux*. 4e éd. Neuchâtel, Paris, Delachaux & Niestlé, 1948. 324 p.

——. "Que deviennent les enfants arriérés?", *Cahiers de pédagogie expérimentale et de psychologie de l'enfant*, no. 12. Genève, Institut des sciences de l'éducation, 1939. 20 p.

DEHAUSSY, J. *L'assistance publique à l'enfance. Les enfants abandonnés*. Paris, Librairie du Recueil Sirey, 1951. 391 p.

DUKER, H. *Experimentelle Untersuchungen über die Steigerung der geistigen Leistungsfähigkeit bei Minderbegabten*. Heilpädagogische Blätter, 1951. 295 p.

FERGUSON, T. *The young delinquent in his social setting*. London, New York, Toronto, Geoffrey Cumberlege, Oxford University Press, 1952. 159 p.

FRAMPTON, M. E. & ROWELL, H. G. *Education of the handicapped*. London, Harrap, 1939. vol. I & II.

FRANCOCCI, G. *Il sordomuto nella scuola e nella vita*. Milano, Bocca, 1942. 264 p.

GREAT BRITAIN. BOARD OF EDUCATION. *Report of the committee of inquiry into problems relating to children with defective hearing*. London, HMSO, 1938. 149 p.

HANSELMANN, H. *Einführung in die Heilpädagogik*. 4 Aufl. Zürich, Rotapfel Verlag, 1953.

——. *Grundlinien zu einer Theorie der Sondererziehung* (Heilpädagogik). Erlendach-Zürich, Rotapfel Verlag, 1941. 251 p.

HILL, T. B. *The education of mentally handicapped children*. Melbourne, Melbourne University Press & Oxford University Press, 1937. 104 p.

INHELDER, B. *Le diagnostic du raisonnement chez les débiles mentaux*. Neuchâtel & Paris, Delachaux & Niestlé, 1943.

INTERNATIONAL CONGRESS FOR THE EDUCATION OF EXCEPTIONAL CHILDREN (FIRST). *Report*. Zürich, Leemann, 1939. 172 p.

INTERNATIONAL CONGRESS ON ORTHOPEDAGOGICS 18-22 JULY 1949. *Proceedings. Rapport du deuxième congrès international pour la pédagogie de l'enfance déficiente 18-22 juillet 1949*. Amsterdam, Keesing, 1951. 534 p.

JOUBREL, H. *Ker-Goat.* Paris, Editions familiales de France, 1945. 166 p.

Jugendkriminalität. Herausgegeben von Friedrich Schneider. Salzburg, Otto Müller Verlag, 1952. 256 p.

LAGACHE, D. "Nomenclature et classification des jeunes inadaptés", *Sauvegarde de l'enfance.* Paris, 1946, nos. 1, 2 & 3.

"L'enfance délinquante", *Educateurs.* Paris, Service central de recherche et d'action pour l'enfance, juillet-août 1946. 120 p.

"Les enfants inadaptés et l'école primaire", *Cahiers de pédagogie moderne pour l'enseignement du premier degré.* Paris, Bourrelier, 1951. 187 p.

LLOYD, F. *Educating the sub-normal child.* London, Methuen, 1953. 148 p.

LUCHSINGER, R. *Lehrbuch der Stimm- und Sprachheilkunde.* Wien, Springer Verlag, 1949. 431 p.

MINISTERO DELL'EDUCAZIONE NAZIONALE. *Le scuole all'aperto in Italia.* Milano, Alfieri Lacroix, 1940. 230 p.

MOOR, P. *Theoretische Grundlegung einer heilpädagogischen Psychologie.* Bern, Huber, 1943. 132 p.

——. *Umwelt, Mitwelt, Heimat.* Hausen a. A., Landerziehungsheim Albisbrunn, 1947. 177 p.

NINTH CHILD GUIDANCE INTER-CLINIC CONFERENCE. 24 Nov. 1951. *Follow-up on child guidance cases.* London, National Association for Mental Health, 1951. 124 p.

PRUDHOMMEAU, M. "Inadaptation scolaire et retard intellectuel", *Cahiers de l'enfance inadaptée.* Paris, 1952, nos. 13, 15.

REY, A. *Arriération mentale et premiers exercices éducatifs.* Paris & Neuchâtel, Delachaux & Niestlé, 1953, 209 p.

——. *Etude des insuffisances psychologiques.* Neuchâtel & Paris, Delachaux & Niestlé, 1947. 2 vols.

SAN FRANCISCO (U.S.A.) *Classified bibliography.* San Francisco, State College, Special Education Department, 1952.

SCHNEIDER, F. et al. *Benachteiligte Kinder.* Freiburg i. Br., Lambertus Verlag, 1953. 243 p.

STERN, E. *Ueber Verhaltens- und Charakterstörungen bei Kindern und Jugendlichen.* Zürich, Rascher Verlag, 1953. 248 p.

TAYLOR, E. A. *Experiments with a backward class.* London, Methuen, 1946. 112 p.

The education of backward children. London, HMSO, 1937. 68 p. (Board of Education, Educational Pamphlets, no. 112).

TRENAMAN, J. *Out of step.* London, Methuen, 1952. 223 p.

UNGDOMSKOMMISSIONEN. *Den tilpasningsvanskelige Ungdom.* København, J. H. Schultz, 1953. 328 p.

VALENTINE, C. W. *Abnormalities in normal children.* London, National Children's Home, n.d. 61 p.

WEIMER, H. *Fehlerbehandlung und Fehlerbewertung.* 2. Aufl. Leipzig, 1931. 97 p.

WIDMER, K. *Schule und Schwererziehbarkeit.* Zürich, Rotapfel Verlag, 1953. 271 p.

WILLS, W. D. *The Barns experiment.* London, Allen & Unwin, 1945. 148 p.

ZULLIGER, H. *Schwierige Kinder.* Bern, Huber Verlag, 1951. 204 p.

CHAPTER X

MENTAL HEALTH AND TEACHING

I. THE TRAINING OF TEACHERS

THE IMPORTANCE OF THE TEACHER'S PART

In the system of personal relationships within which children learn, the teacher is probably, next to members of the immediate family, the most important factor. It is the more surprising therefore that little exact research work has been done to elucidate the complexities of the influence on children of the personalities and actions of their teachers. In the course of a school life of 9 or 10 years, an individual pupil may come into the charge of as many as 15 or 20 teachers;[1] normally, too, the contacts will be more continuous and extensive with younger children, more diffuse and discontinuous during adolescence. Qualitatively, the influence of the teacher varies according to the child's level of affective development: a kind of direct parent surrogate in the eyes of the pre-school or early school-age child, to the adolescent he is an adult the more able to exert influence just because he has not been involved in earlier affective relationships and conflicts.

The classroom group is a society of a structure different from that of the family or of most other groups in which children, adolescents and adults move. Whether obtrusively so or not, the teacher is the leader, the one also who gives or withholds security, and is in the last resort responsible for law and order. In that sense, he represents in the children's eyes the authority both of parents and of adult society at large. His contacts with individual pupils are less intimate than those of a parent, but usually more personal than those of adult authority in general. Directly or by implication, he makes demands and insists on values distinct from those of the home, and which may be in conflict with them. Since he is the only adult, or at least one of a restricted number, in the class environment, and since he represents authority, criticism and value in the learning situation, his influence,

---

1. In some countries, and especially when the child does not attend a secondary school the number may be much smaller—e.g. in German-speaking Switzerland, one teacher normally takes the children for their first three years, another for the next three, and either one or two for the next three. In all rural schools, the number may be smaller.

positive or negative, on his pupils is likely to be great—even though he may strive to concentrate his attention and judgment upon purely intellectual matters. The very formalized nature of most teaching situations—that of a group related as a group to one individual—tends to increase this influence. At the same time, the lack of closer contacts, such as come from family intimacy, emphasizes formal aspects of the teacher's personality.

In relation to the parents, too, he has a part to play. Often he is a respected person of great influence and authority, but, in the minds of some parents, at all events, there is a teacher stereotype based partly on attitudes preserved from their own school days, partly on dramatic and literary presentations of the teacher—often as a comic or pedantic figure. In the teacher-parent relationship, there is implicit a considerable element of jealousy, which readily gives substance to the humorous stereotype or produces overt hostility. Children are, of course, quick to exploit possible differences of opinion between home and school: 'My teacher says . . .', especially in the primary school years, is not infrequently used as a weapon at home. In breaking down such barriers, the personality of the teacher and his ability to communicate with parents are essential elements.

THE SOCIOLOGY OF THE TEACHING PROFESSION

The part played by the teacher in the society in which he lives, his influence on parents and pupils, is directly affected by the social valuation placed upon the teaching profession itself and by its class structure. In almost every country in Europe, the financial rewards of teaching are lower than those of other learned professions; and, in many, lower than those offered by commerce or industry. On the other hand, unlike most professional people, the teacher is a salaried employee enjoying a certain security of tenure, income and future pension rights. The level of public esteem in which the teaching profession is held—and which directly affects both recruitment and the attitudes of teachers to themselves—is in part reflected in the salaries paid, and in part is itself a reflection of the teacher's economic position. Other factors, of course, enter in a way difficult to evaluate. In particular, one might draw attention to the fact that, in many countries, the university teacher enjoys a very considerably enhanced esteem as compared with his colleague in the secondary school, who may have very similar qualifications.[1]

1. See the penetrating essays on 'The Social Position of Teachers' (R. K. Hall, N. Hans and J. A. Lauwerys) and on 'The Nature and Determinants of Social Status' (T. H. Marshal) in *The Year Book of Education 1953*. See also: *Schools under Pressure. I. The Shortage of Teachers*. London, PEP (*Planning* vol. XIX, no. 358).

Whatever the causes, the rewards and esteem of teaching determine in an important way the social structure of the profession. Apart from certain schools like the independent schools of the United Kingdom and other similar ones outside the State system in various countries, teaching staff tends in the main to be recruited from among the middle and working classes. Indeed, teaching in the State systems has been a principal vocational outlet for the intelligent boy or girl from these groups with social ambitions. This tendency has been emphasized in some countries by a system of bursaries and scholarships designed to attract candidates to the profession. Since standards of entry to training, and therefore of qualification for such aid, imply an academic secondary education, which in turn tends to stress a verbal culture, a large majority of entrants to teacher-training will be those who in a certain sense have been educated against the environment in which they have grown up. They will be affected in no small degree by a conflict of values, a conflict between the humanistic literary tradition, however attenuated, of the European liberal culture and the industrial urban milieu from which they may be attempting to escape.

Such potential conflicts may well be accentuated by other circumstances. In many European countries, the past 30 years or more have seen recurrent industrial depression and consequent unemployment; hence, one of the motives in the minds of parents and young people alike for the choice of teaching has been the economic security it offers. In comparison with other professions, however, and unlike commerce or industry, its outlets for ambition are not great and in terms of change of job, mobility is not a marked feature. Advancement within the profession is not clearly a function of achievement; and the change from teaching to educational administration, the inspectorate, or to jobs outside education, for which the teacher's educational level might fit him, is by no means easy. The existence in most countries of different training and salary levels for teachers working in the primary schools, and those, usually university graduates, employed in academic secondary education, tends further to diminish mobility and to produce within the profession itself a certain social stratification and, in some cases, intra-professional tensions.

THE TEACHER'S PERSONALITY

The factors outlined above, important in themselves, are most significant in relation to the personality structure of teachers,[1] and consequently to the system of personal relationships and reactions which

1. It is probable, as Vernon points out (*Year Book of Education 1953*), that teachers are as diversified a group as any other and that 'it is fallacious to talk of the teaching personality in general as something distinct and consistent'.

make up the classroom situation and the whole life of the school. The quality of these relationships is an important factor in many, if not in most, jobs; it is vital in teaching, since the teacher is in daily contact with children in critical stages of their development. Hence, from the viewpoint of the mental hygiene of the community at large, the teacher's psychology, his motives, his degree of maturity, his philosophy and opinions, his personal satisfactions and dissatisfactions, are of the utmost interest. This has been recognized partially by the stress which is sometimes laid, for example, on the importance of political impartiality, on his having or not having particular religious beliefs, upon his private life conforming to particular accepted patterns. Very little attention, however, has been paid to the unconscious factors which may operate in the teacher's relationships with the children he teaches, with his colleagues and with other adults.[1]

His attitudes to individual pupils and to many aspects of his job are likely to be greatly influenced by his own psychological growth. Not a few teachers find it difficult to outgrow the methods by which they themselves were taught. Attitudes to discipline—a topic of significantly marked interest to most teachers—may sometimes be determined by fears of their own aggressive tendencies, fears of the aggression latent in their pupils, reactions against or conformity with the system of their own homes or the schools in which they were taught. It is perhaps partly for reasons such as these that progress in teaching method and changes in the atmosphere of schools are slow to come about in spite of the efforts of training institutions. The teacher's daily job brings him into contact with the immature. The children whom he teaches, with their tendency to project on to the teacher attitudes and fantasies developed within their own families, may arouse in him markedly unobjective likings or dislikings and provoke behaviour on his part over which he has little control. The child to whom he is speaking may symbolize for him the child he feared or wished to be; complexes of jealousy or hostility, ambivalent love and hate, previously felt for a brother or sister may in part determine his evaluations of his pupils and his actions towards them.

THE EFFECT OF THE TEACHER'S CLASSROOM PERSONALITY ON THE CHILDREN HE TEACHES

Some of the ways in which the personality and attitudes of the teacher may influence pupils have been the subject of a number of studies by

1. Much of what follows is based upon papers prepared by the New Education Fellowship for the conference, notably on: D. Jordan, 'The Relationships of Teachers with other Adults'; M. L. Hourd, 'The Teacher in Relation to Himself and the Children he Teaches'; and M. Swainson, 'The Training of Teachers and their Mental Health'. These papers were published in their entirety in *New Era* vol. 33, no. 10, Dec. 1952. Material and ideas have also been taken from *Some Attitudes in Teachers:* an inquiry carried out by P. M. Turquet and T. Alcock under

Anderson and his collaborators.[1] Their work has been based upon the observation of 'dominative' and 'integrative' behaviour in teachers of kindergarten and primary classes. Domination on the teacher's part was broadly defined to include not only those words or actions which brought the teacher into conflict with the class or with an individual child but all those 'social contacts in which the activity of the child or of the group was determined out of the experience or judgment of the teacher'; integrative behaviour on the teacher's part, on the other hand, was assessed on the basis of the way in which she allowed the group's or the individual's activity to be determined in part at least by the judgment and experience of the children themselves. These two categories of behaviour are of major importance, not only because they can be used as dimensions for describing objectively the behaviour of teachers to their pupils, a thing difficult in itself, but because they do seem to provoke reactions in others of generally undesirable or desirable kinds. Studies of pre-school and kindergarten children, for example, reported by Anderson, confirm the common sense view that domination may incite domination and that socially integrative behaviour tends to induce co-operative or integrative behaviour. Thus the teacher who is markedly directive with a class, or who meets the aggressiveness of a pupil with domination or coercion, is likely to stimulate rather than allay aggressive tendencies; whereas socially integrative behaviour on the part of the teacher seems likely to promote co-operativeness in children and, where difficulties have arisen as the result of the child's own behaviour, to break the vicious circle of domination-resistance.[2]

This research, as might be expected[3] showed that 'among contacts

contract to Unesco in 1949-52, and from A. K. C. Ottaway, 'Mental Health in the Training of Teachers', *Bulletin of Education*. Association of Teachers in Colleges and Departments of Education (U.K.), 1951.

1. H. H. Anderson, et al. *Studies of Teachers' Classroom Personalities* I, II and III (*Applied Psychology Monographs* nos. 6, 8 and 11), American Psychological Association, Stanford, Stanford University Press, 1945, 1946. These studies are remarkable for the detailed care and objectivity with which they were carried out. This, of course, has meant that the number of teachers and children observed is relatively small, and the results, whilst highly suggestive, are not conclusive. It would be rash to generalize from the apparently generally permissive atmosphere of the schools studied by Anderson to any given school system in Europe.

2. It is necessary to distinguish between the authority which a good teacher exercises and authoritarianism, between permissiveness which brings children into participation and permissiveness which children accept as an invitation to anarchy. Authority exercised by a mature teacher and based upon understanding and affection for his pupils is accepted and even welcomed by them and is probably essential to their security; it is certainly not incompatible with socially integrative behaviour on the part of the teacher, either in contacts with the class or in contacts with particular children.

3. H. H. Anderson, op. cit., I, 'The Variability of Teachers' Behaviour towards Kindergarten Children'. More dominative contacts, especially with the class as a whole, might be expected, since of course the teacher's job is to direct the activities of her class, organize its existence and the like. Most teachers and psychologists would agree that children need and appreciate some direction and discipline. The important point of these researches is their revelation of the wide differences between teachers in their ability to bring the children into a participating rather than a passive co-operation.

initiated by the teachers, two out of three were dominative'; but there were wide differences between teachers of similar training and dealing with similar groups of children. These differences concerned the numbers of contacts made, the proportion of dominative and integrative contacts, and the number and kind of contacts made with individual children. For example one teacher, observed during 60 different sample periods of five minutes each, made 16 times as many dominative as integrative contacts with her class, as compared with another whose dominative contacts were five times as many as her integrative. Contacts with individual children were more integrative, though with very few exceptions dominative contacts still preponderated; one teacher made three times as many dominative as integrative contacts with individual children, as compared with another who made one and a half times as many integrative as dominative contacts. Perhaps most striking of all was the tendency, revealed in the inquiry, for the teachers to meet the dominative behaviour of individual children by repression rather than by attempts, through integrative behaviour, to break the vicious circle of aggression-domination-aggression.

Subsequent studies showed two other things: that a teacher's behaviour tended to be consistent from year to year, irrespective of the class she was teaching, but that from autumn to winter—that is to say as the teacher got to know her class better—instead of there being an improvement, there tended to be a deterioration.[1]

Such matters are of importance when we consider the effects on the behaviour of the children. It was found that, with the more integrative teachers, children were more spontaneous, showed greater initiative, and made more social contributions, both voluntary and in response to others; with the more dominating teachers there was more inattention, playing with foreign objects, and both conforming and nonconforming behaviour. This seemed to be true for children in kindergarten and in primary school classes. Following the same children from one year to the next, the investigators found that these patterns of response were, at the stage studied, characteristic less of the children themselves than of the classroom situation induced by the teacher.

No broad conclusions can be drawn from this study, since the number of pupils and teachers involved was small, the follow-up period was one year only, and the behaviour observed was relatively undifferentiated and not experimentally related to deeper factors in the personality of the children or of their teachers. But, behind the interactions which Anderson and his collaborators have demonstrated, it

---

1. M. F. Reed, op. cit., III, 'Consecutive Studies of the Schoolroom Behaviour of Children in Relation to the Teachers' Dominative and Socially Integrative Contacts'; H. H. Anderson and J. Brewer, ibid., 'Consecutive Studies from Fall to Winter of Teachers' Dominative and Socially Integrative Contact and Related Changes in Children's Classroom Behaviour'.

seems likely that there is a realm of teacher-pupil influences, conscious and unconscious, of crucial importance to the development of the child's personality.

In considering this we have to be aware of the context in which the teacher's influence is exercised. Children spend some 25 hours a week in the classroom, about one-third or rather less of their waking time. In the primary school this may be mainly with the same teacher, but from year to year in many school systems the teachers change. A given child is exposed normally to the influence of any particular teacher less than one might expect, and considerably less than to that of his own family. Many, if not the majority, of the contacts between teacher and pupil will be neutral, neither greatly contributing to growth nor particularly destructive. Yet teachers and methods, and the interactions of the staff among themselves make up the complex atmosphere of the school, and the very directness of influence implied by the structured situation of the classroom, with its defined purpose of learning, is inclined to increase the suggestibility, positive or negative, of each pupil.

THE EFFECT ON THE TEACHER OF THE BEHAVIOUR OF CHILDREN

The teacher's own response to the children he teaches, and the ways in which the school staff react to each other, to the head, to parents, to the educational hierarchy of which they form part, all go to influence the atmosphere in which the children at school live and learn.[1] If this atmosphere is relaxed and accepting, if it emphasizes co-operation and tolerance, then the pupils are likely themselves to be relaxed and co-operative; if it is tense and aggressive and emphasizes competition, then the pupils themselves are likely to be quick to sense this and to respond with aggression and interpersonal tensions. This reciprocal action and reaction between individual and group seems to be characteristic of any situation in which a number of individuals work together; one neurotic or aggressive person will modify, for example, the whole atmosphere of an office because every manifestation of personal aggression is liable to be echoed in the whole system of relationships. The very immaturity of the children who form the majority of the school group makes the school situation more liable to emotional disturbances of various kinds, since, whereas among

---

1. 'Because one of man's greatest unsolved problems is his relationship to his fellow men, the teacher should have the interests, the attitudes, the knowledge and the skills necessary to teach good human relations, tolerance and solidarity in classroom and home, and in the local, national and world community; the training establishment should recognize the paramount importance of this problem and, both through instruction and practice, qualify the teacher to teach good human relations and world understanding.' Recommendation 36, para. 50 of *XVIth International Conference on Public Education, Proceedings and Recommendations*. Paris, Unesco; Geneva, IBE, 1953.

adults the conscious defences and social habits which protect us from expressing unregenerate and unconscious impulses are well established, they are not so among children.

On the other hand, crude emotional expression among children is generally much less serious than among adults; it is more readily aroused, but also more easily assuaged. What is important is that teachers, and particularly those who have to do with young children, may find their own defences and repressions strongly and continuously challenged by the emotional expression of the children they teach. All but a very few professions, and especially those whose principal 'material' consists of human contacts, impose the emotional strains inherent in personal relationships. Teaching is peculiar in that the very immaturity of the pupil demands of the teacher greater self-restraint, objectivity and self-knowledge than are demanded of any other professional person except perhaps the psychologist or psychotherapist. It is at least partly for this reason that teaching is fatiguing; and perhaps there may be here one of the more or less unconscious motives behind the desire of some teachers that the school should be confined to a purely intellectual training of children.

It is not suggested that all or even the majority of teachers are constantly under an emotional strain to which they are unequal; nor that the challenge which the behaviour of children may present to immaturities in the teacher is continuous or destructive in more than a minority of cases. Yet if the school is to contribute positively to the personal growth of its pupils, we must be aware that the constant interaction of teacher and pupil may stimulate more than the intellect, and in a way which subtly eludes normal conscious control. This should imply that teachers themselves are aware of the process, and sufficiently mature to accept the implications for the pupils of the whole social psychology of the school. The authoritative position held by teachers enables them to conceal from themselves their own immaturity: the fact that in most cases they have gone from school to training college or university and then back to school may have isolated them from the miscellaneous human contacts that speed up maturation in late adolescence and young adulthood. Thus it may well be that some or all the members of a particular school staff have not themselves attained a sufficient personal objectivity to enable them to understand and control the child within themselves, in relation to their pupils, their colleagues or the head of the school.

To a very considerable degree, everyone uses his job as a means, not only of developing his potentialities, but of supplementing his own felt inadequacies. The teacher differs from others in that his material consists of human beings in the course of their growth. This gives him a greater opportunity than most of his fellows of deeper satisfactions, continually renewed as his classes change. In this lies the danger that the pupils may be used for the teacher's own unconscious ends. It is not difficult in any school to find teachers who strive, for example, to shape their pupils in their own image, or who, through a severe discipline, seem in fact to be reacting against their own feelings of guilty identification with the primitive impulses of childhood. It is probably rare nowadays, and it is unlikely that it was ever common, for there to be many seriously abnormal adults in teaching. The Squeers, Thwackums and Viots were probably always more common in literature than in life. Nevertheless without marked abnormality, without even minor neurosis, there are probably not a few teachers whose attitudes towards children in general or towards individual pupils are so coloured by jealousies, the need to dominate, by aggression issuing in sarcasm, by sentimental identification and the like, as to constitute a possible threat to the satisfactory growth of their charges.[1]

MOTIVES DETERMINING THE CHOICE OF A TEACHING CAREER

If indeed this is the case in even a small proportion of teachers, then a study of the motives for the choice of teaching as a profession becomes important. Many adolescents make a deliberate and well informed choice: some young people are attracted to teaching by a genuine love for children; others so value the culture they have themselves acquired that they wish to pass it on to the young; others, still, see in teaching a worthy contribution to social causes they wish to serve. On the other hand, because of the financial security it offers, because of the long holidays, and because it confers a certain minimum social prestige, teaching attracts a number of adolescents who hope that it will be an escape from other less attractive vocations.[2] Some, no doubt, drift into teaching without any clear idea of what is involved. From among all these some excellent, and many competent teachers develop whose positive contribution to their pupils' growth is not negligible.

A certain proportion, the size of which it is difficult to gauge, choose teaching for reasons which may well make them highly vulnerable to its strains, unsatisfactory as teachers, and a threat to the healthy development of their pupils. The very security offered by the profession may attract the unadventurous, in too high a proportion. There may be others who because of disturbances in their growth are fundamentally insecure and have sought an affirmation of themselves in intellectual success. Some perhaps, having identified too strongly with the authority of their own parents, seek an unchallenged authoritarian role; yet

1. 'The number of teachers enjoying adequate mental health is undoubtedly limited'.—*XVIth International Conference on Public Education, Proceedings and Recommendations* loc. cit., p. 141.
2. See the summary of research on this point, p. 63 ff. in *The Year Book of Education 1953*, previously cited.

others, wishing to play the part of the all-providing parent, may come unconsciously into jealous conflict with the real parents of the pupils they teach. Some, obsessed with perfection in themselves, see in teaching both freedom from criticism and the means of enforcing their compulsive standards on others.

Many of those whose reasons, expressed and unexpressed, for taking up the profession are not good ones undergo a considerable change in the process of maturation by experience in the classroom. Others do not: and there are some who enter teaching with every apparent prospect of success, but whose own inner life is so unbalanced that overt difficulties show themselves after they have been teaching some time.

SELECTION

When we remember that, in the course of a vocational life, a primary teacher may spend his days with some forty classes of children and may thereby influence directly the lives of between one and two thousand adults, the question of 'who shall teach?' assumes its full importance. In most European countries selection of students for teaching is based upon academic attainment, physical and moral fitness. In some, prospective candidates are interviewed before being accepted, and probably by this means the more grossly and obviously disturbed are eliminated. In few indeed is the recommendation of the recent Geneva Conference[1]—that psychological tests and interviews should be included in the selection procedure—put into practice.

The reasons for this are twofold. In the first place, few countries are in the happy position of having a considerable surplus of candidates over needs. Most have in fact to stimulate recruitment by the offer of generous training grants. As a consequence there is a strong tendency to accept all but the obviously unsuitable. The second difficulty is more serious. Our means of objectively assessing personality, even when used by those adequately trained in administering and interpreting them, are not highly reliable. Questionnaires, interviews, group and individual projection tests, though by no means useless, have great limitations, especially when we attempt to predict so complex a thing as teaching ability. Indeed, it is probable that there are many combinations of qualities of temperament, personality, intellect and the

---

1. '... It is desirable that all candidates should undergo psychological examination immediately before and during training, with a view to eliminating those possessing anomalies of character or behaviour which are incompatible with teaching; entrance examinations can be with advantage supplemented by interviews and, if necessary, by short periods of probation.'— Recommendation No. 36, para. 26, *XVIth International Conference on Public Education, Proceedings and Recommendations*, loc. cit.

like which lead to different kinds of success in the classroom, and with different age levels of children. It is likely too that certain kinds of 'maladjustment' in the teacher are not harmful to the exercise of his profession and may even be an asset in dealing with some difficult children.

Nevertheless much more could be done than at present to eliminate at an early stage the obvious misfits. Objective assessments of academic and intellectual levels are fairly readily and reliably made; much relevant information on interests, attitudes and conscious motives can be ascertained in a planned interview and from a carefully drawn up questionnaire to the candidate's school. The first month of the course can be treated as a trial period or 'work sample' during which the student is put into many of the situations which arise in teaching, into group activities with other students, and is given an insight into the demands of the profession. This allows a prolonged period of observation by the responsible tutors, aided if possible by the psychological staff. At the end each student might be asked to rate his fellows as well as to write an analysis of his own reactions to these initial experiences. From all these data a decision as to whether or not any student should be accepted can be made with some likelihood of success.[1]

In this general connexion it is important to realize that the teacher in training is usually adolescent. Even at the age of 17 or 18 the processes of psychological maturation are by no means complete; in many countries students are two or even three years younger than this.[2] Thus many of the difficulties of personality growth may be transitory, and others could be eliminated or reduced by wise guidance given in the course of training. The training period itself offers an opportunity for continuous observation of the students, for suggesting before it is too late a change of occupation for those whose personality is clearly unsuitable, and for a direct and conscious attempt by the training college staff to help the majority in the task of growing up into mature, self-aware and balanced adults.

---

1. This is a method based upon the techniques evolved for officer selection during the war and cautiously advocated by Vernon, who points out that for real success a 'favourable selection ratio' must exist. On the techniques of selection used in the army, see P. E. Vernon and J. B. Parry, *Personnel Selection in the British Forces*. London, University of London Press, 1949.
2. The usual age of admission to teacher-training courses in Europe is 17 or 18, though in some countries (for example Austria, Belgium, France, Holland, Luxembourg, Portugal, Spain), it may be two or three years younger. Those who pursue a university course are likely to enter upon professional training somewhat later. Most usually those countries which have an earlier age of entry have correspondingly a longer course of training—e.g. five years in Austria—of which a large proportion is devoted to general education. In most European countries the purely vocational and professional training of the teacher comes during the last year or two before beginning employment. Hence most teachers begin their working career at between 19 and 21 years of age.—*Primary Teacher Training*. Geneva, IBE; Paris, Unesco; publication no. 116.

THE TRAINING COURSE AS AN AID TO GROWTH

In the present conditions of comparative shortage of suitable candidates, it is principally to the training course that we must look to bring about an improvement in the quality of teachers. For at least two years,[1] in some countries for as long as five,[2] the student-teacher is in contact with the training college. A good deal of this time is devoted to continued, general education, and a common criticism[3] is that too little is left for the professional training, and particularly for the guided, practical experience, which are equally necessary. It is generally admitted that the basic training should be either lengthened or considerably supplemented by courses organized for teachers after some years of classroom experience.

The shortness of the training period certainly imposes limitations on what can be done; but, in planning the initial training of teachers and subsequent in-training or refresher courses, priorities should be carefully considered. If indeed, as has been argued earlier, modern conditions demand greater maturity, stability and insight from the teacher than in the past, and if he is called upon to play a constructive rather than a purely conservative part in the development of his society, then it seems to follow that one of the first essentials in the training course is that of ensuring the teacher's own psychological growth.

Such an aim implies three things. Firstly, to an extent determined by their individual capacity, the students must come to grips with themselves, learning to comprehend the unconscious elements which determine their opinions, attitudes and actions and gaining as large a degree as possible of objectivity and detachment. This will involve a consideration both of their own previous development, and of their current problems. In some cases, students may need individual psychological help in getting over, or at least in coming to understand and control, neurotic difficulties. Secondly, they must become aware of the importance of the interpersonal and intergroup relations within which they and their pupils live and learn. This implies experiences of authority, freedom and co-operation which, through discussion and introspection they must come to comprehend and digest emotionally. Finally, there must be a transference to the child and to the classroom situation of what the student has learned about himself and about the psychology of groups. In many ways this is the most critical aspect of training, since if it is to be more than superficial the deeper aspects of the relations among children and between children and teachers must

---

1. Except those who pursue university studies and concentrate their professional training into one year after graduation.
2. In those cases where teacher-training begins at 15.
3. *XVIth International Conference on Public Education, Proceedings and Recommendations,* loc. cit. p. 144.

be brought to light and related to similar situations which the student is experiencing in his training course.

In practice this can be carried out in many different ways, and success will depend upon the capacity of the training staff and upon the flexibility which can be achieved within the programme.[1] Of primary importance is the quality of the training college itself as a community. One of the most common problems with which the young teacher must come to terms is his relationship to his idea of himself as an authority. Intellectually, he may believe in democratic theories of government; emotionally, however, he has probably been conditioned by home and school to a large measure of autocratic authority. It is a revelation to such a student to be in a college in which the community is a co-operative group, where the principal deliberately abrogates a good deal of authority, and where the students study the implications of freedom and responsibility by living them. The establishment of such a college environment is not easy, since to be effective in a dynamic way it can be planned only to a limited extent; it must rather grow, altering its quality with each new member of staff and with each influx of students, and taking several years to mature. But when informed throughout by psychological insight and co-operative understanding, the emotional atmosphere of college or school is the most important factor in the teacher's psychological release and growth.

Within such a framework there is much to be done through the actual content of the courses, particularly the professional courses, and through the methods employed by the staff. The courses should be planned to challenge unconscious assumptions and to put the student in the position of having to do something about these matters if he is to survive. In this, practice teaching can be made an experience which leads to considerable self-questioning. At the same time the tutor should help the students to a hopeful and constructive attitude to their own development, and to a belief in the possibility of change.

The previous education of the students will have been verbally and intellectually biased, giving little enough outlet to creativity and starving many aspects of the personality. Thus practical and artistic activities of all kinds—arts and crafts, music, drama, gardening, etc.— have a more than purely aesthetic contribution to make to the personal growth of teachers in training; they provide a vehicle, in many ways psychologically equivalent to play, for the release of emotion and for the shaping of the whole affective life. They are not frills or ornaments

1. A great deal of what follows in the next three or four pages has been cited verbatim or adapted directly from the paper specially prepared for the conference by M. Swainson, on 'The Training of Teachers and their Mental Health', loc. cit. The work described is based upon practical experience which could be matched, with differences of means and organization, in a small number of the more progressive teacher-training colleges and Institutes of Education in the United Kingdom.

to be squeezed in if time allows or to be taught as merely utilizable techniques for those who teach in primary schools. They have a value in training as a constructive complement to more intellectual studies.

THE COURSE IN PSYCHOLOGY

The course which can most influence the growth of the students is the course in psychology.[1] In the traditional training establishment this course is usually theoretical and is often regarded by the students—not without reason—as having little application either to themselves or to children. It is more important that a teacher should understand himself and be sympathetic to children than that he should have at his finger tips a systematized body of knowledge on learning theory. Psychological insight is not easily gained from books and from lectures; it demands close practical experience in which the whole personality is involved. Hence the core of the course in psychology should be the continued, guided and detailed study of individual children, and of children in small groups, supplemented by some examination and observation of one's self and one's contemporaries. Around this guided experience, the more systematic study of psychology may be readily built. Time can be saved by giving essential factual information in the form of duplicated notes, bibliographies and suggestions for study. The course itself can then be concentrated upon: *social psychology*, stressing the development of interpersonal and intergroup relations with particular reference to the family group, the play group, the psychology of the classroom and of the school as a society; a thorough survey of *child and adolescent development* with special emphasis on emotional growth, and on the particular significance of early childhood and adolescence; and finally a study of the *dynamics of human personality*, including some outline of the psychology of the unconscious, which is clearly necessary to an understanding of the problems of behaviour and adjustment.

Though much may be achieved by a trained psychologist through a course of lectures, discussions and observations as outlined above, there are other methods which should be incorporated in a training aimed at the personal development of the students. For example, it is possible, particularly at the later stages, to arrange for a wide freedom of individual choice of studies, including the choice of a research topic, so that only rarely do two students have an identical programme. Since the issue of freedom and authority is so crucial, students may be

---

1. This assumes that the aims and philosophy of education are fully dealt with, and not merely at an academic level. Psychology as such is a technique and a body of scientific fact; it is not a substitute for values, but a means of understanding oneself and others and thus of assimilating values into the texture of living.

encouraged to take progressively more responsibility for the course, until towards the end they plan it largely themselves. The whole purpose of such techniques is to strengthen the personality in its work of making choices and accepting responsibility, in contrast to the older type of training based largely on imposition of external standards. By this means the individual is helped to develop all his potentialities, to grow from his own roots, to find himself, and discover that inner security which frees him from compulsive dependence upon the opinion of society.

No one, of course, can develop fully except in relation to a free group; hence, since socialization and individuation go hand in hand, stress should be laid on group life as much as on individual development. In a large college, tutorial discussion groups provide the necessary intimate unit in which each student is known well as a person and the shyest may feel valued. The family set-up provides that feeling of 'belonging' which is necessary, particularly at the outset, to give a sense of security. In this informal environment, free criticism of the course and of tutors is possible, and at certain stages even rebellion may be found valuable, so that the student can thus become aware of processes within himself and learn to discriminate between rational and emotionally based criticism. Students can exchange experiences and learn to understand themselves and one another. Sibling problems may be worked out in relation to other students, and parent problems in relation to the tutor. A wise tutor can help an immature student to free himself from parent fixations by playing deliberately whatever form of parental part is required. Throughout the course he may purposely adopt different parts, according to need, ranging from that of the strong leader providing information, advice, inspiration and encouragement, to the colleague who shares equally in discussion, the guide, the detached observer, the guinea-pig (training the student by using his own personality as an example), or the servant of the group. This change of roles helps the student to become aware of what is involved in the idea of 'teacher'.

It should be unnecessary to state that the object of such methods, of the emphasis on the psychology of emotional development, and of the deliberate attempt to lead students to a study and understanding of themselves and of their own growth, is not to induce morbid introspection, nor to train them as amateur psychologists or psychotherapists. It is to lead intending teachers to become, as far as their intelligence and maturity permit, 'transparent to themselves'. Thus they may progressively free themselves from their own illusions and fantasies and be better able to deal realistically with the fantasies and behaviour problems of children. They should be brought to see that no human problem is simple and that psychology supplies an attitude of mind and a method of approach to the study of such problems rather than a series of neat formulae and ready-made answers. They should learn too that there is much they can do to help children to grow up satisfactorily, but that there are occasional situations which require outside help, and more special skill and knowledge than they possess.

Such a constructive use of the teaching of psychology, of the whole atmosphere of the training college and of the methods employed, makes great demands upon the personality, maturity and skill of the tutors, and particularly upon the teacher of psychology.[1] Many of the tutors themselves may need training in the techniques of the tutorial group, and the whole staff has to learn to work as a democratic team. The teacher of psychology requires something more than an academic knowledge of psychology gleaned from books or a theoretical university course. The effectiveness of his work will depend upon his human qualities, upon his ability to temper the directness of the information conveyed to the receptivity of the student, and upon his skill and experience in handling the personal difficulties in individual students which any study of psychology below the purely intellectual level may uncover. As well as having been himself a teacher, he should have had training and experience in the practical applications of psychology to the problems of the classroom, to individual difficult children and adults, and a very thorough knowledge of child and adolescent development.

On the teacher of psychology devolves another duty for which he must take a major responsibility, though he will share it with his colleagues. Some students need personal psychological advice of a kind more specific than tutors can normally give. It is essential that such cases should be ascertained as early in the course as possible. Many sensitive and intelligent neurotics, provided they have tackled and understood their own problems, can become of value as teachers, sometimes more so than the relatively insensitive mentally robust type, since they are frequently more understanding of children's difficulties. But a good many young teachers go into the schools with neuroses untouched by the training course, neuroses which frequently lead to a breakdown during the first few years of teaching, or to severe personality problems in later life with consequent unfortunate repercussions on the children. At the student stage a great many problems which cause severe anxiety are relatively slight in nature and yield to a few sessions with a trained psychological adviser or counsellor.

---

1. XVIth International Conference, Resolution 36, paras. 52 and 49.

This is work which the psychological specialist on the staff of a training college can well undertake, passing on those cases which require more prolonged treatment than he can give to outside psychological or psychiatric services.[1]

OTHER ASPECTS OF TEACHER-TRAINING

The development of an adequate personality in all those who will teach children is a first aim of teacher-training. The attempt to achieve this by the means described above will inevitably contribute to the students' professional efficiency; but, if the schools are to play a constructive part in the development of their pupils and to fulfil some of the aims outlined in earlier chapters, then time must be found in the training course for the acquisition of certain additional techniques and skills.

All teachers should know enough about the problems encountered in the growth of normal children and of the ways in which they may be handled neither to become too anxious about transitory difficulties nor to overlook more serious matters with which the psychological services should be called upon to deal. Some contact during their training with an active psychological service or child guidance centre, in particular through the participation of school psychologists in the training course, can go far to ensure that the student is made aware of such behaviour and developmental problems without being over-whelmed by them. Teachers, too, who in the course of their training have gained some insight into the work of the school psychologist are more ready to collaborate on classroom problems with colleagues trained in psychology.

On the teacher falls the major responsibility for the educational, and later for the vocational guidance of the pupils. Before education was universal and compulsory, and before European schools became diversified, particularly at the secondary stage, in the kinds of studies offered, guidance could be a rough and ready business. An increased awareness and knowledge of the psychology of individual differences and a growing recognition that, in our technological society, a child's future choice of career may be determined by choice of study made as early as the age of 11 or 12, has thrown into relief the need for

---

1. See Section III of the *Report of an Expert Committee on Psychological Services for Schools and other Educational Institutions*, Hamburg, Unesco Institute for Education, 1955. Some universities and large training colleges have developed student guidance services staffed by psychologists and social workers with psychiatric help when that is needed. Others, concentrating more upon psychiatric services, include the work in student health programmes. See: *Problems of Student Health*. Geneva, ISS, 1949; and *La santé à l'université*. Cahier no. 2, Paris, Bureau international des universités, 1954.

continuous observation and recording of the child's whole growth, so that the trends of personal, social, emotional and intellectual development may be detected and so that difficulties may be recognized at a stage early enough for them to be set right by relatively simple means. Where difficulties arise that are beyond the teacher's power to cure, then the school record should contain the relevant facts on which the educational psychologist can base his more profound examination. At the stage of school leaving, the cumulative observations of the teachers should complement the more specialized findings of the vocational guidance specialist.

Such records, however carefully devised, are only as good as the teachers in daily contact with the pupils can make them. The quality and insight of a teacher's observation depends in part upon his general knowledge of children, and of what to look for; in part, upon training in observing and in recording. The training course cannot, except in rare cases, produce the good teacher who is also a perfectly objective, detached and scientific observer of children. It can give its students an insight into the simpler techniques of objective testing, including the precautions necessary in the interpretation of results, and into the methods of observation and of recording, all essential tools of the teacher's craft. The basis can be laid on which experience and subsequent training can build.

Educational and vocational guidance—and still more the attempt to help individual children with particular difficulties—is unlikely to be successful unless teacher and parent co-operate. To do this on more than a superficial level, the teacher not only needs to know something of the psychology of family life, but also to have had some training in how to convey information to parents, and in the techniques of informal education.

Nothing has been said about the general content of the basic training course for teachers, and it would be inappropriate here to examine in detail the various aspects of general culture and of pedagogical skills which it should contain. We should stress that there is a craft of teaching, of how to help children to gain the techniques of knowledge; and this craft has an experimental psychological basis with which the teacher should have more than a nodding theoretical acquaintance. He should, for example, have studied the mental reactions and intellectual mechanisms involved in learning; he should know how to discover the abilities and disabilities of his pupils as they show themselves, particularly in the classroom learning situation. The professional teacher alone in any mixed group of those concerned with the education and growth of children is likely to be the expert on pedagogy; it is essential that his training should make him thoroughly competent in this matter, and that further training should increase his specialist knowledge.

THE TEACHER AS SOCIAL SCIENTIST

There is one overriding consideration which should make us perhaps rethink the whole structure, philosophy and method of our teacher-training. It has been argued earlier that the speed of social change in Europe demands of every adult person a capacity to adapt to and, at the same time, to shape his society. Industrialization and technological change have destroyed, removed or fundamentally changed many of the educative and assimilative influences in the environment which more or less healthily and effectively completed the efforts of the family and the school to bring up children and young people. Traditional social and philosophic interpretations, habits of thought and of action have been assailed, not so much by new integrations, as by the simple perception on the part of more and more people that they just do not apply to modern life. Material progress has destroyed old frameworks of meaning and has gone on too fast to allow others to grow.

Thus the school can no longer concentrate solely upon the preservation and transmission of an intellectual culture, many of the meanings of which have been made irrelevant by atomic fission, international discord and the increasing proximity of huge human groups at different stages of moral evolution. The task of forming the character and personality of children and adolescents cannot be left to the unaided family and to an environment which becomes more and more depersonalized. The teacher is in fact called upon to play the part of an applied social scientist;[1] he must constantly challenge his own assumptions and

---

1. The potential social influence of education has long been recognized; but, by and large, it has been exercised conservatively, and children have been trained for the world of their fathers. In certain instances, whole educational systems have been geared to the mass-production of servile citizens of the State. There is inevitably a danger in expecting schools to shape their pupils for the new society towards which they are moving, but that is a danger which springs rather from the concepts of the society itself, and notably its idea of the value of the individual, than from the efficiency with which the school carries out this social task. It is harder to educate children for a liberal tolerant society based upon the value and dignity of man than for one in which submission to the State and intolerance to other groups are erected as values; hence success has more often attended totalitarian efforts to use education as a means of changing society. The consequence of this has been fear and distrust of this idea of education and an attempt, in some quarters, to thrust the school back into the negative position of merely training the intellect.

One should recall the works of such writers as Castiglione and Ascham, the admittedly partial and limited success of certain of the English independent schools, and the part played by the primary schools in the United States in the development of the American character and way of life from the most heterogeneous and massive immigrations in history (see for example, M. Mead, *The American Character*. London, Penguin Books Ltd., 1944, and C. Gorer, *The American People*. New York, W. Norton, 1948).

It is not without a significance that the rapporteur (R. Dottrens) of the recent Intergovernmental Conference on Primary Education at Geneva (see IBE publication no. 151) stressed this as a major point arising from the conference discussions and drew attention to its relative novelty in thinking about public education. H. Rugg, in *The Teacher of Teachers*. New York, Harper Bros., 1952, carries the matter much further and proposes a detailed plan of teacher training to meet the situation, which he says will arise within a few decades, when man can be maintained by fully automatic machines without having himself to work. See also H. F. Clark, 'Schools Can Change a Community', *Teachers' College Record*. New York, Columbia University Teachers' College, 1943.

examine his own culture in the light of the present and the future of society. He is called on to see that the education he gives his pupils exploits the riches and supplements the deficiencies of their environment and brings them to the point at which they may assimilate the changes which are taking place, and play their part in controlling them. Less and less can the teacher's job be confined to the classroom; less and less can the school isolate itself: it must bring family and community together for the purpose of educating a new generation which, having reinterpreted the faith and culture of its fathers, may control its own destiny. The school must produce men and women who can assimilate in their own lifetime centuries of change without undergoing disruptive social and political strains.

There is no member of the community with a heavier responsibility. It seems therefore somewhat illogical that in many countries the possession of a university degree in any subject (not education) is considered an index of sufficient preparation for teaching, in an academic school, just those children from among whom will come many leaders of society. In other countries a competitive academic examination is the sole instrument of selection—an examination which tells the examiner nothing of the candidate's capacity to teach, though much of his capacity to write answers to examination questions.

Personal maturity and considerable psychological skill are even more essential than high academic attainment; but even these are not enough. A teacher's own experiences of childhood and adolescence are no sure guide to the psychological climate in which his pupils live. Hence he must be sensitively aware of the changing environment in which his pupils are moving, and on this awareness base the aims of his teaching. The cultural and pedagogical content of the teacher-training course must make the student aware of contemporary problems in a concrete way and lead him to seek for means to resolve them in full cognizance of the constants, moral and intellectual, which obtain whatever the form of society. He should be given the skills to reappraise his environment continually and to question what it may mean to his pupils and how it has changed from when he was young. His studies of child development should give him the basis on which to ask how far modern families are capable, even in the early years of growth, of fully meeting the psychological and educational needs of children; and he should be helped to see how, without undermining the parents' authority and responsibility he may aid in the task of bringing up children. He should be led to analyse the roots of prejudice and belief and to confront theories and facts dispassionately, aware that today's favoured hypothesis is tomorrow's popular fallacy. Such a questioning attitude, and the willingness to act in the light of his own maturing insight into his own culture, will not be produced in a student trained on a diet of secondhand information relayed in lectures.

The basic training course, even when it is undertaken at the age of 21 or older, and at the end of university studies, can be expected to do no more than begin to prepare teachers for their task. The attainment of personal maturity can be guided and considerably accelerated, but two or even three years is a short space of time in which to develop a deep insight into oneself and into the educational process. Professional skills, and genuine practical knowledge of child development, cannot be hastily acquired; they have to grow and be confirmed in practice. Those aspects of the teacher's task which turn towards the future of our society demand an even longer period of maturation. The best we can hope for from the basic training course is that it will open the mind of the young teacher to the great socio-moral problems of our time and point some of the ways to their solution.

Education is a profession which makes many and highly varied demands; there is in fact no such thing as 'the teacher' or 'the teacher's task'. Many different kinds of teacher are needed, and many specializations corresponding to different individual gifts and tastes are not only open, but necessary, if the schools are to do their job. Some teachers, for example, have a particular gift for making easy contacts with parents; others are peculiarly able to help the child who is failing; yet others may be apt for and have genuine interest in educational and vocational guidance; some may have the personal qualities which will make a good psychologist; and there are many other aspects of school life and of the contacts between the school, the home and the community which call for particular qualities and a complement of training. There is indeed probably no other profession in which specialization within the framework of a common basic training and common pre-occupations is more necessary—or has been hitherto more neglected, except in the purely academic field. The special course, full-time or part-time, short or extending over six months, a year or even more, and undertaken after the young teacher has already been at grips with the practical problems of teaching, increases within the profession the number of people with complementary special skills.

Such courses may be made to serve a double purpose, particularly where they deal with educational method, with psychology and with aspects of parent-teacher or teacher-child relationships. They should of course improve the teacher's own techniques, which is their major overt purpose; but they can also contribute to the teacher's personal development by confronting him incidentally with the core problems of education, and by involving him in a group-learning situation. For example, a short course on the initial stages of teaching arithmetic is frequently given as a series of lectures or lecture-demonstrations in a more or less didactic fashion. On the other hand, it might consist of a group of teachers discussing the problems of teaching arithmetic in the light of their own experience, aided by a tutor who conceives of his task as being that of gathering together relevant material for the group, of occasionally posing a question, or making a summary of the discussion, and of organizing with individual teachers small experiments in their classes. In the didactic lecture, the tutor is relaying information which may well remain inert; in the second situation the tutor is there much more as a technician who speeds up the work of the group. Active participation has another effect; the relationships betwe members of the group become informal; deeper questions than those of educational technique arise; and a good tutor is quick to profit from them by raising problems for discussion or research without himself being directive.

The responsibility for providing and organizing much of the continued education of teachers should rest largely with the teachers and education authorities themselves, supported by university departments of education, institutes of education and of applied psychology and teacher-training colleges. The training staffs, it should be pointed out, are as likely to benefit from such collaboration as the practising teachers, since the teacher will, given the opportunity, pose the real day-to-day problems of education so apt to be forgotten by those whose direct classroom experience has been overlaid by theoretical study.

This continued education and training has far-reaching possibilities for the whole development of education in any country. Most educational policies are based upon two assumptions. The first is that a certain relatively high level of general intelligence[1] is required of all teachers. Since this is ascertained mainly by the criterion of success in a particular form of secondary education, some 90 per cent of teachers are recruited from the top fifth of the population for verbal intelligence. The second assumption is that, in the primary school at all events, teachers are interchangeable; and that all that is necessary is to have a school staff of a number sufficient to man the classes. Secondary education, and particularly academic secondary education, recognizes the need for the subject specialist. Few schools and school systems, however, have come to realize that within any school there is a need for a balanced team of educational specialists, who, though they may share a common training and do a common job, should also complement one another with specially developed skills.

It may well be asked whether any community can afford to allow teaching to absorb a large proportion of the nation's superior intellects —a proportion which will grow as we move nearer to the small class

---

1. In the English and Scottish school systems *as they are at present constituted*, there are indications that an I.Q. much below 110 is a handicap to efficiency. The general average on verbal tests among students preparing for teaching is much higher. See *Yearbook of Education 1953*, loc. cit. (Vernon), p. 71,

of 25 to 30 children. Certainly all teachers ought to be well educated, but it is worth asking whether affective and personal qualities are not more important than a high level of intelligence for many teachers, for example, those who teach children of pre-school age or in the early primary years. If this is so, then we can accept the entry into teaching of some of those who have not followed academic courses of secondary education, and can for many levels stress personal qualities and a variety of pre-training background and experience.[1] This is not to advocate a general lowering of standards of education or of intelligence. It is to suggest that the intellectual criterion is not the only one of suitability for teaching and that the demands made by teaching at different levels and in different schools should be examined to see whether the net of recruitment could be cast more widely, and whether teacher-training could be more closely adapted to the needs both of the students and of the schools they will serve.

An essential corollary is that greater attention should be paid to ensuring, within each school, a balance of talent, and, generally in the profession, a number of highly trained and highly intelligent individuals available to deal with special problems, to continue the in-training of their colleagues, to act as advisers, heads and directors of schools, and to break new ground in educational technique, curriculum planning and philosophy. In this perspective a co-ordinated programme of further training for practising teachers is essential, ranging from short refresher courses on particular aspects of the teacher's job to intensive and lengthy periods of special training for such functions as that of teacher of handicapped children, school psychologist or counsellor, head teacher, inspector or adviser.

II. TEACHERS WITH SPECIALIST COMPETENCE[2]

In Chapter IX a general outline was given of those groups of exceptional children for whom some form of special educational provision is necessary if they are to realize to the full their impaired capacity. In some countries, and with some special groups, the pioneer educational work with such children has until now been done by devoted amateurs,

1. As was done, with a considerable measure of success, in the post-war Emergency Training Scheme in the United Kingdom. Men and women from many different walks of life, most of them considerably older than students normally accepted for teacher-training, were given one year of full-time training followed by two years of part-time training and supervision. See: M. M. Lewis (ed.), *Teachers from the Forces*. London, Harrap (n.d.).
2. What follows is in part based upon the report drawn up for Unesco by N. L. Gibbs on behalf of the Committee of Professional Psychologists. See also: *National Advisory Council on the Training and Supply of Teachers of Handicapped Pupils: Fourth Report*, London, HMSO, 1954, and U.S. Department of Health, Education and Welfare, Office of Educations: *State Certification Requirement for Teachers of Exceptional Children*, 1954, No. 1.

or by professional teachers who have come more or less accidentally to the job. For certain groups, the blind, and to some extent the deaf, for example, a particular pedagogy has grown up which has been followed by the development of special training for teachers. Compared however with the scientifically based knowledge which research has supplied for the education of normal children, our knowledge of the problems of many handicapped groups and of educational techniques adapted to their special needs is scanty.

Hence, because we know so little, the education of handicapped children has to be experimental and must not be allowed prematurely to crystallize into a body of doctrines cut off from the main stream of educational advance. This experimental approach and the continuing day-to-day research which it implies demand of the teachers a greater background of knowledge than is usual. Moreover, apart from the more strictly pedagogical problems, such for example as the method of teaching blind children braille or deaf children to lip-read, there is a range of psychological problems upon the handling of which the successful education of such children depends. The teacher of physically handicapped, sensorially defective, emotionally disturbed or mentally subnormal children is, even more than his colleagues, called upon to make intimate contact with his pupils' families—a contact which may be the most important factor in allaying parental anxieties or excessive expectations, and in winning a fruitful co-operation in the task of education. Handicapped children of all types present a number of personality problems which demand of the teacher patience, insight and some measure of training so that he can carry out the advice of the psychologist. In many countries, particularly where the population is scattered, special educational provision is made in boarding schools. In such establishments, even more than in day schools, the teaching staff may have to accept a large responsibility for the out-of-classroom lives of the pupils; and in any case the social and personal development of the handicapped child must be an essential preoccupation of all who have to do with him.

On the teacher of handicapped children falls also the task of co-operating with other specialists, medical and psychological, who may from time to time have to do with the child. For example orthopaedic and heart cases call for great resource on the teacher's part. Resentment against forced 'rest' or disappointment at the result of some painful or arduous treatment tend to make children difficult or unhappy or both, and the teacher's understanding and inventiveness can help them to stand up to these stresses if an intelligent interest exists in the various sides of what is a joint task. This implies that the teacher must understand what is being done by the medical staff, and the medical staff must respect the teachers as intelligent colleagues with similar though different responsibilities.

276

Even so general a sketch of the demands made upon the specialist teachers indicates the need for a training which will enable them to discharge their task satisfactorily. The aim of special education is essentially that of helping the handicapped to grow up as normally as possible; hence it is important that the teacher of such children should never become so wrapped up in the world of the handicapped as to lack standards of normality against which to gauge his success and that of his pupils. This suggests that teachers for special schools and classes should be recruited from among those who after the period of basic teacher-training have had considerable experience—at least three to five years would seem desirable—of work with normal children. But special education should not be allowed to become a professional dead end; the specially trained teacher should, if possible, have some periodic or continuous contact with the main stream of education and should have an equal chance of promotion to headships of ordinary schools. Both these considerations lay stress upon the undesirability of training teachers in a speciality immediately upon the completion of basic training, or of having a different and parallel form of basic training.

While much may be done by short courses, and by studies extending part-time over a period, for teachers who are already working in special schools or classes, the main body of specialized teachers, and particularly those who become heads of special schools, should have a thorough training, extending over at least one year, of full-time theoretical and practical work.[1] Such a course should lead to a qualification earning an increment of salary and should be developed in association with training colleges, university institutes of educational research, psychological services and special schools. In addition to an intensified study of educational methodology and of child development, the course should cover study of and practical experience with all types of handicapped child, guided practice in the methodology of teaching the special group chosen, some acquaintance with simpler techniques of educational and psychological research and experiment, and practice and experience in various forms of work with parents. The student should acquire a sound knowledge of the scope and functions of those other services, medical, social and vocational, which impinge upon his field and should be given some insight into the work of the numerous other specialists, with whom he may have to co-operate.

As special educational provision develops within any educational system, it will probably be found that, whereas the majority of teachers need a degree of specialization such as may be achieved within a year's

---

1. Since the war there has been a considerable development in universities in the U.K. of such one-year courses—for teachers of maladjusted, subnormal and deaf children particularly. Similar but shorter courses have been developed in France in specialized colleges.

course, it will be an advantage to provide facilities for a few to undertake more prolonged study and greater specialization leading to a higher university degree or its equivalent. The very uncertainty of our knowledge and the complexity of the difficulties involved demand of those who are to conduct the essential research, and who are to open up new fields of education for different kinds of handicapped children, a training which fits them to tackle the many problems presented by any one disability. It should not be forgotten either that many reforms in the education of ordinary children have arisen from knowledge gained in the teaching of special groups. The highly trained specialist educator with freedom to experiment and to research is likely to have an influence far beyond his apparently limited field.

A word should be said about teachers of retarded and maladjusted children, for whom in most countries no special training as yet exists.[1] The work of such teachers is somewhat different from that of others. The child who is maladjusted or who is retarded in his school work (but not dull in intelligence) presents primarily a *remedial* problem. It is a question of re-education, often on a short-term basis, rather than of special education throughout the whole school life. The teacher frequently has to work alone, either as a specialist in an ordinary school, or moving from school to school or in a class attached to a psychological service. He is often called upon to make the first screening of children who may need his help. Thus he needs a very thorough psychological grounding, including a competence in the more commonly used tests and measures, a good knowledge of the psychology and methodology of the basic school subjects, experience in the various remedial techniques, including the remedial use of play, creative work of various kinds, and free dramatic work, and a trained ability to co-operate in parent guidance. Such workers, carefully selected from among experienced teachers in primary and secondary schools and given a thorough training, can do much to decrease educational retardation and to cure maladjustment before neglect makes them serious.

In view of the fact that the various kinds of specialized training proposed are in their early stages, they are best associated with research in progress. In the stage in which most European countries find themselves as regards special education, it would probably be most effective if two or preferably more different types of course for teachers of handicapped children were associated with an institute of educational and psychological research with a particular interest in the field and at least an experimental diagnostic and remedial service.[2] Where such

---

1. The Institute of Education, University of London, has a one-year course for teachers of maladjusted children, and the Institute of Education, University of Birmingham, a one-year course for those concerned with bright-retarded children.
2. As at Manchester University (Department for the Education of the Deaf) and at Birmingham University (The Remedial Education Centre, Department of Education).

an institute is in a university setting, it is easier to bring both the research and the training into relation with social science, orthopaedic
and pediatric departments. This permits some measure of joint training
for those who will be concerned with handicapped children and
facilitates the interprofessional respect and understanding which is the
basis of sound team-work.

III. PSYCHOLOGICAL SERVICES[1]

If the school is truly to play a constructive part in the healthy development of children and adolescents, it must have at its command the insights and the technical skills which research in educational psychology
has built up over the past century and is daily extending. As has
been indicated earlier, this will in part be achieved through the basic
training and continued training of practising teachers, through the
revision of curricula and methods in the light of a growing knowledge
of the rhythms of child development and of social needs, and through
bringing applied psychology to bear upon the education of parents in
better methods of child-rearing.

Many problems arise, however, in the day-to-day life of the schools,
and many developmental difficulties occur in children which demand
more skill, special training, detachment and time than the class teacher
can give. Moreover, the estimates given in Table 2 (Chapter IX)
indicate that there is a considerable number of children who display
more or less serious maladjustments which call for psychological treatment of a kind that teachers and schools cannot normally undertake.
Recognition of these needs has led many European countries to develop
psychological services of many partial kinds, some inside the educational system itself and some attached to the social or medical services.

The motive behind the establishment of many such services has been
that of treating the more serious forms of maladjustment in children;
and many child guidance clinics,[2] as they came to be called in the
1930's, concentrated upon problems mainly in the psychiatric field,
leaving almost untouched the pressing questions affecting the healthy
mental and emotional growth of the majority of children. Within the
educational system itself have grown up, however, other types of

---

1. This subject was examined in detail by an expert study group convened in 1954 by the Unesco
Institute of Education, Hamburg with the assistance of UN Social Affairs Division, the World
Health Organization, Unesco and the World Federation for Mental Health. It is not proposed
to examine this important subject again in detail here. The reader is referred to the publication
of the Unesco Institute for Education.
2. Or *centres médico-pédagogiques*, or *médico-psycho-pédagogiques*. See 'The History of the Child Guidance
Movement in England', G. Keir, *Brit. Journ. Ed. Psych.* vol. XXII, pt. 1, 1952.

service, by which an educational psychologist is attached to a school or group of schools and acts as adviser to his teaching colleagues on such matters as educational guidance, problems of method and individual difficult cases.[1] A third solution has been the psychologist's office or psychological centre attached to the local educational administration, and working in co-operation with other services to help schools or individual pupils with their difficulties.[2]

Many different organizational patterns are of course possible and are likely to develop in accordance with the experience and needs of different countries. It is possible, after some 40 to 50 years of tentative experimentation in Europe, to suggest the broad functions appropriate to such services and certain principles which they should follow if they are to bring psychology effectively into the service of education.

THE GENERAL ENDS TO BE SERVED

Perhaps the two major problems which the contemporary school faces in a more acute form than ever before in the history of compulsory education are the adaptation of educational content and method to individual differences and the guidance of children between alternatives. These interrelated problems have always existed in education; but we have become more aware of them as education has become universal, and as it has differentiated to meet not only individual needs but also the increasing complexity of modern society. The main responsibility for the guidance of children between different studies, for helping them to adapt to the school, and for the correlation of curricula and method with the rhythms of child growth, is that of the school and of the teacher. It is a process of help and adjustment which should be a continuous part of education; and teachers therefore should be prepared by their training to carry it out. But the teacher's main task is to educate, to be himself emotionally identified with the process of which he is an essential part. Some of the problems of the educational guidance of individual children and of method and curriculum are such that he cannot solve them unaided, either because he lacks time or because he has neither the necessary emotional detachment nor the special training to do so.

We may perhaps illustrate this by an example. A normally intelligent

1. This is the tendency in France and in Belgium, where one also finds voluntary and State-aided *centres psycho-pédagogiques* and *médico-pédagogiques*.
2. Historically, this is the first solution. It was applied by the London County Council in 1913 with the appointment of C. Burt. With some vicissitudes and transformations, it seems likely to become the general pattern in England, just as the psychologist working within a school or school group has so far been the favoured solution in Belgium, Denmark and France. For a fuller analysis of the current position in Europe see the publication of the Unesco Institute previously cited, or *The Year Book of Education 1955*, paper by W. D. Wall on 'Guidance Services in Europe'.

child may develop a specific difficulty, say in learning to read or in arithmetic. Such a difficulty may have a simple cause—perhaps absence at a critical period of teaching; on the other hand, the cause may be complex and related to ramifying influences arising from the past or from his out-of-school environment. The teacher is favourably placed to detect such a child. The determination of possible causes, and the devising of appropriate remedial measures, however, may involve an intensive case-study, including the psychological examination of the child himself and the attempt to assess the effects of environmental and home influences. Such a case-study may well indicate that changes in the environment are necessary if the child is to progress, or that, as well as educational help, the child needs psychotherapy. The teacher, while he would be an essential collaborator in the case-study and might be called upon to assist in remedial work, is not likely to be able to accept a full responsibility.

Teaching continually poses problems of method which can rarely be satisfactorily solved by intuitive judgments or by trial and error procedures. One may instance as examples the controversies which continue to rage around the rival merits of the global and the phonic methods of teaching reading or the teaching of subtraction by equal addition or by decomposition. The determination of the merits of any method is a matter for controlled experiment, and experiment in education is not the elementary business it appears to the naive. Moreover, it cannot usually be conducted in only one class or one school; any problem of teaching method involves the attempt to control or to estimate the influence of a number of interacting factors—the method, the teacher, the child's present level, the effects of maturation, and even the stimulation involved in the mere conducting of an experiment in a school. Hence a number of schools, teachers and classes may be essential to a critical experiment.[1] The more nearly we approach the core problems of education—for example such problems as school readiness, the impact on children's development of active as distinct from didactic methods, the best ages at which to introduce techniques and concepts such as long division or historical time sequence—the more difficult accurate research becomes, and the more caution is necessary both in the statement of hypotheses and in the interpretation of results.

THE DISSEMINATION OF THE RESULTS OF RESEARCH

In devising techniques of educational guidance for the use of teachers, in guiding teachers in their use, and in conducting the research essen-

---

1. E. F. Lindquist (*Design and Analysis of Experiments in Psychology and Education*. New York, Houghton Mifflin, 1953) gives a full discussion of the practical and theoretical problems involved in method experiments.

tial to provide a firm basis for the improvement of education, the educational psychologist has a major technical contribution to make to the work of the schools. Knowledge of child development and of the psychology of education is increasing; and research in most countries is already well ahead of practice. The dissemination of this knowledge among teachers and its practical assimilation are likely to be effected most readily through collaboration between psychologist and teacher over specific and concrete problems rather than by lectures or books. By his training and by the tasks which he discharges, moreover, the psychologist is led to develop towards children, and towards educational problems generally, an attitude different from but complementary to that of the teacher. Whereas the teacher's main task is to induce children to learn, to set up and maintain standards, and to work with a group of children, the psychologist is concerned, not primarily with standards, but with the objective and detached study of individuals, in their affective as well as in their intellectual growth. Thus the psychologist is peculiarly well situated to help his colleague, the teacher, to understand the importance of the emotional and familial factors in the successful education of children, and to call attention to such matters in particular cases that he has been called upon to study. He can informally and unobtrusively make the school aware of practical applications of the principles of mental hygiene, without however making teachers so sensitive to the multiplicity of human relationships as to lose control of their classes or to fail in their normative task.

A psychological service which sets out to prevent maladjustment and to make a constructive contribution to child development must also work with parents. Emphasis has already been laid upon the need for co-operation between home and school; and in most cases parent-teacher co-operation is best based upon the activity of the school staff. The teacher rarely has sufficient knowledge or experience in the psychology of family life to help parents with the intimate psychological aspects of their task. The school staff can and should fulfil the essential function of educational adviser to the parents and of collaborator with them in the upbringing of their children; and to this more general task the psychologist will contribute from his knowledge of child development. But when a particular child is showing signs of educational, social or personal maladjustment, a detailed study of his home circumstances is as important as the complementary examination of the child himself and of his school environment. Not infrequently remedial measures may involve changing the attitudes and behaviour of the family and of the school towards the child. Contacts of this kind are delicate: they require skill and insight which usually come only from a specialized training and an objective impartiality, recognized as such by the parents and by the teacher, which those closely involved in the child's success or failure cannot have. Hence the psychologist working with an individual case frequently finds himself in the position of having to interpret the home to the school and the school to the home, inducing each to modify its demands on a particular pupil in the interests of a more healthy growth.

GUIDANCE AT SPECIFIC PERIODS

The constructive and preventive aspects of a psychological service cannot be dissociated from direct intervention at particular stages in a child's school career. Educational guidance should be a continuous process based upon cumulative records maintained by the schools and should merge into vocational guidance as the adolescent prepares himself for work. But there are a number of occasions at which decisions have to be reached on the basis of evidence gathered specifically for the purpose. The most obvious examples of this are the period of transition from primary to secondary education, and from school to work. In most countries secondary education offers varied opportunities and is to some extent selective; moreover, the choice of type of school and of study, in fact, constitutes a broad vocational choice. The transition from school to work involves not only a careful assessment of aptitudes, and a decision based upon knowledge of what is implied in different fields of employment, but a period of adjustment to the demands made by industry or by professional life. Thus a psychological service would be expected to conduct any special examinations which might be necessary on such occasions, to contribute to the decision taken jointly by parents and school and supervise the child or adolescent during the period of adjustment to the new situation.

DIAGNOSTIC AND REMEDIAL SERVICES

Within the broad action so far outlined, the diagnostic and remedial tasks of a psychological service fall into their natural place, as an essential, but by no means the sole contribution, to the mental health of schoolchildren. Children with gross physical, sensorial and mental handicaps are usually discovered before they go to school, or at least in the first years of schooling. Those handicaps which are not immediately apparent—minor sensory defects, all but the grosser forms of mental subnormality, cognitive difficulties, educational retardation, and social and emotional maladjustments—frequently escape notice until their effects are serious and demand relatively costly and time-consuming remedies. When, however, there is close collaboration between teachers and psychologist, and the school bases its guidance of pupils upon continuous and carefully recorded observation of their development, many such problems are discovered at a stage early enough either for effective special educational provision to be made or for simple remedial measures to be applied by the teachers themselves with a good hope of success.

Even in ideal conditions, certain types of maladjustment will require more careful examination, treatment and supervision than can be provided for within the school or special class. A glance at Table 2 in Chapter IX indicates that we might expect one child in four to show some kind of maladjustment, and that of these about a quarter are sufficiently seriously disturbed as to warrant specialized remedial help. Undoubtedly these estimates include a proportion of those whose problem is basically that of educational failure or of mildly subnormal intelligence. Nevertheless the figures for educational retardation cited in Chapters V and VIII indicate that there is also a group of children whose main difficulty is failure in school. Finally, there is the third group, which may in part overlap the first two, of those who have defects, subnormalities or handicaps which cannot be cured, but which necessitate some form of modified education. It would probably be safe to say that in any school system not less than one-third of the pupils at some time in their career should be carefully examined psychologically and will require some form of special educational, psychological or social help, given either directly by the psychological service or on its recommendation and under its supervision.

Much the larger part of this action will take the form of direct advice to the teachers or the parents as to how they can handle transitory difficulties. Some of it will involve special measures taken within the school, such as the provision of small classes with simplified curricula for the dull, or the setting up of opportunity groups for children who have fallen behind educationally through absence, temporary home difficulties, minor behaviour disturbances and the like. Those whose physical or mental handicaps warrant it will be placed in special schools or classes, and the task of a psychological service will be the initial examination of such children and general supervision and guidance after placement.

A considerable number will remain in need of individual treatment. The mildly or seriously maladjusted may require psychotherapy as well as some form of guidance given to parents and to the school. Children with specific educational difficulties may have to be placed in a small group for a combination of psychological help and remedial education, undertaken either by the psychologist himself or by an assistant trained for the purpose. A small proportion may need psychiatric treatment.

The main responsibility for the educational development of children belongs to the school and the teacher, just as the main responsibility for their personal development falls upon the family. A school psychological service therefore has as its primary aim helping parents and teachers to discharge their joint responsibilities. Its task is mainly advisory; only where there is no alternative should it take over responsibility for a particular child. This principle, kept well in view, avoids the danger of undermining the authority and responsibility of the home and the school by the encroachment of special services—a danger already manifest in some of the developments of social welfare.

To be of full value, a psychological service must be firmly embedded in the educational system. Its work and its research must begin from the problems of the classroom rather than from the laboratory or clinic. At all stages it is dependent upon the full collaboration of the teacher. Thus it must be a service financed by and responsible to the educational authority rather than any other; its task is partly parallel to but independent of that of the school medical services. At the same time it should form the liaison between the school and the social, medical and mental health services of the community, and co-ordinate their activities wherever they impinge upon the work of the school. It should be in direct contact too with authorities responsible for the training of teachers and with institutes and university departments of research in education and psychology.

Either within such a service or functionally connected with it, a number of special units will be required. There is first the whole system of special schools and classes, residential and other, for exceptional children, including classes, schools and hostels for maladjusted pupils. Facilities should also exist for remedial education carried out under psychological supervision by specially trained teachers. For the severely maladjusted and for the psychotic, a psychiatric centre or clinic may be required, which can either form part of the psychological service itself or be developed as a co-operative activity by the educational and health authorities of the district. Similar co-operation will probably be necessary between the school psychological service and the authorities responsible for vocational guidance, placement in industry, commerce and the professions, and follow-up of school leavers. So too if the guidance offered by the service is to be truly comprehensive, and if the healthy mental growth of children is to be ensured, the school psychological service should have the possibility of extending its activities into the pre-school period. Its main preoccupation will of course be schoolchildren; but it should be so financed and organized as to be able to work in nursery schools and kindergartens, and to co-operate with the maternal and child welfare services of the community.

The keynote of such a service must be flexibility and variety of provision, and the capacity to grow as the needs of the schools and of children make themselves felt. To ensure this, two things are essential: a system of finance which is tied not to the case load but to the global service offered, and which recognizes that prevention is less costly, socially and economically, than cure; and staffing which is adequate both in number and in specialization to the many tasks that such a service is called on to perform. The quality and comprehensiveness of a service depend directly upon finance and upon the number and quality of the psychological staff available. The routine educational guidance of schoolchildren can be ensured either by the part-time activities of a number of members of a school staff with a complement of training, or by one specially trained teacher working as a school counsellor for 400 to 500 children. Assuming also that adequate child guidance facilities exist to deal with an annual case load of 200 'problem' children for diagnosis and treatment and that special educational provision, remedial classes, vocational guidance, and the like, are integrated with the service, it has been estimated that not less than two school psychologists would be necessary, in addition, for a school population of some 15,000 to 20,000 children. This estimate is based on the assumption that the service is operating in an urban area where the schools are relatively large and close together, and where transport facilities are good. In rural districts with a scattered population more staff would almost certainly be required.

THE SELECTION AND TRAINING OF THE PSYCHOLOGIST

The essential worker in a school psychological service is the educational psychologist, and upon his quality, training and outlook, success will depend. Essentially he is the specialist upon whom the general educational practitioner, the teacher, will call. He must speak the teacher's language and be able to interpret his psychological insight in practical classroom terms. As well, therefore, as his special training in child development, in methods of conducting psychological examinations, in psychotherapy and the like, he should have a profound insight into education and a practical knowledge of the teacher's task. Such insight can only rarely be developed by those who have never taught; and the necessity of recruiting school psychologists from the ranks of experienced teachers is increasingly being recognized. The practice of psychology, however, whether in the examination and treatment of individual children, in working with teachers or with parents, or in research—and normally all three will be involved—makes heavy demands upon the personality of the psychologist. It imposes an emotional strain which demands great stability and maturity to support. Candidates for training should therefore be carefully selected from among those who have at least three, and preferably five, years of successful teaching experience with normal children, and who have the essential qualities of personality.

The very newness of applied psychology, the relative uncertainty of many of its findings and techniques, the far-reaching demands which are made upon its services, and the responsibility which the psychologist must frequently accept towards the child, the school and the parents, all emphasize the need for a training which is thorough, extensive and practical. For the reputation of the profession itself and for the effectiveness of the services to the schools, therefore, it seems better to have too few psychologists and those highly competent than to multiply those whose inadequate training leads them into errors which may be catastrophic. In those countries where the profession is becoming established, a basic academic training or its equivalent to the level of a good university degree in general psychology is insisted upon. This should be followed by teacher-training and successful teaching experience as suggested above. Finally, before undertaking responsible practice the psychologist should undergo at least two years of training directly for his profession, including theoretical studies and a great deal of supervised practical experience in all aspects of the work he is called upon to do.

TEAMWORK

A fully developed service will, of course, need other workers. The child-guidance centre or clinic, for example, may need the customary team of educational psychologist, social worker and, for many cases, psychiatrist. Specially trained remedial teachers to treat the more difficult cases of educational difficulty, play therapists, speech therapists and vocational guidance experts may all be necessary in a fully developed service covering the needs of a considerable number of schools. In so far as the schools are concerned, it will be the psychologist to whom the task of co-ordinating the activities of these other workers will fall, and on him generally will rest the responsibility for liaison between the schools, the specialized units within the whole psychological service and community medical and social services. It is therefore as important that his training should give him an insight into other specialities than his own as it is that his potential colleagues in psychiatry and social work should have a knowledge of psychology and education. Ultimately, the success of a psychological service will depend upon the team work which develops between teacher and psychologist over the immediate classroom problems and between the various specialists concerned over the problems of individual difficult children. The bases

287

of such teamwork are a measure of common training, mutual understanding, and an acceptance of the responsibilities and insight of the various disciplines that may be concerned.

BIBLIOGRAPHY

ALEXANDER, W. P. *The child guidance service in principle and in fact.* Sheffield, Education Committee, 1943.

BELGIQUE. DIRECTION GÉNÉRALE DE L'ENSEIGNEMENT PRIMAIRE ET NORMAL. *Individualisation de l'enseignement dans les écoles normales.* Bruxelles, Ministère de l'instruction publique, 1948. 48 p.

BOESCH, E. *L'organisation d'un service de psychologie scolaire.* St.-Gall, Tschudy, 1946. 135 p.

——. *L'exploration du caractère de l'enfant.* Paris, Éditions du Scarabée, 1952. 166 p.

BUYSE, R. *L'expérimentation en pédagogie.* Bruxelles, Lamertin, 1935. 468 p.

BOWERS, H. *Research in the training of teachers.* Toronto, Dent & Macmillan of Canada, 1952. 168 p.

CAVALIER, M. L. *L'école publique et ses maîtres.* Paris, Ministère de l'éducation nationale, 1935. 96 p.

DEBESSE, M. "L'enseignement des sciences pédagogiques dans les universités françaises", *Education nationale.* Paris, Ministère de l'éducation nationale, 1953, 33: 5-6: 10.

DERIVIERE, R. "La structure des centres psycho-médico-sociaux", *Revue belge de psychologie et de pédagogie.* Cahier XII, Bruxelles, 1951.

Einundsiebzigstes Jahrbuch des Vereins Schweizerischer Gymnasiallehrer. Versammlung in Solothurn, 1943. Aarau, Sauerländer, 1944. 186 p.

FREY, A. *Pädagogische Besinnung.* Zürich, Artemis-Verlag, 1944. 72 p.

GARCIA HOZ, V. *Sobre el maestro y la educación.* Madrid, Instituto de Pedagogía San José de Calazanz (*Estudios de Educación y Enseñanza,* serie A, no. III), 1944. 196 p.

GEMELLI, A. *L'orientamento professionale dei giovani nelle scuole.* 2a. ed. Milano, Vita e Pensiero, 1947. 186 p.

GREAT BRITAIN. BOARD OF EDUCATION. *Teachers and youth leaders.* London, HMSO, 1944. 176 p.

HERZOG, E. *Persönlichkeitsprobleme des Lehrers in der Erziehung.* München, Kaiser Verlag, 1952. 52 p.

INTERNATIONAL LABOUR OFFICE. *Problems of vocational guidance.* Studies and reports, series J. no. 4. Geneva, ILO, 1935. 193 p.

——. *Les problèmes de l'orientation professionnelle.* Etudes et documents, série J. no. 4. Genève, BIT, 1935. 194 p.

IBE-UNESCO. *Primary teacher training.* Paris, Unesco; Geneva, IBE (publ. no. 117), 1953. 253 p.

——. *Primary teacher training.* Paris, Unesco; Geneva, IBE (publ. no. 149), 1953. 70 p.

IBE-Unesco. *School psychologists.* Paris, Unesco; Geneva, IBE (publ. no. 105), 1948. 106 p.

——. International Conference on Public Education. *Proceedings and recommendations.* Paris, Unesco; Geneva, IBE (publ. no. 151), 1953. 172 p.

BIE-Unesco. *La formation professionnelle du personnel enseignant primaire.* Paris, Unesco; Genève, BIE (publ. no. 116), 1950. 275 p.

——. *La formation professionnelle du personnel enseignant primaire.* Paris, Unesco; Genève, BIE (publ. no. 148), 1953. 74 p.

——. *Les psychologues scolaires.* Paris, Unesco; Genève, BIE (publ. no. 104), 1948. 106 p.

——. Conférence internationale de l'instruction publique. *Procès-verbaux et recommandations.* Paris, Unesco; Genève, BIE (publ. no. 150), 1953. 174 p.

Jadoulle, A. *Le laboratoire pédagogique au travail. Centres d'entraînement aux méthodes d'éducation active.* Paris, Les Editions du Scarabée, 1951. 174 p.

Keilhacker, M. *Der ideale Lehrer nach der Auffassung der Schüler.* Freiburg, i.B., Herder, 1932. 156 p.

Konferenz Schweizerischer Gymnasialrektoren. *Der Gymnasiallehrer, seine Person und seine Ausbildung.* Aarau, Sauerländer, 1942. 122 p.

Kuroczko, E. *O postawę spoxecznq nauczyciela.* Warszawa, P.Z.W.S., 1947. 48 p.

Lafon, R. *Psycho-pédagogie médico-sociale.* Paris, Presses universitaires de France, 1950. 160 p.

Langeveld, M. J. "Over het wezen der paedagogische psychologie en de verhouding der psychologie tot de paedagogiek", *Acta Paedagogica Ultrajectina*, no. 3. Groningen, Djakarta, J. B. Wolters, 1951.

Lippert, E. *Lehrerbildung.* Wiesbaden, Verlag der Hessischen Lesebuchstiftung, 1952. 208 p.

Loveday, M. *Into the breach.* London, Turnstile Press, 1949. 66 p.

Meili, R. *Psychologie de l'orientation professionnelle.* Genève, Editions du Mont-Blanc, 1948. 122 p.

Mialaret, G. *Nouvelle pédagogie scientifique.* Paris, Presses universitaires de France, 1954. 122 p.

Michard, H. & Glossinde, A. *Condition et mission de l'instituteur.* Paris, Aubier, Editions Montaigne, 1945. 224 p.

Oliver, R. A. C. *Research in education.* London, G. Allen & Unwin, 1946. 60 p.

——. *The training of teachers in universities.* London, University of London Press, 1943. 60 p.

Osterrieth, P. "Le centre médico-psychologique pour enfants et adolescents", *Revue du Centre neuro-psychiatrique*, Bruxelles, 1947.

O'Leary, M. "Training of a catholic teacher", *The sword of the spirit.* London.

Planchard, E., *L'investigation pédagogique.* Tamines, Duculot-Toulin, 1945. 168 p.

Sandiford, P., Cameron, M. A., Conway, C. B., Long, J. A. *Forecasting teaching ability.* University of Toronto, Department of Educational Research, 1937. 94 p.

Stellwag, H. W. F. *Begane wegen en onbetreden paden.* 2e dr. Groningen, Wolters, 1954. 401 p.

Teacher education for Württemberg-Baden. The Esslingen plan. Stuttgart, Verlag Klett, 1949. 136 p.

"Technical recommendations for psychological tests and diagnostic techniques", *Supplement to the Psychological bulletin* vol. 51, no. 2, part 2. American Psychological Association, March, 1954.

The year book of education 1953. London, University of London Institute of Education, and Teachers College, New York, Columbia University, 1953. 588 p.

WALL, W. D. "Psychological services for children", *The Times educational supplement.* Section I, 13 April 1951 & section 2, 20 April 1951.

ZULLIGER, H. "Seelischer Gesundheitsschutz in der Schule", in: Meng, H. *Praxis der seelischen Hygiene.* Basel, Verlag B. Schwabe, 1943. 279 p.

CHAPTER XI

SOME UNSOLVED PROBLEMS

The discussions in preceding chapters have been guided by two complementary principles which seem to be at the very root of any attempt to improve the work of European schools so that they not only avoid putting needless strain on their pupils, but make a constructive contribution to a mentally healthy society.

The first of these principles concerns the satisfaction of the basic psychological needs of the growing child and the adaptation of the demands made upon him at home and at school to the rhythms of his growth. Education in the family and in the classroom should largely help the child to achieve and maintain his personal security, and should underline his fundamental acceptability to his parents and to his teachers. At the same time it should foster his bids for independence and enable him progressively to accept the responsibility inherent in emotional and personal freedom. This implies that the demands made on him should be carefully adjusted to his level of development. Premature demands invite failure and tend to undermine his personal security; over-protection or asking too little of him may tend to weaken his independence. The mentally healthy child, adolescent or adult feels sufficiently safe to take a calculated risk. The little boy standing on the stair, wishing to jump, and who says to himself, 'I am afraid—but I will jump', is, at his level of development, healthy. The adult who finds himself at variance with the opinion of his group and who, having carefully examined his own conscience, decides to accept the consequences of a challenge to public opinion is displaying similar behaviour.

If, however, we try merely to adapt education to rhythms of growth, merely to 'follow the child', we do the growing human being no service. Children are not, it is true, so much wax-like material to be moulded by home or school to any desired pattern: nevertheless, conscious shaping there is and must be from the moment the baby is born; and this process of shaping, while it should proceed in tune with the needs and capacities of each human being, must for his own ultimate security also adapt him to norms achieved by his group. In doing this,

291

education gives a direction to growth. It may impede or even destroy it; ideally, it should stimulate and carry it to its full flower. Consistent and wise shaping, steady stimulation of physical, social and intellectual achievement, are essential to the very security and healthy mental growth of children in the European culture. Maturity, in the full sense, is not achieved by the simple flowering of a naturel *élan;* it is partly at least the product of education and the stimulation it quite properly provides.

PROBLEMS FOR RESEARCH

Such principles are easier to state than to apply consistently and wisely in practice when one is confronted with children and with the needs of the society into which they are growing up. Much fundamental research into child development has already been carried out, and we are generally agreed upon certain broad laws of growth which apply at least to Western children. Much too has been done to examine the simpler aspects of formal educational method in relation to the child's capacity to learn. Where research so far has given little help is in following up, throughout growth, the effects upon personality of different kinds of educational experiences, any of which may be immediately 'right' but not of long-term value. We surmise, probably rightly, that the attitudes which underly such things as co-opera-tiveness, democratic thinking, the acceptance of and the ability to work with other groups, are of slow growth and markedly affected by experiences at home and in school. We have, however, little exact information to enable us to decide, for groups of children from different social backgrounds and of different levels of intelligence, what kinds of educational and affective experiences are best and how they may be arranged to help them develop such attitudes. Still less are we near to a systematic psychology of society which will enable us fully to use education as an instrument simultaneously of personal development and of social change. Yet these broad problems in the social sciences touch the very root of mental health in the widest of all applications.

DIRECT TEACHING FOR MENTAL HEALTH

There is another question to which the answer can only be given by carefully controlled and practical research. Many of the older con-ceptions of human responsibility and behaviour have been modified by our knowledge of the psychology of the unconscious life. Greater self-knowledge is perhaps possible now than most people possess, and energies at present bound up in unconscious conflict might be liberated or more positively directed. Although prejudice might not be eradicated altogether, more could be done to bring us to understand and control our irrational thinking, to become aware of unconscious motivations and of the way they affect our dealings with others. It is possible that by using our knowledge of the springs of human behaviour in a direct way in education, we might not merely improve the maturity and mental health of individuals but directly contribute to healthy relationships between persons and between groups in the society to which they belong.

Such an hypothesis underlies some recent work which has been going on in Denmark, the United States and Canada,[1] with, as its principal aim, bringing children to understand the meanings of their own behaviour and that of others.

The Danish scheme is relatively simple. The schools department of the Danish State radio broadcast a series of unscripted conversations between an educational psychologist and a number of boys and girls. This little group spontaneously discussed concrete examples of social and antisocial behaviour. The schools listening in were encouraged to continue the discussion among their own pupils. A more elaborately developed scheme is that begun by Bullis,[2] and now in use in many schools in the United States. Bullis and his collaborators have prepared a series of lesson plans in 'Human Relations in the Classroom'. Each of these consists of a stimulus story, which features an emotional problem for discussion, and which is read by the teacher; the pupils are then encouraged to discuss the problem presented, to appraise the solutions offered, to speculate on the motives behind the actions, and, most important of all, to relate their own experience in similar situations. Each lesson plan ends with the teacher guiding the class to form its own conclusions.

---

1. For a critical examination of some American and Canadian work, see 'Promotion of Mental Health in the Primary and Secondary Schools: An Evaluation of Four Projects', report no. 18 of the Group for the Advancement of Psychiatry (3617 W. 6th Avenue, Topeka, Kansas), Kansas, 1951. The Danish work is described in 'Mental Hygiene—A New School Subject', *Unesco Features*, no. 54, 21 Sept. 1951.

2. See H. E. Bullis: 'A Positive Mental Health Programme', *American Journal of Public Health* vol. 40, no. 9, Sept. 1950; 'The Delaware Human Relations Classes', *Understanding the Child* vol. XX, no. 4, Oct. 1951; 'An Educational Programme for the Development of the "Normal" Personality', *American Journal of Psychiatry* vol. 109, no. 5, Nov. 1952; 'One out of Seven', *Psychiatry* vol. 16, no. 1, Feb. 1953; 'Are we Losing the Fight for Improved Mental Health', *Progressive Education*, vol. 30, no. 4, Feb. 1953; and the textbooks produced for the project: H. E. Bullis and E. E. O'Malley, *Human Relations in the Classroom: Course I and Course II*. Delaware, Delaware State Society for Mental Hygiene, 1948. A Similar scheme, not exclusively concerned with mental health and human relations and not so formalized, is the *Health and Personal Development* series by D. Baruch, E. Montgomery and W. W. Bauer, Chicago, Scott Foresman & Co., 1949. For an account of other schemes, see P. T. Rankin and J. M. Dorsey, *The Detroit School Mental Health Project*. New York, The National Association for Mental Health Inc., 1953, and *Fostering Mental Health in our Schools* (1950 Year Book of the Association for Curriculum Development), Washington, National Education Association, 1950.

In schools in Iowa a rather different technique has been developed by Ojemann.[1] The method is based on the assumption that children can be brought to know and understand basic psychodynamic concepts—just as they can know and understand, for example, basic mathematical ones. The important concepts, according to Ojemann, are those of motivation, of multiple causation in behaviour, and of a distribution of values rather than a dichotomy of right and wrong. Instead of isolating this material in separate lessons, Ojemann has tried to integrate it into the curriculum, wherever such subjects as civics, history, home economics and literature allow for it by their treatment of human relations. The deliberate aim of the supplementary material prepared by Ojemann is to induce pupils to go below the superficial approach to behaviour into the understanding and appreciation of causes. In addition, discussion and dramatic techniques and attempts through various real situations to bring children to grips with the problems in their own lives are being given increasing importance. The outstanding feature of Ojemann's research project is that it envelops the whole school life and affects children throughout their development, basing itself, not on particular lessons or activities, but on the whole life of the school.

The Forest Hill Village project conducted by the University of Toronto is even more elaborate than the preceding ones. It includes a programme of teacher-training, a psychological service to deal with children who are sufficiently disturbed to require treatment, and a parent-education scheme, as well as the 'Human relations classes'. These, unlike the work previously discussed, are totally undirected. The teacher, himself highly trained in psychology, remains in the background, listening, interested, but not expressing any opinions of his own, leaving the children to raise and pursue as they will the topics of discussion.

It will be remarked that these projects carry rather further the suggestions made earlier. In one way or another they are a deliberate attempt to bring children up in an understanding of some at least of their own and other people's motives and to help them to grapple with their own emotional problems as they arise rather than to repress them or put them aside. All those who have observed these attempts agree that many children and adolescents appear to benefit considerably from taking part and that the interest of the participants is very keen.

But there are, or may be, disadvantages. The first two projects (the

---

1. The Ojemann project, an experimental one, is being conducted as a carefully controlled research to determine its effects. It has given rise to a considerable literature since 1939. (R. H. Ojemann and F. R. Wilkinson, 'The Effect on Pupil Growth of an Increase in Teachers' Understanding of Pupils' Behaviour', *Journal of Experimental Education*, December 1939.) A good account of the scheme as it has developed is given in R. H. Ojemann, 'An Integrated Plan for Education in Human Relations and Mental Health', *Journal of the National Association of Deans of Women* vol. XVI, no. 3, March 1953.

Danish one and that in Delaware) are conducted by teachers with very little, if any, special training for the work, though of course they must be fairly permissive if any good is to result. The Iowa project also is based upon the skills of the good teacher who possesses no special psychological insight or training; but it is a more comprehensive attempt to penetrate the whole school programme and activities in such a way as to make pupils and staff aware of the complexity of human relationships. Certainly all three programmes draw attention to the importance of the motives underlying behaviour, and in one way or another direct the attention of pupils and staff alike to the possibility of improvement in understanding oneself and others, in controlling one's own actions, and in deliberately and consciously working for improved personal relations. It might be asked whether more is achieved than would be wrought by less obviously selfconscious methods—such, for example, as deliberate but informal fostering by the school staff of good patterns of behaviour among the children and between staff and children.[1]

The psychologist would ask whether such learning is more than superficial, whether the pupils, simply by getting to know the prepared material, would be affected emotionally, and would change those deeper attitudes built upon early family experience. Directing children's attention to themselves and others in this way may be premature, at least before they have reached adolescence. Finally, we might fear that, if free discussion among children really began to touch upon matters in which the emotions were closely involved, conflicts and personality difficulties would break through which the teacher could not handle. It might indeed be argued that unless such unconscious forces are in some way released and assuaged, the discussion has little value.

The Forest Hill Village project in Canada meets many of these criticisms. The teachers in charge of the undirected groups are specially trained; the project with the children is supported by work with the parents, and there is a fully competent psychological service available to advise teachers on the milder problems, or to undertake treatment of seriously disturbed children, whose difficulties declare themselves more readily under the stimulus of so free a situation.

We must await the research evidence to know if such experiments are succeeding.[2] The initiatives are interesting, and, although to

---

1. There is of course nothing in the techniques used which necessarily emphasizes any particular scale of values. They could be equally well applied in any school where school staff and pupils are in confident relations with each other.

2. So far as the Iowa and Forest Hill projects are concerned (the only ones subject to exact experimental investigation), the results seem to be good. W. Line (private communication), summing up the Forest Hill Village work with primary children, says that great comradeship develops in the group; introverted children do not become aggressive, but they are warmed to themselves and to others by the kinship and the excitement of living. School marks increase; self-confidence is enhanced.

European eyes they may seem somewhat artificial, the objective is probably one that could be attained by other means. Essentially the intention is to provide catharsis for emotions and experiences which might not otherwise be digested and to bring children consciously to attempt a more than superficial understanding and judgment of the behaviour of others and of themselves.

There is something that such experiments do not attempt, except indirectly. All stress that the emotional outlet provided, and the self-awareness and control developed, enable children to use their emotional energy more effectively in school and in life generally. No experiment has yet carried the matter further and attempted to help children and young people to harness the crude creativity of their unconscious lives as a means both of catharsis and construction. Very young children playing with paint, with plasticine and with sand, often appear to be projecting fantasies without much intellectual interference, conscious regulation or control. But the activities of older children, particularly in the classroom, sometimes seem so heavily controlled that little spontaneity is left. Much creative art, plastic, visual, verbal or musical, is in fact based on material which has arisen from the unconscious mind of the artist in a period of excitement and which has then been subjected to a process of intellectual or technical disciplining.[1] It may well be that by concentrating solely upon a purely technical correctness, for example of expression in the mother tongue, we inhibit creativity. By training children to associate freely to a given topic, to draw 'what comes into their head' and the like as an essential preliminary to imposing a disciplined and orderly technical expression, we might be able to stimulate unconscious creativity instead of inhibiting it. Certainly this is attempted in therapeutic work with disturbed children, adolescents and adults, and seems to result in the upsurge of matter which leads to the heart of the problem and brings relief; it may well be that here—if the teacher can create the atmosphere of confidence and emotional freedom in which the child feels safe enough to plumb the depths of his own spirit—is a means not only of catharsis, but of adding to each pupil a new source of riches.

LEISURE

The problem of fostering and exploiting creativity as one at least of the means whereby the human being situates himself in his world, leads

---

1. See for example the remarkable analysis of Coleridge's 'Kubla Khan' and 'Ancient Mariner' by J. L. Lowes, in *The Road to Xanadu*. New York. Houghton & Mifflin, 1927; 2nd ed. London, Constable, 1940. Lowes shows how Coleridge's 'dream' poetry was elaborated—largely unconsciously—out of his prior reading rather than constructed from it. Coleridge's metrical mastery allowed his 'dream' (in the case of 'Kubla Khan') to flow directly into verse without conscious shaping. Similar features may be seen in the work of surrealists (of all epochs), such as Bosch, Dali and Blake.

us directly to the whole question of leisure, at which we have no more than glanced in the preceding pages. It seems regrettably true that many, if not the majority, of people pass their leisure in more or less passive amusements which owe more to the machine than to the participation of the audience. Some of this may be due to fatigue and to dissatisfaction with their employment, some of it to conditions which make sitting in a cinema preferable to staying at home. One is entitled, however, to ask whether education has in fact encouraged the majority of children and adolescents to feel that creative activities can literally re-create the person, and that the antidote to much mechanical work is the affirmation of individuality in making something. Far too few pupils leave school with a sufficient experience and training in any chosen leisure activity to feel confident even of the moderate and personal success which would make them wish to continue it. Yet there are many arts and crafts, many social activities, and many calls which could be made upon personal participation and service, through which even the least talented could find expression.[1]

THE ENVIRONMENT

The problem of how to release and realize creativity in leisure is a special aspect of a broader problem which has been incidentally touched on in preceding chapters, but which demands careful analysis in itself. We have spoken almost as if the sole environments which affect the mental development of the child were the home and the school. In some respects this is true for the young child, since his contacts with the wider environment are relatively slight and usually made through the medium of his parents or teachers. But as the urban child[2] grows older and more independent, a larger and larger proportion of his time is passed in the streets, in the cinema, in cafés, shops, in looking at advertisement hoardings, in reading newspapers and the like.[3] This part of his life is animated by no educational aim and does not have his interests at heart. At best it is a neutral environment; more usually, the growing child, and still more the

---

1. On this whole problem see: H. Durant, *The Problem of Leisure*. London, 1938, and W. Boyd (ed.), *The Challenge of Leisure*. London, The New Education Fellowship, 1936.
2. The proportion of the population in certain European countries who live in towns of 100,000 inhabitants or more are instructive here: United Kingdom, 1951 census, 38.2 per cent; Netherlands, 1947 census, 35.2 per cent; Denmark, 1950 census, 33.5 per cent; German Federal Republic, 1950 census, 27.1 per cent; Belgium, 1947 census, 25.8 per cent; Spain, 1950 census, 23.3 per cent; Sweden, 1950 census, 22.7 per cent; France, 1946 census, 21.7 per cent. If we take 50,000 inhabitants as the standard, the proportion is correspondingly higher—e.g. U.K., 51.1 per cent; Netherlands, 41.3 per cent; Denmark, 36.7 per cent, Sweden, 25.4 per cent.— *United Nations Demographic Year Book*. New York, United Nations, 1952.
3. See H. E. O. James and F. T. Moore, 'Adolescent Leisure in a Working-Class District', *Occ. Psychology* vol. XIV, 1940, vol. XVIII, pts. 1 and 2, 1944.

adolescent, finds himself solicited by commercial interests and exposed to behaviour and ideas from which home and school have largely shielded him, or which they have ignored.

We may here recall that the child growing up in a small, closely knit community, such as a village, is in contact outside his home not only with what is in many ways a simpler environment but also one in which he is rarely out of the supervision of adults who know him and who spontaneously accept a certain responsibility for his well-being. The city street is an environment which is less coherent and intelligible and more impersonal than the village. The adults who are there do not know the child or adolescent and accept no responsibility for him. Much the same may be said of leisure pursuits. Some at least of the activities of a village community actively involve adults, adolescents and children together. The amusements of the city are for the most part impersonal, passive, and do not involve the child or youth in active participation with his elders; entertainment brings him into proximity with others but not into participation with them.

So too the happenings reported in the newspapers, the interpretation of society given on the cinema, the vision of the good life as presented by advertisements, do not come as peripheral happenings unreal by comparison with a small and coherent world; nor are they counter-balanced by the many activities in which the village child takes part with adults with whom he has been familiar since childhood.

Life in towns is not wholly bad; nor is life in the country wholly good. But an increasing proportion of children and young people grow up in towns, and the great modern problems of the depersonalization of life and of the lack of stimulus to creative leisure are posed more acutely in the case of the urban child, and particularly of the urban adolescent. A feeling of belonging to a community, and of having a recognized place within it, grows relatively easily in a village, or even in a small town; it is more difficult to acquire in a sprawling conurb-ation which may not even have the coherence of a town: still less can it be acquired when, as so often happens these days, families move frequently from place to place.

This contemporary situation confronts us with two problems in mental health. The first, in many ways the simpler, is that of protecting children and young people from directly corrupting influences. Most European countries have an extensive system of controls and restrictions: for example, the sale of alcohol to children under the age of 18 is forbidden almost everywhere, entry to cinemas is restricted or films are censored,[1] the sale of pornographic literature is prohibited, and the operation of amusement arcades, fairs and the like is supervised.

1. See P. Bauchard, *The Child Audience;* A Report on Press, Film and Radio for Children *(Press, Film and Radio in the World Today).* Paris, Unesco, 1952.

Though essential, such activity is negative: it does little to give the child or adolescent the idea that his community is actively interested in him. It has recently been suggested that the policeman is the sole representative of the adult world who is always in the streets, and that he therefore is well placed not merely impersonally to protect children from the physical and moral hazards they encounter, but actively, in co-operation with the home and the school, to take a more constructive, personal part both in his contact with individual children and in drawing the attention of the authorities to measures for the general protection of the mental health of the young.[1] Many police forces now have specially trained officers, men and women, for work with young people; most take the opportunity presented by road safety training to enter into contact with schoolchildren in a reassuring and friendly way, and some police forces run youth clubs or sports clubs for adolescents. This largely preventive action might be considerably extended and made more positive if the conception of police work were enlarged to include more directly social tasks, and if the training of policemen and policewomen included some elementary practical instruction in child psychology.[2]

The second problem is that of making more personal, particularly for the adolescent, the world outside his home and school. Most children at the age of 14 or 15 leave school, and many are under no further educational supervision. At this stage of development too the influence of the home on young people tends to decline. Many, if not the majority, find themselves at the beginning of their working lives in very junior positions in their place of work, and for their hours of leisure there are only the cinema, the café and the street. The principal expedient so far devised to meet this problem is the youth club or organization of one kind or another, which, in the past at all events, has often been motivated simply by the desire to keep young people off the streets. Most of these organizations do excellent work in spite of a lack of trained staff, of suitable premises, and of adequate finance. But they often do not touch the very group most in need of service—those urban youths who are drifting, the dull and backward and apathetic, for whom work holds no challenge, for whom home provides little security, respite or support, and who lack the energy to drag themselves out of their apathy. The need to feel oneself needed, to be of value, to someone or to some organization, is very strong in most human beings; it is perhaps strongest of all at the time when the adolescent is on the threshold of independent life. Most modern societies

---

1. Evidence offered to the conference by the International Federation of High Police Officers. The federation, in co-operation with Unesco, United Nations Division of Social Affairs, and the World Federation for Mental Health, has since produced a pamphlet, *The Police and the Mental Health of Children*, based on the work of an international expert group of police officers, social workers, psychiatrists, psychologists and educators.
2. The report mentioned above makes specific recommendations on the content of such training.

appear to the adolescent to have no need for his services. At work he is an easily replaceable 'hand'; at home he is still in some sort in tutelage; the street presents distractions, but calls for no effort or dedication. The youth club may not satisfy young people, burning for recognition, anxious to be accepted as useful; it may seem merely playing at being grown up, or be resented as an adult device to get them out of the way. Rarely does it provide them with a cause to fight or work for, with the comradeship and sense of belonging which self-dedication to a group engaged on a task of recognized value can give.

Here then is a problem in mental health, affecting millions of young people every year, and one in which the schools, industry and parents are vitally concerned. It is that of utilizing effectively and really—not as a palliative or as a remedy—the urge of the young to count for something in the scheme of things, to be needed, to serve their community, and through this to achieve a sense of personal worth, which is the very foundation of security. If worthy causes are not offered, adolescent energies dwindle into apathy or are seduced to unworthy ends; in any case, the opportunity presented by the most formative stage in the growth of attitudes and character is dissipated.[1]

RESPONSIBILITY

In some respects this is a special aspect of what is perhaps the most serious modern problem, that of enabling men and women to adapt to change without relinquishing their responsibility for directing it. It has been many times pointed out that the trend of industrial life is towards centralization, and to an impersonal world in which the individual does not seem to count for much. He loses a sense of worth, of power to influence his own destiny, and is tempted to abandon to a vague 'they' the responsibility for the actions of a group which has grown beyond his comprehension.

Each individual must be equipped to digest change without being overwhelmed by it. Psychological and educational techniques provide the means whereby this adaptation may be aided, and whereby men and women may be produced who are consciously able to analyse the situations which confront them and base their action on intelligent appraisal rather than upon obedience to blind habit. By itself, however, this does not ensure a healthy society or even provide the conditions in which it can grow. Indeed insistence solely on adaptability

---

1. L. J. Barnes, *The Outlook for Youth Work*. London, King George's Jubilee Trust, 1948; *Betaenkning verdrørende Ungdomskoler, Aftenskoler, Ungdommens Fritidsbsekaeftigelse M. V.* Copenhagen, J. H. Schulz A/S., 1952; King George's Jubilee Trust, *Opportunities for Young People to Serve the Community*. London, King George's Jubilee Trust, 1952; H. Métraux, *Schweizer Jugendleben in fünf Jahrhunderten*. Aarau, Sauerlander, 1942; Scottish Education Department, *The Needs of Youth in These Times*. Edinburgh, HMSO, 1945.

and acceptance is probably dangerous socially, politically and morally. If man is in fact to control his destiny, he must accept the responsibility for selecting between ways of life, between different applications of technology, between different philosophical, social and political systems: and such selection cannot be made on psychological grounds, nor on grounds of mental health narrowly conceived. It can only healthily be achieved in terms of a system of values; and no society can provide the conditions in which healthy growth in personality is possible without a commonly accepted framework of ideals.

The expression of these values in human behaviour and attitudes, in the political and social structure of society, and in the whole way of life of a community, will be a compromise, in many ways necessarily imperfect, and subject to changes. Moreover, it has two interrelated aspects which are sometimes in conflict. The behaviour of the individual is regulated by society: he is obliged to do certain things, permitted to do others, and forbidden to do others. This regulation is in one sense, a negative protection of the values generally agreed on by society. Parents, for example, are obliged to send their children to school, thus ensuring the child's right to education; they are not obliged themselves to provide their children with more than the minimum of physical and moral care. The State, through schools and through special services, can take certain positive initiatives which although jealously restricted in democracies, are nevertheless increasing. It can for example, indirectly through economic measures, and directly through encouraging the educative activities of various social agencies, encourage or discourage family life. Thus the State, as well as guarding certain values by restrictions on individual action, can—and increasingly does—play a positive part in embodying them in daily life. In this sense, even the provision of special educational facilities for the handicapped is seen to be a positive expression of values which the individual alone could not ensure.

While, however, the values of a society are expressed negatively or positively in these organized or institutionalized ways, the source of the values by which society lives lies in the individual. No democratic society will for long preserve a system of values abandoned by the majority of its participants. The danger of collective action to implement values individually subscribed to is that it may undermine or remove altogether the responsibility of the individual; if a majority of people are no longer concerned with their responsibility for the implementation of any particular moral principle, they may cease to care for that principle; then it is a small thing to turn the very machinery used to ensure the embodiment of a value in practice into a means of denying it. The machinery of democracy, for example, which exists to protect the freedom and ensure the well-being of the individual, and which rests upon the responsibility of every adult to participate in

301

government, is easily perverted to undemocratic ends when once individual responsibility for government by consent is abandoned.

This superficial excursion into the relation between the values consciously subscribed to and profoundly felt by the individual and the values incorporated in his society through State action, has been undertaken to lay bare the problem of responsibility. From whatever source they are derived and by whatever faith justified, certain values are agreed upon by European society—respect for the value and dignity of the human being, respect for the rights of others, responsibility for one's fellow men irrespective of creed or colour or social class, and the like—and the European States, whilst emphasizing duties, guarantee the rights embodied in the Universal Declaration of Human Rights. Increasingly, through collective action, these rights are being embodied in various legal and administrative forms and carried into the daily lives of men, women and children in an organized way. Unless, however, this action is supported by and evokes conscious participation from the individual, and unless it is kept under constant review by a majority of citizens who are able to test collective action against a consciously held scale of values, it may end in undermining the moral structure upon which mental health rests.

Thus perhaps the core problem of education, even in its narrow relation to the healthy mental growth of children, and still more in its bearing upon the conservation and development of society, is that of helping children and adolescents to come to a knowledge, understanding and critical acceptance of the best values developed by their own society. In this, moral training and moral habit are not enough. Blind adherence to half-understood principles, a series of behavioural patterns adapted to more or less specific situations, may have been sufficient in times when societies changed slowly and when each was composed of a number of more or less un-co-ordinated and uncentralized groups whose interaction provided a series of rough checks and balances. Contemporary society changes more rapidly, and administrative centralization, accompanied by increased efficiency, means that any social measure directly affects everyone, just as any tension reacts upon the whole group. Hence the individual must himself be fully aware that participation in his community implies a series of choices between ways of life, and the constant testing of collective action against a scale of values to which he adheres and which he fully understands. A society which fails in the education of its children and adolescents, in the family, in the school, in the technical college and in the university, to develop this kind of personal responsibility in a majority of its citizens, will not for long remain healthy.

It would be beyond the scope of a work such as this to attempt to define and discuss the values likely to produce the good society. We may here remark that, in the modern world, the responsibilities of the citizen, and therefore his scale of values, do not end with his rights and duties to his own immediate national community. Good human relations, the acceptance of others and of responsibility for their well-being, cannot be confined to an exclusive group. Loyalty to the family and to the school are preliminary stages in the growth towards loyalty to one's community, local and then national. Beyond that, and by no means incompatible with it, is loyalty to mankind: that sense of solidarity with humanity as a whole, irrespective of differences in belief, in education, in language and custom, in political organization, in colour, or in the thousand other ways in which men may differ among themselves, which is the very basis on which international understanding and co-operation must laboriously and slowly be built.

This leads us back to the two principles asserted at the beginning of this chapter. With many defects and with much room for improvement, European education roughly succeeds in adapting itself to the needs and rhythms of growth of its children. Even in ideal conditions, however, children do not grow up spontaneously into well balanced, fully rounded human beings able to participate in the growth of their culture towards the good community. Moreover, if they are expected to do so unaided and undirected, they are likely to become anxious. All of us need, and for all our lives, some norms, some values, within which we can grow and by which we can test ourselves and others and our own society. One of the greatest threats to mental health today is not variety of faith and philosophy, but a kind of homelessness in the sphere of values, the lack of any principle of interpretation by the light of which life can be lived, and by which the worth of the individual can be asserted in the face of his collectivity. Indoctrination, good or bad, is not the answer; nor is a reply to be found in a tolerance based upon the lack of any kind of conviction whatever. Only through an education, at home and in school, by which children and adolescents are steadily confronted with the great modern problems of conscience embodied in national and in international life and action, and relate them to their own personal experiences, can the foundation of a scale of values be laid. Personal security which is based upon a faith accepted without understanding may be fragile. Personal security won by confronting the differences in belief and digesting the resulting tensions gives a vantage point for the understanding of others and for taking the risks involved in shaping a life which depends upon the peaceful co-operation of all mankind.

GENERAL BIBLIOGRAPHY

SECTION I

ARNDT, C. O. & EVERETT, S. "Education for a world society", *Eleventh yearbook of the John Dewey society* New York, Harper, 1951. 274 p.

BARKER, R. G., KOUNIN, J. S. & WRIGHT, H. F. *Child behavior and development.* New York, McGraw-Hill, 1943. 652 p.

BLACKWELL, A. M. *A list of researches in education and educational psychology* (National Foundation for Educational Research in England and Wales, publ. no. 1). London, Newnes, 1950. 173 p.

———. *A second list of researches in education and educational psychology* (The National Foundation for Educational Research in England and Wales, publ. no. 5). London, Newnes, 1952. 128 p.

———. *Lists of researches in education and educational psychology. Supplement I* (The National Foundation for Educational Research in England and Wales, publ. no. 7). London, Newnes, 1954. 57 p.

BRUSSELS TREATY ORGANIZATION. PERMANENT COMMISSION. *The civilization of western Europe and the school.* London, HMSO, 1954. 71 p.

BURT, C. *Contributions of psychology to social problems* (L. T. Hobhouse Memorial Trust Lecture, no. 22). London, Oxford University Press, 1953. 76 p.

BUTLER, J. *Four philosophies and their practice in education and religion.* New York, Harper, 1951. 552 p.

CALO, G. *Educazione e scuola.* Firenze, Marzocco, 1947. 414 p.

CLAPAREDE, E. *Psychologie de l'enfant et pédagogie expérimentale* (2 vols.). Tome I: *Le développement mental;* Tome II: *Les méthodes.* Neuchâtel & Paris, Delachaux & Niestlé.

CONANT, J. B. *Education in a divided world.* Cambridge (Mass.), Harvard University Press, 1948. 250 p.

"Das pädagogische Schrifttum 1949", *Bildung und Erziehung.* Frankfurt, Kern & Birner, 1952. 87 p.

DECROLY, O. & BUYSE, R. *Introduction à la pédagogie quantitative. Eléments de statistique appliqués aux problèmes pédagogiques.* Bruxelles, Editions Lamertin, 1929.

DEWEY, J. *Experience and education.* New York, Macmillan, 1938. 116 p.

304

Enzyklopädisches Handbuch der Heilpädagogik. 2 Aufl. Hrg von A. Dannemann u. A. Halle, Marhold, 1930-34.2 Bde.

FAUVILLE, A. *Eléments de psychologie de l'enfant et de l'adolescent.* Louvain, Nauwelaerts; Paris, Vrin, 1948. 172 p.

FEDERN-MENG. *Die Psychohygiene (Bücher des Werdenden,* zweite Reihe, Band II). Zürich, Bern, Huber, 1949. 423 p.

GOZZER, G. *Tre riforme.* Trento, Arti Grafiche "Saturnia", 1948. 24 p.

HANS, N. *Comparative education.* London, Routledge & K. Paul, 1949. 334 p.

HEHLMANN, W. *Pädagogisches Wörterbuch.* 3 Aufl. Stuttgart, Kröner, 1942. 492 p.

HEINICKE, C. *Bibliography on personality and social development of the child.* New York, Social Science Research Council, 1953. 130 p.

LANGEVELD, M. J. *Begaafdheidsonderzoek en Intelligentiespreiding.* Utrecht, De Haan, 1945.

——. *Beknopte theoretische paedagogiek.* Groningen-Batavia, 1945.

MENG, H. *Seelischer Gesundheitsschutz,* Basel, Schwabe, 1939. 224 p.

MENG, H., SIEGRIST, H., SCHJELDERUP, H., SCHNEIDER, E., WOLFF-HEIM, N., ZULLIGER, H. *Praxis der Kinder- und Jugendpsychologie.* Bern, Huber, 1951. 214 p.

MONROE, W. S. ed. *Encyclopedia of educational research.* New York, Macmillan, 1950. 1520 p.

MOORE, T. V. *Personal mental hygiene.* London, Heinemann, 1947. 331 p.

SPIEL, O. *Psychische Hygiene im Schulalter.* Wien, Verlag für Jugend und Volk, 1952. 32 p.

VALENTINE, C. W. *Psychology and its bearing on education.* London, Methuen, 1950. 674 p.

WASHBURNE, C. *A living philosophy of education.* New York, John Day, 1940. 486 p.

WHITING, J. W. M. & CHILD, I. L. *Child training and personality: a cross-cultural study.* London, G. Cumberlege, 1953. 354 p.

SECTION II

The following are some of the journals which carry papers bearing upon the topics discussed in this book:

American journal of mental deficiency. New York, American Association of Mental Deficiency.

Année psychologique. Paris, Presses universitaires de France.

Archives de psychologie. Genève, Université de Genève.

Avenirs. Paris, Bureau universitaire de statistique et de documentation scolaires et professionnelles.

British journal of educational psychology. London, Methuen.

British journal of psychology. General section. London, Cambridge University Press.

British journal of statistical psychology. London, University of London Press.

Bulletin international des sciences sociales. Paris, Unesco.

Bulletin mensuel de la société Alfred Binet. Paris, Société Alfred Binet.

Cahiers de l'enfance inadaptée. Paris, Editions S.U.D.E.L.

Child development. Baltimore, National Research Council.

Documentación psicopedagógica. Suppl. to *Revista de psicología y pedagogía aplicadas.* Valencia, Salvador Giner.

Elementary school journal. Chicago, University of Chicago Press.

Enfance. Paris, Presses universitaires de France.

Estudios pedagógicos. Zaragoza, Institución San José de Calasanz.

International review of education/Internationale Zeitschrift für Erziehungswissenschaft/Revue internationale de pédagogie. 's-Gravenhage, M. Nijhoff, for the Unesco Institute for Education, Hamburg.

International social science bulletin. Paris, Unesco.

Journal of educational psychology. Baltimore, Warwick and York.

Journal of experimental education. Wisconsin, University of Wisconsin.

New era in home and school. London, New Education Fellowship.

Norsk pedagogisk tidsskrift. Oslo, Noregs Pedagogiske Landslag.

Occupational psychology. London, National Institute of Industrial Psychology.

Paedagogica belgica. Gand, Institut supérieur de sciences pédagogiques.

Paedagogisk psykologisk tidsskrift. København, Munksgaard (Summaries in English).

Pedagogisk tidsskrift. Stockholm & Uppsala, Almqist och Wiksell.

Pour l'ère nouvelle. Paris, Musée pédagogique.

Psychological abstracts. Washington, D.C., American Psychological Association Inc.

Review of educational research. Washington, D.C., American Educational Research Association.

Revista Española de pedagogía. Madrid, Instituto San José de Calasanz.

Revue belge de psychologie et pédagogie. Bruxelles.

Revue internationale de filmologie. Paris, Presses universitaires de France.

Revue internationale de psycho-pédagogie. Bruxelles.

Revue pédagogique. Bruxelles, Labor.

Revue suisse de psychologie (Schweizerische Zeitschrift für Psychologie und ihre Anwendung). Bern, Hans Huber Verlag.

Rivista di psicologia. Florence, Società Italiana di Psicologia.

Sauvegarde de l'enfance. Paris, Union nationale des associations régionales pour la sauvegarde de l'enfance.

Schule und Psychologie. München, Verlag Steinebach.

Schweizerische Lehrerzeitung. Zürich, Schweizerischer Lehrerverein.

Sociological review. University College of North Staffordshire, U.K.

Times educational supplement. London, Times Publishing Co.

Zeitschrift für Angewandte Psychologie und Charakterkunde. Leipzig.

Zeitschrift für Pädagogische Psychologie und Jugendkunde. Berlin, Leipzig.

Wiener Zeitschrift für Philosophie, Psychologie, Pädagogik. Wien, Verlag A. Sexl.

APPENDIXES

I A. THE ASSESSMENT AND RECORDING OF CHILDREN'S PERSONALITY AND PROGRESS

This matter is of so much importance to the adaptation of the methods of the school to individual differences among children, and to wise educational guidance, that we print here parts of the summary of research into this matter prepared by Professor P. E. Vernon.

Personality Diagnosis in Schools, and its Fallibility

Diagnosis of children's personalities is important not only in relation to maladjustment. Most teachers, even those with a strongly traditionalist outlook, get to know their pupils to some extent as individuals, and modify their speech or behaviour to each accordingly; in other words they are practical psychologists. At two stages in particular, their knowledge of pupils' interests along various lines and their judgments of such traits as persistence, stability and resourcefulness can be of value—namely, when the pupils are transferred to various types of secondary school, and when they leave school to enter employment. The capacity to benefit either from academic or technical secondary education does not depend solely on the intellectual qualities that can be measured by examinations and mental tests. Often therefore the head teacher of the secondary school interviews the candidates and their parents, and asks for reports, including assessments of character, from the primary school teachers.[1] When they leave, either he or a 'careers master' reports to prospective employers or to vocational officers. A vocational advisory and/or placement service is available nowadays to the majority of school leavers in all European countries.

Now there can be no doubt that such diagnoses and assessments of children's (or adults') personalities are often very inaccurate and biased. We tend greatly to oversimplify the complexities of personality structure and to jump to conclusions from a few—possibly unrepresentative—incidents, or from such unreliable signs as features and manner. In the course of our upbringing and experience of people, books, etc., we build up our own working hypotheses of human nature, and a series of stereotypes or stock pictures, into which we tend to fit each new person we meet, disregarding those incidents that fail to conform to our expectations. And the better we get to know a person, the more rigid becomes our picture of him, the more bound up with an emotional attitude or sentiment.

---

1. National Union of Teachers. *Transfer from Primary to Secondary Schools*. London, Evans Bros., 1949.

Thus when we are asked to describe his personality, our reports cannot be regarded as an objective summary of his behaviour, but are more an expression of this personal sentiment.[1] It should be remembered also that the individual's behaviour does vary considerably in different situations, and in relation to different observers. Thus differences between their judgments arise partly because the individual develops distinctive patterns of behaviour towards each observer. Another difficulty in personality diagnosis is that the meaning or content of the various trait-names by which we describe people are vague and equivocal: 'sociability', 'instability', 'integrity', etc., do not, like 'height' or 'arithmetical ability', refer to behaviour which everyone recognizes and interprets alike. Again, it is seldom possible to reach any certainty in the interpretation of human motives, since, as psychoanalysis has shown, many of the essential mechanisms and complexes are repressed in the unconscious mind.

What is the evidence for these statements about the fallibility of teachers' judgments? When two or more acquaintances assess the same individuals, even on well constructed rating scales, there are large discrepancies, and the average correlation coefficient seldom exceeds $+0.5$ to $+0.6$, unless the raters have seen the individuals under very similar circumstances and developed similar points of view. When a number of presumably distinct traits are assessed—say, intelligence, stability, honesty, resourcefulness—these are usually found to overlap or intercorrelate rather highly; this is the phenomenon which Thorndike called 'halo effect'. It indicates that raters fail to recognize the subtleties of personality; they tend to attribute all the desirable traits to individuals of whom they approve, all the undesirable ones to those they dislike. Teachers' judgments of their pupils' personalities usually correlate unduly with the pupils' attainments. Indeed investigations in London demonstrated that there was practically no agreement between primary school judgments and secondary school judgments a year or two later, except in so far as both sets of ratings correlated with attainment. Another research into the predictive value of tests, examinations and ratings at the age of transfer to secondary schools was carried out at Dundee.[2] Quite good diagnoses of attainment in grammar schools were obtained from primary school marks and test scores, but when account was taken of primary teachers' judgments of industriousness, and other presumably relevant personality traits, the accuracy of predictions actually decreased.

The studies carried out by Wickman[3] and Laycock[4] over 20 years ago are often quoted. Teachers were asked to rank in order of seriousness a large number of types of maladjustment, and it was found that they generally regarded impertinence, disobedience, aggression, stealing, and destructive or sexual misdemeanours as much more serious than schizoid or nervous tendencies. In so far as the school should be an harmonious community, they were no doubt justified. But it follows that their diagnoses of individuals are too liable to equate maladjustment merely with behaviour that is troublesome to them in the classroom and playground. Similarly, the recent *Survey of Rewards and Punishment in Schools*[5] showed

1. P. E. Vernon, *Personality Tests and Assessments*. London, Methuen, 1953.
2. W. McClelland, *Selection for Secondary Education*. London, University of London Press, 1942.
3. E. K. Wickman, *Children's Behaviour and Teachers' Attitudes*. New York, Commonwealth Fund, 1928.
4. S. R. Laycock, 'Teachers' Reactions to Maladjustments of School Children', *Brit. Journ. Ed. Psych.*, 1934, 4, p. 11-29.
5. National Foundation for Educational Research in England and Wales. *A Survey of Rewards and Punishments in Schools*. London, Newnes, 1952.

that the majority of teachers misjudge the incentives and deterrents that have most effect on the pupils themselves.

Improvements in Assessment

It is easier to point out faults in personality assessment than it is to suggest remedies. There are useful books on interviewing, such as Bingham and Moore's,[1] and Oldfield's.[2] But the understanding of people in general is at present more an art than a science. We certainly cannot claim that a psychological training is a *sine qua non* for the diagnosis and handling of children. Indeed the teacher with a good knowledge of psychology is often too theoretical, too apt to discover elaborate complexes and to neglect the simpler environmental causes of maladjustment or troublesome behaviour which may be obvious to his less sophisticated, but more experienced and practical, colleagues.[3] Diagnosis chiefly involves making certain of all the relevant facts, finding out how persistent and serious is the abnormal behaviour, under just what circumstances does it occur; what are the main pressures operating in the family, among the child's companions, in the classroom; what are his intellectual abilities and physical status, and are these adequate to the demands made on him. The more straightforward explanations should be explored first: for example, the pupil may steal because this is the accepted thing in his circle of friends; he may display temper tantrums or bullying because that is how he gets his own way at home, and so on. Personality maladjustment should not be assumed, nor should the skilled help of the psychiatrist or the educational psychologist be called on until the school, in co-operation with the home, has tried to deal with the situation. Far too many children referred to clinics are either too dull to keep up in school, or are delinquent or spoilt because they have been brought up badly.

At the same time, many who claim to be experienced in handling children are ignorant of quite elementary facts regarding their needs and development. Some teachers are too neurotic or emotionally immature themselves to be able to consider their pupils sympathetically and impartially; and many—as Valentine[4] and others have shown—enter the career without any real interest in it, but rather from such motives as desire for financial security and long holidays. Some types of serious maladjustment, again, are by no means easy to detect. It would appear that more care is being given nowadays to the selection of teachers with suitable personalities and motivation. Ordinary teacher-training is often too crowded to include an adequate course in psychology. Indeed few training institutions possess a qualified psychologist on the staff. Instead, one of the lecturers in education may merely pass on bits of what he or she was taught, early in this century, about instincts, rote-memory investigations, and the like. But here also there are improvements, particularly in the colleges or seminaries where teachers of nursery and infant school, or of handicapped and mentally defective, children are trained. Students are taught more about the characteristics of children of different ages, about individual differences and the need to adjust teaching and teaching materials to the level of each pupil, also about the influence of the 'social

1. W. V. Bingham and B. V. Moore, *How to Interview*. New York, Harper, 1931.
2. R. C. Oldfield, *The Psychology of the Interview*. London, Methuen, 1941.
3. M. F. Cleugh, *Psychology in the Service of the School*. London, Methuen, 1951.
4. C. W. Valentine, 'Reasons for the Choice of the Teaching Profession by University Students', *Brit. Journ. Ed. Psych.*, 1934, 4, p. 237-59.

climate' of the classroom on achievement and adjustment. There is a welcome tendency for such training to be carried out, less by lectures and books, more by making studies of individual pupils and systematic observations of groups, and by discussions with the tutors. It is realized that students who are themselves trained in accordance with psychological principles are more likely to learn psychology which they will actually use in practice. In Scandinavia, Britain and elsewhere, numerous short 'refresher' courses are available for mature teachers on mental testing, vocational guidance, the prevention of maladjustment, and the diagnosis and treatment of educational backwardness.

Cumulative Record Cards

A valuable step towards more systematic study of pupils is the keeping of well designed record cards. All schools already have some kinds of confidential records of pupils' marks, medical examinations, etc. But these are often scattered or incomplete, and much of the valuable information that teachers acquire about individual children is never written down and goes to waste. Cumulative record cards supply a convenient method of collecting together all the relevant material on each child and keeping it in an accessible form.[1] Their value is enhanced because they include independent entries by a succession of class teachers, and because they make possible comparisons of marks, test scores and judgments from year to year: that is, they do not provide merely a single 'cross-section'. For example, the growth of interests, or trends in the curve of intelligence and other abilities, can be observed. Their main use naturally occurs at the stages of transfer from one school to another, or from school to employment. But they are also essential for any educational or vocational guidance within the school, for the planning of individual work, or the grouping of pupils for special instruction, and for referral of pupils for expert study and treatment. (They should, of course, be planned with the advice of the educational psychologist, so that as comprehensive and intelligible a picture as possible can be passed on to the specialist.) Such records are normally confidential within the educational system, though they also provide all the raw material from which testimonials or reports can be written to parents, employers or vocational guidance officers.

The use of such cards is, as yet, rare in European schools, though they are employed in most British primary, and to a lesser extent in secondary, schools. Even in Britain there are great variations in their form, content and adequacy. Some are too superficial or too vague to be of any use; others are so complex and detailed that they demand a great deal of work from the teachers and put people off from consulting them. They should represent a complete case study of each child, which is drawn up by his teacher at least once a year, but also a very condensed study—easy to fill in and easy to file. Their issue should be accompanied not only by a clear explanatory leaflet, but also by constant propaganda and training, so that teachers will use them effectively and uniformly. Teachers are naturally reluctant to spend much extra time on them, unless it is clear that they are of value to themselves and their colleagues. They should be made to realize, therefore, that the records assist them in getting to know each pupil better,

---

1. C. M. Fleming, *Cumulative Records: Notes on their Content and Uses*. London, University of London Press, 1945; W. Glassey and E. J. Weeks, *The Educational Development of Children*. London, University of London Press, 1950; H. R. Hamley et al., *The Educational Guidance of the School Child*. London, Evans Bros., 1937.

in making fuller contacts with the parents, and in developing the sympathy, combined with impartiality, which is the essence of the modern approach to education.

The emphasis will naturally vary somewhat at different ages, and different cards should therefore be drawn up to cover the years normally spent in the infant, primary and secondary schools (a separate card, or page, for each year is apt to be confusing.

They should usually include space for the following entries:

1. Identification particulars.
2. School attendance totals; types of absences and reasons.
3. Relevant features of physique and health (adapted from the medical officer's reports).
4. (a) Family pattern; special home circumstances (e.g. step-parent, mother at work, etc.); parental occupation. (b) Observations on sources of strain in the home, discipline, etc. The ordinary teacher cannot usually make detailed inquiries into such matters; but any relevant information that he can pick up in interviews with the parents should be recorded.
5. Abilities and attainments. (a) Objective test results, including names of tests, age or percentile scores (not merely 'I.Q.'). (b) Term or examination marks. Rank positions in a given school class are perhaps preferable to percentage marks or to letter grades or ratings (A, B, C, D, E, etc.), since these have no uniform meaning. (c) Public examinations entered; certificates or prizes awarded. (d) Voice and speech ratings. (e) Notes on any special aptitudes—artistic, etc. (especially among secondary pupils). (f) Notes on athletic or other extra-curricular participation; positions held (prefect, captain, secretary of club, etc.). (g) Suggestions regarding general level and type of employment, rather than specific jobs (at later ages only).
6. Personality. The previous information is mainly factual, but the remaining items require mere interpretation, and raise serious problems of assessment.[1] The usual method is to list a few important personality traits, with definitions, and to have these rated on a five-point scale, advising the teachers that in a large group of pupils, 10 per cent, 20 per cent, 40 per cent, 20 per cent, 10 per cent (or some other approximation to the normal curve) would be expected to fall respectively into these five grades. Sometimes the five steps are concretely defined, along the lines of a 'graphic' rating scale; sometimes coarse scales with only three steps—strong, average, weak—are substituted. The traits should be specified as unambiguously as possible, and should cover the kinds of behaviour that teachers have opportunities to observe. If marked fluctuations occur from time to time in a child's behaviour, dual ratings can be given. The various gradings can usefully be pictured on a chart or profile. A typical list of traits for primary school children might include: (a) vitality and energy; (b) stability vs. impulsiveness, over-emotionality; (c) sociability and extraverted characteristics; (d) initiative and resourcefulness; (e) perseverance and good habits of work; (f) reliability, trustworthiness.

We have seen already some of the biases and errors to which judgments of personality are prone; they include the 'halo effect', misinterpretation of the content or meaning of the traits, great variations in applying numerical or other standards, the tendency to be over-generous in all ratings or to avoid

---

1. P. E. Vernon, *Personality Tests and Assessments*, op. cit.

extreme (high and low) ratings. The devices just mentioned aim at reducing these biases—probably not very successfully. The most effective way of producing reasonable uniformity and impartiality among raters is likely to be thorough training in objective observation of children and in the use of the scale, with periodic checks. Most record-card ratings are not, in fact, of much value by themselves. They help to stimulate the teacher to take an all-round view of each pupil, but they should usually be accompanied by a brief, but free, personality sketch, which includes supporting evidence. This is a more natural way of conveying to later users the child's outstanding characteristics, as seen by his teachers.

7. Interests. Again a short list of general types of interest may be assessed, for example: (a) intellectual (reading, scientific, etc.); (b) aesthetic; (c) practical (mechanical, domestic, etc.); (d) social-gregarious; (e) physical-athletic. Space should be allowed for noting more specific hobbies and leisure pursuits.

Tests of Intelligence and Attainments

Children's abilities are normally assessed in schools by means of oral questioning, class exercises, and examinations. For most educational purposes these are quite adequate, and they occur so frequently that they supply a more comprehensive picture of each pupil's strengths and weaknesses than do a few short psychological tests given on a single day. Nevertheless they are inferior to tests for diagnostic purposes, for the following reasons.[1]

1. Their marking is largely subjective, and liable to be influenced by the teacher's general impression of the pupil, or by the examiner's personal inclinations. Even if new-type examinations are set, whose marking is objective, the choice of questions and answers will vary widely from one examiner to another. In psychological tests the items are chosen and constructed by experts, and subjected to preliminary trials to prove their suitability. The conditions for giving the tests, and the scoring, are carefully standardized to eliminate variations due to the examiner.

2. The typical examination contains a few long questions, hence the luck of the particular questions set largely affects pupils' performance. The test contains numerous short items, chosen to sample the whole field of ability or attainment systematically. The reliability of the test—that is the consistency of the pupils' performance on parallel or repeated tests—is generally established.

3. An examination tends to test a mixture of qualities—intelligence, knowledge of subject matter, capacity to formulate this knowledge in acceptable language, spelling and handwriting, temperamental stability and persistence, etc. The psychological test tries to measure one clearly defined ability or attainment at a time. True, a study of a pupil's script may throw light on specific good and weak points, but this too can be done more accurately by a diagnostic test in, say, reading or arithmetic.

4. An examination is unstandardized and, while it shows a pupil's standing relative to the rest of the class or other group that has taken it, it does not—like the test—enable him to be compared with norms for his own age. Marks on different examinations cannot be compared, unless they are scaled by statistical treatment.

1. F. J. Schonell and F. E. Schonell, *Diagnostic and Attainment Testing*. Edinburgh, Oliver and Boyd, 1950; P. E. Vernon, *The Measurement of Abilities*. London, University of London Press, 1940.

5. The psychologist normally follows up his tests to find how closely they predict, for example, educational or vocational success. The predictive value of most examinations is a m..tter of guesswork and is usually much lower than their authors assume, on account of the unreliability just mentioned.

Difficulties and Precautions in Testing

A good deal of testing is done by teachers in British and European schools, though far less than is common in the United States of America. Except perhaps in nursery and infant schools, or in some schools for the handicapped, few of these teachers are properly trained, and grave errors are often made in administration, scoring and interpretation. (Some children have even been wrongly certified as defectives on the results of tests applied by psychologically untrained medical officers.) This naturally brings testing, and psychology generally, into disrepute, it is doubly unfortunate, because of the harm done to particular children, and because the majority of teachers still tend to be suspicious of psychological testing, perhaps imagining that it may undermine their own authority and judgment. The proper use of tests is hampered also because not enough well constructed and well standardized ones are published in Europe, and because those that are available are undeniably costly. Thus the authorities often grudge the expense and time involved.

Some of the main dangers and difficulties will now be discussed. The results of any test may be untrustworthy if the instructions are not followed, if conditions are unsuitable, or scoring inaccurate. Timing may be wrong; children may copy from one another; distractions and disturbances may occur; tests may be applied at unsuitable age-levels where they fail to discriminate effectively. Most group tests can be given correctly by those who take the trouble to study and carry out the instructions. Individual testing of attainments and aptitudes requires more skill and experience, and intelligence testing with versions of the Binet-Simon or with performance tests demands especially thorough training. While good rapport and co-operation are naturally desirable, there is evidence to suggest that health or fatigue, also motivation, have remarkably little effect on test scores, except among very young and among emotionally unstable children. A test must be long enough to be statistically reliable. About 45 minutes for each main ability is generally found suitable at 11 years, though some attainments tests are much shorter. Performance and aptitudes tests of 5 to 10 minutes are often worthless unless combined into a fairly lengthy battery.

Test Norms

The norms for most children's tests are expressed in mental and educational ages, from which can be calculated mental ratios or intelligence quotients and reading, arithmetic and other quotients. This system is convenient, but delusively simple. It assumes that mental or educational growth is linear until it stops abruptly at a certain maximum, which is variously estimated at 14 to 16 years. Actually such growth tends to be parabolic, that is it tails off slowly after about 11 years in the average individual, and (as Dearborn and Rothney[1] show) it is far from regular in different individuals. The eventual maximum probably depends largely on

1. W. F. Dearborn and J. W. M. Rothney, *Predicting the Child's Development.* Cambridge, Mass. Sci.-Art, 1941.

the amount and quality of education or mental stimulation received after 11 years.[1] Thus units of M.A. (mental age) and E.A. (educational age) are not equal in size, particularly during adolescence, and fluctuations inevitably occur in I.Q.s or E.Q.s for this reason. Another difficulty with these quotients is that their spread or standard deviation differs from test to test, and at different ages. Thus 130 I.Q. on one test with an S.D. of 15 may be equivalent to 150 on another test with an S.D. of 25. It would be much more logical if the norms for all tests, especially from the age of 11 onwards, were expressed in percentiles or standard scores determined at each age level. Only in this way could a given degree of superior or inferior ability on any test at any age be expressed as a constant numerical index. This is already done in the case of most adult and some children's tests (e.g. the Wechsler and the Moray House tests). Unfortunately the widely used Terman-Merrill test shows particularly large variations in spread, so that its I.Q.s are most difficult to interpret. Even the median or average scores at different ages are not always correct in some tests, for it is far from easy to secure truly representative samples on which to standardize. The norms for educational tests were seriously upset by wartime disturbances of schooling, and the lost ground has not yet been fully regained.[2] De Groot[3] gives evidence of a drop of about five points in I.Q. on verbal intelligence tests in Holland at the end of the war, where the average child missed at least 18 months' schooling. Even the expert is often insufficiently aware of these difficulties: non-experts such as teachers naturally take out-of-date and unsatisfactory norms on trust, and thus arrive at inaccurate diagnoses of their pupils' abilities.

Test Content

The statistical naivety of many people who administer tests also results in their discovering puzzling discrepancies between different tests of, nominally, the same abilities. Some familiarity with factorial research would show them why two or more intelligence tests, for example, often conflict.[4] Such tests all measure the same general intellectual factor, or g, to a certain extent; but they also embody varying amounts of such group or specific factors as: verbal ability (v), spatial judgment (s or k), rote memory, number ability, logical reasoning, facility in doing multiple-choice tests, ability to work at speed, and factors dependent on the level of difficulty of the items, and so forth. Thus verbal and non-verbal (or performance) tests of intelligence never intercorrelate perfectly, and a child's I.Q. on such tests may vary 20 to 30 points on account of differences in content and form. A major advantage of the Binet-Simon tests is that they cover so wide a range of content. But even these cannot be assumed to measure intelligence in general, or for all purposes. The name of the test should always be stated. Similar difficulties arise in educational and vocational testing. Thus a graded-word oral reading test gives far from perfect predictions of silent reading or comprehension ability.

It follows that verbal intelligence tests give better predictions of scholastic abilities, because they have group factors in common, than do pictorial, perform-

---

1. P. E. Vernon, 'Recent Investigations of Intelligence and its Measurement', *Eug. Rev.*, 1951, 43, p. 125-37.
2. Ministry of Education. *Reading Ability*. London, HMSO, 1950.
3. A. D. de Groot, 'The Effects of War upon the Intelligence of Youth', *J. Abnorm. Soc. Psych.* 1949, 43, p. 311-17.
4. P. E. Vernon, *The Structure of Human Abilities*. London, Methuen, 1950.

ance or other non-verbal tests. The latter, however, usually overlap more closely with mathematical, technical and scientific abilities at secondary and college levels. Another corollary deserves mention. The teacher of a backward class may find his pupils much better at performance tests than they are at verbal tests. Again a grammar school teacher, on testing his pupils a year or two after entry, may note an apparent decline in average I.Q. Such occurrences may arise from inaccurate test norms, but they are more probably attributable to statistical regression effects when imperfectly correlated tests, with different factor make-up, are compared. Great caution is needed, therefore, in drawing any psychological conclusions from them.

Uses of Tests

When the above sources of error or misinterpretation are allowed for, psychological tests have a great variety of important applications to schoolchildren, which may be summarized as follows:[1]

1. Surveys of the level of intelligence or of attainment, and its distribution in a school class, or a whole school, or district, for comparison with wider, e.g. national, norms. The 1932 and 1947 mental surveys carried out by the Scottish Council for Research in Education are outstanding examples.[2] Reference may also be made to the studies of postwar illiteracy and reading backwardness in England.[3]

2. Experimental researches into factors or conditions that influence attainments, such as comparisons of rural and urban schools, studies of delinquents, etc.

3. Assessments of the effectiveness of new teaching methods, visual aids or other devices, contrasting arrangements of the curriculum, etc. It is essential to apply objective tests to experimental and control groups before and after the introduction of such methods in order to avoid the possible bias of the teacher in marking ordinary written work, or judging from general impressions of the class response.

4. Testing has repeatedly brought out the enormous range of individual differences within a class, not only in intelligence but also in attainments. Despite teachers' efforts to bring all their pupils up to given standards, and despite early promotion of bright pupils, or holding back of dull ones, it is usual to find a range of reading or arithmetic ages in any one class from about 3 years above to 3 years below the average. That is, some children in a class mostly consisting of 10-year-old read as well as the average 13-year-old, others as poorly as the average 7-year-old. Teachers can thus make valuable use of tests for grouping within a class, and adjusting the work to suit the various levels of intelligence and attainment. The claim sometimes made that classes should be organized on a mental rather than a chronological age basis, so that each would be homogeneous in ability, does not appear to have received experimental support. Probably the social and emotional difficulties of putting together very bright youngsters and old dullards, and the bad effects on

---

1. F. J. Schonell, 'The Development of Educational Research in Great Britain', *Brit. Journ. Ed. Psych.*, 1947-50; F. J. Schonell and F. E. Schonell, *Diagnostic and Attainment Testing*. Edinburgh, Oliver & Boyd, 1950.
2. Scottish Council for Research in Education: *The Intelligence of Scottish Children*. 1933; *The Trend of Scottish Intelligence*. London, University of London Press, 1949.
3. Ministry of Education, *Reading Ability*, loc. cit.

some children of knowing that they are regarded as stupid, outweigh the intellectual advantages of streaming. Moreover, we have pointed out that different abilities overlap only to a moderate extent; hence there are few children who cannot shine and achieve the satisfaction of success at *something* within the varied curriculum of an up-to-date school.

5. Individual diagnosis. Teachers frequently fail to spot a highly intelligent child, who is not using his ability, either because of emotional difficulties or through sheer laziness; or alternatively the dull child who, though backward in his work, is doing better than might have been expected. It is particularly helpful to compare results on several educational tests with one another and with the child's mental and chronological ages, perhaps in the form of a graph or profile. Schonell has distinguished the backward (those whose educational ages are less than 80 or 85 per cent of their chronological ages) from the retarded (those with E.A.s much below their M.A.s). It is the latter who particularly repay study and remedial measures. There are, however, strong technical objections to the calculation of achievement or accomplishment quotients $\left(\dfrac{\text{E.A.}}{\text{M.A.}} \text{ or } \dfrac{\text{E.Q.}}{\text{I.Q.}}\right)$ especially from the results of non-verbal intelligence tests. They are very unreliable, and they fail to allow for the normal statistical regression effect.

Individual work can be planned, and instructional materials of a suitable level or difficulty chosen, on the basis of such results.

6. Diagnostic tests, and observations of types of errors, help the experienced psychologist to discover the specific difficulties of the backward pupil, and to guide his course of remedial instruction. Such testing should be combined with a full investigation of educational history, home circumstances, and emotional adjustment, as pointed out—for example—by Burt[1] and Schonell.[2] For backwardness is often merely a symptom of deeper causes, which must be corrected if progress is to be made. Although most effectively done by the trained educational psychologist or the child guidance clinic, such diagnosis is not outside the scope of many teachers who are prepared to give the time to individual pupils.

7. Similarly in vocational guidance, tests of intelligence, educational and vocational abilities must be supplemented by inquiries into interests, relevant experience, opportunities, etc., if a complete picture is to be obtained.[3] We have pointed out the unreliability of judgments made in interviews, but we should also refer to the apparent success of properly trained psychologists and teachers in the vocational field.

8. The expert can derive from tests considerable additional qualitative information on intellectual and personality traits by observing the manner in which a subject responds to performance and assembly tests. The way the child reasons, his persistence or impulsiveness, his speech and expressive movements, provide valuable insights. Considerable caution is needed, since it is only too easy to jump to premature conclusions. For example, separate Binet items (rote memory, numerical, practical, etc.) do *not* provide reliable indications of special abilities or disabilities. Uneven performance on the Wechsler sub-

1. C. L. Burt, *The Young Delinquent*. London, University of London Press, 1937.
2. F. J. Schonell, *Backwardness in the Basic Subjects*. Edinburgh, Oliver and Boyd, 1942.
3. C. A. Oakley et al. *Handbook of Vocational Guidance*. London, University of London Press, 1937.

tests, or particular patterns of performance, have proved disappointing in diagnosis of particular types of neurosis and psychosis.[1]

9. Major decisions, such as transfer of children to special schools for the subnormal or defective, should be taken only after expert and thorough testing. And in view of the mutability of the I.Q., mentioned above, periodic retesting should be carried out to discover which children are capable of returning to the normal streams.

BIBLIOGRAPHY

In addition to the books cited in the text, the reader is referred to the following:

AMERICAN EDUCATIONAL RESEARCH ASSOCIATION. *Educational and psychological testing*. Washington, D.C., 1953.

DIEDERICH, E. & W. *Das pädagogische Schrifttum 1945-1948*. Wiesbaden, Pädagogische Arbeitsstelle, 1951-52. 2 vols.

GAL, R. *L'orientation scolaire*. Paris, Presses universitaires de France, 1946. 148 p.

GULLIKSEN, H. *Theory of mental tests*. New York, Wiley, 1950. 486 p.

KIENZIE, R. *Schülerbeobachtung und Schülerbeurteilung*. 2 Aufl. Esslingen/a/N., Schneider, 1949. 134 p.

KLIMPFINGER, S. *Die Testmethode in der Persönlichkeitsbegutachtung*. Wien, Rohrer, 1944. 110 p.

LEFEVRE, L. *Le professeur psychologue*. Paris, Presses universitaires de France, 1949. 144 p.

The nineteen thirty-eight mental measurements yearbook. Buros, O. K., ed. New Brunswick, Rutgers University Press, 1938.

The nineteen forty mental measurements yearbook. Buros, O. K., ed. Arlington, Virginia, The Gryphon Press, 1941.

The third mental measurements yearbook. Buros, O. K., ed. New Brunswick, Rutgers University Press, 1949.

The fourth mental measurements yearbook. Buros, O. K., ed. Highland Park, New Jersey, The Gryphon Press, 1953.

MIALARET, G. *L'éducateur et la méthode des tests*. Paris, Editions du Scarabée, 1953. 135 p.

PIERON, H. *Progrès de la technique, 1939-1945*. Berne, Francke, 1947. 315 p.

SCHENK-DANZIGER, L. *Entwicklungstests*. Wien, Verlag für Jugend und Volk, 1953.

SPIEL, O. & ZEMAN, H. *Der wiener Erziehungsbogen*. Wien, Verlag für Jugend und Volk, 1953. 55 p.

WAEYENBERGHE, A. VAN. "Une batterie de tests d'instruction pour l'orientation scolaire", *Revue des sciences pédagogiques, Cahier VIII*. Bruxelles, 1947.

---

1. A. I. Rabin and W. H. Guertin, 'Research with the Wechsler-Bellevue Test, 1945-1950', *Psych. Bull.*, 1951, 48, p. 211-48.

I B. A NOTE ON THE INNATENESS AND CONSTANCY OF INTELLIGENCE

As is stated in the text (Chapter VII), sheer all-round intellectual efficiency increases from birth to some time in the mid teens when it begins to taper off. The abler group tends to continue developing longer than the average and the duller to reach its maximum earlier. After the age of 13 the annual increments become increasingly smaller but some very slight increase doubtless continues for some years. There is too considerable evidence[1] that intelligence does not go on developing in adolescence unless stimulated by higher education. Moreover the fact that a mean mental age of 14 or 15 is reached by a population of a similar mean chronological age and not exceeded by an otherwise similar population two or three or more years older may merely indicate a lack of discriminatory power in the test used.

This brings us to the controversial topic of the innateness of intelligence as measured by our tests, and the constancy of I.Q.s[2]. Considerable changes are in fact found when children are retested. Over a five-year period (say 5 to 10, or 11 to 16), the average child is likely to vary only 7 or 8 points up or down, and many are still more stable. But variations as large as 30 or 40 points may occur in rare instances. I.Q.s obtained before the age of 5 are even more unstable, Most of this variation is due to unreliability in the tests used, inefficient testing, wrong norms, or variations in units of measurement, and differing factor content. There are also definite practice effects if children are retested too frequently, and still more serious distortions if they are coached on the actual, or on parallel, tests by misguided teachers or parents.[3] Nevertheless some genuine rises and falls, or trends spread over considerable periods, do occur, though less frequently perhaps than the parents of dull children imagine when they talk of 'late developers'. The famous Iowa studies[4] and other researches in America have indicated the possibility of really large alterations in I.Q. consequent on such environmental changes as adoption by foster-parents, attendance at nursery schools, etc. Most psychologists regard these claims as exaggerated, but are nevertheless willing to accept a more fluid conception of intelligence than they did 30 to 50 years ago. Although the potentialities for intellectual development are hereditarily determined (probably by multiple genes), such development would seem to occur only under appropriately stimulating environmental conditions, and to be dependent on harmonious emotional integration. Thus within any one cultural group, where home influences and education do not vary very widely, the I.Q. may mainly reflect heredity. But wider environmental differences, as between highly educated parents with one or two children and the lowest socio-economic groups with big families, or between western and eastern Europeans, or American whites and negroes, probably have much larger effects—not only on intelligence

1. See for example: Jones and Hsai, *J. Ed. Psych.* vol. XXV, no. 3, 1933.
2. P. E. Vernon, 'Recent Investigations of Intelligence and its Measurement', *Eug. Rev.*, 1951, 43, p. 125-37. The rest of this paragraph draws heavily upon the working paper by Vernon previously cited.
3. These range from about 5 to 15 points of I.Q., depending more on the similarity of the coaching or practice material to the actual test, also on the recency of the practice rather than on its amount.
4. B. L. Wellman, 'Iowa Studies on the Effects of Schooling', *Thirty-Ninth Yrbk. National Society for the Study of Education.* 1940, p. 377-99.

as measured by our tests, but also as expressed in daily life, in school work or in employment. Such environmental differences are most marked in the formative pre-school years, and during adolescence and adulthood when only a proportion of the population receives the stimulus of higher education. Among those who get no true secondary or further education, and whose jobs or leisure pursuits provide little mental 'exercise', intelligence reaches its maximum earlier and declines more rapidly than among the privileged minority. But we still know far too little regarding what kinds of upbringing and education supply the most effective nourishment. It follows that tests cannot be used legitimately for making interracial or other genetic comparisons, where upbringing has been dissimilar; and this applies to performance and non-verbal just as much as to verbal tests.[1] There is much evidence again, that children who are seriously maladjusted fail to realize their full intellectual, as well as educational capacities.

Compare also: C. Burt, *Intelligence and Fertility*, London, Eugenics Society, 1948; R. Zazzo, *Le devenir de l'intelligence*, Paris, Presses universitaires de France, 1946.

I C. MENTAL FACULTIES AND THE TRANSFER OF TRAINING

Although the doctrine of mental faculties and the related one of transfer of training in its crude form have been exploded by empirical psychological research[2] their over-simplified convenience has extended their dominance in the minds of administrators, teachers and the lay public. An examination of contemporary curricula in primary and still more in secondary schools reveal how many classroom demands are in fact motivated almost solely by their supposed general value as mental disciplines.

It is perhaps worth while therefore briefly examining the old faculty psychology and theories of transfer of training. These doctrines, widely held from medieval times, taught that the mind consisted of a number of 'faculties', such as 'memory', 'reasoning', 'judgment', 'observation', and that through a formal training given by a particular subject, a particular faculty was improved generally in all its spheres of function. Latin or mathematics were for example considered not only to convey specific skills and information to the pupil but to develop memory or reasoning in general. Behaviouristically speaking, that is to say, the pupils were expected to transfer or apply their trained memory or reasoning power to problems differing widely in nature from the school subjects in which the training had been achieved. Memory, trained by memorizing Latin paradigms, would for example show greater ease in retaining geometrical proofs, and the reasoning power trained while studying mathematics would allow more competent and critical evaluation of political issues. This over-simple theory attracted empirical

---

1. S. Biesheuvel, 'Psychological Tests and their Application to non-European Peoples', *1949 Yearbook of Education*. London, Evans Bros., 1949.
2. See for example: I. R. Hilgard, *Theories of Learning*. New York, Appleton Century Crofts, 1948; T. G. Andrews, et al., 'Transfer of Training', *Encyclopaedia of Educational Research*. Ed. W. S. Monroe, New York, Macmillan, 1950; H. R. Hamley, 'Formal Training, a Critical Survey of Experimental Work', *Brit. Journ. Ed. Psych.* 1936, 6, p. 236-49; C. Burt, 'Mental Abilities and Mental Factors', *Brit. Journ. Ed. Psych.* vol. XIV, pt. II, June 1944.

investigation by psychologists in the late nineteenth century. The early experiments of James[1] and of Thorndike and Woodworth[2] led Thorndike to declare that transfer of training from the learning situation to new situations only took place in so far as the latter contained elements identical with the former. This conclusion, which meant of course a total rejection of the doctrine of formal discipline, seemed to be borne out by Thorndike's large-scale investigations on the transfer value of school subjects.[3] Transfer from the study of Latin or mathematics seemed to be practically non-existent. Since 1929 however, Thorndike himself has been led to revise his narrow connexionism,[4] and the great number of experiments carried out during the last two or three decades tend to show that transfer of a wider range than Thorndike's theory of identical elements had implied can be obtained. But transfer does not occur automatically nor does it occur as the result of training supposed faculties. It occurs only if the pupils are led to derive generalizations from particular facts, if principles are clearly formulated and if, after completing a piece of mental or physical work, the pupils consciously develop insight into the methods of attack and the ways of proceeding used.

I D. MENTAL FACTORS

A great deal of research and discussion has been devoted to this important topic. The reader is referred to C. Burt, *The Factors of the Mind*, London, University of London Press, 1940; L. L. Thurstone, *Primary Mental Abilities*, Chicago, University of Chicago Press, 1939; G. H. Thompson, *Factorial Analysis of Human Ability*, London, University of London Press, 1939; P. E. Vernon, *The Structure of Human Abilities*, London, Methuen, 1950. The general ability or *g* is usually identified with innate all-round intelligence. The group abilities are so called because they enter into one group of related activities and not into another. This three-factor theory as it is called should not be confused with the older faculty theory. It is based on the fact that if a matrix of correlations and covariances derived from the scores achieved by a sample of children on a variety of cognitive tests is mathematically analysed, it can be shown that (a) all the tests cohere to a certain degree implying that success is determined in part by a general or *g* factor; (b) that certain groups of tests are distinguished from other groups of tests when this *g* factor is extracted. These subgroups cohere in virtue of a factor or factors common to them but not to other groups; (c) there remains a residual which is peculiar to the variance of each test and which may be either a specific factor or a factor of error in the test.

If we invert the analysis and correlate not tests with tests but persons with persons a similar picture emerges. Furthermore, with widely divergent measures

1. W. James, *Principles of Psychology*. New York, Holt, 1890.
2. E. L. Thorndike and R. S. Woodworth, 'The Influence of Improvement in One Mental Function upon the Efficiency of Other Functions', *Psych. Rev.*, 1901, 8, p. 247-61, 384-95, 553-64.
3. E. L. Thorndike, *Educational Psychology*. New York, Teachers College, Columbia University, 1916.
4. E. L. Thorndike, 'Mental Discipline in High School Studies', *J. Ed. Psych.*, 1924, 15, p. 1-22, 83-98.

and at different age levels, although the relative weights of the general, group and specific factors vary and although certain of the group factors may be eliminated by the omission of particular measures, this structure persists; and, in spite of differences, the upshot of much research work is to suggest very strongly that human cognitive activity consists functionally, in any one operation, of the interaction of the general capacity with one or more group abilities and specifics. Such a theory is supported by commonsense observation when we observe the way in which, for example, two people equally able generally may show very different levels of success in mathematics, science, music or the learning of a foreign language.

It is difficult to say—and indeed cannot be said conclusively—whether these group factors are innate aptitudes which mature in the course of development or whether they represent a structuring of the mind imposed by experience and education. Most psychologists are agreed however on their crucial importance in determining educability at the secondary stage and as a component in the development of interests in the second decade. In so far as vocational guidance is based upon the analysis of ability, it too must take account of the importance of special ability in the prediction of success at work.

There are of course alternative views possible—see for example G. H. Thompson, op. cit. supra. American and some British psychologists have carried the analysis of group and special abilities much further than is indicated above. On the other hand a distinction has been drawn between the meanings to be assigned to 'capacity' and 'aptitude'. Ambiguities exist not only of a terminological but of a theoretical kind, particularly as concerns the part played by heredity. An author like P. Naville for example rejects the notion of 'aptitude' along with psychological heredity. H. Piéron on the other hand reserves 'aptitude' for the heredity substratum and the term 'capacity' for the actual possibility of success which depends upon maturational and environmental factors. Hence 'capacity' alone is subject to measurement and reveals 'aptitude' indirectly.

II. WASTAGE AND FAILURE IN SECONDARY EDUCATION

Comparatively few systematic studies have been published dealing with the extent of failure to profit from various forms of selective secondary education in Europe. The following figures from various sources, not all of which are directly comparable, are of value therefore in documenting the statements made in Chapter VII, and revealing a situation which seems to warrant extensive research.

In Belgium (Hotyat et al, *The Instruction, Education and Mental Health of Belgian Children and Adolescents*, para. 6, p. 114 ff.) it seems that while some 30 per cent of the age group commence the secondary course, up to the end of the fourth year wastage annually is between 20 and 30 per cent—in fact only just over one-third of all entrants complete the fourth year.

In Denmark it appears that about 40 per cent of children enter the Examination Middle School, of whom one-third withdraw at the end of the compulsory schooling period. (*World Handbook of Education Organization and Statistics*, Unesco, Paris, p. 115.)

In 1948-49 in Finland, official figures indicate that 44.5 per cent of those who completed the primary course in 1947-48 enrolled the following year in general secondary schools; and for every 100 pupils completing the primary course in 1947-48 there were, after four years at general secondary schools, 10.6 pupils who passed the *baccalauréat*. For every 100 pupils in the first year of secondary school in 1948-49, 23.9 pass the *baccalauréat* four years later. [Tilastollisessa Päätoimistossa (Central Statistical Office), *Kansanopetustilasto, Kansakoululaitos Lukuvuosina 1948-50* (Statistics of primary education, 1948-50), Helsinki, 1951. *Oppikoulut. Tilastollinen Katsaus Oppikoulujen Tilaan ja Toimintaan Lukuvuonna, 1949-50* (Statistics concerning institutions of secondary education, 1949-50), Helsinki, 1951. *Tilastokatsauksia* (Bulletin of statistics), no. 11-12, November-December 1952; no. 11, November, 1953. *Suomen Tilastollinen Vuosikirja, 1952* (Yearbook of statistics, 1952), Helsinki, 1953.]

In France (1949-50) approximately 21 per cent of pupils are, at the age of school leaving, in the *enseignement du 2e degré—classique ou moderne*—and a further 11 per cent are in the *enseignement technique*. For 100 pupils entering the sixth class in 1944-45, 95 registered for the first part of the *baccalauréat* in 1949-50. Of these, 41 per cent were successful. (Bureau universitaire de statistique, *Recueil de statistiques scolaires et professionnelles, 1949-1950-1951*. Paris, 1951. See also 'Le baccalauréat en 1952 et 1953', *Education nationale* no. 8, 25 Febr. 1954, and 'L'enseignement du second degré public et ses effectifs', *Avenirs* no. 55, June 1953.)

In Holland about 10 per cent of pupils of the age of 13 enter modern secondary schools, *gymnasiums* and *lyceums*. Some 46 per cent of these leave without obtaining a leaving certificate (*De ontwikkeling van het onderwijs in Nederland*. 1951.)

In Italy, 23.8 per cent of those who in 1948 were in the fifth primary year entered the *scuola media unica*. It is from this intermediate school that at the age of 13 pupils are recruited for the more academic and specialized higher secondary education; hence it is of interest to note that 59.5 per cent of those who entered in 1947 the *scuola media* were to be found in the third year in 1949, and of these 42.5 per cent entered the higher secondary schools in 1950 (19.8 per cent classical, 6.1 per cent scientific, 16.6 per cent normal). These figures suggest that about 9 per cent of the total age group in fact enter this form of education after a process of continuous guidance and selection. Of these somewhat more than half obtain their *maturita* certificates. (Istituto Centrale di Statistica, *Annuario Statistico dell'Istruzione Italiana, 1949-50; 1950-51*. Rome, 1952; 1953. 2 volumes).

In Portugal some 11.5 per cent of pupils enter the secondary schools; of these (in 1951) about 9 in 10 finish the sixth year, and one in four the seventh. (Instituto Nacional de Estatística, *Estatística da Educação, 1948-1949; 1949-1950; 1950-1951; 1951-1952*, Lisbon, 1950; 1951; 1952; 1953.)

A recent study in Fife, Scotland, reveals that less than 10 per cent of a year group reaches the Scottish Leaving Certificate, and that those passing represent approximately 4 per cent of the age group. (H. Fairlie, 'The Pool of Ability', *Scottish Educational Journal* vol. XXXVI, no. 50, 1953.)

In Switzerland (figures supplied in a private communication by M. Chevallaz and M. Dottrens) it seems that between 40 and 60 per cent of those who enter the *collèges classiques* of Lausanne and Geneva gain the *maturité* or *baccalauréat*. They further point out that, for example, in one school in 1934-35 in the four classes leading to the *maturité*, of 499 pupils, 89 were not promoted, 73 had to resit examinations, 25 failed completely, 137 or 27 per cent failed in one way or another. In a subsequent year the percentage was 25 per cent. In 1942-45, of

215 pupils entering in 1942, 47 per cent only were continuing their studies normally in 1945 (46 had left, i.e. 21.4 per cent).

In the United Kingdom some 28 per cent of all children attend the secondary grammar schools, and in each year before the reform of the School Certificate and Matriculation examinations some 60 per cent of candidates qualified. It should be remembered too that not all those entering the schools in fact presented themselves for examination. For the years 1948-49 and 1949-50 for example, 26 per cent of the girls and 22.4 per cent of the boys left State-aided grammar schools in England and Wales before the age of 16 (*Times Ed. Suppt.* 24 August 1951). Hence—if success in the examination is in fact even a rough measure of the success of the education given, which is of course disputable—only rather less than half of the pupils in such schools showed themselves able to profit from the education they received.

III A. MALADJUSTMENT

It has been and continues to be asserted that *all* maladjustment derives from upsets of a *sexual* kind in the *early* years of life. As has been argued elsewhere (see Chapter VI), while the importance of the early years cannot be denied, other periods of growth seem also to be critical for the development of personality, and maladjustment may arise whenever the individual is placed in a situation of conflict from which he is unable to emerge without severe repression of a powerful psychobiological drive. The evidence we have is insufficient either to warrant the thesis of the exclusively sexual nature of early disturbance or that of the unique importance of the first three to five years of life.

Hadfield states[1] 'love is not merely sexual; love is protective as well as sexual and the need for protective love and security is of far greater importance in the development of psychoneurosis than the sexual'. Valentine[2] makes a logical analysis backed by evidence from numerous observations of children of the theory of infantile sexuality and reveals many of its fallacies. Similarly, while the importance of the personal relationships within the family cannot be denied, we are by no means certain that there is a simple and direct relationship between, say, parental disharmony and maladjustment or neurosis; nor is there any reason to suppose that conflicts will not develop, and ultimately produce neurosis if, for example, the self-assertive impulse is frustrated at any stage.[3] Hence it seems more in accordance with the evidence tentatively at least to accept a theory of multiple causation and to conceive of maladjustment as (a) a disequilibrium brought about by the interaction of the individual and an environment which denies satisfaction to *any* of the primary needs; and as (b) a state generally of slow growth and representing an accumulation of experiences rather than a dramatic clash with the environment or 'trauma'.

In what is probably the only attempt at a thorough statistical analysis of the conditions reported among 273 maladjusted children, and of the frequencies of various conditions in a series of 394 maladjusted children compared with an

1. J. A. Hadfield, *Psychology and Mental Health*. London, Allen & Unwin, 1950.
2. C. W. Valentine, *The Psychology of Early Childhood*. London, Methuen, 1942.
3. W. McDougall, *Abnormal Psychology*. London, Methuen.

equal number or normal children, Burt[1] and Howard come to the following conclusions. There is little evidence of homogeneity in the maladjusted group, but one bipolar factor indicates a broad classification into environmental conditions and personal conditions respectively, with another suggesting a cross classification into intellectual and emotional conditions. Judged by a correlational study of the maladjusted and normal groups, a wide variety of conditions shows significant correlation with maladjustment. The most important appear to be the following: (a) in the school, the presence of an uncongenial teacher, the assignment to a class where the work is too difficult; (b) in the home, lack of affection, overstrict discipline, presence of a step or foster-mother, death of the child's own mother, drunken parents, illegitimacy and lack of adequate facilities for recreation; (c) as regards intellectual characteristics, general educational backwardness, often (though not always) the result of innate intellectual disability, either general or specific; (d) as regards emotional characteristics, general emotional instability, excessive extraversion, excessive introversion (often accompanied by anxiety states, conflicts or feelings of inferiority) and (among the older children) adolescent instability. There are appreciable variations according to age, locality and social class.

III B. MATERNAL DEPRIVATION

Pestalozzi (1764-1827) seems to have been one of the first to point out, especially in *Wie Gertrud ihre Kinder lehrt* (letters 13 and 14), Zürich 1801, the paramount importance of the mother-child relationship. J. Bowlby (*Maternal Care and Mental Health*, Geneva, World Health Organization, 1952) has summarized the considerable research literature which has grown up on this subject since 1925. The work cited by Bowlby has produced a mass of evidence on the effects of maternal deprivation and a large number of strikingly dramatic cases of psychic 'trauma' leading sometimes in later life to delinquency. However, there exist many instances where the child has been separated at an early age from its natural mother, permanently or temporarily, without any demonstrable ill-effect other than a more or less severe but transitory disturbance. Many of these cases have been able to form a more or less permanent affective relationship with a mother substitute, some appear to have profited by special nursery school education with a direct therapeutic aim (see the paper specially prepared for the conference by M. David, F. Créange and A. M. Schoendoerffer, 'Problems Confronting Nursery School Teachers in a Group of Children Between 1 and 3 Years of Age, Separated From Their Families') and others from the more diffuse relationships possible in children's communities or other institutions run on 'family' lines. See also C. W. Valentine, *Abnormalities in Normal Children*, London, National Children's Home, n.d.

---

1. C. Burt and M. Howard, 'The Nature and Causes of Maladjustment among Children of School Age', *Brit. Journ. Psych. Stat.* vol. V, pt. I, March 1952.

IV A. THE REGIONAL CONFERENCE ON EDUCATION AND THE
MENTAL HEALTH OF CHILDREN IN EUROPE, PARIS,
27 NOVEMBER TO 17 DECEMBER 1952

Unesco's Programme

The present book is the direct outcome of Resolution 1,251 of the Programme of
Unesco for 1952, by which the Director-General was authorized: 'to organize, in
collaboration with the United Nations (Division of Social Affairs and Unicef,)
the World Health Organization and competent international organizations, a
regional conference on the problems of education in relation to the mental health
of children in Europe'.

In January 1952 the secretariat of Unesco called together a small working
group from the secretariats of the United Nations, the World Health Organization, the International Labour Organisation and Unicef to discuss the technique
of the conference and the means by which the United Nations agencies concerned could effectively collaborate. A definition of the aims of the conference
was embodied in a paper accepted by the Executive Board of Unesco at its
Twenty-eighth Session (28 EX/Decisions Item 7.1) and formed the basis of
document EMH/28, sent to all participants. This paper stated:

'. . . The main topic of inquiry will be what is conventionally understood by
education—the period of compulsory schooling (roughly from the age of 5 or 6
to the age of 14 or 15). Within this, the conference will concentrate upon a full
examination of the interaction between the method, organization and atmosphere
of the European schools, on the one hand, and the development of the personality
of their pupils on the other. The stress will be on the normal development of
normal children, since these make up by far the majority of those who will form
the citizens of the future.

'The school cannot, however, be thought of entirely in isolation. Hence,
though emphasizing the mental health role of the school, both positive and negative, the conference will, to a limited extent, consider those influences which bear
upon the child outside the classroom. Among these, as of primary importance,
may be noted the educational function of the family, extra-curricular activities,
and the like. Similarly, topics like pre-school education, education for the highly
intelligent, vocational guidance, and preparation for and adjustment to working
life, appear among the problems raised.'

The Constitution of the Conference

A task of this type can be accomplished only by a relatively small, highly expert
group, working together for a lengthy period. Four elements should play an
adequate part: (a) official representatives of interested Member States; (b) Independent experts with special knowledge; (c) representative experts aware of
the broad problems in other parts of the world; (d) competent international non-
governmental organizations.

The Executive Board of Unesco at its Twenty-eighth Meeting decided that the
following European Member States should be invited each to send a qualified
representative: Austria, Belgium, Czechoslovakia, Denmark, France, German
Federal Republic, Greece, Hungary, Italy, Luxembourg, Monaco, Netherlands,

Norway, Poland, Sweden, Switzerland, Turkey, United Kingdom, Yugoslavia. To this group, by invitation of the Secretary-General of the United Nations (Division of Social Affairs and the Technical Assistance Administration) and the Directors-General of Unesco and the World Health Organization, was added a body of experts whose special knowledge, experience and independence would complement the contribution of the national delegates. In addition, to secure a broad basis in the experience of other great regions, experts were invited from Latin America, India, the Arab States[1] and the United States of America. In this way the membership of the conference was kept representative, workably small and highly expert. A detailed list of participants is given in Appendix IV B.

To have invited the international non-governmental organizations for the full three weeks would nearly have doubled the size of the conference, yet their experience, technical knowledge and viewpoints are of great value. Each non-governmental organization accordingly was invited to suggest topics for the agenda, to prepare objective reports on subjects of interest to them, and to delegate an expert representative to meet members of the conference for a minimum of one half-day session.

The Working Technique of the Conference

The conference worked mainly in small groups, each with a technically qualified rapporteur-secretary experienced in international conferences. Throughout, these rapporteurs, appointed by Unesco, served as aids to the chairman of the working groups and as liaison officers with the secretariat. Co-ordination was assured by a steering committee and by occasional plenary sessions. In all, five plenary sessions were held of half a day each, and 25 sessions of groups, of which five were devoted to hearing evidence from the non-governmental organizations.

The conference agenda called for a balance between many specialized professional points of view. Hence each working group was so constituted as to include representatives of the administrative, educational, psychological and medical professions, and to contain official delegates and invited experts. Such a cross-disciplinary approach, though not without initial difficulties of adjustment, led to a deeper exploration of the complex problems involved.

The broad lines of the agenda had been determined by the suggestions made by governments and by non-governmental organizations. The conference decided that each group should take a section and elaborate its own agenda further. This enabled each group to pursue its work in some depth. The steering committee, the exchange of provisional reports between groups, occasional plenary sessions, the notification to all groups of topics of general interest, and the setting up of ad hoc groups on special subjects, ensured that there should be no serious omission or overlapping.

Working Papers

During the 12 months which preceded the conference, 15 representative European experts, working in close contact with each other and with the secretariat of

---

1. The representative from the Arab States, A. H. El Koussy, was unfortunately at the last moment unable to come. He did however largely contribute to the discussion of the book in manuscript.

Unesco, prepared digests of the research information available on the topics to be covered. So far as was possible each of these was an objective synthesis principally of European work and made directly in relation to European school systems. In addition, each of the international non-governmental organizations which expressed its wish to collaborate was invited to prepare a carefully documented and factual statement on those items of the agenda which fell within its competence. Certain of the European National Commissions for Unesco, the International Labour Organisation and the United Nations Division of Social Welfare also prepared and submitted documents.

This documentation formed the technical background to the discussions of the conference; and much of it, in one form or another, is incorporated in the present work. It has served a further useful purpose. Since December 1952 a total of 19,940 copies of this material in its duplicated form has been supplied to libraries, to individual experts, to non-governmental organizations and to small working parties in 27 countries, studying special problems arising out of the conference. As will be seen from Appendix IV D, a number of these documents are now available in printed form.

The Present Book

The present book is something more than, and different from, a simple account of the conference. In the 18 months following the conference, the members of Unesco secretariat responsible for the whole activity drafted each chapter, basing their work upon the specially prepared papers, upon the working reports of the groups into which the conference divided, and upon such other material as came to hand. These chapters were circulated in their draft form to the participants, to representatives of non-governmental organizations likely to be interested, and to individuals. In all, well over 60 men and women expert in different fields and coming from 15 European and 5 non-European countries read and criticized either single chapters or the whole work.[1] Each person who received part or the whole of the book was asked not merely for general cirticisms and suggestions, but for specific supplements of information and for further bibliographical and other data. In many cases, information and suggestions received were the work of a group of people in the country concerned. Thus, while the principal task of drafting, collating and ordering this material was that of the secretariat of Unesco, the whole work represents an example of international collaboration among scholars from many countries and many disciplines.

The Follow-up of the Conference

The conference and the resulting book are a step in a long-term programme aimed at fostering the healthy mental development of children through education conceived in its largest sense. It is set against a background of supporting activities which continue to develop as needs make themselves felt. From 1951 onwards Unesco has joined with other agencies of the United Nations in a series of expert committees to study such topics as: *Mental Hygiene in the Nursery School* (Paris, Unesco, *Problems in Education* no. IX, 1951); *The Physically Handicapped Child* (Geneva, The World Health Organization, *Technical Report Series*, no. 58, 1952);

---

1. See the list of participants in Appendix IV B, and the Acknowledgements.

and *The Mentally Subnormal Child* (Geneva, The World Health Organization, *Technical Report Series*, no. 75, 1954).

Many of the international non-governmental organizations have, either centrally or through their national branches, set up committees and study groups to continue the study of particular topics. Among these should be mentioned: the Catholic International Child Bureau, which has continued study of the 'Influence of Religious Education', through its national branches; the Conference of Internationally Minded Schools, which devoted its summer conference (Pendley Manor, Tring, U.K., August 1954) to 'The Teacher and the Modern World'; the Consultative Council of Jewish Organizations, which has set up an expert committee to study the 'Effects of Prejudice on Mental Health'; the International Federation of High Police Officers, which took the 'Action of the Police in Protecting the Mental Health of Children' as the theme of its international conference (Paris, 1954); the International Union of Family Organizations, which, centrally and in its national branches, has set up committees for the study of 'Parent-Teacher Co-operation'; the New Education Fellowship which, through its journal the *New Era* and through its national branches, has stimulated discussion of the conference agenda; the World Federation for Mental Health, which has placed 'Education and Mental Health' upon the programme of the Fifth World Congress for Mental Health (Toronto, Canada, 1954); the World Organization for Early Childhood Education, which devoted its Fifth World Assembly (Copenhagen, Denmark, 1954) to the 'Selection, Training and Further Training of Nursery School Teachers'; and the World Union of Catholic Women's Organizations, which has undertaken a study of the 'Education of Mothers'.

Certain of these international non-governmental organizations, and certain national bodies, have, in close collaboration with Unesco and with the participation of other United Nations Agencies, called together small international cross-disciplined study groups. For the reports of these groups see Appendix IV D.

IV B. LIST OF CONFERENCE PARTICIPANTS

Representatives of Member States

Austria: Dr. L. Haensel, Councillor, Federal Ministry of Education, Vienna.

Belgium: Prof. R. Buyse, professeur à la Faculté de philosophie et de lettres de l'Université de Louvain.

Denmark: Mr. O. M. Nielsen, Headmaster of a Coursvejens skole, Copenhagen.

France: Miss P. Mezeix, inspectrice générale des classes et écoles de perfectionnement, Paris.

German Federal Republic: Dr. E. Loeffler, Ministry of Public Education, Stuttgart.

Italy: Prof. G. Gozzer, Ministry of Education, Rome.

Luxembourg: Dr. G. Schaber, professeur a l'École normale d'instituteurs, Luxembourg.

Monaco: Rév. Père G. Shugrue, aumonier du Lycée de Monaco.

Netherlands: Dr. J. A. A. Verlinden, Head, Department of Research and Documentation, Ministry of Education, The Hague.

Sweden: Mr. A. Faltheim, Councillor, Royal Swedish Board of Education, Stockholm.

Switzerland: Mr. G. Chevallaz, directeur de l'École normale d'instituteurs et d'institutrices, Lausanne.

United Kingdom: Mr. J. H. Goldsmith, H.M. Staff Inspector, Ministry of Education, London.

Yugoslavia: Mrs. S. Jelić, Professor of Education at the Training College for Nursery School Teachers, Zagreb.

Representatives from non-European Areas

India: Prof. M. V. Gopalaswami, Professor of Psychology, University of Mysore.

Latin America: Prof. O. Robles, Professor of Psychology, National University of Mexico.

United States of America: Prof. W. Olson, Dean, School of Education, University of Michigan (vice-president, chairman of Group III).

Experts Invited by the Specialized Agencies

Unesco

Prof. E. Boesch, professeur de psychologie à l'Université de la Sarre, Sarrebruck.

Prof. A. Fauville, professeur de psychologie, président de l'Institut de psychologie appliquée et de pédagogie a l'Université de Louvain, Belgium.

Prof. R. Gal, conseiller technique pédagogique du Ministère de l'éducation nationale, chargé du Service de la recherche pédagogique, Paris, France (vice-president, chairman of Group II).

Prof. E. T. Rasmussen, Professor of Psychology, University of Copenhagen, Denmark.

Prof. A. Rey, professeur de psychologie à l'Institut des sciences de l'éducation. Geneva, Switzerland (vice-president, chairman of Group IV).

Prof. F. J. Th. Rutten, Professor of Psychology, Director of the Laboratory of Psychology, University of Nijmegen, Netherlands (president).

Short-term consultants

Prof. C. H. Dobinson, Professor of Education, University of Reading, United Kingdom.

Prof. G. Heuyer, professeur à la Faculté de médecine de Paris, France.

Dr. A. G. Hughes, Chief Inspector, Education Officer's Department, London County Council, United Kingdom.

Prof. M. J. Langeveld, Professor of Education and Psychology, University of Utrecht, Netherlands.

Prof. G. Mauco, directeur pédagogique du Centre psycho-pédagogique du lycée Claude-Bernard, Paris, France.

Prof. P. E. Vernon, Professor of Educational Psychology, Institute of Education, University of London, United Kingdom.

United Nations/Technical Assistance Administration

Miss G. Chesters, Special Adviser to the Children's Department of the Home Office, United Kingdom.

Secretariat

Miss M. V. Pohek, Deputy Head, Social Division, Technical Assistance Administration.

World Health Organization

Dr. H. M. Cohen, Principal School Medical Officer, City of Birmingham, United Kingdom (vice-president, chairman of Group I).

Dr. M. Ponzo, Professor of Psychology in the Faculty of Medicine in the University of Rome, Italy.

Mrs. G. Seitz, Clinical Psychologist, Erica Institute, Sweden.

Dr. A. Sunier, Director of Mental Health Services, City of Amsterdam, Netherlands.

Short-term consultant

Dr. A. Berge, directeur du Centre médico-pédagogique Claude-Bernard, Paris, France.

Secretariat

Dr. K. Kjellberg, Regional Health Officer, Regional Office for Europe.

Non-Governmental Organizations

The following were represented by expert witnesses: Agudas Israel World Organization; Consultative Council of Jewish Organizations; International Bureau of Education; International Catholic Child Bureau; International Federation of Children's Communities; International Federation of High Police Officers; International Union of Family Organizations; League of Red Cross Societies; Pax Romana; The New Education Fellowship; World Association of Girl Guides and Girl Scouts; World Federation for Mental Health; World Organization for Early Childhood Education; World Union of Catholic Women's Organizations.

Rapporteurs

Dr. M. Duncan, Child Psychiatrist, Child Guidance Clinic, Chichester, United Kingdom (Group III).

Mr. R. Mallet, psychologue, adjoint au délégué permanent du Comité de recherche pédagogique, Paris, France (Group II).

Dr. M. Revault d'Allonnes, médecin consultant du Centre Claude-Bernard, neuro-psychiatre d'enfants, médecin à l'École des parents, Paris, France (Group IV).

Dr. P. Volkov, Editor *New Era*, London, United Kingdom (Group I).

Unesco Secretariat

Miss U. M. Gallusser (Department of Education).
Dr. W. D. Wall (Department of Education).

IV C. WORKING MATERIAL PRESENTED TO THE CONFERENCE

Experts

Dr. H. Aebli, professeur à l'École normale supérieure de Zürich, Switzerland:
'Experimental Evidence Concerning the Psychological Principles underlying
the Choice of Educational Methods and Curricular Content Appropriate to
Various Development Stages.'

Anonymous: 'A Brief Commentary on Primary Education in Western Europe.'

Dr. Cle J. M. H. Souren, Roman Catholic Central Bureau for Instruction and
Education, The Hague, Netherlands: 'The Relationship Between Education
and Educational Methods, on the One Hand, and the Structure and Ideology
of the Family and Society, on the Other.'

Dr. M. David, Fondation Parent de Rosan, Paris, France: 'Problems Confronting
Nursery School Teachers in a Group of Children between One and Three
Years of Age, Separated from their Families.'

Miss G. de Failly, Centre d'entraînement aux méthodes actives, Paris, France:
'Teaching in Holiday Camps. Training of Staff. Centres for Training in
"Active Education".'

Prof. R. Gal, Centre national de la recherche pédagogique, Paris, France:
'French Contribution to the General Effort to Adapt Education to Modern
Needs.'

Mr. J. Genevay, École d'organisation scientifique du travail, Paris, France:
'The Problem of the Transition from School to Working Life.'

Prof. F. Hotyat, Centre de travaux de l'Institut supérieur de pédagogie de
Morlanwelz, Morlanwelz, Belgium: 'The Instruction, Education and Mental
Health of Belgian Children and Adolescents.'[1]

Dr. L. Lang, Ministry of Education, Vienna, Austria: 'The Pedagogical Position in Austria.'

Dr. R. Lindahl, The Training College, Gothenburg, Sweden: 'Theoretical and
Practical Training in Educational Psychology for Teachers in Sweden.'

Prof. G. Mauco, Centre psycho-pédagogique du lycée Claude-Bernard, Paris,
France: 'Psychological Problems of Adolescence.'[1]

Prof. E. A. Peel, University of Birmingham, United Kingdom: 'External Examinations in the Education System.'

Dr. I. Rother, The Training College, Celle, German Federal Republic:
'Teaching the Basic Educational Skills.'

Dr. J. A. A. Verlinden, Ministry of Education, The Hague, Netherlands: 'Contribution of the Method of Teaching and the Syllabus to Training for Living
in Society.'

Prof. P. E. Vernon, Institute of Education, University of London, United Kingdom: 'The Assessment and Objective Testing of Children.'[2]

---

1. Available in published form. See Appendix IV D.
2. For substantial extracts, see Appendix I A.

332

National Commissions

Austrian Ministry of Education: 'Outline of a Study of New Functions and New Working Methods in Kindergartens.'

French National Commission for Unesco: 'Answer to the Questionnaire on Mental Health in Schools' and 'Report on School Psychological Services.'

The Swedish Royal Board of Education: 'Education and the Special Problems of Children in Sweden.'

United Kingdom National Commission for Unesco: 'Suggestions for the Agenda of the Conference.'

United Nations Agencies

International Labour Office: 'Vocational Guidance and Information.'

United Nations, Division of Social Welfare: 'Social Work and Education.'

Non-Governmental Organizations and other Bodies

Consultative Council of Jewish Organizations: 'Antisemitism and the Mental Health of Children in Europe. Influence of Education.'

International Catholic Child Bureau: 'Considerations on Pre-School Education' and (in French only) 'La sélection et la formation des éducateurs extra-scolaires.'

International Federation of High Police Officers: 'The Police and the Protection of the Mental Health of Children.'

International Union of Family Organizations: 'Investigation on the Co-operation Between Parents and Teachers.'

League of Red Cross Societies: 'The Contribution of the Junior Red Cross towards the Development of the Personality of Children and Adolescents.'

Pax Romana: 'The Religious and Moral Education of Children.'

The New Education Fellowship: 'Suggestions and Working Material submitted for consideration as part of the Conference Agenda.'[1]

World Association of Girl Guides and Girl Scouts: 'Education through Leisure-Time Activity' and 'International Holidays'.

World Federation for Mental Health: 'Child-Rearing Practices and the Social, Intellectual and Emotional Growth of Young Children.'[2]

World Organization for Early Childhood Education: 'Survey of Pre-School Education throughout the World.'

World Union of Catholic Women's Organizations: 'The Modern City and the Mental Health of Children.'

In addition to the above, the following presented reports without being represented:

International Children's Centre: 'Observations on the Training of Teams of Experts Presented by the International Children's Centre.'

International Union for Child Welfare: 'The Psychological, Educational and Social Adjustment of Refugee and Displaced Children in Europe.'

The British Psychological Society: 'Memorandum on the Schools Psychological

---

1. Published in *New Era*, vol. 33, no. 10 (see articles by Balint, Hourd, Jordan, and Swainson listed in Appendix IV D).

2. Available in published form. See Appendix IV D.

Services in Europe' and 'The Training of Teachers for Work with Handicapped Children' (Miss N. L. Gibbs).

The Catholic Education Council: 'The Catholic Position in Education.'

IV D. PUBLICATIONS ARISING OUT OF THE CONFERENCE

The following publications either give a detailed account of aspects of the conference or reproduce certain of the working material prepared for it.

BALINT, E. 'The therapeutic value of play in school', *New era* vol. 33, no. 10, Dec. 1952. United Kingdom.

BOESCH, E. 'L'Unesco et l'enseignement européen', *La revue universitaire de la Sarre*, Sarrebrück, 1953.

CENTRE DE TRAVAUX DE L'INSTITUT SUPÉRIEUR DE PÉDAGOGIE DU HAINAUT, MORLANWELZ. 'L'instruction, l'éducation et la santé mentale des enfants et des adolescents belges', *La revue pédagogique*, no. 9, Nov. 1953, and following numbers. Belgium.

HÄNSEL, L. 'Seelische Gesundheit des Kindes und Schule', *Pädagogische Mitteilungen*, Stück 10, 1953. Austria.

HOURD, M. L. 'The teacher in relation to himself and the children he teaches', *New era* vol. 33, no. 10, Dec. 1952. United Kingdom.

JORDAN, D. 'Relationships of teachers with other adults', *New era* vol. 33, no. 10, Dec. 1952. United Kingdom.

MAUCO, G. 'Les échecs scolaires et les difficultés d'adaptation aux niveaux secondaire et supérieur', *Sauvegarde de l'enfance*, April 1954. France.

REVAULT D'ALLONNES, M. H. 'Un récent travail de groupe', *L'école des parents* no. 4, 1953. France.

SWAINSON, M. 'The training of teachers and their mental health', *New era* vol. 33, no. 10, Dec. 1952. United Kingdom.

WALL, W. D. 'L'Unesco et la psychologie de l'éducation', *La revue internationale de psycho-pédagogie* vol. 1, 1954. Belgium.

WORLD FEDERATION FOR MENTAL HEALTH. *Mental health and infant development.* London, Routledge & K. Paul, 1955.

The present book (no. 11 in the Unesco series *Problems in Education*) can also be considered as one of a collection of studies on the subject of 'Education and Mental Health' which will be published by Unesco itself, or by non-governmental organizations in co-operation with Unesco.

The following list gives the other titles in this collection and the addresses of the organizations from which they can be procured.

*Mental hygiene in the nursery school.** Paris, Unesco, 1953, 33 p., 1/-.

*The police and the mental health of children.*** Fédération internationale des fonctionnaires supérieurs de police, 22, rue de la Banque, Paris-2e, 1954, 54 p., 2/-.

*The training of teachers.** Conference of Internationally Minded Schools, F. Button, Secretary, CIS, 5 Warwick Road, Reading, Berks. 40 p.

---

* In English and French.

** In English and French; plans are being made for a Spanish edition.

Periods of stress in the primary school.* National Association for Mental Health, 29 Queen Anne Street, London, W.C.1, Great Britain, 1955, 50 p.

La pédagogie du calcul. École normale supérieure de Saint-Cloud, Saint-Cloud (Seine-et-Oise), France, 1955. 50 p. approx.

Psychological services for schools and other educational institutions.*** Unesco Institute for Education, Feldbrunnenstrasse, Hamburg, German Federal Republic, 1955. 150 p.

---

*   In English and French.
*** In English, French and German.

AUTHOR INDEX[1]

Adams, R. H., 116.
Aebli, H., 57, 105, 123, 154.
Alexander, W. P., 126.
Allen, 53.
Allport, G. W., 22.
Alstyne, D. van, 67.
American Council on Education, 149.
American Educational Research Association, 84.
Anderson, H. H. et al., 257.
Anderson, H. H. and Brewer, J., 258.
Andrews, T. G. et al., 320.
Arvidson, S., 126.
Asher, P. and Schonell, F. E., 226.
Association for Curriculum Development, 293.

Balint, E., 70.
Ballard, P. B., 192.
Bantock, G. H., 86.
Barker, R. G. et al., 62.
Barnes, L. J., 169, 300.
Baruch, D., Montgomery, E. and Bauer, W. W., 293.
Bauchard, B., 298.
Bauwens, L., 90.
Bender, L., 218.
Bierer, J., 49.
Biesheuvel, S., 320.
Binet, A., 107, 111, 112, 215.
Binet, A. and Henri, V., 189.
Bingham, W. V. and Moore, B. V., 310.
Birch, L. B., 119.
Boutonier, J., 34, 36.
Bowlby, J., 325.
Boyd, W., 297.
Bradford, E. J. G., 126, 127.
Brogan, C., 124.
Brosse, T., 246.

Bühler, Ch., 24, 61, 62, 66, 69, 107, 108.
Bühler, K., 66.
Bullis, H. E., 293.
Bullis, H. E. and O'Malley, E. E., 293.
Bureau universitaire de statistique (France), 323.
Burki, M. F., 130.
Burroughs, G. E. R., 194.
Burt, C., 111, 114, 115, 116, 118, 125, 126, 155, 156, 169, 172, 215, 235, 237, 240, 280, 317, 320, 321.
Burt, C. and Howard, M., 237, 325.
Buyse, R., 121.

Care of Children Committee, 246.
Carmichael, L., 84.
Carnivet, N., 202.
Cast, B. M. D., 192.
Castle, E. B., 163.
Catholic Education Council (United Kingdom), 97.
Central Statistical Office (Helsinki), 323.
Chevallaz, G. M., 323.
Child Welfare Congress (Zagreb), 214, 219.
Clark, H. F., 271.
Cleef, E., 118.
Cleugh, M. F., 310.
Commissione Nazionale d'Inchiesta per la Reforma della Scuola (Italy), 90, 172.
Council for Curriculum Reform, 163.
Culpin, M. and Smith, M., 161.
Cummings, J. D., 238.
Curr, W., 122.

---

1. Authors whose works are in the chapter biblographies are not indexed here.

339

SUBJECT INDEX

343